Discourse Analysis and Media Attitudes

Is the British press prejudiced against Muslims? In what ways can prejudice be explicit or subtle? This book uses a detailed analysis of 140 million words of newspaper articles on Muslims and Islam, combining corpus linguistics and discourse analysis methods, to produce an objective picture of media attitudes. The authors analyse representations around frequently cited topics, such as Muslim women who wear the veil and 'hate preachers'. The analysis is self-reflexive and multidisciplinary, incorporating research on journalistic practices, readership patterns and attitude surveys to answer questions including: what do journalists mean when they use phrases such as *devout Muslim* and how did the 9/11 and 7/7 attacks affect press reporting? This is a stimulating and unique book for those working in the fields of discourse analysis and corpus linguistics, while clear explanations of linguistic terminology make it valuable to those in the fields of politics, media studies, journalism and Islamic studies.

PAUL BAKER is Professor of English Language in the Department of Linguistics and English Language at Lancaster University.

COSTAS GABRIELATOS is Senior Lecturer in English Language in the Department of English and History at Edge Hill University.

TONY MCENERY is Professor of English Language and Linguistics in the Department of Linguistics and English Language at Lancaster University.

Discourse Analysis and Media Attitudes

The Representation of Islam in the British Press

Paul Baker, Costas Gabrielatos and Tony McEnery

CAMBRIDGE
UNIVERSITY PRESS

CAMBRIDGE UNIVERSITY PRESS
Cambridge, New York, Melbourne, Madrid, Cape Town,
Singapore, São Paulo, Delhi, Mexico City

Cambridge University Press
The Edinburgh Building, Cambridge CB2 8RU, UK

Published in the United States of America by
Cambridge University Press, New York

www.cambridge.org
Information on this title: www.cambridge.org/9781107008823

First published 2013

Printed and bound in the United Kingdom by the MPG Books Group

A catalogue record for this publication is available from the British Library

Library of Congress Cataloging-in-Publication data
Baker, Paul, 1972–
    Discourse analysis and media attitudes : the representation of Islam in the British
press / Paul Baker, Costas Gabrielatos, and Tony McEnery.
        p. cm.
    Includes bibliographical references and index.
    ISBN 978-1-107-00882-3
    1. Islam–Great Britain.   2. Muslims–Great Britain.   3. Islam–Press coverage.
4. Islamophobia–Great Britain.   5. Public opinion–Great Britain.
I. Gabrielatos, Costas.   II. McEnery, Tony, 1964–   III. Title.
    BP65.G7B35 2013
    305.6′970941--dc23

                                                                            2012031146

ISBN 978-1-107-00882-3 Hardback

Contents

Figures

Tables

Concordances

Acknowledgements

This book would not have been written without the funding we received from the Nuffield Foundation (grant reference SGS-01198/G) and the Economic and Social Research Council (ESRC) (grant reference RES-000-22-3536). The Nuffield Foundation funded a pilot project on the representation of Islam that led to our ESRC grant, the findings of which are reported in this book.

We would also like to express our sincere thanks to Shenaz Bunglawala, Bandar Al-Hejin, Kim Knott, John Richardson and Linda Woodhead, who, in different ways, helped enormously in the writing of this book.

1 Introduction

Introduction

On 18 October 2006 the British tabloid newspaper the *Daily Star* carried the front page headline 'BBC PUT MUSLIMS BEFORE YOU!'. The headline was accompanied by a picture of a woman in a face-covering niqab making a two-fingered gesture. Despite the fact that the 2001 census recorded 1,588,890 Muslims living in the United Kingdom, comprising 2.78 per cent of the population,[1] the use of the word *you* to address the reader directly appears to discursively exclude the possibility that a Muslim could buy the newspaper or even read the headline.

It is unlikely, though, that *Daily Star* editors would think that Muslims would never see the headline. Instead, the article seems to have been intended to create an 'us' and 'them' distinction. On one side is the presumably non-Muslim majority readership of the newspaper, represented as overlooked by the BBC (a British public service broadcaster that is funded principally by an annual licence fee). On the other are Muslims, implied to be the recipients of undeserving privilege. One interpretation of the accompanying picture is that the Muslim woman is making an insulting gesture towards all non-Muslims, particularly *Daily Star* readers.

This article is an explicit case of British journalism fanning the flames of conflict between the mostly white, nominally Christian (though mainly non-churchgoing) majority of people living in the United Kingdom and the minority of Muslim residents, many whom were born in the United Kingdom, although their parents or grandparents may have come from countries such as Pakistan, India or Bangladesh. While Ford (2008) reports that most British people have become more accepting of ethnic minority groups, McLaren and Johnson (2007) and Eatwell and Goodwin (2010) have noted that public concerns about topics such as immigration, law and order and Islam have become more salient since 1999. In general, attitudes towards Muslims in the United Kingdom have not been positive. For example, according to the

---

[1] From the Office for National Statistics; www.ons.gov.uk/ons/index.html.

British Social Attitudes survey in 2003, 62 per cent of Britons believed that British Muslims were more loyal to Muslims abroad than to British non-Muslims (McLaren and Johnson 2007). Another survey, carried out by the Exploring Islam Foundation in 2010, found that 40 per cent of British adults (in a sample of 2,152) felt that Muslims had not had a positive impact on British society. Half the respondents linked Islam with terrorism, while only 13 per cent and 6 per cent believed that Islam was based on peace and justice, respectively. Sixty per cent said they did not know much about the religion, although, perhaps more encouragingly, a third said they would like to know more.[2]

At the time of writing, there is a sense that opposition to Muslims has grown in recent years in the United Kingdom. A group called the English Defence League was formed in 2009, and since then it has conducted anti-Islam demonstrations in cities and towns including Birmingham, Bradford, Leeds, Leicester, London, Newcastle, Oldham and Preston. Many of these places have relatively high numbers of Muslims, and some of these demonstrations have resulted in conflict, street violence and arrests. This growing opposition is hardly confined to the United Kingdom but seems to be part of a larger trend: attitudes towards Islam in other parts of Europe, and the United States, appear to be hardening. In 2010 a proposal to build a Muslim community centre two blocks north of the site where al-Qaeda terrorists flew two hijacked planes into the Twin Towers in New York City in 2001 resulted in protests about a 'Ground Zero mosque'. In France, the Senate approved the banning of the face-covering burqa in all public places, while other European countries including Belgium, Italy, the Netherlands, Austria, Denmark, the United Kingdom and Switzerland have seen discussions about similar bans. The Swiss government banned the building of new minarets (towers that are distinctive features of mosques) in 2009. Such events suggest that a sense of animosity between 'the West' and 'the Muslim world' has intensified since 11 September 2001.

This book focuses on the role that the British national press has played in representing Muslims and Islam, particularly in the years following the 9/11 attacks. We have chosen to focus on the printed media because we believe that it plays an important role in shaping opinions as well as setting agendas regarding the importance of certain topics. As an indication of the 'news value' of Muslims, between 2000 and 2009 the word *Muslim* and its plural appeared 121,125 times in the national British press (about thirty-three times a day on average), suggesting that this is a topic that the UK press feels is worthy of considerable focus.

---

[2] See www.inspiredbymuhammad.com/campaign.php.

The media present information about world events to masses of individuals. As it is never possible to present a completely impartial, accurate and full account of an event, instead the media offer *representations* of events, through the use of language (spoken or written) and/or images (still or moving). Such representations are often restrained by space and time limitations; journalists need to prioritise particular events, as well as certain people's perspectives or opinions, over others. Additionally, summaries of events may be coloured by the political priorities of newspapers or the abilities of the journalists who are writing for them. In the United Kingdom, national newspapers function as more than mere 'mirrors' of reality. Instead, they have the role of constructing ideologically motivated versions of reality, which are aimed at persuading people that certain phenomena are good or bad, leading John Richardson (2004: 227) to describe journalism as an 'argumentative discourse genre'. Thus, British national newspapers attempt to exert (often successfully) social and political influence, though, as discussed below, newspapers must also balance this aim with reflecting the views of audiences. As Gerbner *et al.* (1986) have shown, the media have a long-term effect on audiences, small at first, but compounding over time as a result of the repetition of images and concepts. Although our main goal is to examine how language is used to represent Muslims and Islam, more specific aims involve focusing on whether there have been changes in representation over time, and whether there are differences between newspapers. We are also interested in identifying the various techniques or strategies that newspapers employ in order to legitimate or justify certain representations, particularly those that may be controversial or would otherwise result in people complaining about the newspaper.

In this chapter, we first describe the context of our own study: the British national press. We then locate our study among others that have examined the representation of Islam and Muslims in various media around the world. Following that, we outline two types of linguistic analysis, which we combined in order to conduct our research: critical discourse analysis, a process that combines close analysis of language with consideration of social context; and corpus linguistics, which uses computational tools to uncover linguistic patterns across very large amounts of text. After describing how we collected the articles to be analysed in this book, we consider the limitations of our approach, and then give an overview of the remainder of the book.

Before we can examine the ways that the British press have written about Muslims and Islam, it is useful to look at the British press in general. The following section gives a brief account of different ways of classifying British newspapers, as well as examining issues surrounding readership, influence, political bias and complaints processes.

The British press

The British press is composed of a wide range of different types of newspapers, distinguished by frequency of appearance (daily, Sunday, weekly), political stance (left-leaning, right-leaning, centrist or 'independent'), style (broadsheet, tabloid or 'middle-market') and coverage (national, regional). In deciding which newspapers to focus on, we were initially constrained by availability. We used an online searchable archive (Nexis UK), which gave us access to the text (but not the images) of a wide range of newspapers. While it would have been interesting to examine regional newspapers, and to compare whether areas with higher populations of Muslims had different news coverage from others, we eventually decided to focus on news reportage at the national level, reasoning that such newspapers would be more readily available to the entire population of the United Kingdom, and thus potentially more influential. It is certainly the case that regional newspapers have a role to play in the way that the country views Islam; for example, a 2006 article on Muslim women and the veil in the *Lancashire Evening Telegraph* written by the then leader of the House of Commons, Jack Straw, triggered a national debate on veiling (see Chapter 8). It is the fact that this story was picked up by the national press that is of key interest to us. We have included both daily and Sunday editions of newspapers. The Sunday editions tend to be longer (sometimes as a result of supplemental magazines or sections), and often have different editors from the daily editions. Traditionally, the Sunday editions of British newspapers have been responsible for breaking or covering sexual or political scandals.[3] For the purposes of our analysis, we have classed *The Observer* as the Sunday version of *The Guardian*, and the now defunct *News of the World* as the Sunday version of *The Sun*.[4] One Sunday newspaper, *The People*, has no daily equivalent. Our data set also contains a weekly newspaper called *The Business*, which converted to a magazine format in the autumn of 2006 and then closed in 2008. These two latter publications contributed only a small proportion of our data.

Readers of this book who are unfamiliar with the national British press may benefit from further information. The national British press works within a system of capitalist democracy, meaning that people choose to buy print newspapers from a range of possible options (often from local

[3] Examples include David Beckham's affair with Rebecca Loos (broken by the *News of the World* in 2004), Max Mosley's private sadomasochistic sexual acts with prostitutes (*News of the World*, 2008) and MPs' expense claims (*Sunday Telegraph*, 2009).

[4] As the *News of the World* did not contain much text, we have tended simply to conflate it with *The Sun*. However, *The Observer* tends to be a longer newspaper, so we have often viewed it separately from *The Guardian*.

shops, newsagents, supermarkets, petrol stations or kiosks at railway or bus stations).[5] By the beginning of the twenty-first century national newspapers also published online versions, which were mainly free to access at the time that the corpus was collected (although some newspapers have since begun to charge for access). Such online access, combined with the high status of the English language and the fact that the United Kingdom is a relatively rich and culturally influential country, means that the British press has a potential reach beyond its own shores. British newspapers compete for readers and do not receive government funding. As Sparks (1999: 45–6) points out, newspapers 'do not exist to report the news… They exist to make money.'

To survive, a newspaper needs to be attractive to readers, enough of whom will maintain some form of 'brand loyalty' to that newspaper. The period under examination (1998 to 2009) saw talk of a crisis in print journalism, with sales figures suggesting that newspapers were in decline[6] and losing readers to other sources such as twenty-four-hour television news or online news, although Conboy (2010: 145) argues that newspapers are adapting to the paradigm shift by incorporating their products to online formats, as noted above.

Some academic research indicates that newspapers have considerable power to influence public opinion (see van Dijk 1991). For example, Lido (2006) has demonstrated that the negative portrayal of asylum seekers in the press had a direct and immediate effect on readers' assumptions about asylum seekers. Brescoll and LaFrance (2004) examined news stories about sex differences, and found that readers tend to accept explanations about sex differences as being scientifically valid, rather than being linked to the newspaper's political standpoint, while Dietrich *et al.* (2006) found that subjects who read a newspaper article that linked mentally ill people to violent crime subsequently had an increased likelihood of describing a mentally ill person as dangerous and violent. The power of influence possessed by the press therefore seems well established.

One significant way that newspapers can impact on society is by their perceived ability to influence the outcome of national elections. Linton (1995) and McKee (1995) have both attributed the defeat of the Labour Party in the UK general election of 1992 to *The Sun*'s pre-election anti-Labour campaign that year. Sanders, Marsh and Ward (1993) and Gavin and Sanders (2002), who concentrated on news reporting of the economy, found

---

[5] Some local newspapers are free, relying heavily on advertising, and are either delivered to homes or can be picked up from kiosks or collection points in towns or cities.

[6] For example, sales of all daily newspapers between 2007 and 2008 dropped – by as much as 10.3 per cent for *The Independent* or as little as 1.43 per cent for *The Sun* (www.guardian.co.uk/ media/table/2009/jan/09/abc-december-national-newspapers).

that there was an indirect influence exerted by press coverage on voting perceptions. However, research does not always indicate that newspapers can affect elections. For example, Norris *et al.* (1999) looked at a shift in some British newspaper coverage from the concept of 'sleaze' to 'Europe' during 1997, and conclude that this shift did not impact on the outcome of the 1997 general election.

In line with other writers on news media, including Martin Conboy, Norman Fairclough and Ron Scollon, we view the relationship between newspapers and readers or audiences as complex, with each influencing the other. Conboy (2010: 7) writes that '[n]ewspapers have always created readers, not news, as their primary function', and argues that viewing the role of newspapers as mirroring society is 'lazy-minded' (Conboy 2010: 4). However, he also points out: 'Newspapers over time have adapted to articulate particular variants of language for particular social groups' (Conboy 2010: 6). Newspapers thus help to bring the concept of particular social groups into being – Anderson's (1983) concept of 'imagined communities' being relevant to note here. However, readers are not passively constructed; meaning is created from interaction between a text and its readers (McIlvenny 1996), and a newspaper's fortunes may suffer if it falls too far out of step with the social group buying it. For example, Gibson (2003) argues that the *Daily Mirror*'s anti-war stance on Iraq in 2003 was a factor in its circulation dropping to below 2 million for the first time in seventy years. Additionally, individual members of audiences possess multiple identities (based on gender, nationality, region, social class, age, sexuality, ethnicity, religion, political views, etc.), and particular identities may become extremely salient if newspapers do not take this into account. *The Sun*'s negative and inaccurate coverage of the 1989 Hillsborough football stadium disaster (in which ninety-six people died) resulted in many people in Liverpool boycotting the paper – a boycott that has lasted to the time of writing.[7] Newspapers thus construct society and the identities of their readers, but if they wish to be successful they must also construct themselves in relationship to their readers.

One way of classifying newspapers relates to style and format. A distinction can be made between tabloids and broadsheets. Tabloids are generally smaller in size, have short articles, use puns in headlines, tend to focus more on national stories, particularly about celebrities, sport and entertainment, and employ a more populist and informal writing style. Broadsheets are normally larger, contain more text, have more focus on international news and political analysis, and generally use a more formal writing style. Tabloids tend to be

---

[7] *The Sun* made the unsubstantiated claim that Liverpool fans urinated on the bodies of the dead and attacked rescue workers. In September 2012, after the publication of an official report concluding that no Liverpool fans were responsible for the disaster, the then editor, Kelvin MacKenzie, apologised for the article.

more popular with working-class readers whereas broadsheets are more commonly bought by the middle classes, which, in Britain, refers to professionals (see Figure 3.2). For the period under examination, the tabloid/broadsheet distinction becomes problematic for a number of reasons. First, some newspapers are easier to classify than others. A newspaper such as *The Sun* could be thought of as being a typical tabloid, having its title in a red nameplate (tabloids are sometimes called 'red tops') and printing many stories about celebrities and sport. The *Daily Mail*, on the other hand, is of a similar size to *The Sun*, but contains longer articles and has a more formal writing style than *The Sun*, as well as having its title in black ink. However, while the *Daily Mail* seems to feature more political articles, it often appears to articulate a 'tabloid' world view, associated with populist politics or even a politics of fear, suggestive of attempts to create moral panic (see, for example, an analysis of its construction of gay people as promiscuous and proselytisers by Baker 2005). Some people refer to the *Daily Mail* and the *Daily Express* as 'middle-market' newspapers rather than tabloids.

To make matters more complicated, there are aspects of broadsheets that make them appear closer to tabloids. For example, the broadsheet newspaper *The Guardian* has a daily supplement, referred to as a 'tabloid section', that focuses on more populist reporting of celebrity gossip and quirky and 'human interest' stories. Additionally, most broadsheet newspapers have become smaller in size over time. *The Times* and *The Independent* are now the same size as tabloids (and are sometimes referred to as 'compacts'), whereas *The Guardian* has reduced its size to what is called a 'Berliner' format. Thomas (2005: 154–5) argues that the popularity of tabloids has impacted on all forms of news reporting, with a move in the elite press towards populism. Distinctions between newspapers are thus made with regard to multiple factors and are gradient in nature rather than binary. As well as noting that the distinction between tabloid and broadsheet is impressionistic and personal, we also need to take into account the fact that newspapers can change style over time, or even within a particular issue.

Another way of conceiving of the differences in focus and style between newspapers is to use the terms *popular* and *quality*. As Tables 1.2 and 1.3 show, *The Sun*, *Daily Mail* and *Daily Mirror* are the three most popular newspapers, whereas the traditional broadsheets *The Guardian* and *The Independent* are the least popular. However, the right-leaning broadsheets, or 'qualities', *The Times* and *The Daily Telegraph* are actually more popular than the *Daily Express* and the *Daily Star*. *Popular* therefore more accurately refers to 'populist' than number of copies sold or read. The term *quality*, on the other hand, refers to newspapers that take a more serious approach to news reporting, with a higher proportion of political or international stories and more in-depth analysis. Pricing tends to correlate with sales to an extent: in

September 2006 the highest-selling newspaper, *The Sun*, cost 35p whereas the two lowest-selling papers, *The Guardian* and *The Independent*, cost twice as much).[8] In this book we maintain the tabloid/broadsheet distinction, as it is the one that most British people are familiar with, although we acknowledge that the terms are broad and do not always apply.

A second important distinction is to do with political affiliation. Post-structuralists would maintain that it is impossible to write from an unbiased stance (arguing that the aim to be unbiased is in itself a 'position'). Even a news source such as the BBC News website, which claims no political affiliation, could be said to contain biases within its reporting (from the choice of stories that it prioritises to the opinions it decides to quote or foreground in a particular article). Nonetheless, even armed with the knowledge that bias is unavoidable, visitors to the United Kingdom are sometimes surprised at how partial British newspapers appear to be. Newspapers declare allegiance to particular political parties and urge their readers to vote accordingly. For example, the 1992 election win for the Conservative Party was reported by *The Sun* on 11 April as 'It was the Sun wot won it!'. Despite their political standpoints, newspapers are not normally blindly loyal to a particular party (and even less so to leaders of parties). Many newspapers backed Tony Blair's 'New' Labour Party in 1997, including the right-leaning *Sun* and the left-leaning *Guardian*. However, in later years many newspapers became negatively disposed towards Labour, and in the 2010 election *The Guardian* backed the Liberal Democrats while *The Sun* favoured the Conservatives. The political terms 'left' and 'right' are relative, multifaceted and therefore problematic, and we use them to indicate a broad overall stance, while acknowledging that within a newspaper there may be some columnists who have been chosen precisely because they represent an antagonistic view (the Conservative Member of Parliament Anne Widdecombe was briefly employed as an 'agony aunt' by *The Guardian*, for instance), and that there are different ways of being 'left' or 'right'. For example, someone could hold leftist economic views, and advocate that all property should be government-owned, that there should be wage equality and that the state should provide benefits for those who are less able. Yet the same person could hold rightist social views, in arguing that homosexuality and abortion are wrong, that the death sentence is an acceptable form of punishment and that immigration should be highly regulated. Consequently, we use the terms *right-leaning* and *left-leaning*, rather than *left-wing* and *right-wing*, in this book, as the latter two terms suggest that a newspaper occupies an extreme position. When

---

[8] The correlation is not perfect, though. The broadsheet newspaper *The Daily Telegraph* cost as much (70p) as *The Guardian* and *The Independent* in September 2006, but sold more newspapers than the less expensive tabloids the *Daily Express* (40p) and the *Daily Star* (35p).

Table 1.1 The British national press

	Left-leaning	Right-leaning
Tabloid	*Daily Mirror* and *Sunday Mirror*	*The Sun* and *News of the World* *Daily Star* and *Daily Star Sunday* *Daily Express* and *Sunday Express* *Daily Mail* and *Mail on Sunday* *The People*
Broadsheet	*The Guardian* and *The Observer* *The Independent* and *Independent on Sunday*	*The Daily Telegraph* and *The Sunday Telegraph* *The Times* and *The Sunday Times* *The Business*

compared with newspapers across the world or throughout other periods in history, the British press does not currently occupy the most extreme political positions possible; the newspapers are not at the 'wing'. Table 1.1 shows our (admittedly impressionistic) view of where the newspapers we included in our corpus fall in terms of their style and political position.

Readers will have noticed that the majority of the tabloids are right-leaning, whereas the broadsheets appear to be more evenly spread. At a first glance, this would appear to suggest that the corpus of newspaper articles we have collected will be somewhat skewed to the right. However, it should be borne in mind that the tabloids generally contain less written text than the broadsheets; it should also be noted that, for some of the right-leaning newspapers (*The Business*, the *Daily Express*, *The Star*, *The Sun* and *The Daily Telegraph*), the archiving of data in Nexis UK was rather patchy for the years 1998 and 1999.

Along with political affiliation, it is worth taking into account where the newspapers generally stand on religion. Taira, Poole and Knott (forthcoming) carried out a profiling of newspapers based on the analysis of stories about Geert Wilders, a Dutch conservative politician who was banned from entering the United Kingdom in 2009 because of concerns over his anti-Islam views, and a visit by the Pope to the country in 2010. They placed British newspapers on a pro-/anti-religious continuum. At one end of the continuum were two pro-Christian newspapers, *The Daily Telegraph* and the *Daily Express*. Next to them were the *Daily Mail* and *The Sun*. At the opposite end of the continuum were more secularist newspapers, which were sometimes openly critical of religion. These included *The Independent* and *The Guardian*. In the middle of the continuum were the *Daily Star*, the *Daily Mirror* and *The Times*. It can be seen that, generally, the pro-Christian newspapers were also right-leaning, whereas the two secularist newspapers were left-leaning.

Another factor when considering newspapers also needs to be taken into account: newspapers contain more than 'hard news', or stories about important current political and social events. They also feature a great deal of 'soft news', consisting of celebrity gossip, 'human interest' stories (which often have little impact on anyone except for those directly related to the story) and reviews and commentaries about books, films, music, plays, gadgets, computer games, fashions, restaurants and holiday destinations. Such articles are also found in magazines and thus could be viewed as belonging to genres of entertainment, or even advertising, rather than news. Additionally, newspapers employ columnists or commentators, to write on particular topics (often on a weekly basis). Such columnists may or may not be representative of the newspaper's general stance, and one columnist may work for multiple newspapers. Some columnists were well known to the public for other reasons before they started writing columns (such as the British television presenters Jeremy Clarkson and Robert Kilroy-Silk), while others became well known through their journalism (such as Julie Burchill and Richard Littlejohn).

Columnists are generally granted more freedom than journalists, who engage in the 'hard' reporting of facts. Their columns normally aim to be entertaining, provocative or populist, and as a result are more openly opinionated than other forms of journalism. During the period we focused on, the British press was regulated by the Press Complaints Commission (PCC), which describes itself on its website[9] as 'an independent self-regulatory body which deals with complaints about the editorial content of newspapers and magazines (and their websites)'. The PCC contains an editors' code of practice, which was originally written in 1991 and had almost thirty changes made to it by 2011. The PCC's website describes the code as not constituting a legal document but, instead, setting a benchmark for ethical standards and acting as 'the cornerstone of the system of self-regulation to which the industry has made a binding commitment'. The code (about 1,400 words in length) is divided into sixteen main sections, which cover areas such as accuracy, discrimination and privacy. The discrimination section, for example, reads:

(i)   The press must avoid prejudicial or pejorative reference to an individual's race, colour, religion, gender, sexual orientation or to any physical or mental illness or disability.
(ii) Details of an individual's race, colour, religion, sexual orientation, physical or mental illness or disability must be avoided unless genuinely relevant to the story.

---

[9] See www.pcc.org.uk/index.html.

In October 2011 a search for complaints on its website relating to the word *Muslim* found forty-six cases, the majority of which were complaints regarding inaccurate reporting of facts. These complaints tended to result in the newspaper in question apologising, printing a retraction and/or removing the inaccuracy from its website. For example, a complaint about an article in *The Sun* (7 October 2006), which claimed that 'Muslim yobs...wrecked a house to stop four brave soldiers moving in after returning from Afghanistan', resulted in the newspaper printing the following retraction:

Following our report 'Hounded out' about a soldiers' home in Datchet, Berks, being vandalised by Muslims, we have been asked to point out no threatening calls were logged at Combermere Barracks from Muslims and police have been unable to establish if any faith or religious group was responsible for the incident. We are happy to make this clear.[10]

When it can be established that a newspaper has made a factual error, the PCC appears to have been effective in achieving an apology or retraction. This relates to the section on accuracy, which states:

(i)   The Press must take care not to publish inaccurate, misleading or distorted information, including pictures.
(ii) A significant inaccuracy, misleading statement or distortion once recognised must be corrected, promptly and with due prominence, and – where appropriate – an apology published. In cases involving the Commission, prominence should be agreed with the PCC in advance.
(iii) The Press, whilst free to be partisan, must distinguish clearly between comment, conjecture and fact.

However, Petley (2006: 56) describes a complaint made to the PCC about an article by celebrity columnist Robert Kilroy-Silk in the *Daily Express* (16 January 1995). The article contained the line 'Moslems everywhere behave with equal savagery'. The complaint was rejected, on the grounds that '[t]he column clearly represented a named columnist's personal view and would be seen as no more than his robust opinions'. Similarly, Robin Richardson (2004: 68) reports on a complaint made to the PCC about an article written by columnist Carol Sarler in the *Daily Express* (15 November 2001). Sarler wrote: 'Every Moslem state in the world today is a cauldron of violence, corruption, oppression and dodgy democracy: the direct opponents of everything a liberal holds dear; yet at your peril do you mention it.' She also referred to the Qur'an as 'no more than a bloodthirsty little book'. Again, a complaint to the PCC was

---

[10] Despite *The Sun*'s retraction, at the time of writing, the article was still available from the newspaper's website, without the retraction present.

rejected, as 'the article, headed as comment, was clearly distinguished as the opinion of the columnist, in accordance with terms of the Code'. Richardson (2004: 68) concludes that '[i]t is clear that the PCC is not an adequate bulwark against Islamophobia in the media', while Petley (2006: 61) argues that 'the PCC is quite hopeless as a bulwark against negative representations of Muslims and Islam in the press. Since it is paid for by newspapers and its Code Committee is stuffed with editors, some of whose papers are front runners in the Islamophobia stakes, I find it extremely difficult not to regard it as part of the problem rather than part of the solution.'[11]

Of course, individuals can also take newspapers to court if they feel that they have been unfairly represented or treated. For instance, in 2008 world motorsport boss Max Mosley successfully won a legal action against the *News of the World*, which claimed that he had participated in an orgy that had Nazi overtones. The newspaper had to pay £60,000 in damages, as well as covering Mosley's legal costs (£450,000). However, the ability to take newspapers to court is usually beyond the means of ordinary people, for many of whom the best hope is to secure a retraction and apology forced by the PCC if they feel aggrieved by the press.

Another form of 'text' in newspapers consists of letters, e-mails or text messages from readers. As with columnists, these texts tend to comment on news stories, providing less accountable opinions that may also be interpreted as being from a different 'voice' from the reporting tone of the editorial of the newspaper. In quoting parts of articles in this book, we have noted when such articles are actually letters or from columnists. We are not convinced that readers are always able to disassociate the opinions of a columnist or a letter writer from the overall stance of the newspaper, particularly because editors are ultimately able to choose which points of view are articulated in their newspaper. Such opinions are 'there', in print, and they have the power and potential to influence others. A columnist has something of the glamour of a celebrity whereas a letter writer could represent the voice of the 'ordinary person' or the 'invisible majority'. Readers often have little way of tracing the identities of letter writers or of finding out the extent to which such views are representative of the newspaper's readership[12] or the views of the wider populace, though they may

---

[11] In March 2012 it was announced that the Press Complaints Commission would close and be replaced by a new body, in the wake of its poor response to a scandal involving journalists hacking into people's telephones.

[12] Some newspapers conduct polls of their readers, asking them to telephone a number if they agree or disagree with a particular proposition. Such polls can be money-making endeavours for the newspaper. For example, a poll on 8 February 2008 in *The Sun* asking whether the Archbishop of Canterbury, Rowan Williams, should be sacked for commenting on sharia law cost voters 10p per call. While such polls are often reported the following day as strongly supporting a particular position (often in congruence with the newspaper that ran the poll), they are perhaps not perfect indicators of reader opinion, and definitely not good indicators of

make inferences about the extent to which the letter has been chosen because it reflects the political views of the newspaper.

Another issue we need to address is why we choose to focus on newspapers to examine the representation of Islam rather than, say, television or radio broadcasts, blogs, twitter feeds or focus group interviews. There are a number of reasons, some involving practical considerations, others based more on the notion of 'influence'. Practically, newspaper data nowadays is relatively easy to obtain in electronic form, particularly if one is interested in the first decade of the twenty-first century. Thousands of articles can be downloaded onto a personal computer's hard drive in a couple of minutes, and very specific searches can be carried out of newspaper databases, so that only articles from a specific time period or newspaper or articles containing certain words will be retrieved. This has allowed us to consider (almost) every newspaper article published in the UK national press that referred to Islam, however briefly, in the period from 1998 to 2009. This gave us a much larger dataset to analyse than what we could have gathered if we had engaged in the expensive and time-consuming transcription of television or radio news. A less pragmatic reason is that British newspapers make no secret of their political standpoints, and actively attempt to influence the populace (for example, by backing particular political parties during elections). This makes them distinct from the broadcast media. Yet it could be argued that newspapers have a limited readership and hence, relative to broadcast media, a limited influence. Some evidence for this view can be gained from the Audit Bureau of Circulations (ABC), which shows that actual sales of newspapers appear to be quite low (see Table 1.2) relative to the United Kingdom's population.

However, we need to take into account the fact that more than one person may read a newspaper, and that newspapers have online sites where their articles can be obtained. When considering 'influence', it is perhaps better to consider estimates of numbers of readers rather than purchases. The National Readership Survey[13] carries out surveys of 36,000 adults each year in order to obtain information about newspaper and magazine readership

---

national opinion. For example, *The Sun* (13 July 2005) reported on a poll of its readers to see if they agreed with allowing Professor Tariq Ramadan, an Egyptian scholar, into the United Kingdom. The newspaper reported that 98.7 per cent (23,475 readers) wanted him banned from the country. Although it is likely that the majority of *Sun* readers wanted to ban Professor Ramadan, it should be noted that, in many newspaper polls, participation is self-selecting (e.g. people first choose to buy a particular newspaper that represents their views, and then they choose to telephone a number in order to vote), and that people who feel strongly about something may be more likely to vote. Additionally, such polls often appear at the end of highly biased articles. One may also speculate that people who would be likely to disagree probably would not buy the newspaper in the first place.

[13] See www.nrs.co.uk.

Table 1.2 Newspaper sales, December 2008

Daily newspapers		Sunday newspapers	
Sun	2,899,310	News of the World	2,987,730
Daily Mail	2,139,178	Mail on Sunday	2,060,731
Daily Mirror	1,346,916	Sunday Mirror	1,195,711
Daily Telegraph	824,244	Sunday Telegraph	597,934
The Times	600,962	Sunday Times	1,155,589
Daily Express	728,296	Sunday Express	638,556
Daily Star	725,671	Daily Star Sunday	342,019
Guardian	343,010	Observer	420,323
Independent	200,242	Independent on Sunday	163,545
		People	592,306

Note: There are no figures for *The Business* as this publication closed in February 2008.
Source: ABC, derived from www.guardian.co.uk/media/table/2009/jan/09/abcs-pressandpublishing and www.guardian.co.uk/media/table/2009/jan/09/abc-december-national-newspapers.

Table 1.3 Readership estimates, July 2008–June 2009

Daily newspapers		Sunday newspapers	
Sun	7,860,000	News of the World	7,850,000
Daily Mail	4,846,000	Mail on Sunday	5,466,000
Daily Mirror	3,566,000	Sunday Mirror	3,893,000
Daily Telegraph	1,843,000	Sunday Telegraph	1,672,000
Times	1,801,000	Sunday Times	3,194,000
Daily Express	1,624,000	Sunday Express	1,676,000
Daily Star	1,471,000	Daily Star Sunday	888,000
Guardian	1,205,000	Observer	1,374,000
Independent	679,000	Independent on Sunday	646,000
		People	1,431,000

Source: National Readership Survey.

patterns. Their estimates for the UK readership of daily and Sunday newspapers are shown in Table 1.3.

From this table it can be seen that, in general, people tend to read newspapers more often on Sundays, tabloids are more popular than broadsheets, and the right-leaning newspapers tend to be read more than the left-leaning ones. The combined daily readerships of two right-leaning tabloids *The Sun* and the *Daily Mail* are about seven times higher than the two left-leaning broadsheets *The Guardian* and *The Independent*. So, while newspaper sales appear low, Table 1.3 suggests that a reasonably high proportion of the adult population regularly reads newspapers. With almost 30 million votes cast in

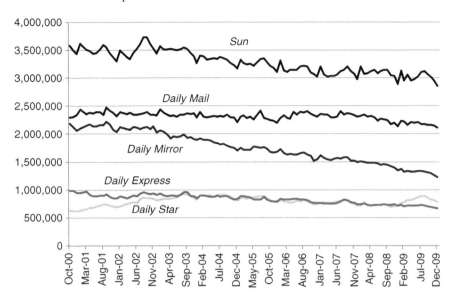

Figure 1.1 Newspaper sales (tabloids), October 2000–December 2009
Source: ABC

the 2010 British general election[14] and a 65.1 per cent turnout,[15] indicating approximately 46 million people of voting age, the readership of the daily newspapers – at about 24 million – amounts to more than half the voting population at that election.

Yet a tendency towards declining newspaper sales has been documented over the first decade of the twenty-first century (see Figures 1.1 and 1.2).[16] It should be noted that the scales in terms of numbers of sales shown in the Y axis are different for the two figures, as the tabloids sell many more copies than the broadsheets. The best-selling newspaper, *The Sun*, sold about half a million fewer copies in 2010 than it did in 2000, dipping below 3 million. The *Daily Mirror* shows the most marked decline, which can perhaps be partially attributed to a series of decisions it made between 2002 and 2005 when it tried to dissociate itself from the 'red top' label by changing its logo

---

[14] See www.politicsresources.net/area/uk/ge10/result_summary.htm.

[15] See www.ukpolitical.info/Turnout45.htm.

[16] The question of whether 9/11 and 7/7 – two events that caused large rises in the number of stories about Muslims and Islam – were also responsible for increases in newspaper sales is worth considering here. The 9/11 attacks did not result in a marked increase in tabloid sales, although there were small increases for the broadsheets. However, this pattern was different for 7/7, with most newspapers showing a small increase in sales between May and July 2005.

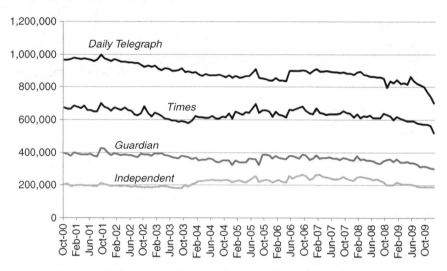

Figure 1.2 Newspaper sales (broadsheets), October 2000–December 2009
Source: ABC

from red to black. Unlike other tabloid newspapers, the *Mirror* opposed the United Kingdom's participation in the invasion of Iraq. Then, in 2004, it published photographs of the Queen's Lancashire Regiment abusing Iraqi prisoners. These photographs were later found to be faked, which resulted in the sacking of the paper's editor, Piers Morgan. This scandal, and the *Mirror*'s anti-war stance, may have resulted in some readers turning away from the newspaper.

An interesting insight into the influence of newspapers on UK politics was provided by Lance Price, a media advisor to the prime minister, Tony Blair, from 1998 to 2001. In *The Guardian* (1 July 2006) Price wrote: 'No big decision could ever be made inside No 10 [Downing Street] without taking account of the likely reaction of three men – Gordon Brown, John Prescott and Rupert Murdoch. On all the really big decisions, anybody else could safely be ignored.' Murdoch is the founder, chief executive officer and chairman of News Corporation, which owns *The Times* and *The Sunday Times, The Sun* and the (now closed) *News of the World*.[17] He also has a large stake in a satellite television network, Sky, which has its own news

---

[17] In July 2011 the *News of the World* closed as a result of the exposure of a phone-hacking scandal in which people working for the newspaper illegally hacked into the mobile telephones of a number of people, including victims of the 7/7 attacks, relatives of British soldiers who had been killed in Afghanistan and Iraq, the murdered schoolgirl Millie Dowler, the mother of another murdered girl, Sara Payne, and a number of celebrities.

channel. News Corporation also owns other media and news sources around the world, including the American news channel Fox News, and Star TV, which broadcasts to Asia. Since the 1980s, apart from *The Times*, which supported the Conservatives in 1997, Murdoch's newspapers have backed the winning political party in every UK national election.[18]

As a result, even with declining sales of newspapers, their large readership and the focus upon newspaper opinion by politicians in the United Kingdom mean that we feel that there are strong justifications for our focus on traditional print journalism in this book.

Having provided a brief introduction to the British national press, we now narrow our focus to consider existing research that has examined how the media (particularly the British media) have represented Islam and Muslims.

Islam and the media

This book is by no means the first to have examined the representation of Islam and Muslims in the 'Western' media, although our approach differs from earlier studies both in terms of scope and methodology. However, it is useful in this initial chapter to consider how others have approached the subject, as well as outlining what they found.

In general, the picture is one that has repeatedly highlighted negative bias. Said's 1981 book *Covering Islam* (revised in 1997) argues that the media control and filter information, selectively determining what Westerners learn about Islam. He claims that the media portray Islam as oppressive, outmoded, anti-intellectual, restrictive, extremist, backward, dangerous and causing conflict. The examples in Said's book are wide-ranging, consisting of reports of print and television sources, mainly from the United States, but also including some from the United Kingdom. A main focus is concerned with the reporting that took place during and after the Iranian hostage crisis, when fifty-two American citizens were held hostage by Iranian militants in the US embassy in Tehran for 444 days from 1979 to 1981. The examples that Said describes are convincing, although it is difficult to know how they were selected, or whether certain cases were chosen because they showed the most negatively biased representations. Subsequent studies have certainly supported his findings. For example, Awass (1996) also examined the American media, and he concludes that it depicted Islam as a threat to Western security, associating the religion with fundamentalism and terrorism. Later studies have attempted to lend more weight to their findings by backing them up with quantitative evidence. Accordingly, Dunn, who focused on two Australian newspapers (2001: 296), notes how Muslims were constructed negatively – 'fanatic,

---

[18] See www.guardian.co.uk/news/datablog/2010/may/04/general-election-newspaper-support.

intolerant, fundamentalist, misogynist [and] alien' – 75 per cent of the time, whereas positive constructions accounted for 25 per cent of cases.

Similarly, Poole (2002) analysed all articles on British Muslims in *The Guardian/Observer* and *The Times/Sunday Times* between 1993 and 1997, as well as stories in *The Sun* and *Daily Mail* taken from 1997. She finds that British Muslims were frequently represented as irrational and antiquated, threatening to liberal values and democracy, involved in corruption and crime, extremist and fanatical, and influenced politically by Muslims outside the United Kingdom.

John Richardson's book *(Mis)Representing Islam* (2004) uses techniques from critical discourse analysis (CDA: described in the following section) to carry out a qualitative examination of linguistic and social practices within British broadsheets over a four-month period in 1997. He finds four common argumentative themes associated with the reporting of Islam: as a military threat, as being associated with terrorists/extremists, as a threat to democracy and as a sexist or social threat. Richardson concludes that British broadsheets engage in three processes, separation, differentiation and negativisation, and 'predominantly reframe Muslim cultural difference as cultural deviance, and increasingly, it seems, cultural threat' (2004: 232).

In the same year a report by Robin Richardson of the Commission on British Muslims and Islamophobia addressed a range of contexts and institutions relevant to the representation of Islam, including the media. The report comments on the extremely negative views of some newspaper columnists (2004: 11, 21–2), but also notes that some newspapers acted in a 'responsible' way after 9/11, printing headlines and articles that emphasised that the vast majority of Muslims were peaceful and law-abiding. Such headlines include ones from *The Sun* ('Reach out to Muslims as friends'; 17 September 2001) and the *Daily Mirror* ('Don't blame the Muslims'; 14 September 2001).

Akbarzadeh and Smith (2005), who examined the Australian newspapers *The Age* and *Herald Sun* between 2001 and 2004, find that crude Islamophobic reporting was rare, but argue that 'recurring language used to describe Islam and Muslims (such as "Islamic terrorism", "Muslim fanatics") can come to be representative of all Muslims and Islam as a religion' (2005: 4). They note that the mass media depict Muslims as immature, backward and foreign, and that the context of stories that Muslims appeared in (often war and conflict) would leave a negative impression on readers. However, they also note that about half the stories in *The Age* and a quarter of those in the *Herald Sun* demonstrated some care in their choice of words in order to present Australian Muslims as diverse rather than a homogeneous group and to avoid stereotyping.

Billig *et al.* (2006), who examined press reporting during two-week periods prior to the British general elections of 1997, 2001 and 2005, find very few articles about Muslims in the two early periods (thirteen and nineteen, respectively), but a larger number in 2005 (2006: 141), showing how Islam had become an increasingly politicised topic. Billig *et al.* report how press articles tended to represent Muslims as voting with different priorities from non-Muslims (with allegiance to Iraqi Muslims trumping all other issues), despite the fact that this contradicted the views of British Muslims quoted in the articles.

Poole and Richardson's (2006) edited volume *Muslims and the News Media* takes a number of different approaches to analysis, considering not only articles themselves but also how various processes of production and reception can offer insights into the representations found. For example, Richardson's own chapter (2006) includes a quantitative analysis of the religious identity of people who are quoted in articles about Islam, finding that Muslim sources tend to be quoted when they are critical of their own religion. In another chapter, focusing on production processes, Cole (2006) examines employment statistics on ethnic minority reporters in British news-rooms, while a third chapter, by Petley (2006), is concerned with the process of reception, considering the role of the Press Complaints Commission in responding to complaints about Islamophobic articles.

Moore, Mason and Lewis (2008) use content analysis in applying a cate-gorisation scheme to 974 articles on Islam in the British press from 2000 to 2008, as well as examining a smaller sample of visuals appearing in the articles. They find that stories that focused on extremism or differences between Islamic culture and 'the West' increased over time, whereas stories that focused on attacks on Muslims or problems that they faced decreased. Their visual analysis finds high usage of police 'mugshots' to portray Muslims, a greater number of pictures of Muslim males compared to females and a high number of pictures of Muslims engaged in religious practices.

This review, while not exhaustive, serves to show an emerging pattern of negative representation, coupled with briefer glimpses of positive or more responsible reporting in studies of Islam in the press. The review also shows a move towards sampling larger amounts of articles that cover longer time periods, in order to get an impression of a general picture (which can be quantified) rather than selecting a few articles, which may or may not be representative. Moreover, analytical approaches have involved critical dis-course analysis, visual analysis, content or quantitative analysis or various combinations of these approaches. Our approach also combines different, though compatible, techniques, which are described in more detail in the following two sections.

Critical discourse analysis

In writing this book, we draw on theories from critical discourse analysis, an approach to the analysis of discourse that holds that language is a social practice and examines how ideologies and power relations are expressed in language. Critical discourse analysis involves the close examination of language in texts, as, for example, in showing how particular linguistic phenomena (word choice, sentence structure, metaphor, implicature, argumentation strategy, etc.) can be used to represent a particular stance. This type of linguistic analysis is multidisciplinary, as it is informed by different fields of study (see Wodak and Meyer 2009: 1–2), including critical linguistics (Fowler *et al.* 1979), which focuses on how grammatical systems are related to social and personal needs. Additionally, critical discourse analysis combines linguistic analysis with a consideration of different contexts. In order to interpret and explain our analyses, they must be interrogated from different social, historical and political contexts. References to events that have occurred (either recently or in the distant past) in the United Kingdom, as well as the wider world, help to explain why certain linguistic patterns of representation of Islam are found while others are not. Perhaps the two most salient world events (at least for British newspapers) in the reporting of Islam were the 9/11 attacks on the United States in 2001 and the 7/7 attacks on the London transport network in 2005. As will be seen in Chapter 4, both attacks resulted in large 'spikes' in terms of the amount of newspaper stories referring to Islam or Muslims, and they can also reasonably be viewed as the source of the general increase in interest in Islam over the period studied in this book. Other contexts, such as the increase in immigration of Pakistani and Bangladeshi Muslims to the United Kingdom after the end of World War II, resulting in a sizeable so-called 'British Muslim community', and the overall political situation, also need to be taken into account. The broader political context is dominated by the Labour Party, which came to power in the United Kingdom in 1997 and remained in control until 2010. During this period Labour's policies on asylum seekers, immigration, multiculturalism and issues surrounding 'cultural sensitivity' were often felt to be too 'soft' by the right-leaning press. Given that, as noted, Muslim immigration into the United Kingdom also forms part of the context of our study, this too is likely to contribute to how certain articles represented Islam. Importantly, the Labour government's decision to combine forces with the United States to invade Afghanistan and Iraq in 2001 and 2003, respectively, resulted in criticism of a different kind, with some quarters of the press viewing Labour as following American interests, and, particularly in the case of Iraq, engaging in an unjustified war that could alienate Muslims. Other factors – a move in the United Kingdom towards secularism, and the growing influence of equality politics, particularly rights for women, ethnic minorities and gay men and lesbians – can also help to explain the sometimes conflicting representations of Muslims found in the British press.

The context outlined above is fairly immediate, but it is also pertinent to take into account context that goes beyond our own experiences of the last couple of decades. A quote (popularly attributed to Mark Twain) goes as follows: 'History does not repeat itself, but it does rhyme.' One question that this book aims to address is the extent to which the representations of Islam found in the modern British press appear to echo or rhyme with long-standing ways of thinking, and towards the end of this book we compare the representations of Islam found in the early twenty-first-century press with those from nineteenth-century British newspapers.

As well as focusing upon context, as discussed, critical discourse analysts also point out that texts are not isolated occurrences and do not materialise out of nowhere. Instead, they are produced by particular people for particular reasons, with certain restrictions or expectations placed upon them. They may be widely distributed or there may be restrictions on who has access to them. They may be subject to censorship or the style of language used may mean that some texts are simply inaccessible to certain people. The meanings of texts are also negotiated by audiences, who may react to a text in a wide range of different ways – some that the text producer may have desired, some that may be unexpected or unwanted. Additionally, parts of texts or whole texts may refer to other texts or may themselves be referred to in later texts. In order to make sense of the full impact of a text, then, we need to take into account these intertextual references. This can sometimes involve looking at how a single article is later reported on or discussed; a frequent example involves the letters page, which normally contains comment on articles that appeared in previous issues. Newspapers can also comment on the reporting practices of other newspapers (engaging in a form of critical analysis themselves). At other times, intertextuality can involve the reproduction of parts of texts or references to texts from outside the set of newspapers under examination (e.g. a quote from a film or a well-known speech, a book review, a report featured in an overseas newspaper, etc.).

Interdiscursivity, or the way that texts are constituted from diverse discourses and genres (Fairclough 1995: 134–5), is another factor that can be examined. For instance, newspaper articles may incorporate styles of writing from multiple genres into the same article – 'hard news', 'entertainment', 'political rhetoric' or 'advertising'. Additionally, if we view discourses as ways of representing the world or particular phenomena within it, then we may find that particular discourses within an article may support or contradict each other. For example, we found that some liberal newspapers seemed to draw on a 'gender equality' discourse to argue that Muslim women should not wear the veil. However, at the same time, such an argument could also be viewed as oppressive, as it positions Muslim women who *do* wear the veil as problematic. Such a notion of 'discourses' as ways of representing the world means that the discourses that the analyst identifies are subjective and open to reinterpretation.

In considering how to interpret a text, a key question posed by CDA is 'Who benefits?'. Critical discourse analysts are often engaged in a form of 'action research', in that they wish to highlight particular inequalities or biases that appear within certain texts. While, theoretically, CDA can be conducted from any political perspective, it has often been used by left-leaning analysts who are concerned with highlighting how powerful people or groups are able to claim and maintain power. Theorists such as Antonio Gramsci, Michel Foucault and Karl Marx have been influential on the development and implementation of CDA. The action research dimension of CDA has led to a number of offshoots of the approach; one strand of CDA, for example, called eco-critical discourse analysis (Harré, Brockmeier and Mühlhäusler 1999; Stibbe 2006), has focused on both exposing ideologies that are potentially damaging to the environment and finding discursive representations that contribute to ecologically sustainable societies. Although the individual goals and foci of many CDA practitioners may differ, there is generally a broad consensus towards creating a fairer, more transparent society, in which people are given more opportunities, and vulnerable groups are empowered rather than exploited (though people may, of course, disagree with how this should be done, or how concepts such as *fairness*, *opportunity*, *vulnerable group*, *exploitation* and *empowerment* are defined). CDA is not against power per se but more concerned with abuses of power. One strand of CDA, called positive CDA, focuses on highlighting what texts 'do well' and 'get right' (Martin and Rose 2003; Martin 2004). Theoretically, it should be possible to conduct critical discourse analysis from any position, although it is very rare to find CDA practitioners explicitly arguing from perspectives that deny the Holocaust or global warming, or favour viewpoints that others would label homophobic, sexist, racist or in favour of 'Big Business'.

Thus a concern that could be raised about CDA is the extent to which its analysis can be said to be overtly biased. Although some CDA practitioners do not begin their analysis determined to 'prove a point', questions may be raised about the extent to which pre-existing positions may have influenced the way that the analysis is carried out. For example, if I am convinced that a certain newspaper is homophobic, I may look through articles that reference homosexuality and then choose five such articles that clearly do demonstrate homophobia. However, in an early stage of the analysis, I may have decided to overlook another 200 articles that present more positive representations of gay people. While my analysis of those five articles is clear evidence of homophobia, it is not the full story. More importantly, the analysis may lead readers to infer that the five articles are representative of the attitudes expressed in the newspaper. Widdowson (2004: 102) has therefore raised the concern that the analysis is shaped by the desired result, which is influenced by the researcher's own political agenda.

Clearly, though, all forms of analysis, being conducted by human beings, are inevitably subject to various biases. On one level, humans tend to demonstrate cognitive biases. For example, we tend to pay more attention to negative rather than positive experiences (the negativity bias; see Baumeister *et al.* 2001), we develop preferences for things we are familiar with (the exposure effect; see Zajonc 1968), we tend to give preferential treatment to people who we perceive as being members of our own group (the in-group bias; see Tajfel 1970, 1982) and we tend to remember distinct and unique items that 'stand out like a sore thumb' (the von Restorff effect; see von Restorff 1933). These cognitive biases, along with many others, can impact on the way that we select data for research and analyse, interpret and explain it.

At another level, our own identities and experiences may bias us. Our parents, teachers and friends are likely to have influenced our thinking about a particular topic, as well as what we read or hear in the media. As we grow older, such biases can become further entrenched, as humans have a tendency to seek out and pay attention to sources that confirm their existing points of view while ignoring those that are oppositional (the confirmation bias; see Plous 1993). Aspects of our identity (our religion, ethnicity, gender, age, sexuality, etc.) may also have a role to play in how we attend to and make sense of particular representations. We have a tendency to be interested in people who resemble us in some way. Conversely, Goffman (1963: 14) and Epstein (1998: 145) have both noted that stigmatised aspects of an identity can become very salient, subsuming other types of identity. Other factors, such as the extent to which we have interacted with people from a particular identity group, and whether we view ourselves as different from them or in competition with them for resources (such as jobs or social housing), can also impact on how we view them. Finally, we are constrained by the discourses that circulate in the society we live in. Foucault (1972: 146) notes that 'it is not possible for us to describe our own archive, since it is from within these rules that we speak'. Put another way, the newspapers we analyse are also the newspapers that we read, and have read for many years. These newspapers will have already played a part in creating the views of the analysts who then go on to examine them.

It would therefore be disingenuous to claim that we (the authors) are unbiased. Nor would we expect to produce an analysis that everyone will agree with. Some readers may attempt to explain our findings as stemming from our own identities (e.g. 'They are not Muslims themselves so they missed out on various insights'). As with all books, with a set of word limits and deadlines, we have had to make decisions to prioritise certain aspects of analysis over others. No analysis of the representation of a particular social group can claim to be exhaustive or unbiased. So why bother carrying out such research at all?

We have made two attempts to address this issue of bias. The first involves researcher reflexivity, or the methodological principle of using self-awareness to reflect on the research process and how our own identities as researchers may have impacted on it. The fact that there are three of us has been helpful, in that we have been able to challenge each other's perspectives in the process of writing this book. We have also presented different parts of this work at conferences and workshops, to different audiences, as well as seeking the opinions of Muslims and non-Muslims, who have provided a range of differing views on our interpretations of the data. We therefore do not subscribe to a view that there is a single or 'correct' interpretation of our data, but instead argue that there are multiple interpretations, each appearing valid to the interpreter.

We also acknowledge our own biases, and here attempt to make explicit a set of tenets that we had in mind when analysing and interpreting the newspaper data. These were based on admittedly rather broad notions of respecting others, 'playing fair', doing to others as you would have done to you and striving for accuracy (e.g. not misleading readers). We were thus interested in cases of reporting that could be interpreted as not adhering to these tenets. We feel that we are generally in keeping with CDA's focus on abuse of power, rather than viewing all power as negative, as well as keeping the question 'Who benefits?' in mind as we carried out our analyses.

With respect to our own views on Islam, we note that we sometimes have contradictory or opposing perspectives (something we also found to be pervasive in the press, even when journalists were well-meaning). We acknowledge that we are products of a 'Western', liberal, secular, academic culture, and that this has impacted on the way we carried out our analyses and the way we interpreted the results. We have also found it useful to consider a distinction made by the Runnymede Trust (1997), between 'open' and 'closed' views of Islam. A closed view would be phobically hostile to Islam, viewing it as monolithic, static and authoritarian, totally separate from 'the West', inferior and primitive, an aggressive enemy, with Muslims constructed as manipulative, devious and self-righteous. However, an open view would see Islam as diverse and dynamic, with internal debates, as being interdependent on the West, sharing a common humanity, different but equal, and as a cooperative partner to work with on shared problems. Legitimate criticisms of Islam would be made in such a spirit of openness. Robin Richardson (2004: 26) writes that this distinction is 'fundamental in all considerations of media coverage', and in conducting our analysis we have attempted to keep it in mind, particularly when encountering articles that appear to be critical of Islam.

Our second way of attempting to address bias is also methodological, involving taking a corpus linguistics approach to our data collection and analysis. This is discussed in more detail in the following section.

Corpus linguistics

Corpus linguistics is the 'study of language based on examples of "real life" language use' (McEnery and Wilson 1996: 1). In the same way that a scientist may test a new drug on a smaller, representative sample of a population, corpus linguists test out or discover linguistic theories by collecting a smaller, representative sample of language. Generally, corpus linguists attempt to create a balanced *corpus* (Latin for *body*) of language, which is representative of the variety of language that they are interested in. A corpus of nineteenth-century English literature might contain samples of writing from a range of different authors, although we would try to balance these samples so that no single author or type of writing was over-represented. The larger and more well-balanced the corpus, the more confident the researcher can be that any findings can be extrapolated to that particular language variety as a whole.

However, an important principle behind corpus linguistics is that, once the corpus has been assembled, the way that it is analysed is very distinct. Rather than simply reading the whole corpus (which would take a long time) or picking out parts at random, at the initial stage of analysis the corpus linguist relies on computer software, which can quickly and accurately perform complex calculations on the corpus as a whole. Such calculations are often based on frequency information, sometimes with attendant statistical tests, though they can also involve presenting data in particular ways that make it easier for human beings to identify linguistic patterns.

The advantages of this approach, particularly for anyone wanting to carry out critical discourse analysis, should – we hope – be clear. First, the larger amount of data being studied means that any findings we make are more credible than those based on a handful of examples. Second, we can obtain a much better picture surrounding the frequency of particular phenomena. As Conboy (2010: 5) notes of newspapers, 'Heteroglossia is Bakhtin's conceptualisation of the fact that all language transactions take place in the context of potentially alternative expressions.' Put simply, newspapers have lots of ways of writing about a given topic, and they continuously make decisions, choosing one particular way out of a potentially large, perhaps infinite, set of choices. A corpus analysis will allow us to see which choices are privileged, giving evidence for mainstream, popular or entrenched ways of thinking. Echoing Gerbner's views on 'cultivation theory' in the media

(Gerbner *et al.* 1986), Fairclough (1989: 54) writes: 'A single text on its own is quite insignificant: the effects of media power are cumulative, working through the repetition of particular ways of handling causality and agency, particular ways of positioning the reader, and so forth.' A similar point about repetition is made by Stubbs (2001: 215), who argues that '[r]epeated patterns show that evaluative meanings are not merely personal and idiosyncratic, but widely shared in a discourse community. A word, phrase or construction may trigger a cultural stereotype.' A corpus analysis of hundreds or thousands of news articles is well positioned to identify such media repetitions, occurring day after day, gradually influencing their readership.

A third advantage of taking a corpus approach is that the large amount of data has the potential to reveal choices that are much less frequent (though not necessarily those that *never* occur, as discussed in the following section). Such positions, being minority ones, may have been otherwise overlooked by researchers, who did not know to look for them.

This indicates a major benefit of what is called the *corpus-driven* approach (Tognini-Bonelli 2001): the fact that the researcher allows the research to be driven by whatever is found to be salient or frequent in the corpus. Linguistic choices or patterns that run counter to intuitive prediction are thus identified and need to be accounted for. The potential in limiting bias, forcing the researcher to confront realities of frequency or saliency, is not to be underestimated. Importantly, such an approach enables replicability – the fact that another researcher, using the same corpus and the same tool, will be directed to the same frequencies. Of course, there are other, less 'naive', ways of analysing a corpus. A *corpus-based* (Tognini-Bonelli 2001) approach gives the researcher more control, and instead the corpus is used more as a way of testing out existing hypotheses. For example, a researcher who believes that a certain newspaper uses a variant form of the word *Muslim*, such as *Moslem*, more than others can query such a word in the corpus and obtain exact frequencies. Additionally, as discussed in the following section, a corpus analysis does not follow a specific set of procedures in a particular order but can also take different routes.

The availability of powerful personal computers and large amounts of electronic texts has made corpus linguistics an increasingly popular method. Indeed, its status as method has resulted in it making inroads into a wide range of linguistic subdisciplines, including sociolinguistics, language teaching, linguistic description, stylistics, historical linguistics, forensic linguistics and feminist linguistics. Its influence on discourse analysis can be traced back to the 1990s, with papers by Caldas-Coulthard (1995), Hardt-Mautner (1995) and Krishnamurthy (1996) demonstrating the utility of corpus approaches to this field. Other early proponents of the approach include Stubbs (1996, 2001) and Partington (2004), who coined the term *corpus-assisted discourse studies*. We have also previously used and developed this method: Baker (2006)

(1) Context-based analysis of topic via history/politics/culture/etymology. Identify existing topoi/discourses/strategies via wider reading; reference to other CDA studies.
(2) Establish research questions/corpus-building procedures.
(3) Corpus analysis of frequencies, clusters, keywords, dispersion, etc. Identify potential sites of interest in the corpus along with possible discourses/topoi/strategies; relate to those existing in the literature.
(4) Qualitative or CDA analysis of a smaller, representative set of data (e.g., concordances of certain lexical items or of a particular text or set of texts within the corpus); identify discourses/topoi/strategies.
(5) Formulation of new hypotheses or research questions.
(6) Further corpus analysis based on new hypotheses; identify further discourses/topoi/strategies, etc.
(7) Analysis of intertextuality or interdiscursivity based on findings from corpus analysis.
(8) New hypotheses.
(9) Further corpus analysis, identify additional discourses/topoi/strategies, etc.

Figure 1.3 Framework for combining CDA and corpus linguistics
Source: Baker *et al.* (2008: 295).

provides an overview of the methodology, with a number of case studies, and we have implemented the approach to investigate the representation of a number of other subjects, including gay men (Baker 2005), swearing (McEnery 2006) and refugees and asylum seekers (Baker and McEnery 2005; Gabrielatos and Baker 2008; Baker *et al.* 2008). A pilot study for this book (Baker 2010) involves a broad comparison of the representation of Islam between tabloid and broadsheet newspapers from 1998 to 2005, focusing on keywords – words that were statistically significantly more frequent in one of these data sets when compared against another. The intention of this book is to go beyond that pilot study, by focusing on a longer time period (1998 to 2009), carrying out a more detailed investigation of some of the issues that were initially raised (such as stories about extremist 'scroungers') and also employing different forms of analysis, which include examining nineteenth-century newspapers in order to explore historical context. We also wish to combine the quantitative corpus-driven forms of analysis with the qualitative analytical tools more commonly found in critical discourse analysis. These include the identification of intertextuality, as well as legitimation strategies (Van Leeuwen 2007), or ways that help the newspapers to justify their stance (particularly if it is controversial), and perspectivisation (Reisigl and Wodak 2001: 81), or the ways that journalists position their point of view.

Figure 1.3 shows a framework for combining CDA with corpus linguistics, which we developed as part of an earlier study that examined the representation of refugees in the British press (Baker *et al.* 2008). This framework contains a number of stages and involves moving back and forth between quantitative and qualitative techniques of analysis, with each stage informing the next stage and aiding the creation of new hypotheses. The framework is thus cyclical and potentially endless.

In this way we have combined critical discourse analysis and corpus linguistics approaches, by alternating between them as described in the figure. For example, the corpus approach helps in the identification of frequent words or phrases that occur in our data, helping to give an initial focus for a more detailed analysis. We hope, then, that our combination of methods, along with engaging in researcher reflexivity, has resulted in a credible analysis.

Limitations of our approach

One aspect of reflexivity is to cast an equally critical eye over one's own research methods. Thus, in this section, we acknowledge a number of potential limitations of an approach that combines the quantitative analysis of millions of words of data with more qualitative analyses of text and context derived from critical discourse analysis.

First, as noted earlier, the corpus of articles that we examine was taken from online archives, and, as such, contains only the words themselves, rather than a combination of words and pictures. A study by Moore, Mason and Lewis (2008) carried out a content analysis of 974 newspaper articles on Islam, including an analysis of visuals. They find that '[t]he visuals used also indicate the focus on cultural/religious differences, with Muslims seen engaged in religious practice in a way non-Muslims rarely are, and with Muslim men being far more visible than Muslim women' (Moore, Mason and Lewis 2008: 4). They also find evidence that 'Muslims are identified simply *as* Muslims rather than as individuals or particular groups with distinct identities' (2008: 28; emphasis in original). Clearly, pictures play an important part in helping a reader to make sense of a particular news story. However, we do not wish to simply replicate Moore, Mason and Lewis's visual analysis, and we concede that it is not always possible for an analyst to do everything.

A second limitation concerns the way that we found newspaper articles. Following a mixture of introspection, the reading of articles and some trial and error, we created the following set of search terms with which to query the online database:

Alah OR Allah OR ayatollah! OR burka! OR burqa! OR chador! OR fatwa! OR hejab! OR imam! OR islam! OR Koran OR Mecca OR Medina OR Mohammedan! OR Moslem! OR Muslim! OR mosque! OR mufti! OR mujaheddin! OR mujahedin! OR mullah! OR muslim! OR Prophet Mohammed OR Q'uran OR rupoush OR rupush OR sharia OR shari'a OR shia! OR shi-ite! OR Shi'ite! OR sunni! OR the Prophet OR wahabi OR yashmak! AND NOT Islamabad AND NOT shiatsu AND NOT sunnily

It should be noted that '!' acts as a 'wild card' for the purposes of the database, so that 'Muslim!' would yield articles containing the words *Muslim* and *Muslims*.[19] Additionally, we incorporated the 'NOT' operator in order to exclude some words that did not refer to Islam, such as *sunnily*, which otherwise would have been included due to our incorporation of *sunni*!

This search elicited 200,037 articles consisting of almost 143 million words, but, without reading every single article from every newspaper produced during the time period from 1998 to 2009, we cannot be 100 per cent certain that we have found every single article that referenced Islam. For example, at a late stage in the research we read an article in a left-leaning 'quality' newspaper that referred to new Conservative activists being sent to 'Madrasa-style training camps' in order to learn Conservative policy. We had not included *madrasa* in our search terms. The article did not mention Muslims in any other way, although we found it notable that a concept associated with Islam was being used in quite a negative way in the article, which was critical of the Conservative Party in the United Kingdom. A similar issue occurs when an article is about Islam only because it refers to a certain Muslim by name only (such as Abu Hamza, a frequently referenced person in the corpus). We did not search for specific names, so this may have limited the number of articles about individual Muslims that could have told us something interesting about the representation of Islam in general. We also noticed that, occasionally, some references to Islam were made 'in passing' in newspaper articles, rather than being the main focus of the article. We did consider whether it was actually worth including such articles at all. However, we decided that they did have a part to play in terms of the overall picture. Why, for example, would a sports column report 'in passing' on the religious status of one of its players? Finally, as the analysis progressed, we realised that a small number of articles had mistakenly been included in the corpus as a result of some of the search terms having multiple meanings. For example, *Mecca* can refer to the birthplace of the prophet Muhammad, but it can also refer to a British bingo hall chain of the same name. While we could address such issues by deleting the erroneously retrieved articles, we took the decision to keep all articles that had been elicited through the search terms, so as to facilitate the replication of our study using the same terms by other researchers, while acknowledging that the search did not yield 100 per cent of all potential articles on Muslims, and did result in a small number of articles in which Islam appeared to be only peripheral or not a focus of the article at all. However, as we were focusing on very frequent patterns, the effect of such articles was minimal.

Before concluding the discussion of corpus linguistics, let us consider some potential criticisms of the corpus approach. One is that the corpus approach

---

[19] In fact, the database search facility automatically included plurals of nouns.

sometimes appears simply to confirm what people already know. We found evidence of this when presenting some of our results at conferences. For example, a finding that 9/11 caused a sharp increase in the amount of articles about Muslims was occasionally met with the response 'So what? That's obvious!' In some cases, we have agreed that the results have confirmed our own hypotheses, but on closer consideration we have wondered whether this was actually true. In fact, we started out with very few expectations about what we would find in the corpus, and sometimes, when results appeared, it was easy to think 'I already knew that'. Such a phenomenon is a cognitive bias with its own name: the hindsight bias (Fischhoff 1975). Also more informally called the I-knew-it-all-along effect, it is the tendency for people to see events as being more predictable than they were before they took place.

An argument for 'uncovering the obvious' is that it at least gives more credibility to other non-obvious findings. Demonstrating that our method works is helpful to other researchers, who may wish to replicate our procedures with their own sources of data. Additionally, corpus approaches can give exact quantifications of vaguer suspicions; it may appear obvious that 9/11 caused more news stories to be written about Islam, but what was the percentage increase, how long did the effect last and in which newspapers was the increase most notable? Moreover, as time passes, findings that are 'obvious' now may not be so clear to people who were born many years after 9/11. This is particularly true of the study of the nineteenth century towards the end of this book. Many of the things that a reader then may have thought were obvious are far from obvious now. Setting out a clear record of such findings is therefore useful to future generations. In any case, not all findings will be obvious (at least, not to everyone). For example, before starting this analysis, we did not expect to be conducting a detailed analysis of the phrase *Muslim world*. While *world* is the second most frequent word to follow immediately after *Muslim*, the significance of the phrase *Muslim world* seems to have been underplayed in other research that has used more qualitative methods to analyse the representation of Islam in the news.

Another limitation of taking a corpus approach is that the corpus can only ever reveal its own contents. We can use procedures that foreground the frequency and saliency of various phenomena in the corpus in order to gain an impression of mainstream or minority discourses or ways of representing the world, but the corpus cannot reveal what is not there. To give an illustrative example, in a previous piece of research we carried out, on the representation of asylum seekers in the British news, we found that some newspapers regularly used the phrase *illegal asylum seeker*, which they used to refer to people who sought asylum while misrepresenting their circumstances (Gabrielatos and Baker 2008: 30–2). We argued that the term was nonsensical because everyone is entitled to seek asylum. However, when we presented frequency information about which newspapers tended to use this construction the most, one response we received from a specialist in immigration issues was that our research came from a position that assumed that the concept of asylum seeking, and the processes around it, were unproblematic and not in need of criticism in themselves. Indeed, the idea of critiquing asylum was not one that we had considered, nor had we uncovered it from our analysis of the corpus. Instead, our understanding and acceptance of asylum and the processes around it were a kind of 'naturalised discourse' (see Fairclough 1989:75). We had taken issue with what we felt was a misreading of the meaning of *asylum*, but not the concept of asylum itself. We do not wish to address whether it is beneficial to problematise the notion of asylum here, but instead note that a corpus approach may help us to 'step outside' our own discourses, albeit only to the extent to which alternative discourses are present (and discoverable via corpus methods) within the corpus. Otherwise, we need to rely on other sources, such as reflexivity and receiving feedback from others.

Overview of the book

The remaining nine chapters of this book cover the media representation of Islam from a number of different perspectives. In order to begin our analysis from a reasonably objective position, Chapters 2 to 4 take a somewhat naive or corpus-driven approach to our data. We do not start these chapters with any specific hypotheses to explore but, instead, are more interested in finding out what is in the corpus overall or how specific parts of the corpus might differ from other parts.

Thus Chapter 2 tackles our main corpus data as a whole – 143 million words of British newspaper articles about Muslims from 1998 to 2009. We begin by looking at the most common patterns of representation, in particular examining the words *Muslim, Muslims, Islam* and *Islamic*. This analysis uses Sketch Engine, a sophisticated online corpus analysis tool that is able to identify salient patterns of particular words within different grammatical structures. Sketch Engine can distinguish between *Muslim* as a grammatical subject and object, so it is possible to answer questions such as: 'What sort of actions are Muslims commonly represented as having done to them, and what sort of actions are they represented as doing to others?' We also examine common predication strategies that attribute qualities to Muslims, by looking, for example, at the sorts of adjectives that are frequently used to describe them.

Then we ask: 'What is this corpus about?' By conducting an analysis of the most frequent content words (nouns, verbs and adjectives) in the corpus, we identify particular semantic groups that are frequently addressed in the data. While some of these groups are likely to be typical of all news reporting, and others would be expected to occur in articles about Islam, we argue that an 'unexpected' semantic group is to do with conflict, which seems to be the main context in which Islam is discussed in the news.

While Chapter 2 considers the corpus as a whole, Chapters 3 and 4 break the corpus into smaller parts in order to carry out comparative analyses. Chapter 3 considers differences between newspapers, particularly by examining the extent to which there are differences between the 'popular' and 'quality' newspapers. This is done by comparing the two sets of newspapers together using a keyword analysis that identifies words that are statistically more frequent in one data set when compared against another. Such words can then be grouped together and examined in more detail to reveal unique strategies. The chapter looks at particular uses of language – showing, for example, how at the beginning of the time period being examined there was confusion regarding the spelling of particular words, and how different newspapers reacted to a request from the Muslim Council to avoid a certain spelling that had Islamophobic connotations. As well as comparing tabloids and broadsheets, we also use the keywords technique to examine words that are very salient in only one newspaper – a method that can tell us much about the preoccupations of individual newspapers.

Chapter 4 considers how the representation of Muslims has changed over time. We show how the frequency of reporting changed over the years as newspapers focused on different types of stories at different points, and how certain concepts went in and out of fashion. We also look at whether there is an increasing focus on Muslims (the people) as opposed to Islam (the abstract concept).

Having carried out a number of corpus-driven analyses, we then take the findings from Chapters 2 to 4 in order to focus on a set of more specific topics or ways of constructing Muslims. Chapters 5 to 8 combine a mixture of corpus-driven and corpus-based methods as we begin to ask more specific questions of the data, in order to follow up hunches or interesting lines of analysis that had been shown up earlier. Chapter 5 considers some of the most frequent ways that Muslims are referred to collectively. Terms that appear to be used to group large numbers of Muslims together, such as *Muslim world*, *Muslim community*, *Muslim leaders* and *Muslim country*, are found to be extremely frequent in the corpus. Therefore, in this chapter we consider the concepts of collectivisation and differentiation, asking to what extent newspapers represent Muslims as a homogeneous group, different from other groups such as 'the West'. The chapter also considers the extent to which newspapers attempt to acknowledge different branches within Islam, with an examination of terms such as *Shia* and *Sunni*.

In Chapter 6 we examine a set of words relating to the strength and nature of belief, such as *extremist*, *radical*, *fanatic*, *fundamentalist* and *militant*.

These words are found to be frequent modifiers of *Muslim*, though different words are foregrounded by different newspapers at different time periods. We also find it useful to look at other words such as *progressive, moderate* and *mainstream*, in order to examine how newspapers make an evaluative distinction between different types of belief. Additionally, we consider a set of words that appear to reference a position somewhat between radical and moderate belief: *orthodox, pious, committed* and *devout*. To what extent do journalists find such types of belief to be newsworthy, and are they actually used to imply a halfway point between extremism and moderation?

Chapter 7 focuses on the construction of Muslims as receiving benefits, which leads on from the analysis of 'fanatics' in the previous chapter; it is found that some newspapers tend to focus on a small number of so-called Muslim fanatics who are reported to be on benefits, although over time we show how this discourse seems to expand to include other types of Muslims and other ways of receiving financial help. The chapter considers how such Muslims were constructed linguistically in the tabloids (e.g. as *spongers* and *scroungers, raking in benefits* while preaching hate). The chapter asks whether these stories, which initially appeared in the tabloids, were able to influence the discourse of the broadsheets. Additionally, the chapter considers the extent to which the topic of Muslims on benefits was used as part of a larger discourse, critical of the Labour government's welfare state.

Chapter 8 considers topics that relate to gender. Two very frequent phrases in our corpus are *Muslim men* and *Muslim women*, and it is thus pertinent to focus on the construction of gender as it relates to Islam. Two particularly frequent stories are identified – the use of the veil for women and the radicalisation of Muslim men – both of which were highly frequent after the 7/7 attacks. Our analysis of the veil considers the extent to which newspapers position women who veil as choosing to do so, being forced into it or doing it as a form of politicisation. The analysis of the radicalisation of Muslim men focuses on the extent to which this is viewed as a threat, whether newspapers construct Muslim men as passive or active agents (that which is 'blamed' for the problem) and how the newspapers attempt to construct solutions for radicalisation.

Having considered our main corpus of articles from the early twenty-first century, Chapter 9 takes a different stance, by reporting on the analysis of a corpus of nineteenth-century British newspaper articles about Muslims, in order to compare the representations found there with those that have been uncovered in Chapters 2 to 8. In this chapter we ask: 'To what extent does twenty-first-century news echo the representations of Muslims from up to 200 years previously, and, if any representations have occurred only recently, why would this be the case?'

Finally, Chapter 10 summarises the main findings of the analysis, and attempts to explain the findings by linking them to the social and political context, as well as comparing our findings to relevant studies. In Chapter 10 we reflect further on the methodology we have used, and consider some of the directions that related research projects could take in the future. We review a few of the more problematic cases of language use that were found in the corpus and ask whether there is value in requesting journalists to curb certain practices. We therefore make some cautious recommendations with regard to those reporting and representational practices that we consider ultimately damaging and counterproductive for creating a cohesive society. Finally, we end the chapter by looking at who is likely to have benefited from the way that Muslims and Islam have been written about in the British press in the early years of the twenty-first century.

2 Sketching Muslims: the big picture

Introduction

This chapter consists of two sets of analysis that aim to uncover the 'big picture' when the corpus is considered as a whole. If our general research question is 'How are Muslims and Islam represented in the British press?', then it makes sense to focus first on how the words *Muslim* and *Islam* are actually characterised in the corpus. To this end we make use of word sketches – a relatively recent concept in corpus linguistics that identifies and groups together the salient lexical patterns of particular words within different grammatical structures.

The second form of analysis in this chapter broadens our scope somewhat to ask the question 'What is this corpus about?'. While the answer to this may already be obvious – it is about Muslims and Islam – it is useful to consider the contexts and topics within which Muslims and Islam are written about. Therefore, we collectively consider the most frequent nouns, verbs and adjectives in the corpus, grouping similar types of words together in order to see what kinds of themes emerge. Having obtained an answer to this question, we end the chapter by conducting some additional checking procedures. For example, we consider whether the results obtained from this corpus would also be found if corpora of *general* news articles were examined – or, in other words, whether our findings are specific to news articles about *Islam*, or whether they are simply typical of all types of news.

However, before beginning the analysis part of this chapter, it is worth spending some time discussing the corpus tool that we used for most of the analysis in this chapter and throughout the book, Sketch Engine. Additionally, for readers who are less familiar with corpus linguistics, it is worthwhile outlining some of the procedures and analytical concepts that are pertinent to our analysis. Therefore, in the section below we also discuss concepts such as collocation, semantic preference, discourse prosody and concordances.

Beginning the analysis

Once collected (see Chapter 1), our Islam corpus comprised almost 143 million words, spread over 200,000 articles. After collection, we installed the corpus in the online corpus analysis tool Sketch Engine[1] (Kilgarriff *et al.* 2004). This tool can be used, among other things, to identify collocates of words. A *collocate* is a word that occurs frequently within the neighbourhood of another word, normally more often than we would expect the two words to appear together because of chance (see Baker, Hardie and McEnery 2006: 36–8). The identification of collocates can be useful for discourse analysis because they can help to reveal ideological uses of language. For example, in a previous study on refugees (Gabrielatos and Baker 2008), the word *refugee* was found to collocate with the word *flood*. When all the cases of these collocates were investigated by reading the sentences that contained both words, it was found that the relationship was not normally due to cases of flooding that resulted in people being displaced from their homes and becoming refugees but was, instead, due to the metaphorical construct *flood of refugees*. Gabrielatos and Baker argue that such a phrase represents refugees in a particular way, dehumanising them and constructing them negatively as an unwanted natural disaster.

Many corpus analysis tools simply present the collocates of a word in a list, either ordered alphabetically, in terms of frequency or in terms of strength of collocation. There are numerous ways that a collocation's frequency or strength can be calculated. First we must decide on a span, a range either side of a word within which we consider candidate collocates. There is no 'standard' within corpus linguistics circles with regard to what such a span should be, although the default settings on Sketch Engine and another popular analysis tool we used for the analysis in this book, WordSmith, have set the default span at five words either side of the search word. We have used this span because it seems to offer a good balance between identifying words that actually do have a relationship with each other (longer spans can throw up unrelated cases) and giving enough words to analyse (shorter spans result in fewer collocates).

Having decided on a span, we then must use a technique for calculating collocation. Baker (2006) describes various techniques. The most basic technique simply counts the number of times two words are found together within the specified span. However, this method tends to favour very frequent grammatical words, such as *the* and *of*, so it is not always helpful in identifying exclusive relationships. To illustrate, it is somewhat more interesting to know that a relatively rare word such as *flood* collocates with a word such as

---

[1] See www.sketchengine.co.uk.

refugees than that a frequent grammatical word such as *the* collocates with *refugees*. Therefore, other techniques (such as *mutual information*) tend to take into account the cases when two words occur together as well as apart from each other, and assign higher priority to those that are generally found together; such a technique allows us to make claims about the *strength* of collocation. Other techniques (such as *log-likelihood*) are based on testing the null hypothesis that two words appear together no more frequently than we would expect by chance alone, considering their frequency in the corpus and the size of the corpus. These techniques produce measures that tell us how *confident* (statistically speaking) we can be that two words are a collocate.[2]

A useful feature of Sketch Engine is that it not only identifies collocates but also specifies the grammatical relationship between them. When a corpus is installed in Sketch Engine, each word is assigned a grammatical 'tag', such as 'proper noun', 'adjective', 'base form of verb', '-s form of verb', etc. As a result, when Sketch Engine identifies collocates, it also takes into account the positions of the collocates in relation to each other, and the grammatical tags of each collocate, in order to identify grammatical relationships. The collocates of a word within particular grammatical structures are thus grouped together; this is referred to as a word sketch.

Figure 2.1 shows a screenshot of a word sketch of the word *Muslim* (when used as a noun) in our corpus.[3] It can be seen that Sketch Engine has grouped the collocates of *Muslim* into five grammatical patterns, or frames. The first group shows words that occur in the frame {*Muslim and/or x*}.[4] Additionally, this frame includes cases when *Muslim* appears at the end {*x and/or Muslim*}. This pattern is useful in telling us about the other sorts of groups or people who tend to get associated with Muslims. It is interesting to see which other belief-based groups tend to occur with Muslims: *Sikhs*, *Buddhists* and *atheists*. The most frequent group is *Sikhs*, which occurs eighty-three times in this frame. The *Sikhs* group also shows the strongest relationship, having a log-dice score of 8.98.[5]

Two related frames are in the second and fourth columns of Figure 2.1. The frame in the second column is {[verb] + *Muslim*}, giving cases when *Muslim*

---

[2] In order to extract collocations that are both lexically interesting and statistically significant, we combined the two metrics: a word was accepted as a significant collocate if it combined a mutual information score of at least 3 with a log-likelihood score of at least 6.63 ($p \leq 0.01$). For details, see Gabrielatos and Baker 2008: 11.

[3] This word sketch considers both *Muslim* and *Muslims* when tagged as a noun.

[4] Frames are given within braces. The part of speech of frame collocates, as well as the collocates themselves (when a list of examples is given), are enclosed in square brackets.

[5] For each word sketch, as well as each collocate within a sketch, Sketch Engine provides a measure of its salience, using the logDice metric. Salience is computed on the basis of the frequencies of the node, the collocate and the collocation within a given frame. For details on logDice, see http://trac.sketchengine.co.uk/raw-attachment/wiki/SkE/DocsIndex/ske-stat.pdf.

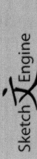

user: Costas Gabrielatos   **corpus:** Islam-UK

Concordance
Word List
Word Sketch
Thesaurus
Find X
Sketch-Diff
? Help on main menu

Save
Change options
Turn on clustering

More data
Less data
Switch menu position

Muslim *(noun)*   Islam-UK freq = 37677 (221.1 per million)

and/or	1697	0.9	v+N	6348	2.8	adj+N	6192	2.4	N+v	3341	2.3	N+n	2060	2.1
Sikh	83	8.98	practise	213	9.25	devout	839	11.57	convert	517	10.34	cleric	204	7.75
Buddhist	22	7.19	marry	201	8.41	British-born	119	8.97	pray	27	6.52	heartland	10	6.3
atheist	18	6.97	become	600	7.41	strict	137	8.52	complain	16	5.75	scholar	22	5.99
brit	10	5.75	offend	34	6.64	moderate	106	8.08	refuse	20	5.54	fanatic	24	5.92
Muslim	34	5.4	bear	108	6.63	fanatic	60	8.02	want	49	4.89	sect	12	5.79
Christian	16	4.67	appoint	22	5.73	Bosnian	109	7.9	study	12	4.8	preacher	16	5.49
%	13	4.06	insult	11	5.46	non-practising	39	7.68	try	26	4.59	shrine	11	5.29
population	19	3.91	veil	10	5.38	committed	40	7.43	wear	28	4.3	community	114	5.17
mother	20	3.86	behead	10	5.21	observant	31	7.29	join	18	4.29	population	42	5.04
community	46	3.86	arrest	32	4.85	-year-old	148	7.26	attend	12	4.24	extremist	40	4.95
father	22	3.85	be	3367	4.8	British	674	7.19	believe	27	4.16	militia	16	4.79
person	16	3.84	recruit	11	4.72	fundamentalist	58	7.11	mean	16	4.16	organisation	38	4.71
citizen	12	3.76	suspect	12	4.71	pious	30	7.09	do	102	4.01	group	138	4.51
wife	17	3.47	meet	35	4.71	fellow	63	6.94	carry	18	3.99	protester	10	4.48
worker	14	3.39	accuse	20	4.68	young	305	6.93	serve	12	3.77	leader	93	4.31
son	15	3.21	jail	10	4.62	radical	74	6.83	live	30	3.69	plot	12	3.73

Figure 2.1 Word sketch of *Muslim* as a noun

is the object of a verb – or, rather, when someone else carries the process of the verb out on a Muslim. As the verbs here include *behead*, *recruit* and *suspect*, this means that the corpus contains phrases such as *Muslim was beheaded*, *Muslim was recruited* and *Muslim was suspected*. The fourth column has the frame {*Muslim* + [verb]}, which gives the opposite pattern: cases when Muslim is the subject (or doer) of the verb. Here we have cases in which Muslims are described as *converting*, *praying*, *complaining*, *refusing*, etc.

The third and fifth columns give cases when adjectives and other nouns, respectively, modify the word *Muslim*. There are cases of Muslims being referred to with adjectives such as *devout*, *strict*, *pious*, *radical*, etc., as well as noun phrases such as *Muslim cleric*, *Muslim scholar* and *Muslim preacher*. When a group of collocates of a particular word all seem to have a similar meaning or function, then this can be called a *semantic preference* of that word (Stubbs 2001: 65). For example, words such as *devout*, *strict*, *pious*, etc. indicate that *Muslim* has a preference for the concept of strong belief. It is sometimes possible to take this kind of analysis a stage further, particularly when a set of related collocates, examined in context, seems to suggest a particularly negative or positive stance and thus reveals a discourse (or way of representing an aspect of the world). For example, in the second column of Figure 2.1, the collocates *behead*, *suspect*, *arrest*, *accuse* and *jail* suggest that the word *Muslim* (as an object) carries a negative *discourse prosody* (Stubbs 2001) related to criminality. A single word may have multiple semantic preferences and discourse prosodies, particularly in cases when people tend to disagree over how a concept should be represented. Additionally, the boundary between semantic preference and discourse prosody can sometimes be blurred. So, although we labelled the 'strong belief' adjectives as comprising a 'neutral' semantic preference, we might also note that some of them, such as *fanatic*, tend to have rather negative meanings, and some people might therefore argue that *fanatic* contributes to a negative discourse prosody, referencing not just strong belief but dangerously extreme belief.

It should be noted that the process of assigning grammatical classification to words, so called 'tagging', in the corpus is not 100 per cent accurate. It is carried out automatically via a computer programme that uses rules, some of which are based on the positions of words, some are based on accessing a lexicon that knows that certain words or word endings will always have certain tags, and some make use of probabilities. As a result, occasionally errors can creep in to the tagging. Most taggers achieve around 95 to 97 per cent accuracy, although texts that contain large numbers of unfamiliar words or unusual grammatical structures may contain higher error rates. The tagging of the Islam corpus is reasonably good, but it is not perfect, and the errors can mean that some collocates are identified as being part of the wrong frame. For example, in the first frame

Concordance 2.1 Muslims who complain

1	displaying a picture of Jesus Christ because a	Muslim	complained ... well, tough. I would
2	to be escorted off the premises after the	Muslim	complained. Mr Langmead was only reinstated
3	Dog watch: but a	Muslim	complained about the advert featuring Rebel
4	of the Al Muhajiroun group. One moderate	Muslim	complained that community leaders 'face
5	Pooh and Piglet. Bosses acted after a	Muslim	complained about pig-shaped stress relievers
6	totally mad. Has anyone actually heard a	Muslim	complain about Christmas? MARK O'NEILL
7	is utter rubbish. I do not know a single	Muslim	who has complained about non-Muslims celebrating
8	boards. Not once did I hear or read of a	Muslim	complaining about this, although it showed
9	Bury, after complaints and a petition. One	Muslim	reportedly complained that it was 'insulting
10	Christian denominations. I have yet to hear a	Muslim	complain about an image of Mary, whom they

{*Muslim and/or x*}, the collocate *school* occurs in phrases such as *Muslim and non-Muslim schools*. Here, *Muslim* seems to be functioning more as a modifier of *school* than acting as a noun in its own right. The relationship is therefore between two modifiers, *Muslim* and *non-Muslim*, rather than *Muslim* and *school*. As a result of cases of mistagging, it is usually necessary to examine *concordances*, in order to check that a relationship actually functions in the way that Sketch Engine claims. A concordance is simply a table showing all the cases of a word, phrase or pair of collocates in their immediate co-text. Concordance 2.1 shows a concordance from the frame {*Muslim* + [verb]}, where the verb is *complain*. Although there were sixteen cases of this in the corpus, we have shown only ten, in order to save space.

The concordance shows cases when Muslims are described as complaining about things (e.g. line 3 is from a reader's letter reporting on Muslims complaining about an advert). However, it is interesting to note that there are a number of cases in which people appear to be questioning whether Muslims actually complain at all. This occurs in lines 6 to 8 and 10, and line 9 hedges the complaint with the word *reportedly*. While it is often easy to get the 'gist' of how a particular word, phrase or collocational pair is used in context through reading concordance lines, in some cases we require even more co-text, and the line needs to be expanded so that we can access the rest of that article. For example, by expanding concordance line 3, it transpires that the article is from the *Daily Mail* and is about a police advertising poster campaign that featured a picture of a dog called Rebel, and was subsequently complained about by a Muslim who said that dogs were considered unclean in his culture and that the posters were offensive to his community. The *Daily Mail* article is critical of the Muslim who made the complaint. All the concordance lines are from right-leaning newspapers. It seems that complaining Muslims are not considered as newsworthy to left-leaning newspapers.

Word sketches

Having outlined some of the key techniques that we used in our analysis, we now turn to reporting the main findings of the word sketch analyses that we carried out. In order to obtain an initial idea of the 'big picture' of the corpus, we decided to focus on a small number of words that were both frequent and also very relevant to the representation of Islam and Muslims. As a result, we generated word sketches of four very frequent words: *Muslim, Muslims, Islam* and *Islamic*. As Table 2.1 indicates, *Muslim* is the most frequent word of the four, *Islam* the least.

Below, we summarise some of the key points that emerged from looking at these word sketches. As shown in Figure 2.1, the word sketch of *Muslim* revealed a number of frames that indicated various semantic preferences and discourse prosodies. When *Muslim* is tagged as a noun, its adjectival and noun modifiers tended to be grouped in the categories shown in Table 2.2.

As already noted, one way that Muslims are characterised is in terms of the extent of their belief. Some words indicate extremely strong belief (*firebrand, fanatical, hardline*), while only one word, *moderate*, is suggestive of a less strong belief. These words are considered in more detail in Chapter 6. Another set of collocates indicates words that appear to collectivise Muslims (*sect, community, population, world*). These words are the focus of Chapter 5. A smaller set of words is concerned with crime or war, and echo the verbs found when *Muslim* was in the object pattern.

However, *Muslim* could also be tagged as an adjective (this occurred for about 70 per cent of the cases of the word *Muslim*). The *Muslim* (adjective) form produced a different word sketch, which had two main frames

Table 2.1 Frequencies of main words referring to Islam in the corpus

Word form	Frequency
Muslim	126,913
Muslims	73,775
Islamic	89,720
Islam	54,562

Table 2.2 Adjectival and noun modifiers of Muslim *(as a noun)*

Category	Collocates
Belief (level of)	*devout, strict, moderate, fanatic, committed, observant, fundamentalist, pious, radical, orthodox, faithful, fanatical, hardline, extremist, firebrand*
Location	*British-born, Bosnian, Bangladeshi, Pakistani, Kashmiri*
Collective	*sect, community, population, organisation, group, state, world, nation, country, area, majority, dozen, minority*
Crime/war	*militia, plot, prisoner, protester, terrorist*

{*Muslim* + [noun]} and {[adverb] + *Muslim*}. The first frame contained collocates that referred to types of people (e.g. {*Muslim* [*woman, girl, youth, man, pupil, student, family*]}). Other words related to collective groups: {*Muslim* [*community, world, population, country, group, nation, organisation, state*]}. There were two words in this frame that pertained to religion in general – {*Muslim* [*cleric, faith*]} – although other words referenced religious extremism: {*Muslim* [*extremist, fanatic, fundamentalist*]}.

The second frame, {[adverb] + *Muslim*}, consisted of words that indicated frequency or strength: {*predominantly, mainly, overwhelmingly, mostly, largely, strictly, exclusively, especially, predominantly, strongly, entirely, heavily, particularly*}. The word sketches of *Muslim* as a noun and adjective therefore mainly reinforce each other, suggesting that Muslims are constructed as having strong (sometimes dangerously strong) beliefs and as existing in large groups.

What about the plural form, *Muslims*? Although the sketch of *Muslim* tagged as a noun also encompasses the plural form, it is worth looking at just the plural form alone, particularly in light of the frequent presentation of Muslims as members of groups (see above). Here a word sketch shows that two broad categories or representation are being referenced. The first contains frames with collocates relating to conflict, mostly denoting forms of prejudice or aggression against Muslims:

- {[*action, aggression, atrocity, attack, backlash, campaign, crime, crusade, discrimination, genocide, hatred, injustice, prejudice, reprisal, violence*] *against Muslims*}
- {[*killing, massacre, oppression, persecution, plight, slaughter, treatment*] *of Muslims*}
- {[*commit, discriminate, fight*] *against Muslims*}

A related group of frames relates to the (perceived) results of the above stances:

- {[*alienation, radicalisation*] *of Muslims*}

- {[*attack, backlash, complaint, criticism, pressure, protest, reaction, response*] *from Muslims*}
- {[*attack, demonstration, protest, uprising, violence*] *by Muslims*}
- {[*alienation, anger, concern, extremism, fear, fury, outrage, radicalisation, resentment*] *among Muslims*}

Secondly, the frame {[noun] *of Muslims*} contains collocates denoting their number (*number*) – either in absolute terms (*hundred, million, thousand*) or as a proportion of a population (*majority, minority, per cent, %, proportion*). An interesting use in the last frame is that of the collocate *majority*. Although there are some cases in which it denotes the religious orientation of a country's population, in more than three-quarters of its instances it refers to Muslims whose attitudes and practices are deemed acceptable by the author of the article. It is telling that, in most instances of the frame, *majority of Muslims* is qualified by the adjectives *decent, law-abiding, moderate, peace-loving, peaceable* and *peaceful*. Such cases are sometimes attributed to the prime minister, Tony Blair, speaking after the 7/7 bombings:

'We know that the vast and overwhelming majority of Muslims are decent law-abiding people who abhor these acts of terrorism every bit as much as we do,' Mr Blair said (*Independent*, 8 July 2005).

Of the eighty-nine cases of *majority of Muslims are* in the corpus, sixty-six of them are used in constructions such as the one above, either to describe most Muslims as law-abiding and decent or to say that they are opposed to violence, terrorism and extremism. Only one says the opposite (legitimating the claim by attributing it to an Islamic scholar):

The majority of Muslims are 'passive terrorists' who secretly condone terror attacks on the West, an Islamic scholar has warned (*Sunday Express*, 17 July 2005).

However, a closer look at the sixty-six cases of positive representation reveals another pattern, as shown in the following examples:

No one doubts that the vast majority of Muslims are peaceful and law abiding. But the furore that resulted from the publication of certain cartoons depicting Islam in a Danish newspaper showed how Islamic radicals could create chaos in European capitals (*Daily Mail*, 26 September 2007).

We live in a world in which, although the vast majority of Muslims are not terrorists, the vast majority of terrorists are Muslim (*Daily Telegraph*, 20 August 2007).

The vast majority of Muslims are not terrorists, but most of the terrorists who threaten us claim to be Muslims. Most countries with a Muslim majority show a resistance to what Europeans and Americans generally view as desirable modernity, including the essentials of liberal democracy (*Guardian*, 15 September 2005).

Here, eighteen out of the sixty-six cases (27.3 per cent) state that the vast majority of Muslims are peaceful or not terrorists in order to either go on and focus on a dangerous minority or to question the claim:[6]

Even now we are told that we must celebrate diversity, since the vast majority of Muslims are moderate and Islam is really a peace-loving religion. That kind of propaganda always seemed dubious (*Daily Express*, 20 February 2006).

The use of *number* in the frame indexes a variety of topics; however, the most prominent ones are the increasing number of Muslims in Britain, the apparent rise in extremist views among British Muslims and the alleged radicalisation of young British Muslims. Examples of each case are shown below:

The report found in the past decade a rise of 275,000 in the number of Muslims who were born in Pakistan or Bangladesh living in Britain. The increase is equivalent to twice the population of Oxford (*Daily Express*, 14 December 2009).

While efforts after the 11 September attacks on America focused on the threat to the UK from outside the country, antiterrorist police now believe the number of British Muslims suspected of supporting terrorism, either directly or indirectly, runs into 'thousands of people' (*Independent*, 4 September 2006).

Indeed, our security establishment has only very recently begun to wake up to the real extent of this threat and to the fact that, while most British Muslims are opposed to violence, large numbers of young Muslims are being radicalised. Yet even now, that establishment still doesn't fully grasp the nature of what it is up against (*Daily Mail*, 28 May 2007).

Moving on from *Muslim(s)*, we also considered the words *Islam* and *Islamic*. While *Muslim* is a form that references the people who practise the religion, *Islam(ic)* refers to the religion itself, and so is a more abstract and impersonal concept. Of the two words, the adjective *Islamic* is more frequent, though it actually has far fewer frames than the noun *Islam*, and can be dealt with first. The main pattern of *Islamic* is as a modifier of nouns that reference people, groups or concepts characterised as extreme or dangerous in some way {*Islamic* [*extremist, militant, fundamentalist, terrorist, extremism, radical, fanatic, militancy*]}. A second pattern involves *Islamic* modifying nouns that reference Muslims as an organised group (*community, group, society*) and, more frequently, that of Islam as a political entity (*country, law, nation, party, regime, revolution, republic, state*). Only in a minority of cases is *Islamic* used to modify nouns directly relating to religion (*cleric, faith*), although some collocates present it as an object of study (*scholar, school, study*), and others refer to its cultural aspects (*art, culture, dress*).

---

[6] Similar patterns were found for the related phrase *most Muslims*.

A final frame is {[adverb] + *Islamic*}, and here the adverbs tend to reference strength or amount: {[*devoutly, predominantly, strictly, purely, mainly, truly, strongly, especially, largely, particularly*] *Islamic*}. This is the same frame that was found with the sketch of *Muslim* as an adjective. However, an interesting exceptional adverb in this category is *insufficiently*, although this tends to be used in descriptions of situations in which Muslims are described as being punished for being insufficiently Islamic by people or states that are implied to be too extreme and punitive.

It comes to something when a cleric is disbarred from running in the parliamentary elections in the Islamic Republic of Iran, particularly when he is disqualified for being insufficiently Islamic. But that is what happened to Hojatoleslam Hadi Rabbani, an MP from Shiraz who was disqualified for 'lack of practical adherence to Islam' (*Independent*, 14 March 2008).

Generally, then, *Islamic* tends to hold a negative discourse prosody of extremism, as well as a semantic preference for collectives, particularly involving political entities. As *Islam* has more frames associated with it, we now spend more time discussing the word sketch of this word.

One set of interrelated topics indexed by collocates in a large number of frames of *Islam* (particularly those involving noun collocates) is that of the nature and aspects of Islam as a religion. However, it must be noted that in the majority of cases the discussion of these aspects is embedded within a context of conflict. A good number of collocates relate to the discussion of Islam not being a uniform religion ({[*branch, brand, form, strain, strand, sect, version*] *of Islam*}, {*sect in Islam*}, {*approach to Islam*}) and its being multifaceted ({*aspect of Islam*}), as in the following two examples:

In moves reminiscent of the Taliban, which in 2001 destroyed two statues of Buddha, the Somali hardliners have desecrated the tombs of saints worshipped by Sufis, a mystical branch of Islam despised by the extremists but widespread among ordinary Somalis (*Times*, 11 July 2009).

In fact, fasting Ramadan – but not the marathon prayer sessions and Quranic recitals associated with the holy month – is the only aspect of Islam that I have ever stuck to religiously (*Guardian*, 29 August 2009).

As a result, there is a lack of (full) consensus as to its doctrine ({*interpretation of Islam*}), and its tenets can, therefore, be misunderstood ({*understanding of Islam*}, {[*misconception, prejudice*] *about Islam*}).

It is believed that Casablanca, a cosmopolitan city where many women wear Western clothes and most people follow a liberal interpretation of Islam, has been singled out by hardline Muslims for its 'decadence' (*Sunday Telegraph*, 18 May 2003).

Nagina, the first Muslim to use the room for daily prayers, said: 'Everyone went out of their way. I feel so special knowing they've made such an effort.' There are no mosques in Windsor. Muslims who want to attend Ramadan prayers must travel into Slough, three miles away. Otherwise they need to ask their employers to provide a suitable room. Nagina, from Slough, said: 'I was worried I might not get it because there are many misconceptions about Islam' (*Daily Mirror*, 30 September 2006).

However, some collocates indicate that there is common ground, such as {[*principle, tenet*] *of Islam*}, {[*forbid, prohibit*] *by Islam*} and {[*allow, forbid*] *in Islam*}:

A central and fundamental tenet of Islam is the command that there is no compulsion in religion. Thus, it is not the headscarf that symbolises the subordination of Muslim women in any given society, rather, it is the arrogance and temerity of men (*Independent*, 22 December 2003).

Finally, the above issues seem to have necessitated the provision of (clarifying) information to those not familiar with issues related to Islam by more knowledgeable parties, as well as debate regarding its nature: {[*conference, debate, expert, lecture, programme, speech, series*] *on Islam*}, {[*book, debate, documentary, film, truth*] *about Islam*}:

Dr Youssef Choueiri, of Exeter University, an expert on Islam and its fundamentalist strains, backed the view that Moslems keep fighting through the fasting festival. He said: 'Ramadan is the most important date in the Islamic calendar. It's supposed to be a time of peace, goodwill and charity. But Moslem nations would not hesitate to go on fighting. It's not a violation of God's will' (*Sunday Express*, 4 November 2001).

Compared to the word sketches of *Muslim*, a larger number of collocates of *Islam* relate directly to issues of conflict:

- {[*critic, criticism*] *of Islam*}
- {[*hostility, opposition*] *to Islam*}
- {[*threat*] *from Islam*}
- {[*conflict, confrontation, problem, struggle, trouble, war*] *with Islam*}
- {[*battle, clash, conflict, confrontation, struggle, tension, war*] *between Islam and X*}, where 'X' is either 'the West', or another religion (mostly Christianity, but also Judaism)

It must be clarified that the use of *Islam* in contexts of conflict does not necessarily indicate that hostile or sceptical attitudes towards Islam are presented as justified; instances such as the following are quite frequent:

Tolerance is clearly better than intolerance, but that has blinded us to its inadequacies. It is no accident that two of the most liberal countries in Europe, which prided themselves on their tolerance, have hatched a deep hostility to Islam – Denmark and the Netherlands (the latter is even considering banning the burqa in all public spaces) (*Guardian*, 27 February 2006).

However, even when the above attitude is criticised – as in the next example – it is to claim that hostility and criticism are pervasive:

It wasn't just me who found the title, tone and content of the debate disturbing. The liberal rabbi, Pete Tobias, described it as a 'damaging and hurtful exercise', sinisterly reminiscent of the campaign a century ago to alert the population to 'the Problem of the Alien' – namely the Eastern Jews fleeing persecution who had found refuge in the capital. My view is that it was symptomatic of a much wider and deeper hostility to Islam and, contrary to the claims of the panellists, to Muslims too (*Sunday Telegraph*, 25 November 2007).

A larger group of frames imply the presence of conflict in less direct ways. Islam is (explicitly or implicitly) discussed as an unwelcome or dangerous religion: {[*rise, spread*] *of Islam*}:

It is worth remembering that the rise of Islam represents a miraculous case of the triumph of human will. With little more than their beliefs to gird them, the Prophet Mohammed and a small number of devoted followers started a movement that brought the most powerful empires of their day crashing to the ground. On September 11, the attackers undoubtedly imagined themselves to be retracing the prophet's steps (*Guardian*, 8 December 2001).

Sooner or later the Left are going to have to make up their minds as to which lobby they wish to cringe to. You can support homosexual liberation or the spread of Islam but not both (*Mail on Sunday*, 8 January 2006).

This last example, by the opinion columnist Peter Hitchens, does not explicitly disapprove of Islam, although the phrase *spread of Islam* carries an implication of disapproval. The verb form *spread* carries a negative discourse prosody. If we examine its collocates in another corpus, the 100-million-word British National Corpus (BNC) of general English, we find words such as *disease, infection, AIDS, virus, rumours* and *fire*. Generally, things that spread are not good.

Moreover, in the majority of cases of the latter frame, *Islam* is modified by the adjectives *extremist, fundamentalist, militant* and *radical*. In the same vein, it is presented as a religion that is inflexible, intolerant and too sensitive to deviations from, or comments on, its doctrines: {*enemy of Islam*}, {[*affront, offensive, traitor*] *to Islam*}, {[*blasphemy, offence, conspiracy*] *against Islam*}:

My father was euphoric and decided to go back to Tehran for a few weeks. He was still poking fun at things he didn't agree with, and when the Ayatollah imposed the hijab on women, my father wrote this joke about a man who had his wife flogged because she'd shown her hair to some dinner guests. The joke was that it was a hair that had fallen into the soup she was serving. The mullahs made a big fuss and my father was declared an enemy of Islam. One day, a 1,000-strong mob surrounded his offices shouting that he was going to die (*Daily Mirror*, 20 June 2009).

A resulting concern seems to be that of people converting to Islam: {[*conversion, convert* (noun), *convert* (verb)] *to Islam*}:

The Old Bailey heard how her 18-stone son spent months chatting to Muslim fanatics on the internet. He converted to Islam at 17 and changed his name to Mohamad Saeed-Alim in honour of the 9/11 bombers. In 2003 he told a psychiatrist he wanted to become a martyr and police were alerted. But his threat was dismissed (*Sun*, 31 January 2009).

The most salient frame in the word sketch of *Islam* was {[noun] *against Islam*}. Another frame that had a very similar function, {[noun] *on Islam*}, was also identified. Both frames tended to attract many collocates and had the word *war* as their most frequent collocate of *Islam*. As a result, we decided to examine the frame {*war against/on Islam*} in more detail. A close reading of expanded concordance lines revealed an interesting pattern: the target frame tended to appear in juxtaposition with another frame, {*war against/on terror**}.[7] The function of the juxtaposition was usually to forward or report the argument that the wars in Afghanistan and Iraq are/were not the former, but the latter − as in this example:

But Israel's best interests will not be served by poking sticks in the Palestinians' eye at a time when the West is straining every muscle to persuade the Muslim world that the war against Osama bin Laden is not a war against Islam. The Americans may be very close to Israel, but Mr Sharon will be making a mistake of historic dimensions if he forces them to choose between maintaining their alliance with Israel and winning the wider war against terror (*Independent*, 26 September 26).

However, there were also instances when the opposite is argued, as in the following example, or (rarely) a neutral stance is projected (i.e. both views are reported with no explicit or implicit comment). As the above example demonstrates, the juxtaposition was not necessarily within the same sentence.

Izzadeen told listeners: 'Everyone knows, Muslims and non-Muslims, that the war on terror is a war against Islam, and I'm telling you something, if they don't stop this there is going to be a very strong reaction from the community' (*Daily Mail*, 23 September 2006).

In turn, the recurrence of the latter pattern resulted in the frequent co-occurrence of the words *Islam* and *terror(ism/ists)* within the same text. This observation gave rise to the question of whether the high frequency of *terror** was simply a characteristic of the juxtaposition of these frames, or a more general co-occurrence between *Islam** and *terror** in the corpus. A first step was to compare the corpus frequencies of *Islam** and *terror**, which turned out to be comparable (see Figure 2.2).

---

[7] The asterisk denotes all forms of the term, in particular *terror, terrorism, terrorist* and *terrorists*.

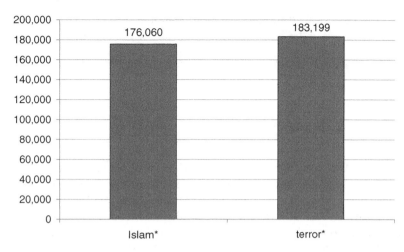

Figure 2.2 Frequency comparison of *Islam** and *terror** in the corpus

To understand the significance of the frequency similarity between the two groups of types,[8] we need to remind ourselves that *Islam** was one of the query terms that was used to create the corpus, and therefore would be expected to have a very high frequency in the corpus. *Terror**, on the other hand, was not a query term, and its very high frequency (actually higher than that for *Islam**) needs to be explained. On the lexical level, the following question can be posited:

Does the use of the term Islam* *attract the use of the term* terror*?

To address this question, we carried out a collocation analysis of the five main forms within *Islam**, namely *Islam, Islamic, Islamism, Islamist* and *Islamists* (henceforth denoted collectively by *Islam$^+$*).[9] In order to establish the strength and statistical significance of each collocation, both mutual information (MI) and log-likelihood (LL) scores were taken into account, using the thresholds described earlier in this chapter. The analysis showed that the five forms of *Islam$^+$* collocate with almost all the four main forms of *terror**, namely *terror, terrorism, terrorist* and *terrorists* (henceforth referred to as *terror$^+$*).[10] Table 2.3 shows the collocate pairs in detail. A tick mark indicates that both MI and LL

---

[8] A distinction is made between types and tokens. Types are distinct word forms. Tokens are all word forms in a list (or corpus) irrespective of whether some are repeated. For example, the following list contains ten tokens, but only four types: *chair, chair, desk, desk, desk, bookcase, bookcase, bookcase, shelf, shelf*.

[9] The five forms of *Islam$^+$* account for 95 per cent of all forms of *Islam** in the corpus (167,382 out of the total 176,060).

[10] The four forms of *terror$^+$* account for 92 per cent of all forms of *terror** (168,620 out of the total 183,199).

Table 2.3 Collocations of Islam$^+$ *and* terror$^+$

	terror	terrorism	terrorist	terrorists
Islam	✓	✓	(✓)	✓
Islamic	✓	✓	✓	✓
Islamism	✓	✓	--	--
Islamist	✓	✓	✓	✓
Islamists	✓	✓	✓	✓

values were at/above the threshold, whereas a tick mark in parentheses indicates that only the LL value was at/above the threshold, and a dash indicates a lack of collocation (i.e. both MI and LL values were below the threshold). There were no cases when only the MI score exceeded the threshold.

In addition to the almost invariable collocation between *Islam*$^+$ and *terror*$^+$, these forms co-occur in more than one-third (37.9 per cent) of corpus texts.[11] More precisely, *Islam*$^+$ frequently co-occurs with *terror*$^+$ not only within a span of five words but also over longer spans within corpus texts – particularly after 9/11. This strengthens the conclusion that the strong collocation of *Islam*$^+$ with *terror*$^+$ is not the result of their strong and perhaps multiple collocations in a small subset of corpus articles, but is a result of their more general frequent co-occurrence in corpus texts. What highlights even more clearly the association between Islam and terror is the proportion of texts that *Islam*$^+$ and *terror*$^+$ co-occur in after terrorist events. Taking 9/11 and 7/7 as examples, we examined the co-occurrence of *Islam*$^+$ and *terror*$^+$ in a period of one month after (and including) the event. As shown in Table 2.4, the proportion of co-occurrence is more than double the average immediately after 9/11, and almost double immediately after 7/7.

A content-oriented question arising from the above results is whether the 'incremental effect' (Baker 2006: 13–14) of the lexical co-occurrence of *Islam*$^+$ and *terror*$^+$ reflects a particular *discourse* – in the sense of 'a set of meanings, metaphors, representations images, stories, statements and so on that in some way together produce a particular version of events' (Burr 1995: 48).[12] More precisely, a second question can be formulated thus:

In the corpus newspapers, taken as a whole, does the discussion of issues pertaining to Islam frequently involve issues of terrorism?

At this point we also need to consider the existence of the two highly salient frames discussed above, {[noun] *against Islam*} and {[noun] *on Islam*}, and

[11] The proportions of co-occurrence within individual texts were derived from Nexis UK, using techniques adapted from Gabrielatos (2007).
[12] For a summary of different conceptions of the term *discourse*, see Baker (2006: 3–5).

Table 2.4 Proportion of corpus texts in which Islam⁺
and terror⁺ *co-occur around 9/11 and 7/7*

	Percentage of texts
11 September–10 October 2001	81.7
7 July–6 August 2005	71.6

the fact that these frames were populated by collocates denoting conflict of some description, such as *war, attack, assault, crusade, battle* and *debate*. It is not unreasonable, therefore, to posit a more general content-oriented question:

Are the reports and discussions pertaining to Islam and its faithful frequently linked to, or even framed within, issues of conflict, and, if so, to what extent?

This question was addressed by examining which other non-query word types are most frequently found in the texts derived by the query term outlined towards the end of Chapter 1. At this point we also need to consider that the corpus was designed so that all newspaper articles in it contain at least one of the query terms. Simply put, the corpus comprises articles in which issues related to the religion of Islam and/or its faithful are a topic – central or peripheral, explicit or implicit. Therefore, words that occur frequently in the corpus can be expected to reflect the most frequent, and arguably the most important, topics related to Islam and Muslims in the national UK newspapers in the period in focus, 1998 to 2009.

A closer look at highly frequent content words

Given that the four word forms in *terror*⁺ have, on average, individual frequencies of about 40,000,[13] it seemed useful to examine other non-query content words[14] – that is, words that are expected to reflect the subject matter of the corpus articles, with a frequency of 40,000 and above (henceforth referred to as '40k types'). The corpus contains only 147 40k types – a mere 0.03 per cent of the content types in the corpus. However, this tiny proportion of types accounts for 15.1 per cent of the content tokens in the corpus (about 10 million tokens). This is a strong indication of the centrality of 40k types to the content of corpus articles, seen collectively. An examination of concordance lines (expanded as appropriate) showed that the majority of these 40k types (eighty-five, accounting for 57.8 per cent of all types) are clear indicators of

[13] The frequencies are: *terror* (44,220), *terrorism* (43,564), *terrorist* (45,818) and *terrorists* (34,923).
[14] The words examined were nouns, adjectives and verbs – but not adverbs.

the topics dealt with in the corpus articles (henceforth referred to as '40k topic indicators'). The rest of the 40k types have a range of meanings and functions too wide for any particular topic to be clearly indicated, and comprise general lexical verbs (e.g. *come*, *say*, *take*), lexical markers of modality (e.g. *think*, *want*, *need*) and general adjectives (e.g. *good*, *little*, *new*). The 40k topic indicators, although no more than a mere 0.02 per cent of the content types in the corpus,[15] account for 9.5 per cent of the corpus content tokens. Because of their very high frequency in the corpus, it can be argued that 40k topic indicators are salient to the discourses surrounding the query terms, or, at least, that they reflect the most frequent topics in the corpus.

Figure 2.3 shows the overall frequencies of the 40k topic indicators. At the top of the figure, the two core query terms that were used to collect the corpus data (*Islam**, *Muslim**) are included, for the purposes of comparison. We believe it is remarkable that only one of the 40k topic indicators is directly related to religion (light grey), whereas a good number of types (thirteen) directly refer to armed or violent conflict, and the attendant issue of death, as well as the law (black). An even larger number (twenty-nine) refer to countries or regions involved in war or armed conflict of some description, in which religion is, or is perceived by some to be, directly or indirectly one of the main causes of that conflict (dark grey). The rest (forty-two) refer to issues of governance and leadership, time, money, quantification and human aspects, such as age and sex (dotted outline). Although not automatically related to issues of conflict, when we examined how these words occurred in the corpus we found that they often referred to the willing or unwilling participants in a conflict, their representatives or leaders, or the place and time of conflict.

This preliminary analysis suggests that, although the query consisted of terms purely relating to Islam, its faithful, and attendant religious practices, many of the most frequent types in the corpus articles directly or indirectly refer to issues of conflict. However, we need also to query whether the 40k topic indicators, a mere eighty-five types, barely representing 10 per cent of the content tokens in the corpus, can be safely seen as indicative of the main corpus topics. Could it be that, if a much larger proportion of corpus types were examined (i.e. if the examination included much less frequent types), different topics would emerge? To express the question through a popular metaphor:

As far as corpus topics are concerned, are the 40k topic indicators the tip of the iceberg?

---

[15] These were extrapolated using type frequencies of adverbs and function words in the BNC (Leech, Rayson and Wilson 2001).

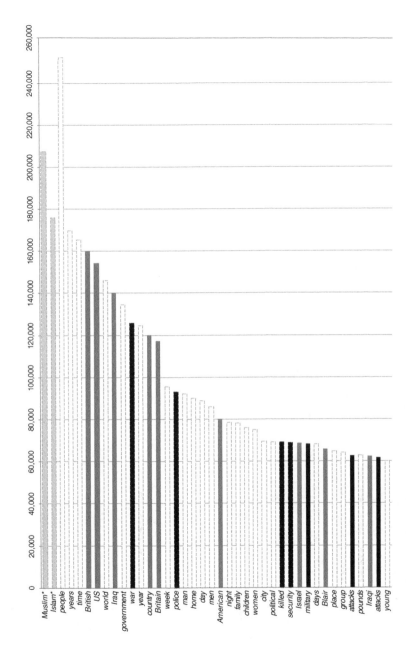

Figure 2.3 40k topic-indicators and their corpus frequencies

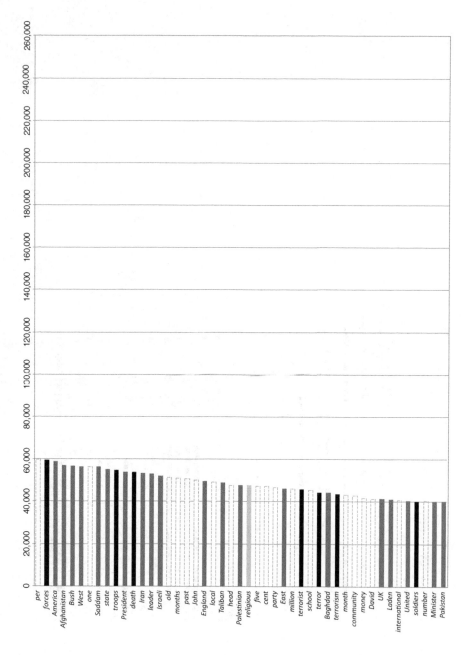

Figure 2.3 (cont.)

Expanding the analysis to lower-frequency words

To address the above reservations and question, and to pursue and expand this line of investigation further, all content words with a frequency of at least 4,000 (henceforth '4k content types') were examined.[16] Although the 4k content types account for only 0.5 per cent of the corpus content types, collectively they constitute almost two-thirds (61 per cent) of all the content tokens in the corpus.[17] The first observation to emerge from this part of the analysis was that the classification used for the 40k content types (i.e. the distinction between topic indicators and types not clearly indicating topics) was rather limiting for the classification of 4k content types. Unsurprisingly, the examination of a significantly larger number of types revealed a much more complex picture – one that seems to reflect the composition of natural discourse. More specifically, three broad groups of 4k content types emerged, according to their discourse function in the corpus articles:

- types indicating *topics* ('topic indicators')
- types indicating *contextual elements* (e.g. participants, place, time: 'context indicators')
- types with *general meaning* (i.e. types that are essential for discussing the topics, but are not clear topic indicators themselves, such as general adjectives, modality/attitude markers: 'co-text types')

Figure 2.4 shows the frequency distribution of the three broad groups of 4k types, in terms of tokens. The frequency of the query terms is also given, for reasons of comparison.

The following subsections define and exemplify the categories into which the 4k types in each broad group can be divided. Each category is subdivided (when appropriate) into subcategories according to the meaning and function of the types they contain. The categories of topic indicators are examined last, as they are the most interesting and useful to the analysis.

Context indicators

The types in this category provide information on different contextual elements, such as participants (individuals, groups or nations), location, time and quantity. Simply put, these types answer the questions 'Who?', 'Where?', 'When?' and 'How many/much?' (see Table 2.5).[18] Types referring to

---

[16] The 4k content types also include the 40k content types.
[17] There are 2,982 4k types, accounting for 42,748,872 content tokens.
[18] Topic categories are denoted through SMALL CAPITALS.

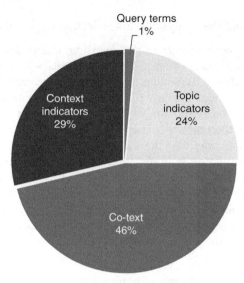

Figure 2.4 Broad categories of 4k types: frequency distribution in terms of tokens

participants and place had to be conflated, because names of countries, regions, cities, etc. are used in the corpus as indicators of either place or participants (e.g., the type *UK* is used to refer to the country or its government).

Co-text types

The content types in this category (Table 2.6) are essential for discussing the topics indexed by the topic indicators, but are not (clear) topic indicators themselves.

Topic indicators

The most populous topic category, by far, in terms of the number of both the types and the tokens it comprises, is that of CONFLICT (Table 2.7). It has more than five times the number of types and tokens than any other single category of topic indicators and, on its own, contains more types and tokens than all other categories combined. As its name suggests, all words in it relate to conflict, irrespective of whether it manifests itself in the form of verbal argument (whether in the sense of problem-solving-oriented discussion or verbal confrontation – including threats) or in the form of violent or armed conflict, and the related issues of damage, injury, ill-health and death.

Table 2.5 The 4k context indicators

Subcategory	Types n = 532	Tokens n = 9,273,434	Definition	Example types
GOVERNANCE/POLITICS	133	2,186,522	Heads of state, politicians, politics, governmental groups	authorities, Blair, BNP, cabinet, CIA, congress, dictator, elections, minister, officials
NAMES	110	1,157,855	First/last names of individuals	Ibrahim, Mike, Williams
REGION/COUNTRY	81	2,409,187	Names of continents, regions encompassing more than one country, and countries	Afghanistan, Dubai, East, International
ETHNICITY/NATIONALITY/ ORIGIN/RESIDENCE	71	1,432,138	Identification of people in terms of their ethnicity, nationality, origin or place of residence	Afghan, Bosnian, homeland, residents, tribal
AREA/CITY/COMMUNITY	68	979,351	Names of, or types related to, cities and areas within, or smaller than, cities	Berlin, capital, city, local, metropolitan, settlement, urban, village
TIME	67	1,798,820	Reference to time points/periods and time orientation	ancient, contemporary, dawn, decade, era, hours, interim, month
QUANTIFICATION	63	1,408,826	Reference to numbers and quantities – in absolute or comparative terms	bigger, crowd, decline, enough, fewer, greater, largest, miles, million, several, thousands
ORGANISATIONS/ LEADERS	34	679,237	Non-governmental groups and their leaders or representatives	activists, al-Qaeda, chair, chief, commission, institutions
BUILDINGS	20	299,537	References to buildings and their component parts	apartment, castle, door, hotel, house, roof, room, villa
GEOGRAPHY	15	129,607	Geographical locations	bay, coast, forest, mountain, river

Table 2.6 The 4k co-text types

Subcategory	Types n = 126	Tokens n =1,719,500	Definition	Example types
General content words	1,411	18,220,192	Words that do not index topics, but are essential to the discussion of topics	*bring, call, card, central, circumstances, discover, joke, keep, look*
Modal marker	80	1,288,242	Expression of attitude to likelihood or desirability of something	*ability, allow, capacity, chance, claim, demand, hopes, impossible, ordered, predicted, promises*
Emotion	40	396,741	Expression of reaction to topics and events	*afraid, angry, concerned, desperate, fear, feelings, loved, passion*
Colour	8	121,292	Names of colours	*black, blue, colour, green, grey, orange, red, yellow*
Material	6	34,517	Types of materials	*metal, plastic, wood*
Animal	6	33,153	Names of animals	*animal, dog, fish, horse*

As would be expected, types belonging to CONFLICT have a predominantly negative meaning (e.g. *invasion, racism*); however, related positive words are also included, as they are used in the discussion of negative topics. For example, the word *moderates* is used in discussions of extremism or fundamentalism to juxtapose, explicitly or implicitly, two stances – moderation and extremism – or to relate the efforts of groups or individuals described as 'moderate' to avert or minimise conflict:

Last week, moderate Muslim opinion spoke out more convincingly on terrorism than hitherto (*Daily Telegraph*, 9 July 2007).

The latter group are also often presented as targets or victims of violence. Simply put, discussions of peace or moderation tend to arise when war or extremism become an issue:

Abu Qatada, described by MI5 as 'Osama Bin Laden's right-hand man in Europe', has published fatwas on the internet from Long Lartin calling for holy war and the murder of moderate Muslims (*Sunday Times*, 15 November 2009).

The next category, RELIGION/CULTURE/EDUCATION/SOCIETY (RCES) comprises types indexing the topics that would be expected to be found in the articles returned by the query if discourses on Islam and Muslims

Table 2.7 *The 4k topic indicators indexing the topic of conflict*

Subcategory	Types n = 418	Tokens n = 5,278,904	Definition	Example types
violent/ armed conflict	145	1,883,949	Armed or violent conflict	*guns, invasion, military, war*
violence/ damage	85	1,055,092	Reporting of or reference to instances of (threat of) physical/psychological violence towards humans, and damage in property.	*attack, blast, bloody, bomb, brutal, casualties, destruction, explosion, fire, hurt, injured, rape, refugees, suffering, threatening, victims, violence*
law/crime	55	688,748	References to law-breaking and punishment	*charged, conviction, crime, criminal, detainees, drugs, (il)legal, jail, judge, legitimate, prisoner, suspects*
argument	30	286,171	Differences in opinion, goals, etc.	*argue, agreement, criticism, debate, division, resolution*
death	27	441,639	References to violent death	*buried, death, died, genocide, kill*
problem/ danger	19	206,764	Reference to (potentially) problematic/dangerous actions or situations	*chaos, corruption, crisis, dangerous, emergency, panic, problem, risk, trouble, worry*
exclusion/ inclusion	15	120,118	Issues of racial (in)tolerance	*ban, discrimination, diversity, racism, tolerance*
peace/safety	15	245,719	Although, nominally, these words refer to positive notions, they are used in discussions of their lack and need	*aid, calm, friend, peace, protection, safety, welfare*
extremism	12	103,780	References to extreme views and/or practices	*extremists, fundamentalists, hardline, moderate, radicals*
health	9	69,412	References to ill-health	*disease, doctors, medical*
terror	6	177,512	Reference to terrorism or terrorists	*hijackers, terrorists, towers*

Table 2.8 The 4k topic indicators indexing topics of 'RELIGION',
'CULTURE', 'EDUCATION' *and* 'SOCIETY'

Subcategory	Types n = 89	Tokens n = 1,171,095	Definition	Example types
religion	46	548,069	Religions, deities, devout, religious groups, beliefs and practices	*beliefs, bible, Christians, clerics, converted, faith, Hindu, heaven, prayer, sacred, worship*
culture/art	24	268,666	References to cultural aspects	*art, civilisation, heritage, music, traditional*
education	16	236,059	References to education and related institutions and participants	*academic, education, pupils, schools, students, teachers*
society	3	118,301	Issues pertaining to society	*public, social, society*

revolved around the tenets, beliefs and religious, social and educational
practices associated with Islam and its faithful (Table 2.8). It is, therefore,
pertinent to point out that this category is much less populous than CONFLICT.
A useful way of perceiving this difference is this: on average, for every RCES
token contained in the articles returned by the query there are five CONFLICT
tokens.

Table 2.9 shows a range of other topic indicators that refer to more specific
subjects. These include HUMAN ASPECT, which contains mainly nouns
describing human attributes referring to age (*baby, teenager*) and kinship
(*family, parents*), as well as related types referring to everyday events and
activities (*birthday, wedding*). Other categories in Table 2.9 include
FINANCE/BUSINESS, which contains types denoting financial institutions
(*banks*), economic metrics and tools (*income, debt, budget*) and related words,
and RESOURCES, the types that index discussion of wealth in terms of
resources, or their dearth as a result of conflict. Finally, Table 2.9 contains
four less populated categories, indexing issues of TRANSPORT/TRAVEL,
MEDIA/COMMUNICATION, LEISURE/SPORT and FOOD/DRINK.

Examination of the frequency breakdown of the 4k topic-indicating tokens
(Figure 2.5) shows that almost half of them (48.9 per cent) relate to issues of
discrimination, conflict, crime, violence, death and suffering − whereas
the 4k tokens directly or indirectly related to religion (RCES) account for
only 16.3 per cent, one-third (5.5 per cent) of which are query terms. In other
words, non-query RCES tokens account for only 10.8 per cent of the topic-
indicating tokens in the corpus articles. The latter observation is significant, in

Table 2.9 Other 4k topic indicators

Category	Types	Tokens	Definition	Example types
human aspect	80	1,688,662	References to • people's age, sex, and appearance • family/kinship relations • events/ceremonies	adult, baby, birth, birthday, boy, childhood, couple, dad, divorce, family, fat, home, parents, relatives, teenager, wedding, wife, youths
finance/ business	57	752,022	References to issues of finance, economy, business and commerce	banks, benefit, budget, customers, debt, financial, funding, GBP, income, market, spending, tax, wealth
transport/ travel	48	475,730	Means of transport, and lexis related to travel	airlines, arrived, cars, convoy, flight, helicopter, journey, passenger, passport, station, traffic, travel, vehicles
media	27	377,032	References to the dissemination of news	journalists, magazine, media, papers, radio, report, reporter, television, video, website
food/drink	14	110,731	Lexis related to foodstuffs, drinks and meals, and related actions	beer, breakfast, coffee, dinner, drink, eat, food, fruit, lunch
leisure/ entertainment	11	91,852	Lexis related to leisure activities and entertainment	cafe, cinema, entertainment, holiday, pub, restaurant, tourism, tourists
sport	9	84,630	Sport and athletic events	championship, cricket, football, Olympic, rugby, sport, tennis
resources/ energy	7	81,421	Natural resources	electricity, fuel, gas, water
precious metals	3	22,027	Metals	gold, silver
communication	5	43,091	Reference to means of communication	internet, (tele)phone, satellite

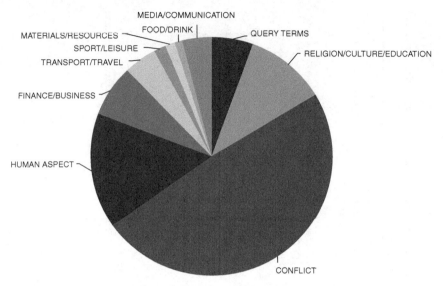

Figure 2.5 Frequency breakdown of 4k topic-indicating tokens

that it strongly indicates that the query (which, it must be reiterated, comprised terms related to Islam, its faithful, and related religious practices) returned newspaper texts in which content tokens related to conflict were almost five times more frequent than tokens related to religion. What is more, the examination of expanded concordance lines suggests that the 4k topic indicators belonging to other groups – in particular, HUMAN ASPECT – are predominantly employed in the reporting and discussion of conflict-related issues.

However, we need to entertain the hypothesis that the picture emerging from the quantitative breakdown of the 4k topic-indicating tokens may be the result of the extremely high frequency of particular 4k types. In order to examine this possibility, the frequency of types (rather than tokens) within topic categories was also examined. As Figure 2.6 shows, there is no significant change in the relative proportion of categories when examined in terms of number of types rather than tokens. Types in the conflict category account for just over a half (51 per cent) of the 4k topic indicators, and those related to religion account for only 16.4 per cent (the proportions for 4k topic-indicating tokens were 48.9 per cent and 16.3 per cent, respectively).

The analysis so far seems to lead to the clear conclusion that the 40k types were indeed the tip of the iceberg, as they proved to have provided reliable indications of the main topics in the corpus. However, the examination of the much larger group of 4k content types has revealed a much richer and more

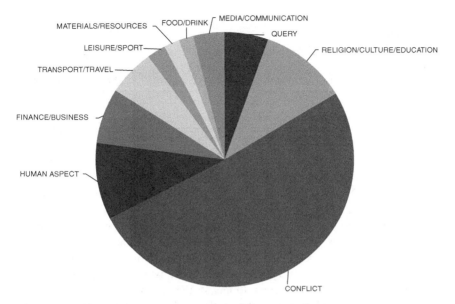

Figure 2.6 Frequency breakdown of 4k topic-indicating types

detailed picture. A methodological conclusion that can be drawn here is that the examination of a small number of high-frequency words can indeed pinpoint central topics in a corpus, albeit lacking in the provision of detailed insights. However, focusing on our own corpus, the most salient finding is that the British press most frequently positions Islam and Muslims in stories or contexts that relate to conflict.

Prominence of CONFLICT: a corpus characteristic or a newspaper trend?

At this point we need to examine the possibility that the high proportion of CONFLICT tokens in the corpus may not be a characteristic of the reporting on Islam and Muslims, but simply a general trend in newspaper reporting – that is, it may be due to newspapers predominantly reporting on negative and controversial events and issues (e.g. military action, crime, disasters). To this end, we decided to compare the collective frequency of CONFLICT tokens in our corpus (which we refer to here as 'Islam-UK') with a corpus of more general news articles on a wide range of topics. We chose the newspaper sub-corpus of the British National Corpus. The BNC consists of 100 million words of written and spoken British English, of which about 10 million words are from newspapers (henceforth referred to as 'BNC-news').

Table 2.10 Frequency comparison of 'CONFLICT' *tokens in Islam-UK and BNC-news*

Corpus	Total size (tokens)	Number of conflict tokens	Percentage of conflict tokens	Difference	Log-likelihood
Islam-UK	142,962,543	5,278,904	3.70	+34.5%	24,618.53
BNC-news	9,897,378	272,131	2.75		

As Table 2.10 shows, CONFLICT tokens in Islam-UK are more than a third (34.5 per cent) more frequent than in BNC-news, and the difference is statistically significant.

Even if we separate the Islam-UK corpus into sections of one year each and examine only the year that had the lowest relative frequency of CONFLICT tokens (2000), that year still contains more CONFLICT tokens than BNC-news, again with extremely high statistical significance (LL = 1750.03). However, we also need to ensure that this frequency difference is not due to the high frequency of a small number of CONFLICT tokens in Islam-UK. A keyword comparison (which compares the relative frequencies of all words in both corpora) established that more than two-thirds (69.1 per cent) of CONFLICT types are key in Islam-UK when compared against BNC-news. In light of the above, it seems that we can be reasonably confident that the high relative frequency of CONFLICT tokens in Islam-UK is not merely a common feature of the reporting practices of UK national newspapers, but reflects frequent topics in reporting issues pertaining to Islam and/or Muslims, and, consequently, is a salient characteristic of the discourses on Islam/Muslims.

There is a further concern with the keyword analysis reported above: the time spans of the two corpora do not overlap; the BNC contains texts from the late 1980s up to 1994, whereas Islam-UK spans 1998 to 2009. In order to derive indications of whether the keyness of CONFLICT tokens in the previous comparison reflected the different time spans, we also carried out a frequency comparison of the group of CONFLICT tokens in a sub-corpus of Islam-UK containing articles published in 2005 to 2007 with the newspaper sub-corpus of BE2006 (Baker 2009), a corpus of written British English in which 82 per cent of the texts were published between 2005 and 2007. As Table 2.11 shows, CONFLICT tokens are again significantly more frequent in Islam-UK, by virtually the same proportion as in Table 2.10. Therefore, it seems that Islam-UK does indeed contain CONFLICT tokens significantly more frequently than articles in national British newspapers taken collectively.

Table 2.11 Frequency comparison of 'CONFLICT' tokens in Islam-UK and BE2006-news

Corpus	Total size (tokens)	Number of conflict tokens	Percentage of conflict tokens	Difference	Log-likelihood
Islam-UK (2005–7)	44,120,772	1,894,614	4.29	+33.2%	517.78
BE2006-news	174,963	5,626	3.22		

Conclusion

This chapter has shown that the presentation of Islam and Muslims in UK newspapers in the twelve-year period from 1998 to 2009 was predominantly carried out in a context of conflict, and the religion and its faithful were frequently portrayed as causes for concern, if not sources of threat. It is notable that the term *terror** occurs more often than *Islam** in a corpus in which *Islam** was one of our search query terms.

For both *Islam* and *Muslims*, the majority of frames included a number of collocates indexing conflict, while an examination of the most frequent content words in the corpus found that over one-half of such words directly related to conflict. What is more, even when the discussion was on aspects of doctrine and religious practices, it was often embedded in a context of conflict. In the case of *Muslims*, its collocates are related to conflict in more varied ways, which can be seen to be connected causally to form a vicious circle: Muslims as victims of discrimination and violence, whose feelings of victimisation lead not only to their voicing their concern but also to their acting upon it, resulting in their becoming the actors of violence. A related concern is that of their number, particularly in Britain, as well as the propor-tion of those seen as holding extremist views. In the latter case, although the vast majority were perceived to pose no threat (as they were *moderate* and *law-abiding*), there was also concern voiced in the corpus articles that the number of those that do pose a threat is rising – particularly among the younger generations.

The above points do not paint a coherent picture of Islam and Muslims. What seems to be in operation is, on the one hand, the drawing of overgener-alisations from the attitudes and actions of a minority among Muslims, which is then applied to Islam and Muslims in general, and, on the other, attempts to counter the image of Islam and Muslims as sources of conflict. This is confounded by the existence of different approaches within Islam, as well as different conceptions of the nature of those differences. At the same time,

Islam is also treated as a political entity, and quite often countries and regions are labelled by their dominant religion rather than other characteristics (e.g. their political system). Overall, although the presentation of Islam and Muslims in the UK press is anything but uniform, the common ground seems to be their treatment as a difficult issue that needs to be addressed.

While this chapter has considered the larger patterns across the whole corpus, it would be premature to end the analysis at this point. We have uncovered a number of key representations, such as words relating to religious extremism or collectivisation, that are worthy of more detailed examination, and they are the subject of later chapters. Additionally, we need to consider variation between individual newspapers. This is the subject of the following chapter.

3   Muslim or Moslem? Differences between newspapers

Introduction

Having looked at the broader picture across the whole corpus, this chapter and the one following it focus on breaking different sections of the corpus into smaller parts and examining how these sections differ from each other. Here we compare different newspapers, first making a broad distinction between tabloids and broadsheets, and then looking at the distinctive lexis of each newspaper individually. Some questions that we explore in this chapter are as follows. Which newspapers tend to be more personalising in their reporting, referring to Muslims (the people) more than Islam (the religion)? What topics and political debates do certain newspapers tend to focus on in their discussion of Islam, and are there any notable idiosyncrasies in particular newspapers, such as spelling choices or the format of readership feedback that help to disclose that newspaper's stance towards Islam?

As described in Chapter 1, our corpus comprises articles about Muslims and Islam that were collected from a searchable database of British national newspapers. We have taken a number of daily newspapers along with their Sunday equivalents (where they exist). In one case we have used a Sunday newspaper which has no daily equivalent (*The People*, which is aligned to the Mirror Group of newspapers), and we have also included *The Business*, a weekly newspaper that ended publication in 2008. Figure 3.1 shows the number of articles collected from each newspaper. It can be seen that the broadsheets tend to make up the bulk of the corpus, although it should not be assumed that these newspapers are more interested in Islam than the tabloids. The broadsheets simply tend to be larger newspapers with more articles, so would be likely to have more articles about most subjects.

In Chapter 1 we noted that the tabloid newspapers tended to outsell broadsheets, although some of the most notable declines in sales over the first decade of the twenty-first century involved two of the most 'popular' newspapers, *The Sun* and the *Daily Mirror*. We also considered the potential for newspapers to have political influence, both in terms of leading large numbers of people to vote for certain political parties and in terms of the

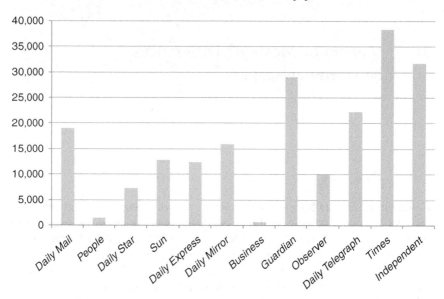

Figure 3.1 Number of articles collected from each newspaper in the corpus

political influence of large media empires, whose power may extend beyond newspapers to television and online news, and may have directly influenced political policy.

Before beginning this chapter's analysis, it is useful to consider the type of readership of some of Britain's newspapers and how this may relate to the way that Muslims are represented within them. Figure 3.2, created with information taken from the Newspaper Marketing Agency, shows the social class profiles in terms of percentages of the readership of each newspaper.[1] The National Readership Survey has developed a social grading system in the United Kingdom in order to classify readers, and this system has become a standard in market research (Wilmhurst and Mackay 1999).

Social groups are broadly defined by letters of the alphabet from A to E, with A representing the 'upper middle class' of people, who work in higher managerial, administrative or professional jobs. B consists of the 'middle class', who have intermediate managerial, administrative or professional jobs. C1 is 'lower middle class', comprising 'supervisory or clerical and junior managerial, administrative or professional jobs'. C2 is the 'skilled working class', comprising skilled manual workers, while D is 'working class',

[1] The data has been taken from www.nmauk.co.uk/nma/do/live/factsAndFigures. Figures for the *Daily Star*, the *Daily Express* and *The Business* were not available.

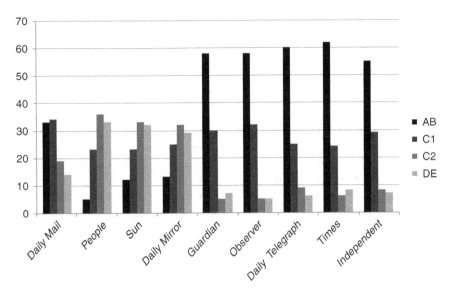

Figure 3.2 Social class profile of newspaper readerships

meaning semi- and unskilled manual workers. Finally, those in group E are at the lowest level of subsistence, consisting of casual or lowest-grade workers, as well as pensioners and those who depend on the welfare state. They could be viewed as Britain's 'underclass'.

From Figure 3.2 it is fairly easy to discern which newspapers are the broadsheets, as these are the newspapers that tend to have more than a half of their readership in the AB social classes: *The Guardian*, *The Independent*, *The Observer*, *The Daily Telegraph* and *The Times*. Additionally, we can identify tabloids as having more than 50 per cent of their readership in the C2 and DE groups. By this definition, the *Daily Mirror*, *The People* and *The Sun* are tabloids. However, the *Daily Mail* does not fit into either pattern, with its readership split almost equally across three groups: AB, C1 and C2DE. As described in Chapter 1, we have broadly categorised the *Mail* as a tabloid in instances when we were forced to choose between a tabloid/broadsheet distinction for the purposes of comparisons, although we acknowledge that a more accurate description of the *Mail* would be 'middle market'.

The social class of a newspaper's readers is likely to impact on the way that particular stories are selected as newsworthy, as well as the way that they are then written about. In the United Kingdom there is a reasonably strong correlation between social class and income.[2] Some newspapers may assume

---

[2] See, for example, www.nrs.co.uk/lifestyle.html.

that their typical readers have a certain 'world view', based upon their social class (in combination with other factors, such as political affiliation). For example, tabloid newspapers may be more likely to view their readers as being less financially secure and thus concerned about 'threats' such as immigration, which could result in competition for low-level jobs. However, there is also an enormous amount of variation within the social groupings, and people may read multiple newspapers or may 'change' social groups over time.

Newspapers are able to gather great amounts of demographic information about their readers, as well as relying on feedback through letters, e-mails and telephone polls. Such information helps them to tailor their stories to an idealised or 'imaginary' reader (Ballaster *et al.* 1991: 2), who will be viewed as having the typical concerns and interests reflected in that newspaper. It is with this idea of an 'imaginary' reader in mind that we turn to consider how the newspapers actually differ from each other.

Examining frequencies

The initial question that this chapter intends to answer is 'Do certain newspapers show a particular preference for referring to *Muslim(s)*, the people, or *Islam(ic)*, the religion?'. Figure 3.3 shows the overall frequencies of the terms *Muslim, Muslims, Islam* and *Islamic* for each newspaper.

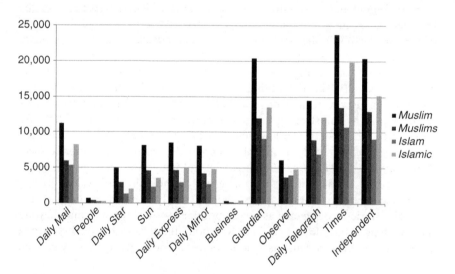

Figure 3.3 Frequencies of main terms relating to Islam for each newspaper

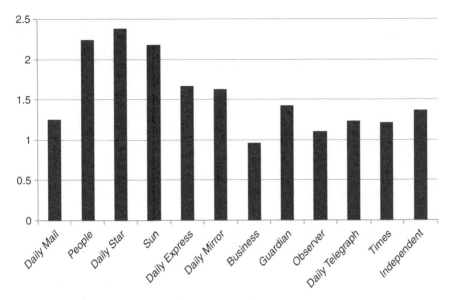

Figure 3.4 Ratio of *Muslim(s)* to *Islam(ic)* for each newspaper

As expected, the overall frequencies of the words under examination are higher in the daily broadsheets (*The Guardian*, *The Daily Telegraph*, *The Times* and *The Independent*), while the two newspapers that appear weekly (*The People* and *The Business*) have very small frequencies. *The Observer*, which also appears only once a week, has frequencies that are closer to some of the daily tabloids, reflecting the fact that this newspaper contains much more text per issue than a tabloid. For each newspaper, the frequencies of the four terms are pretty similar: *Muslim* is the most frequent, followed by *Islam*, then *Muslims*, then *Islamic*. The exceptions to this pattern are the three weekly newspapers: *The People*, *The Observer* and *The Business*. *The People* has the order *Muslim*, *Muslims*, *Islam*, *Islamic*, *The Observer* has *Muslim*, *Islamic*, *Islam*, *Muslims*, while *The Business* has *Islamic*, *Muslim*, *Muslims*, *Islam*. It is notable, then, that the Sunday tabloid tends to place more emphasis on the people who practise the religion rather than the religion itself, while this seems to be the opposite case for *The Business*. However, all the frequencies in these two newspapers are relatively small, so perhaps the most salient point is that readers of such papers will rarely come across articles about Muslims *or* Islam.

Another way of considering the information in Figure 3.3 is to think about the overall ratio between *Muslim(s)* and *Islam(ic)*. This is shown in Figure 3.4. Here, the longer bars indicate the newspapers that tend to favour the personalising *Muslim(s)* over the more abstract *Islam(ic)*. All newspapers except for *The Business* show this preference, having a ratio higher than 1:1. The preference for writing about Muslims as people seems to be more pronounced in the tabloids, especially the *Daily Star*, *The People* and *The Sun*. It is interesting that the middle-market newspaper the *Daily Mail* seems to be closer to the broadsheets in terms of this ratio.

While the analysis so far tells us about which newspapers favour which terms, it does not reveal anything about the different sorts of contexts Muslims and Islam are written about. In order to do this we need to use another technique, called keyword analysis.

Broadsheets versus tabloids

A quick and simple 'way in' to comparing different parts of the corpus against each other is to obtain lists of keywords. Put simply, a keyword is a word that occurs more frequently in one corpus than in another corpus. However, the difference needs to be statistically significant, and it is relative to the overall size of the two corpora being compared. Generally, statistical tests can be used to determine which words have a significant difference in frequency between two corpora. If the Islam corpus is split into two, with all the broadsheet articles comprising one section, and all the tabloid articles comprising the other, then we can obtain lists of words that are key in one section when compared against the other. Table 3.1 shows the broadsheet and tabloid keywords (100 of each) that were most statistically significant when using log-likelihood tests.[3] To give an example of the difference in frequencies involved, the word *terror* occurs 22,188 times in the tabloids and 22,032 times in the broadsheets. This may not appear to be a particularly large difference, but consider that the broadsheet part of the corpus contains almost 103 million words while the tabloid part contains only 40 million words and the difference is put more clearly into perspective: the tabloids refer to the word *terror* more than twice as often as the broadsheets.

---

[3] Corpus linguists regularly have to impose 'cut-off' points in their data analysis. With a keyword analysis this is particularly difficult, because the standard cut-offs for statistical significance used in the social sciences (e.g. a p value of less than 0.01 or 0.05) would result in hundreds or thousands of keywords to account for, especially when working with large corpora. We have therefore simply chosen to focus on a more manageable number, looking at the 100 keywords from each corpus that were strongest in terms of statistical significance (this meant that we could focus on the words that we were most certain actually were key). In fact, when going beyond the top 100 keywords, we found evidence of similar sorts of patterns (e.g. more words to do with politics in the broadsheets, more words referencing extremism in the tabloids). Therefore, 100 words for each newspaper category provides a representative overview, without overwhelming the reader with too much information.

Table 3.1 Top broadsheet and tabloid keywords

Category	Broadsheet keywords	Tabloid keywords
Grammatical words	*the, of, that, its, in, between, is, an, as, which, by*	*was, all, up, out, after, at, back, off*
Pronouns		*I, her, she, my, our, me, we, he, him, I'm, your, you, he's, they, she's, I've*
Adjectives	*final, most, contemporary, middle*	*just, last, top*
Verbs		*get, got, didn't, wear*
People	*Mr*	*Dad, boss, miss, bosses, chiefs, girl, wife, fans, family, pals, pal, kids, couple*
Reporting	*comment, writes*	*added, said, revealed, yesterday, told, exclusive, claimed, warned, spokesman*
Royalty		*Diana, Fergie, Diana's, Dodi, Fayed, princess*
Education	*MSc, PGDip, university, MA*	
Media and sport	*media, art, novel, review, books, television, book, journal, press, journalists, arts, writers*	*TV, Harrison*
Politics/ economics	*political, government, president, elections, administration, state, economic, UN, movement, election, opposition, politics, democratic, policy, oil, reform, regime, conservative, debate, Lab*	*PM, Blair, taxpayers, Tony*
Places/ nationalities	*London, international, Palestinian, Israeli, Israel, US, Iran, American, overseas, foreign, Iraq, Washington, Iraqi, Palestinians, States, western, Arab, Baghdad, Gaza, Iranian, Israel's, Jerusalem, national, Kurdish, Syria, India, Lebanese*	*English, England, Britain, pub, Brits, home, Brit*
Religion	*Shia, Sunni, Islamist, secular, Jewish*	*Moslem, Moslems, Muslim*
Abstract concepts	*power, century*	*holiday, Christmas, ten, love*
Islamic groups	*Taleban, Hamas, Fatah, Hizbollah, Hizbullah, Qa'eda, Qaida*	*Qaeda*
Terror/ extremism		*Hamza, fanatics, Bakri, hate, Choudary, fanatic, maniacs, hook, Omar, terror, terrorists, Bin, bomb, Laden, bomber*
Crime		*cops, police, jail, PC*
Conflict	*military, General, occupation, revolution, conflict*	*hit*

As with Chapter 2, the method of categorising keywords is a fairly subjective process. Concordances were first carried out on the words in order to ensure that their actual usage in context was understood. Some words clearly have a single 'obvious' meaning, so we know that *American* refers to people or things from the United States, and is unlikely to be anything else. Other words can have multiple meanings. Still others have many referents, such as names. For example, we would guess that, in the context of our newspaper corpus, *Blair* would refer to the British prime minister, Tony Blair. In the vast majority of cases this is true, but *Blair* occasionally refers to other people who have that surname. Yet, as the majority of cases referenced Tony Blair, we categorised *Blair* as a political word. That said, we could have simply had a category for 'names of people' and put *Blair* in that, along with other names such as *Bakri*, *Diana* and *Harrison*. Instead, we felt it would be more relevant to categorise names according to the context in which they most frequently appeared.

When creating categorisations and assigning words to them, ideological issues are often raised. It was particularly difficult to make distinctions between the final four categories (Islamic political groups, terror/extremism, crime and conflict) as these concepts overlapped. We acknowledge, therefore, that the categorisation system is not definitive, and should be intended more as a guide to the different sorts of topics that distinguish tabloids and broadsheets.

With these disclaimers in mind, Table 3.1 is revealing in a number of ways. First, it tells us something about the different ways in which these two types of newspaper use language when reporting. It is notable that the tabloids make more use of personal pronouns. In particular, the first- and second-person pronouns *I*, *my*, *we*, *me* and *our* suggest a more 'involved' (Biber, Conrad and Reppen 1998: 151–2) style of writing, whereas the broadsheets' use of grammatical words such as *the* and *of* are indicative of nouns and noun phrases, which suggest a more 'informative' (151–2) reporting style. It is also of interest that there are a number of tabloid keywords that are indicative of reported speech or news reporting: *said*, *added*, *warned*, etc. The keyword *yesterday* was put in this category, as it occurs regularly in constructions such as *was revealed yesterday* and *it emerged yesterday*:

A further link to Bin Laden emerged yesterday with the discovery that Reid, identified by British police from fingerprints sent by the FBI, was a worshipper at a London mosque with one of the suspects detained over the September 11 outrages (*Daily Express*, 27 December 2001).

NINE out of ten British Asians back UK action in Afghanistan, a poll revealed yesterday. And half want Brits fighting for the Taliban tried for treason if they return. Among Muslims, 87 per cent said they were loyal to Britain – despite 64 per cent opposing the US-led campaign (*Sun*, 23 November 2001).

The tabloids therefore seem to make more effort to highlight the 'newsworthiness' of their journalism, with keywords such as *revealed* (implying that hitherto secret information is being given) and *exclusive* (implying that no other newspapers have the story).

Other keywords are suggestive of different levels of formality. The formal *Mr* is a broadsheet keyword, whereas more informal terms such as *boss*, *cops* and *pals* are key in the tabloids. While the broadsheets write the word *television*, the tabloids use the shorter term *TV*. Some of the keywords are revealing about popular tabloid and broadsheet story types. The tabloids have keywords that reference royalty, with the British royal family often being written about (including the relationship between *Princess Diana* and *Dodi Fayed*), while the broadsheets have many more keywords that are concerned with politics and different types of media (*novel, book, press, arts, music*, etc.). It is interesting that the broadsheets tend to write about a wide range of different places around the world, whereas the place keywords in tabloids are all focused on Britain. This also reflects a major difference in reporting focus: the broadsheets cover international news while the tabloids tend to be mainly concerned with what is happening at home. A supporting point is found by looking at the political keywords in the tabloids, the name *Tony Blair* and the acronym *PM* (prime minister). The tabloids seem to be more concerned than the broadsheets with the man who was the leader of the United Kingdom for most of the period under analysis. Additionally, the tabloids' more frequent use of words that describe family members and relationships (*mum, dad, wife, family, couple, kids, daughter, husband* and *mother*) suggests an emphasis on news stories that are at a more individual and personal level. The tabloids seem to relate news to the immediate contexts of their readers, whereas the broadsheets are more concerned with the 'broader' picture.

The broadsheet 'place' keywords suggest some of the contexts within which Islam is written about: the Palestine–Israel conflict, Iraq (a country with a leader considered to be problematic for the West at the start of the period studied, and which later experienced a prolonged insurgency involving troops from the Western powers) and Iran (a country considered to be problematic for the West throughout the period studied), India, Syria and the United States, the superpower that was the target of the 9/11 attacks and then went on to fight a 'war on terror', which involved invading Afghanistan and Iraq, with the help of other countries including the United Kingdom.

In terms of words that specifically refer to religion, it is notable that the broadsheets have two keywords, *Shia* and *Sunni*, that refer to different branches of Islam. The presence of these keywords suggests that the broadsheets are more likely to make distinctions within Islam, rather than simply using a broader term such as *Muslims*. These terms are considered in more detail in Chapter 5.

Another tabloid focus seems to be on extremism, with the word *fanatics* occurring as key in these newspapers. This word suggests a particular way of positioning Muslims who are seen to have extreme beliefs, and provided an early reason for examining this word, along with other words that focused on the type and strength of belief that Muslims hold (see Chapter 6). Additionally, four names associated with extremism were key in the tabloids: *Osama Bin Laden*, (Omar) *Bakri*, (Anjem) *Choudary* and (Abu) *Hamza*. A related keyword, *hook*, referred almost exclusively to the prosthesis on the right hand of Abu Hamza. While Osama Bin Laden is globally known as the architect of the 9/11 attacks on the United States, Choudary, Bakri and Hamza are perhaps less familiar names internationally. All three lived in the United Kingdom, and are described by the tabloids as 'hate preachers'; they were often pilloried for being in receipt of benefits. The subject of Muslims on benefits is explored in more detail in Chapter 7.

Vanishing Moslems

Particularly after the 9/11 attacks in September 2001, the British media began to report more stories about Islam (see Chapter 4), which led to newspapers needing to find ways to represent concepts and groups that were initially written in Arabic script but now required translations (or transliterations) to the English alphabet. Perhaps unsurprisingly, there was a lack of consistency, not just across newspapers but also within them, which led to certain spellings being keywords, although, for some words, newspapers eventually developed standards and became more consistent.

For example, one spelling inconsistency was concerned with the group that claimed responsibility for the 11 September attacks. The tabloids are more likely to refer to this group as *al Qaeda*, whereas the broadsheets use *al Qa'eda*, *al Qa'ida* or *al Qaida*. This is indicated by the fact that *Qaeda* is a tabloid keyword while *Qa'eda* and *Qaida* are broadsheet keywords. It was mainly *The Guardian* that used *al Qaida* (though it was also used by the *Daily Star* and *The People*). *The Independent* seems to have preferred *al Qa'ida* (though *The Sun* also used this spelling), while *The Daily Telegraph* used *al Qa'eda*. The difference in spelling is also reflected between the American Associated Press (referred to as AP, which used *al Qaida*) and the London-based Reuters (which used *al Qaeda*). The tabloids appear to have used the Reuters spelling conventions more regularly, while the broadsheets, particularly *The Guardian*, complied with the

AP guidelines. However, the most common spelling overall, in both sets of newspapers, was *al Qaeda*, with the tabloids, *The Times*, *The Observer* and (to an extent) *The Daily Telegraph* tending to favour this spelling over others.

Similarly, there has been inconsistency between newspapers over the spelling of the name of a Shia Muslim militant group and political party based in the Lebanon: *The Guardian* used *Hizbullah* more than other newspapers, whereas *The Daily Telegraph* used *Hizbollah*. Another spelling, *Hezbollah* (which was not a keyword), was most popularly used by *The Times*, although it was also common to some tabloids, such as the *Daily Mail*.

Sebba (2007: 56) highlights how orthography and spelling are social practices. Therefore, spellings, especially those that appear to be unconventional, are interesting from a discourse analytical perspective. They can signal something about the way that a text producer wishes to represent a particular concept and his/her stance towards it. Although the above examples do not seem especially ideological, a notable distinction arises around the spelling of *Muslim*. The word *Muslim* occurs 126,913 times across the whole corpus, with its plural occurring 73,775 times. However, the corpus also contains 7,009 references to the terms *Moslem* and *Moslems*, with 97 per cent of the cases of this spelling occurring between 1998 and 2003. Between 2004 and 2009 this spelling is much less frequent, reflecting the fact that it was mainly discarded by journalists, who seem to have agreed that *Muslim* is the 'standard' spelling. The term *Moslem(s)* is not equally spread across different newspapers either. The *Daily Mail* accounted for 68 per cent of all cases, while another 23 per cent appeared in the *Daily Express*. Together, then, these two right-leaning tabloids accounted for over 90 per cent of the references to *Moslem(s)* and were responsible for the fact that both *Moslem* and *Moslems* emerge in our top keywords when the broadsheets and tabloids are compared against each other.

As Figure 3.5 shows, while, collectively, all the newspapers (except for the *Daily Mail* and the *Daily Express*) had low frequencies for these spellings, which slowly decreased further over time, the patterns for the *Daily Mail* and the *Daily Express* are very different. The *Daily Mail* looks as if it intended to drop using the spelling in 2000, but in 2001 it used it more than ever, as did the *Daily Express*. However, the spelling peaked in 2001, and by 2003 the *Daily Express* matched the profile of the other newspapers, having dropped the *Moslem* spelling. The *Daily Mail* seems to be the only newspaper that used *Moslem(s)* in 2003, and it was not until the following year, 2004, that it abandoned the spelling in favour of *Muslim*.

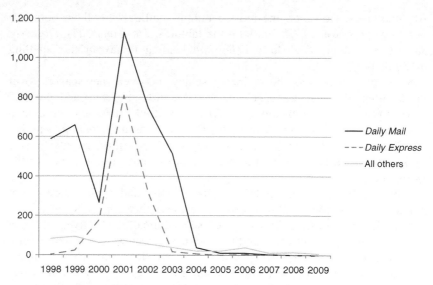

Figure 3.5 Frequency of *Moslem(s)* over time, 1998–2009

As reported by Baker (2010: 324), the Media Committee of the Muslim Council of Britain (MCB) wrote to the editors of these two newspapers on 16 July 2002 and asked them to standardise their spellings of common Arabic words. They specifically objected to the spelling *Moslem*, as they noted that it can be pronounced 'mawzlem', which is similar to the Arabic word for *oppressor*. Looking at Figure 3.5, then, it is notable that the *Daily Express* seems to have complied with the Muslim Council's request fairly quickly, but the *Daily Mail* appears to have continued using *Moslem* for about a year after it was contacted.[4] We can only guess as to why the *Mail* appeared to drop *Moslem* in 2000, then returned to the word in 2001, and continued to use it for up to a year after it was asked to stop using the spelling, eventually dropping it in 2004. Possibly, it decided to take a more aggressive stance towards Islam as a direct result of the 9/11 attacks but then eventually bowed to the pressure of being the only newspaper still regularly using *Moslem*. Everything else aside, we would suggest that the trajectory of *Moslem* in the British press is evidence of a subtle form of hostility from the *Daily Mail*.

---

[4] In May 2003 the *Daily Mail* used *Moslem(s)* 121 times. This dropped to twenty-three times in June and then three times in July, so mid-2003 appears to mark the turning point when the word was largely abandoned.

Unique keywords

So far we have addressed differences only between broadsheets and tabloid newspapers. However, as discussed in Chapter 1, this is a problematic distinction for a number of reasons. It does not take into account so-called 'middle-market' newspapers such as the *Daily Mail*, which was categorised as a tabloid for the purposes of the above analysis. Additionally, it ignores general political stance, so the left-leaning *Guardian* is considered alongside the right-leaning *Telegraph*. The above analysis does suggest that there are stylistic and topic differences between newspapers if we group them in this way, but it is also useful to consider the newspapers individually, in order to obtain a clearer idea about what makes each newspaper unique, particularly in terms of how it writes about Muslims and Islam.

Therefore, twelve additional sets of keyword analyses were conducted. This time, each newspaper was compared against the remainder of the corpus. So, for example, the frequencies of all the words in *The Sun* were compared against the collective frequencies of the words across all the newspapers except for *The Sun*. This was done for each of the twelve newspapers. After that, the 100 keywords with the highest log-likelihood values were considered for each newspaper, and, in order to focus on what made each newspaper unique, only the keywords that were unique to the top 100 keywords list in one newspaper were noted (these words are shown in Tables 3.2 to 3.13). For example, the word *veil* is one of the top 100 keywords when the articles in the *Daily Express* are compared against all the other articles in the Islam corpus. However, the word *veil* is not a top 100 keyword for any of the other newspapers, so this suggests that the *Express* is particularly interested in writing about Islam in the context of the veil. Another *Express* top 100 keyword is *terror*. However, this word is also a top 100 keyword for *The People*, the *Daily Star* and *The Sun*, so, while *terror* is clearly an important topic in the corpus, it is not especially associated with any single newspaper. The following tables therefore give only the keywords for each newspaper that are uniquely in its top 100 keywords list.

An examination of the unique keywords is revealing about the different preoccupations of each newspaper. It should be noted that these words are not unique in the sense that they never occur in any of the other newspapers' articles, but they are unique to the top 100 keywords list for each newspaper and are therefore a good indicator of topics and concepts that a particular newspaper is concerned with. Some of them, when explored in more detail, help to reveal ideologies.

There are a large number of proper nouns dispersed throughout the unique keywords, although there are various reasons why they appear. Often they can refer to the names of journalists or columnists associated with particular newspapers. For example, *Younge* in *The Guardian* refers to the journalist Gary Younge, while *Dominik Diamond* is the name of a *Star* columnist, and *Deidre* refers to *The Sun*'s regular agony aunt column, 'Dear Deidre'.

With several hundred keywords to account for, it is beyond the remit of this chapter to give attention to all of them. Instead, we have tried to focus on a smaller number of keywords that are more directly related to representations of Islam and Muslims. We have also tried to keep our coverage as wide as possible, by considering a few terms from each newspaper. Let us deal with the broadsheets first.

The broadsheets

Interestingly, every word in the top 100 keywords for *The Times* (Table 3.2) was unique to this newspaper, suggesting that *The Times* has a very distinctive form of language use compared to the other newspapers, although it should be noted that *The Business* (Table 3.3) also has a very high number of unique top 100 keywords. It would perhaps be expected that *The Business* would appear to be fairly distinctive, as it is the only newspaper that focuses on a specific topic: business news. A look at its keywords suggests this, with many business-related words such as *asset*, *banking*, *boom* and *cuts* appearing. These words often appear because of the fact that *The Business* reports on global financial stories that involve countries with a high population of Muslims. For example, on 24 October 1999 there is a story about an election in Indonesia, and what this will mean for foreign investment. The new president of Indonesia is described as 'an influential and moderate Muslim leader'.

Table 3.2 Words that are unique to the top 100 keywords in The Times

Newspaper	Unique top 100 keywords
The Times	*ably, ABTA, adaptions, adjudicator, Akhmad, Amersham, archeologists, Ashling, atavistic, Austravel, automotive, babble, Bannerman, bantamweight, Boden, bonhomie, Bradbury, Callier, Cass, chow, Cochrane, companionship, consecrated, dealerships, Dobriskey, Dodds, dropout, eastwards, ebookers, enlivened, enrol, entertainments, exrtracurricular, Faruq, Fayyad, fini, Finkel, Fordham, Franco's, fungus, Ganguly, Gravesend, groans, Hakimullah, Hawton, horticulture, impede, industrials, insurgencies, intelligently, introductions, Jakarta's, Kamm, Kingfisher, labor, Lagnado, Laurels, leaden, LNG, LU, magisterial, Mahler, Mansell, Matravers, McFarlane, Mead, Midwest, Minh, Morgan's, Mushtalk, Nav, netball, O'Brien's, overstate, Pacquiao, Padi, pang, peaceable, Pendle, Prasad, quandary, Rasoul, Ripon, Rowlands, Samui, sanctuaries, Seri, shovel, Sibohan, SM, Smethwick, Somak, Suroor, variegated, Vermes, Whittle, wholesaler, Yanbu, zealotry, Zim*

Table 3.3 Words that are unique to the top 100 keywords in The Business

Newspaper	Unique top 100 keywords
The Business	*advertising, airlines, analyst, analysts, asset, assets, banking, Barak, barrel, barrels, Beijing, betting, bingo, bond, boom, boost, Brazil, businesses, casino, casinos, company's, consumer, consumers, contract, contracts, corporate, cuts, data, debt, decline, develop, developing, digital, Dow, earnings, economies, emerging, equity, estimates, executives, existing, exports, farmers, federal, firms, fixed, gambling, gaming, GPD, goods, gross, Hezbollah, Hong, index, infrastructure, invest, investments, investors, Kong, Korea, Las, leisure, Mahathir, Malaysia, managing, operators, ownership, presidency, product, products, profit, profits, projects, rank, recession, recovery, reforms, reserves, returns, revenue, revenues, Saudis, shareholders, Shi, ski, smaller, stake, sub, taxes, trading, unemployment, Vegas, welfare*

In a smaller number of cases, there are stories in which Islam and finance are more clearly linked together. For example, on 8 February 2004 *The Business* writes: 'The Islamic House of Britain is set to become the first Islamic retail bank in Europe when it receives a banking licence from the Financial Services Authority next month.' The article gives a description of a contract called a *mudarabah*, or 'trust partnership', and describes how the bank will work, pointing out that Islamic banking products are structured so that profits are not made at the expense of customers. The article therefore appears to be a fairly straightforward descriptive and uncritical account of the new bank.

Another set of keywords in *The Business*, such as *bingo* and *casino*, are a result of a small number of articles appearing in the corpus by accident due to the presence of *Mecca* in the search term that was used to build the corpus. As noted in Chapter 1, *Mecca* can refer to a British bingo hall chain, as well as being used in other gambling contexts such as describing Las Vegas as a 'gambling Mecca'. These 'accidental' or metaphorical terms provide some interesting cases of how words from Islam have entered the English language with extended meanings, although, for the purposes of this chapter, they are less useful in directly telling us much about how Islam is represented.

It is more difficult to explain why *The Times* has the most top 100 unique keywords. It has a lot of keywords that are proper nouns, but also some quite rare words, such as *atavistic, bonhomie, enlivened, magisterial, quandary* and *variegated*, which may be indicative of *The Times* aiming its articles at readers who are expected to have large vocabularies or a high level of education (Table 3.1 shows that *The Times* has the highest number of people from social class AB in its readership). One interesting keyword relating to Islam that *The Times* uses is *zealotry*. This word is not especially frequent (it occurs only fifty-one times in *The Times*), but it occurs far more in this

Table 3.4 Words that are unique to the top 100 keywords in The
Daily Telegraph

Newspaper	Unique top 100 keywords
The Daily Telegraph	*Amberin, Ambrose, America, Anton, Aug, Blomfield, brig, butcher, café, coalition, col, correspondent, Coughlin, Damien, diplomatic, Dorment, EDA, electorate, ES, Fairweather, Gardham, Gedye, gen, Gilmore, headliners, Hizbollah, however, Howse, Inigo, Iran's, Isambard, Islamic, Lab, LD, Mandrake, McElroy, Mujahideen, nuclear, officials, Pathan, PBK, Petre, Philip, Philps, Poole, PP, PS, Qa'eda, Qa'eda's, Quetteville, Rayment, Rennie, Sandhu, senior, Sherwell, sir, Smucker, Spillius, states, Sukhdev, Taliban, Teheran, Teheran, Teheran's, telegraph, terrorist, Thurs, Toby, Tues, turnout, Tweedie, UKIP, Washington, Woy*

newspaper than any of the others. In *The Times*, *zealotry* is often used to refer
to religious zealotry, and particularly 'Islamic zealotry'. For example, one
journalist describes Saudi Arabia as 'a nation built on Islamic zealotry but
dependent for its wealth and security on the secular, materialist West' (1 June
2004) and another article contains the headline 'Briton "brainwashed into
religious zealotry by Finsbury Park cleric"' (5 July 2003). Although *zealotry*
is not as frequent as words such as *extremist* or *militant* in *The Times*, it seems
to be used as a particularly marked and negative way of referring to very
strong beliefs, like terms such as *fanatic* and *firebrand*, which tend to be more
associated with the tabloids (Chapter 6 demonstrates that extremism words
are proportionally used more often in the tabloids). Perhaps, then, some
journalists in *The Times* wish to distance themselves from appearing too
obviously similar to the tabloids, so they avoid calling Muslims *fanatics*
or *extremists*. However, by using a different term that references the same
concept but in a more abstract and lexically unusual way, *zealotry*, they are
able to refer to a tabloid concept.

Another *Times* keyword is *peaceable* (forty-nine occurrences), which occasionally refers to *Muslims* (e.g. 'British Muslims are mainly peaceable,
law-abiding citizens'; 17 August 1999). As with *zealotry*, this word seems to
be a function of the newspaper's tendency to use somewhat rarer synonyms than
the other newspapers, which would tend more towards using a word that has a
broader meaning, such as *peaceful* (which can mean calm or favouring peace).

The other conservative broadsheet newspaper, *The Daily Telegraph*,
is notable for having *Islamic* and *terrorist* in its top 100 unique keywords
(Table 3.4). In Chapter 2, we saw how *Islamic* tends to be connected with
extremism, conflict, strength of belief, organised groups and political entities.
These meanings also hold true when just *The Daily Telegraph* is considered.

Table 3.5 Words that are unique to the top 100 keywords in The Independent

Newspaper	Unique top 100 keywords
The Independent	*against, ago, an, army, as, been, between, both, city, death, did, during, east, end, even, far, few, first, from, how, in, independent, Iraqi, left, little, many, may, men, might, minister, most, much, no, not, on, one, only, other, over, own, part, party, place, PLC, president, publishing, right, same, September, since, some, south, state, there, these, this, troops, under, war, well, west, where, which, world*

Here, common contexts of *Islamic* include *Islamic Jihad*, referring to a group that is often involved in conflicts in the Middle East (542 occurrences), *Islamic militants* (382 occurrences), *Islamic extremists* (405 occurrences) and *Islamic terrorist(s)/terrrorism* (676 occurrences).

Similarly, the presence of *terrorist* as another *Telegraph* keyword is indicative of a greater linking of stories that directly relate Muslims and Islam to terrorism in *The Daily Telegraph* than other newspapers. As shown in Table 3.1, a tabloid keyword is *terrorists*, while the tabloids also make more reference to *Bin Laden* than the broadsheets, so it is interesting that, when all the newspapers are considered separately, the word *terrorist* emerges as key in a broadsheet, *The Daily Telegraph*. This newspaper's references to *terrorist* are not incidental or 'in passing' cases, unrelated to the context of Islam, but mainly refer to 9/11.

One newspaper that stands out as unusual in terms of its unique keywords is *The Independent*, which appears to favour grammatical (as opposed to lexical) words more than the other newspapers (Table 3.5). While *The Times* tends to have a preponderance of rare nouns, adjectives and verbs as key, most of *The Independent*'s keywords are very frequent prepositions, determiners and auxiliary verbs such as *as, been, both, did, from, in, no, on, there, these, this* and *which*. Such words do not reveal much about representations of Islam, but are more typically associated with writing style. Biber, Conrad and Reppen (1998: 104) note that the frequent use of prepositions (as part of prepositional phrases that 'integrate high amounts of information into a text') is characteristic of genres that are more concerned with information production than showing involvement between the writer and reader. Therefore, some of *The Independent*'s keywords may be indicative of a particularly informational style of journalism. The presence of the keywords *army, death, troops, Iraqi* and *war* suggests that *The Independent* especially writes about Islam within contexts of conflict (e.g. the Iraq war).

The Guardian (Table 3.6) is notable for having words for various higher-level education degrees (*MBA, PGCert, PGDip, MPhil, MA, MSc*). This is not due

Table 3.6 Words that are unique to the top 100 keywords in The Guardian

Newspaper	Unique top 100 keywords
The Guardian	*abstract, Aglionby, analysis, AOS, appended, Borger, Cofe, cooperation, correction, debate, ECON, education, emails, Ewen, Falluja, fin, final, Freedland, FT, Gadafy, Gaza, GD, Goldenberg, Hizbullah, Hizbullah's, human, Intl, Islamist, Israel's, leftwing, MA, Macaskill, management, MBA, McGreal, mngt, Mojahedin, movement, MPhil, MSc, Norton, novel, occupation, Palestinian, Palestinians, PGCert, PGDip, policy, politics, Qaida's, rightwing, serv, state, Steele, students, Suzanne, Tehran, thinktank, Tisdall, UN, uni, university, unlimited, Vikram, Wollacott, Younge*

to *The Guardian* writing articles about Muslims with degrees, but because of its publication of educational supplements that list postgraduate courses across the United Kingdom, including courses such as Contemporary Islamic studies and Islamic political economy. Perhaps more importantly, *The Guardian* seems to be more interested in writing about various conflicts in the Middle East particularly involving Palestine and Israel. While *The Daily Telegraph* has *Islamic* as one of its keywords, *The Guardian* has *Islamist* (occurring 2,388 times). Apart from the fact that *Islamic* is used mainly as an adjective and *Islamist* mainly as a noun, there are strong similarities in how the two words seem to be used across the whole corpus. Both words occur in contexts that relate them to extremism, militancy and terrorism. *The Guardian* mainly uses *Islamist* to distinguish a set of Muslims who advocate (usually an extreme form of) Islamic political rule.

One interpretation of *The Guardian*'s relatively frequent use of *Islamist* is that it is an attempt at 'responsible' reporting, which tries to avoid attributing extremism, terrorism and militancy to the more generalising *Islamic*, or the personalising *Muslim*. We understand the term *Islamist* to refer to someone who advocates the ideology that Islam is not only a religion but a political system. However, the term does not appear to be explained in the corpus, and its close orthographical similarity to *Islam* and *Islamic* might mean that some readers do not grasp the distinction. On 9 November 2002 a writer in *The Independent* asks: 'So what is an Islamist? Obviously it has something to do with the Islamic religion, but there's no parallel word such as "Christianist". Words are needed to distinguish between the many different ways the Islamic religion interacts with Muslim political life.' In *The Guardian*, on 9 September 2011 (during the period after our corpus collection), columnist Mehdi Hasan writes: 'The term "Islamist" – one I have, admittedly, used myself – is especially problematic.' He goes on to state that he has been called an Islamist by his critics, even though he has declared opposition to an Islamic state.

Table 3.7 Words that are unique to the top 100 keywords in The Observer

Newspaper	Unique top 100 keywords
The Observer	*about, are, Beaumont, are, black, book, books, Burke, business, Chucky, Cohen, directed, dollars, Doward, ECB, economic, economist, economy, eighties, escape, Euro, Euros, Eurozone, Faisal, film, Flett, focus, Gaby, Greenspan, growth, Hinscliff, HK, Hoddle, is, Jason, like, magazine, market, markets, metonymic, mins, MPC, music, nineteenth, nineties, OFM, OMM, OSM, patronymic, productivity, rate, rates, Riddell, screengrabs, seventies, Shayler, story, tax, there's, though, toponymic, treasury, twentieth, Vulliamy, week, Xbox*

The Guardian also has the political distinctions *rightwing* and *leftwing* in its top 100 unique keywords. These words (especially *rightwing*) are sometimes used to refer to other newspapers. For example, Richard Littlejohn is referred to as a 'rightwing *Sun* columnist whose remarks about race, gender and homosexuality earned him a place on the shortlist for Bigot of the Year' (14 July 1999). There are also references in *The Guardian* to the *rightwing press, rightwing hacks* and *rightwing newspapers*. On 24 December 2002 a leader column argues: 'Ever since September 11 the rightwing press here have been united in a virulent Islamophobia.' *The Guardian*, then, is critical of other sections of the British press, although it also comes under attack from other newspapers itself (see the discussion of Jeremy Clarkson's *Sun* article in Chapter 5).

The final broadsheet, *The Observer*, which is considered to be the Sunday version of *The Guardian*, appears to have few keywords that relate directly to Muslims or Islam (Table 3.7). For example, three keywords, *toponymic, patronymic* and *metonymic*, relate to a long special supplementary article on the origins of British surnames that briefly mentions how some surnames come 'from the Muslim world', while numbers such as *seventies* and *nineteenth* tend to refer to time periods (e.g. the 1970s) and relate to articles about culture, history and tourism, in which references to Islam are mainly incidental. The high number of business-related words is due to *The Observer*'s 'Business' supplement. Unlike *The Business*, *The Observer* does not necessarily write about Islam in relation to business more than other newspapers, but the author of some of these business articles is called Faisal Islam, which helps to explain why these articles appeared in the corpus – the result of having the word *Islam* in the search algorithm for collecting data.

The tabloids

What about the keywords in the individual tabloids? The *Daily Express* (Table 3.8) uses the keywords *veil* and *wear*, which relate to Muslim women wearing the veil. This practice was so frequently found to be problematised in

Table 3.8 Words that are unique to the top 100 keywords in the Daily Express

Newspaper	Unique top 100 keywords
Daily Express	*asylum, August, British, Broster, claimed, column, correctness, Cyril, DP, edited, extremists, Fagge, Flanagan, Formullah, Gabriel, Hickey, immigration, Ingham, Kilroy, letters, MacVicar, McKinstry, Memmler, Milland, officers, O'Flynn, Padraic, Pilditch, police, princess, publication, Scott, sharia, Shiach, Shipman, taxpayers, veil, warner, wear, Whitehead*

the corpus (and not just in the *Daily Express*) that we decided to focus on it in more detail (see Chapter 8). The *Express* also tends to refer proportionally more to *extremists* than other newspapers (as with the tabloid keyword *fanatics*, this is analysed in further detail in Chapter 6). The keywords *immigration* and *asylum* tend to occur in stories about terrorists or terrorist suspects who are also Muslims and asylum seekers (often failed asylum seekers). For example, on 25 August 2005 the *Daily Express* writes about 'asylum seeker Yasser Al-Siri, who boasted that his lawyers will ensure he is never extradited to Egypt where he faces execution for the murder of a six-year-old girl in a bomb blast'.

There are a number of other interesting keywords in the *Daily Express* that are worthy of exploration: the words *taxpayers, correctness* and *sharia*. The presence of *taxpayers* relates to stories that involve British taxpayers covering the cost of various claims made by Muslims, who are generally characterised as undeserving. Some of these stories are covered in more detail in Chapter 7, but for now we can note that particularly frequent cases involve Muslim preachers who are receiving benefits, as well as Muslims who have used legal aid in court cases. Such stories are used to argue that Britain is no longer a place to be proud of, as the following letter to the *Daily Express* demonstrates:

This country of ours – of which we were once so proud – is falling to pieces at incredible speed. Last week, we the taxpayers financed a successful court case (in the sum of £70,000) brought by a 16-year-old Muslim schoolgirl who claimed that her 'human rights' had been breached after her school in Luton – incidentally run by a lady Muslim head teacher who has bent over backwards to accommodate modest Muslim dress in the design of its school uniforms – sent her home for wearing a jilbab. Apparently this pupil is now considering further legal action, seeking compensation. Another hefty bill for British taxpayers if she succeeds (13 March 2005).

A related *Express* term that also laments the state of the United Kingdom is *(political) correctness*, a label given to behaviours or attitudes that are seen to be overly sensitive, resulting in a lack of common sense or unfairness.

Table 3.9 Words that are unique to the top 100 keywords in the Daily Mail

Newspaper	Unique top 100 keywords
Daily Mail	*antiterrorist, antiwar, ark, baby, because, bedroom, Blair, Camilla, children, Cofe, could, couple, daughter, Dempster, didn't, Doughty, Ephraim, Ed, family, father, friend, friends, fulltime, girl, Gordon, guerrilla, guerrillas, had, Hardcastle, have, hers, Hickley, him, his, husband, if, Kadamba, Kalman, knew, Labour, learned, Letts, life, Littlejohn, love, man, married, marry, McLauchlan, met, middleclass, miss, money, mother, Mrs, never, old, papers, parents, PC, pictured, primary, Sarwar, school, Seamark, sixties, so, their, they, was, wedding, when, who, wife, would, yearold*

For example, on 2 August 2005, just weeks after the 7/7 bombings of London, an *Express* leader column argues that 'political correctness is to hamper the operation to weed out the few Muslim extremists in our midst', implying that it is acceptable for young Asian males to be singled out for police searches.[5]

Another concern of the *Daily Express* is *sharia* law, which is described with the adjectives *barbaric*, *brutal*, *extremist* and *strict*. The newspaper refers to cases in countries such as Nigeria and Afghanistan, where sharia law operates, giving examples of people being sentenced to death by stoning for giving birth outside marriage, or adultery. The *Daily Express* also expresses concerns about sharia law in Britain, as in: 'MUSLIM LAW IS HERE IN BRITAIN; Sharia courts operating in our cities. Secret courts imposing draconian Islamic justice are operating across Britain' (30 November 2006). A term related to *sharia* is *Islamification*, which is not a keyword but occurs most frequently in the *Daily Express*, and is used to express concerns that Britain (or Europe) is gradually turning into an Islamic nation. More than other newspapers, then, the *Daily Express* seems to paint a picture of Islam that is characterised by immigration problems, oversensitivity on behalf of the British establishment, financial burden, brutal laws and encroachment into the United Kingdom.

Of note in the *Daily Mail* is the large number of keywords (Table 3.9) that are linked to people (*baby, children, friend, girl, man*) and relationships between family members: *couple, daughter, family, father, husband, married, mother, parents, wedding, wife*. If there is one newspaper that embodies the somewhat traditional notion of 'family values' then it is the *Daily Mail*.

---

[5] In the *Daily Mail*, the keyword *PC* appears. While this could be an acronym for *political correctness*, it is more often used in the *Mail* to refer to *police constable* or *per cent*. That said, the *Daily Mail* does have the highest usage of the term *political correctness* in the corpus, and it tends to use it in ways that are similar to those found in the *Daily Express*.

Table 3.10 Words that are unique to the top 100 keywords in the Daily Mirror

Newspaper	Unique top 100 keywords
Daily Mirror	*Antonowicz, around, Blackman, blast, bomber, cert, co, Dowdney, Ellis, Gardai, Griffin, Ilbox, Mayhew, mirror, mortgage, Ocack, Oonagh, Osama, Reade, Sheila, Thursday, Wednesday*

Perhaps unexpectedly, given the *Mail*'s defiant use of *Moslem* shown earlier, this stance can result in the newspaper writing of Muslims in approving tones, as in the example below:

The overwhelming majority of Moslems are decent, law abiding people whose commitment to family values is an example to the rest of the country (13 January 1999).

As we will see in Chapter 4, the *Daily Mail* has also defended Muslims who have been criticised for their views on homosexuality, which the *Mail* sees as being against traditional family values.

Children in the *Daily Mail* are often referred to as *small*, *innocent* or *vulnerable* and are frequently viewed as at risk, with common verb collocates being *suffer* and *protect*. One frequent construction refers to the killing or harm of innocent children, particularly in countries involved in conflicts:

Saudi petrodollars have long financed terrorist groups like Hamas, which recently sent a suicide bomber into a Jerusalem pizzeria to slaughter innocent Israeli women and children (26 October 2001).

The *Daily Mail* also shows concern for the children of Muslim extremists:

BARELY 18 months old, he was far too young to know what was happening. He was still so tiny that he had to be carried in his mother's arms. But with a handful of other small children yesterday, an innocent little boy became engulfed in the politics of hatred. When the Muslim men and women around him screamed their poisonous slogans, he tried to mouth along with the words, as if they were merely nursery rhymes. When the chanting crowd punched the air with their fists, he simply looked around in wonder (10 June 2006).

The words *guerrilla* and *guerrillas* are far more common in the *Daily Mail* than other newspapers (it has 60 per cent of all the mentions of these words), and they tend to be linked to stories about Hezbollah, although there are also references to Chechen guerrillas, Moslem guerrillas, Israeli guerrillas and Islamic guerrillas. Such references help to create an association between Islam and conflict, in cases such as: 'Fears were growing last night for four Avon ladies kidnapped by Moslem guerrillas in the southern Philippines' (23 August 2002).

The *Daily Mirror* (Table 3.10) has few unique keywords, although notable ones include *blast*, *bomber* and *Osama*. This reflects a preference on the part

Table 3.11 Words that are unique to the top 100 keywords in The People

Newspaper	Unique top 100 keywords
The People	*back, bars, beaches, Beckham, Bushell, cops, Cork, Daniel, factfile, football, Gillian, holidays, hot, hotspots, KO, Medina, Megan, Mellor, movie, Nigel, paper, people, restaurants, reveal, SAS, season, sport, striker, stunning, Sven, tel, tips, Tunisia, txt*

of the *Daily Mirror* to write articles about conflicts in Iraq, Afghanistan and other places where bombs are set off. Suicide bombers are particularly referenced; for example, a typical article begins: 'Suicide Bomber: An Islamic militant riding a bomb-laden bicycle killed himself yesterday in a suicide attack on an Israeli outpost in the Gaza Strip' (27 October 2000). The *Mirror*'s use of *Osama* (which always occurs in the three-word construction *Osama Bin Laden*) reflects the fact that the newspaper is more likely to use a personalising strategy by referring to the Al Qaeda leader by his full name than other newspapers are.

On the other hand, *The People*'s unique keywords (Table 3.11) tend to focus on two of the more pervasive interests of this Sunday newspaper: sport (*football, striker*) and holidays (*beaches, bars, restaurants* and *hotspots* with *stunning* scenery). A regular feature in this newspaper is called 'Holiday hotspots', with countries such as Tunisia, Morocco and Spain described as having 'Islamic art and architecture' or mosques that are recommended as tourist sites. Unlike some of the other tabloids, *The People* seems to focus more on Islam in terms of culture and travel. However, the presence of sport keywords is mostly due to the small amount of 'noise' in the data and the fact that one of our search terms when building the corpus was *Medina* (there is a footballer called Nicolas *Medina* and a boxer called Manuel *Medina*); as a result, articles about these sportsmen accidentally found their way into the corpus.

The keyword *maniacs* in the *Daily Star* (Table 3.12) was initially thought to be used to describe certain Muslims as having very strong beliefs, similar to *extremists* and *fanatics*. However, this word was actually found to be due to a regular column called 'Text maniacs', which features reader responses that have been sent by text message to the newspaper. As the text messages appear to have been printed exactly as they were sent, without any editing, this also explains the large number of *Daily Star* keywords that are in non-standard English: *aint, av, cant, cos, goin, gud, hav, im, luv, ov, pls, plz, shud, thats, ur, wen, whats, wiv, wont, wot, wud, ya.* The 'Text maniacs' column contains some of the more openly negative representations of Muslims and Islam in the corpus. Below is a sample:

Table 3.12 Words that are unique to the top 100 keywords in the Daily Star

Newspaper	Unique top 100 keywords
Daily Star	*aint, all, anon, av, babe, BB, big, bout, Britney, cant, Chanelle, Choudary, cos, Dave, Diamond, Dominik, Dstar, em, February, goin, gorgeous, gud, hav, im, Kev, Lawton, link, luv, LW, maniacs, mate, ov, pic, pics, pls, plz, ppl, sexy, shud, Steve, telly, thats, ur, wen, whats, wiv, wont, wot, wud, x, Xmas, ya*

kids rnt scum! nowher 2 go! no youth clubs. nothin 2 do! all our money goes on asylum & mosques. samwigan (16 May 2005).

I've never been in trouble in my life and I cant wear a hoody but Muslims can walk about with just two slits showing and thats alright. NEIL (17 May 2005).

MY SON'S HALF PAKISTANI. WILL HE B TARRED BY THE SAME BRUSH AS OTHER MUSLIMS? BUSH + BLAIR MAKE EM ALL SOUND BAD PLEASE STOP WAR. A FLISSIKOWSKI (1 February 2003).

Since end of 1st Gulf War Brit & Yank troops have protected Muslims in north & south Iraq. And how do they treat us in return? Max (13 April 2004).

y r people having a go at anton du beke, there is more important things to worry bout. Like immergration and muslim schools teaching terror acts. Grow up people. Scott (7 October 2009).

WHY DON'T DECENT MUSLIMS TURN ON OMAR BAKRI MOHAMMED? HE'S SCUM. J.WEST (8 September 2004).

Reading the text messages in the *Daily Star*, there is a general impression of reader resentment towards Muslims, who are constructed as receiving preferential interest while hating 'us'. There is also little attempt to 'fact-check' such text messages; a statement such as 'all our money goes on asylum & mosques' is easily disproved, yet its publication could be seen to validate the claim.

However, not all the messages are simply negative. One writer above expresses concern that her son will be tarred by the same brush as other Muslims, and blames George W. Bush and Tony Blair for making all Muslims sound bad. Another writer refers to 'decent Muslims' but asks why they don't turn on Omar Bakri, thus implying that even the 'decent' Muslims are not doing this. However, the main picture is one of hostility towards Muslims.

The Sun's keywords (Table 3.13) indicate this newspaper's preoccupation with Abu Hamza – in the shape of the word *hook*, as noted, referring to the prosthetic device that he wears. *The Sun* constructs Hamza as a pantomime villain, calling him *Captain Hook* on eighty-two occasions, while the word *hook* is employed in a number of puns. One *Sun* headline reads: 'Our soft lawyers let evil Hamza off the hook' (30 April 2004), while another reads: '£200K right hook: Hamza's

Table 3.13 Words that are unique to the top 100 keywords in The Sun

Newspaper	Unique top 100 keywords
The Sun	*all, Anila, Baig, chiefs, code, cop, dear, Deidre, evil, ex, hook, jail, journal, July, Kavanagh, last, NOTW, Omar, opinion, Parker, Pascoe, Platt, rant, sun, sun's, Syson, ten, up, Watson, Wooding, WVM*

lawyer hits YOU for massive legal aid bill' (9 February 2004). The newspaper also ran a campaign to have Hamza deported called 'Sling your hook':

The Sun gave hook-handed fanatic Abu Hamza a right earful yesterday – by blasting him with pop songs. We carefully chose ten hits that would get across our 'Sling your hook' message loud and clear. And we played them at top volume from our Sun bus as Hamza tried to give his weekly sermon of hate outside Finsbury Park Mosque in North London. Our tunes included the Madness classic *Night Boat to Cairo* – suggesting Hamza, 46, return to his Egyptian homeland (9 February 2004).

Readers' letters also focus on Hamza's hook, with one reader simply referring to him as 'Hook': 'Unless Hook can support the people he brought here, they should be sent back to where they came from' (17 September 2003). On 17 October 2004 *The Sun* wrote an article that combined its hatred for Hamza with its outrage at the financial benefits he gains from taxpayers and its continuing fascination with his hook: 'RANTING cleric Abu Hamza is to be given a new hook – on the National Health Service. The taxpayer will pick up the bill for the aluminium replacement, which could top £5,000.'

Two related *Sun* keywords are *rant* and *evil*. People described as *ranting* in *The Sun* include a number of high-profile Muslims – Abu Hamza, Omar Bakri, Osama Bin Laden, Yasser Arafat – but also the MP George Galloway, who is described as 'treacherous' and a 'slimy Saddam supporter' for his opposition to the war on Iraq (1 April 2003). However, *The Sun* also describes the leader of the British National Party, Nick Griffin, as ranting:

Defiant BNP leader Nick Griffin last night challenged police to take him to court over his sickening views… Griffin, 45, launched his rant over last night's BBC1 expose *The Secret Agent*, which nails thugs within the British National Party… The BBC revealed one BNP member who wanted to shoot Muslims, another who had beaten up an Asian and others guilty of intimidation (16 July 2004).

In this case, *The Sun* sets itself in opposition to the BNP, a party that is to the right of the mainstream British political parties, and consequently in this case *The Sun* appears to be a defender of Muslims. This example shows the danger in labelling newspapers with terms such as *right-wing* and *left-wing*; political labels are always relative.

The final *Sun* keyword to be examined is *evil*. *The Sun*'s relatively frequent use of *evil* (1,136 occurrences) compared to other newspapers is notable in itself, although a close look at the word reveals that it is used in a number of different contexts. Unlike most of the other newspapers, *The Sun* frequently uses moral absolutes, regularly labelling Omar Bakri, Abu Hamza and Osama Bin Laden as *evil* (the *Daily Express* and, to a lesser extent, the *Daily Star* and the *Daily Mirror* also refer to people as *evil*). *The Sun* also quotes political leaders who use the term, including George Bush, who talks of a battle of 'good versus evil' (26 September 2001), and Tony Blair, who says the 'fight on terror is a war against evil, not Islam' (6 October 2001). The newspaper is critical of people who do not approve of the word. For example, on 16 February 2002 an opinion piece by former US defence secretary Richard Perle described EU commissioner Chris Patten as 'patronising' and having 'worrying views'. Perle writes:

When the President talks about the 'Axis of Evil', he is describing some of the nastiest regimes of the 20th and 21st centuries. If Mr Patten is upset by the word 'evil', how would he describe them? And what would he do about them? He seems prepared to do nothing except to countenance their continuing evil.

However, another reason why *evil* is a keyword in *The Sun* is that, two days after the 9/11 attacks, it published an article entitled 'Islam is not an evil religion'. The article argues:

If the terrorists were Islamic fanatics then the world must not make the mistake of condemning all Muslims... There are Muslims in Ireland who ARE Irish and there are Muslims in Britain who ARE British. They may have a different culture but they love their countries and they respect democracy.

This article is frequently referred to in subsequent *Sun* articles, when the newspaper reiterates that Islam is not evil. So, while *The Sun* is somewhat atypical of the British press in that it frequently describes particular people or concepts as evil, at an important point it stresses that Islam is not evil.

Conclusion

The analyses in this chapter indicate that, when it comes to reporting on Islam and Muslims, the British press is not monolithic. Instead, it embraces a range of concerns and stances, with different newspapers focusing on certain types of news story, or attempting to present stories about Islam filtered through their particular ideological position. Consider, for example, how *The Sun* views the world through a framework of moral absolutes in which the presence of evil exists – echoing the sentiments of George Bush and Tony Blair, who also employed the world *evil* in response to the terrorist attacks of 9/11. On the other hand, the *Daily Express* tends to link stories about Muslims to traditionally right-leaning concerns about immigration and asylum seeking, as well as worrying that British government policy in relation to Islam is resulting in political correctness and, ultimately, more expense for taxpayers. The *Daily Star* also pursues a right-leaning ideology, and this is especially apparent in the text messages of its readers, who tend to feel that Muslims unfairly receive preferential treatment, perhaps as a result of what they have read about Muslims in that newspaper (see also Chapters 5 and 7).

Some of the stances of other newspapers appear to be more subtle, and are also more difficult to categorise as positive or negative. For example, the *Daily Mail*'s choice to use the word *Moslem* rather than *Muslim*, for a year after other newspapers abandoned that problematic spelling, and in spite of the fact that the Muslim Council of Britain asked it to stop, tells us something about its unwillingness to cooperate, even before we have examined what contexts *Moslem* is used in. While the *Mail* sometimes paints Muslims (or Moslems) as extreme and involved in conflict, on other occasions the newspaper writes approvingly of Muslims who have 'traditional family values' and set a good example to the rest of the country, as well as defending Muslims who have been accused of homophobia. Additionally, consider how the left-leaning *Guardian*'s use of the term *Islamist*, to refer to a certain type of political and militant Islam, sometimes mirrors the right-leaning *Daily Telegraph*'s use of 'Islamic'. Both terms attract negative discourse prosodies, and, for some readers, the difference may appear to be mostly cosmetic. For others, it will be much more meaningful.

The lexical choices of other newspapers reveal more about style; contrast the *Daily Mirror*'s personalising trait of writing *Osama Bin Laden* in full with *The Times*' preference for rare words such as *zealotry* and *peaceable*. Other terms tell us about focus; the tabloids are much more concerned with events at home, and what the presence of Muslims in the United Kingdom will mean for the day-to-day lives of their readers. On the other hand, the broadsheets write more about Islam from a global perspective, although this trend stems from their covering wars (especially *The Independent*) and overseas acts of terrorism (especially *The Daily Telegraph*) more frequently and in more detail than the tabloids. Moreover, although the broadsheets write about Islam in the context of culture and politics, the tabloids seem to focus more on terrorism and extremism, especially writing more about high-profile 'villains' such as Osama Bin Laden, Abu Hamza and Omar Bakri.

Some of the differences between newspapers that were uncovered in this chapter have provided the basis for more detailed qualitative analyses, which comprise some of the later chapters of this book. However, in the following chapter, we consider variation across the corpus from another perspective, by examining change over time.

4   The 9/11 effect: change over time

Introduction

In the previous chapter we considered variation between different news-papers, focusing in particular on the broadsheet/tabloid distinction. In this chapter we consider another kind of variation: change over time. The period between 1998 and 2009 saw a number of highly significant events that involved Muslims or were related to Islam. How did such events impact on the ways that the British press represented Muslims? For example, to what extent did the terrorist attacks of 9/11 and 7/7 result in a monumental shift in such representations, and for how long? What news stories led to 'spikes' or increases in frequency in reporting, and at what points did stories about Muslims involved in conflict peak?

For the sake of simplicity, in this chapter we have considered a year as a discrete period, allowing us to break the corpus up into twelve parts. This gives a manageable number of distinctions, although to an extent it disguises the fact that events do not neatly begin in January and end the following December. The 9/11 attacks, which perhaps represent the strongest 'shift' in the representation of Islam in the corpus, happened in September 2001. Therefore, the period of '2001' could be divided into two parts, reflecting pre- and post-9/11 sections. As a result of the 9/11 effect, the discourse around Islam in December 2001 is probably closer in nature to the discourse in January 2002 than it would be to August 2001. However, a twelve-part analysis retains sufficient complexity while still allowing a manageable analysis to be undertaken.

As with Chapter 3, we have used a number of different techniques in order to compare different parts of the corpus. We have used keywords again (words that are statistically more frequent in one corpus or part of it, when compared to something else), deriving keywords for each year of the corpus by comparing the frequencies of each year against all the other years. This allowed us to identify unique keywords for each year, though it also tended to tell us more about news stories that began and ended in one calendar year. To gain a view of stories that straddled multiple calendar years, we have supplemented the keywords approach by looking at sets of similar keywords that are key in multiple time periods. This method is useful in that it shows the 'shelf life' of certain topics or concepts, or how the words associated with a particular concept may alter over time. Additionally, we have continued our focus on the four most frequent words in the corpus that refer to Islam: *Muslim*, *Muslims*, *Islam* and *Islamic*. We also return to a finding that was made when we examined the corpus as a whole in Chapter 2, asking whether the general focus on the topic of conflict is constant across the time period under examination.

However, we begin this chapter with a closer look at how the number of articles about Muslims in the British press changed over time.

Frequency of stories

Our data collection period was from January 1998 to December 2009. Figure 4.1 shows the number of articles per year of the corpus. A couple of disclaimers need to be made before we discuss this figure. First, the collection of articles prior to 2000 was not possible for some newspapers, due to the fact that Nexis UK did not begin archiving them until later. There was no data for the *Daily Express*, *The Business*, the *Daily Star*, *The Sun* and *The Daily Telegraph* in 1998, while the latter three also did not archive in 1999, and the *Daily Star* only began

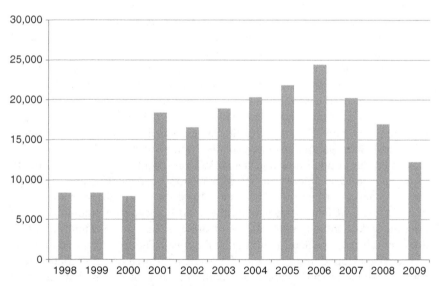

Figure 4.1 Number of articles collected in each year of the corpus, 1998–2009

archiving in December 2000. Furthermore, *The Business* stopped publishing in 2008. Therefore, the data should be considered to provide a relatively 'full' picture only for the years 2001 to 2009.

Additionally, when considering change over time, trends will be more heavily influenced by the broadsheet newspapers, which tend to have more articles (see Chapter 3). Accordingly, if the broadsheets proportionally increase their coverage of stories about Muslims, this will be reflected as a greater change than if the tabloids do the same. Figure 4.1 therefore probably tells us more about broadsheet coverage than tabloid trends.

That said, it is interesting to note the high number of articles in 2001 (even taking into consideration the fact that data from some newspapers is missing, there would still be a large increase between 2000 and 2001). The increase in articles over time between 2002 and 2006 is also notable, suggesting that 9/11 may have kick-started media interest in Muslims, but that it continued over the decade. It is notable that the terrorist attacks on the London transport network occurred the year before the largest number of articles in the corpus, suggesting that this 'home-grown' event was of great importance to the British media, perhaps even more so than the 9/11 attacks. However, the final part of Figure 4.1 suggests a sharper decline in interest in Islam, with 2009 having the fewest articles since 2001.

In order to take into account the fact that there were some periods when the data collection was not complete, another way of considering change in frequency over time is to look at the average number of articles in a particular time period, across the set of newspapers that *were* available for collection then. Figure 4.2 gives this information, and, in order to give a more detailed picture, the unit of analysis is months rather than years.

Figure 4.2 suggests that, prior to 9/11, interest in Muslims in the British press was actually decreasing, having peaked in late 1998 when stories about conflict in the Balkans were common (at least for the newspapers that were being archived during this period). However, the 9/11 attacks appear to have triggered a notable change, with the largest spike occurring in September 2001, and then another, slightly smaller, spike in 2005 as a result of the attacks on the London transport network. Thus, two terrorist attacks seem to cause the greatest amount of interest in stories about Muslims, although the focus appears to be reasonably short-lived. However, the overall trend is of an increase of interest over time: the trend line shows a gradual rise, and after the spikes, although the number of stories about Muslims tends to fall, it does not fall as far back as it was before the spike. The American-led invasion of Iraq also resulted in a spike in 2003, while a terrorist attack in Madrid also caused a spike, as did a debate on veiling in the United Kingdom, inspired by an article by the leader of the House of Commons, Jack Straw. Another spike, in 2007, was caused by the war in Somalia. The overall effect is a

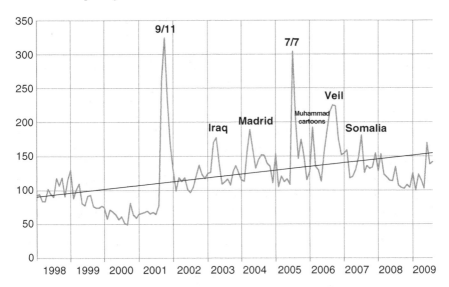

Figure 4.2 Average number of articles referring to Muslims and Islam per month of the corpus, 1998–2009

ratcheting up of the focus of the newspapers on Islam. The cause of this ratcheting up confirms the findings in Chapter 2, that Muslims and Islam tend to be focused on in the context of conflict: terrorist attacks, wars and political debate surrounding whether Muslim women should or should not wear veils.

Figures 4.1 and 4.2 are useful in showing the general trend over time, as well as allowing us to see which news stories tended to trigger large spurts in coverage about Muslims and Islam. However, we should not assume that each spike is necessarily the result of a single event. For example, the 2006 spike was mainly caused by the debate on veiling, but there was another story at that time, involving the first anniversary of the controversial publication of Danish cartoons that depicted the prophet Muhammad. Additionally, Figure 4.2 might cause us to focus on the spikes while disregarding the periods when there were fewer stories. Therefore, as a way of providing a clearer focus of what was happening during each year of the corpus, there is a need to consider keywords.

Unique keywords

Following the procedure carried out in Chapter 3, which compared keywords across different newspapers, the top 100 keywords for each year of the Islam corpus were derived by comparing the data from each year against the other eleven years. Almost all these keywords were found to be unique to the top 100 keyword lists, reflecting the fact that the keywords of each year tended to be relatively transient, based as they are upon specific news events. This was unlike the examination of keywords newspaper by newspaper, when certain keywords were more likely to reveal a continuing focus in a particular paper over a long period of time, such as the *Daily Express*'s interest in political correctness and taxpayers. Perhaps unsurprisingly, Table 4.1 also shows a high proportion of proper nouns relating to people and places, although occasionally certain words reflected a focus on a particular concept that became important to a certain story. For example, the nouns *seekers* and *inspectors* in 2002 involve stories about, first, concern over numbers of asylum seekers in the United Kingdom (with a focus on cases involving Iraqis and Afghans) and, second, weapons inspectors in Iraq, with a subsequent interest in the possibility of Iraq holding 'weapons of mass destruction'.

Table 4.1 presents a selection of twenty-five of the top 100 keywords for each year of the corpus. The keywords were selected in order to provide a representative picture of the main news topics associated with each year. We have avoided listing keywords that are very similar; so, for example, in 2001, rather than listing the keywords *Taliban* and *Taliban's*, we have listed only *Taliban*.

Echoing a main finding from Chapter 2, Table 4.1 shows that many of the keywords refer to conflicts involving Muslims across the world. However, this raises the question: did particular events result in more reporting about Muslims in terms of conflict? Moreover, was the effect cumulative? For example, did the 9/11 attacks result in Muslims and conflict becoming a 'newsworthy' story, resulting in an increasing emphasis on such stories in future years?

CONFLICT in the corpus: diachronic development

Having established that issues of conflict are dominant in the corpus articles, we now turn our attention to the frequency development of CONFLICT tokens over the twelve years that the corpus articles span. This is done in two complementary ways, by looking at the development of (a) the percentage of words in each year of the corpus that refer to conflict and (b) the average number of words about conflict per article, for each year. The dual approach to the frequency development of CONFLICT tokens is necessitated by the observation that, in the corpus, broadsheet articles are, on average, about 80 per cent longer than tabloid articles. Therefore, the examination of percentages in terms of words may be skewed towards broadsheets. Examination of the development of frequencies in terms of articles (irrespective of

Table 4.1 Keywords associated with each year of the corpus

Year	Keywords	Topics and events
1998	*Abubakar, Acourt, agreement, Albanian, Albright, Algiers, Brunei, Chechenia, Clinton's, Diana, duchess, fatwa, Fein, impeachment, Indonesia's, Jakarta, Lewinsky, prince, princess, Rushdie, Sinn, Sudan, Suharto, Ulster, Unionist*	Bill Clinton's impeachment Good Friday agreement in Northern Ireland US bombing of Sudan
1999	*Albania, Balkan, Belgrade, Caucasus, Chechnya, cleansing, ethnic, Kosovan, Macedonia, Megawati, millennial, Milošević, Moscow, NATO, Nostradamus, refugees, Russia, Sarwar, Serbia, Slobodan, Timor, village, Yeltsin, Yemen, Yugoslavia*	War in Kosovo and Chechnya Slobodan Milošević indicted Referendum in East Timor Millennium celebrations
2000	*Arkan, Assad, Ballesteros, Fergie, guerrillas, Hague, hostages, Jerusalem, Jewish, Jolo, Kanungu, Lombok, peace, Philippine, Putin, rebels, reformers, repeal, Rezala, Sayyaf, silicon, SLA, temple, Tyson, Wahid*	Killing of hostages in Philippines Middle East peace talks Repeal of section 28 of Local Government Act 1988
2001	*action, Afghan, aircraft, alliance, anthrax, atrocities, Atta, bombing, Bora, caves, fight, hijackers, Kandahar, Moslems, Mujahedin, network, Oldham, Pakistan, Pentagon, plane, strikes, surrender, Taliban, targets, terrorism, Tora, trade, united, we, west*	9/11 War on Afghanistan Anthrax attacks in United States
2002	*Bali, Bethlehem, camp, contestants, Cuba, Dutch, Fortuyn, Gujarat, Hindu, India, Indonesia, inspectors, Jemaah, Jenin, jubilee, Karachi, Kashmir, Malvo, Mombasa, Nablus, Nigeria, Pen, Pim, Qaeda, queen, seekers, Vajpayee*	Bali bombing Assassination of Pim Fortuyn Miss World finals in Nigeria
2003	*Baath, Basra, Blix, destruction, featherweight, forces, guard, Gulf, Hussein, infantry, Kurds, Kuwait, looters, loyalists, oil, Powell, regime, Republican, resistance, resolution, ricin, soldiers, Tigris, Tikrit, UN*	Invasion of Iraq
2004	*Abu, Basque, beheaded, Beslan, Bigley, Blunkett, Brahimi, cleric, contractors, Fallujah, Ghraib, handover, hostage, interim, Iraqi, Ken, kidnapped, killed, Madrid, marines, militants, rebel, sovereignty, Spain, WMD*	Kidnapping of Ken Bigley Bombing in Madrid Abu Ghraib scandal

Table 4.1 (cont.)

Year	Keywords	Topics and events
2005	*Bakri, bombers, Britain, cardinals, Clarke, constitution, Edgware, electorate, EU, Galloway, insurgency, Khan, Londoners, police, Shias, suicide, Sunnis, suspects, Syrian, terror, tsunami, tube, turnout, UKIP, vote*	London transport attacks British general election Reporting of Indian Ocean tsunami (Boxing Day 2004)
2006	*Azmi, Barot, Beckett, Beirut, cartoon, ceasefire, Danish, Darfur, debate, faith, Hizbollah, Lebanon, Mahmood, Misbah, Mogadishu, niqab, nuclear, profiling, prophet, raid, rockets, speech, Straw, veil, wear*	UK veiling debate Humanitarian catastrophe in Darfur Danish cartoons of Muhammad
2007	*airport, Banna, bear, Benazir, Bhutto, British, Cofe, Crocker, Eagleton, Ethiopian, Glasgow, Ibrahim, Johnston, kidnap, Musharraf, sailors, Shilpa, Siddique, Sudan, surge, teacher, teddy, troop, Turney, Warsi*	Attack on Glasgow airport Assassination of Benazir Bhutto British teacher held in Sudan for naming teddy bear 'Muhammad' Iranian capture of British sailors
2008	*Abdulla, archbishop, Beijing, Boris, Calzaghe, Canterbury, code, court, crunch, Dev, Galway, Hillary, Jacqui, Karadzic, Khan, Khy, McCain, Mumbai, Olympics, Palin, pirates, senator, sharia, Solzhenitsyn, Taj, Tibet*	Credit crunch American elections Beijing Olympics Archbishop of Canterbury and sharia law
2009	*Ahmadinejad, BNP, burqa, Choudary, Dhabi, Dubai, EDL, expenses, Gaddafi, Gaza, Griffin, Guantanamo, Hasan, Libya, Lockerbie, Mahmoud, Megrahi, Mousavi, protests, recession, swine, Tehran, Twitter, Uighur, Wilders*	British right-wing organisations MPs' expenses scandal Global recession Rise of social networking sites Lockerbie bomber returned to Libya

their length) will supply a different perspective – this time of frequencies being skewed towards tabloids.[1]

In terms of the relative frequency per 100 words (which is skewed towards broadsheets), the emerging picture is of a clear rise (50 per cent) after 2001 (arguably triggered by 9/11), and then an overall slight downward trend (Figure 4.3). However, at all points since 2001 frequencies are at least 20 per cent higher than in 2000. The overall picture is only slightly different when the average proportion of CONFLICT tokens per article is examined (Figure 4.4).

---

[1] Given that tabloid articles are, on average, significantly shorter than those in broadsheets, the same number of CONFLICT words would result in a much higher proportion for tabloids than broadsheets.

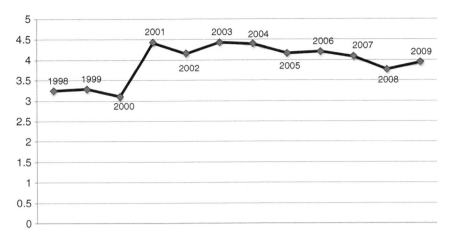

Figure 4.3 Diachronic development of the proportion (%) of CONFLICT tokens in each annual sub-corpus, 1998–2009

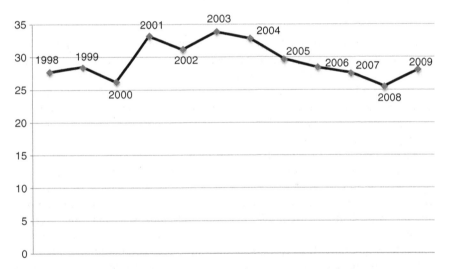

Figure 4.4 Diachronic development of the average frequency of CONFLICT tokens per article in each annual sub-corpus, 1998–2009

However, there are two interesting differences between Figures 4.3 and 4.4. First, the frequency increase of CONFLICT tokens from 2000 to 2001 is roughly the same irrespective of whether it is examined through the proportion of the total words in each annual sub-corpus (Figure 4.3) or the average number of CONFLICT tokens in individual articles (Figure 4.4) – in fact, it is slightly more pronounced in the former case. As was noted above, the former measure

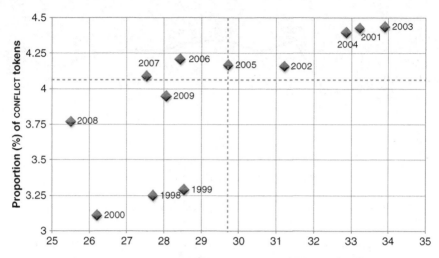

Figure 4.5 Plot of normalised annual sub-corpus frequency and average frequency per article of CONFLICT tokens

is mainly influenced by the broadsheet newspapers in the corpus, whereas the latter is more influenced by tabloids. Second, the post-2003 frequency decline of CONFLICT words is less pronounced in Figure 4.3 (skewed towards broadsheets) than Figure 4.4 (skewed towards tabloids). This suggests that the link between Islam/Muslims and issues of conflict is not a characteristic of either the broadsheets or the tabloids but of the UK national press as a whole – at least, during the time period in focus.

As the two ways of measuring the diachronic frequency development of CONFLICT types are complementary, a clearer picture emerges when both are considered in combination (Figure 4.5). The higher and more to the right a year is depicted, the more prominent issues of conflict are in the corpus articles published that year. The two dotted lines represent the average frequencies in the whole corpus, and their intersection acts as a reference point, to which the other annual sub-corpora can be compared.

Examining the positions of the different annual sub-corpora in Figure 4.5 reveals a number of interesting patterns. The 2001 sub-corpus and the sub-corpora for the three years following (2002, 2003 and 2004) have frequencies clearly above average. For 2005 (the year of the 7/7 London bombings), the frequency of CONFLICT is closest to the corpus average. In order to interpret the above, we need to remind ourselves of three interacting points. First, the trigger for the frequency increase from 2000 to 2001 (Figures 4.3 and 4.4) was 9/11. This is supported by the fact that the frequency of the group of query terms also peaks in the 2001 sub-corpus. Second, the corpus was designed so that it contains articles in which Islam and/or Muslims are a topic (central or peripheral). Third, the corresponding increase (2000 to 2001) in the frequency of CONFLICT types can reasonably be ascribed to the connection in the UK press of the 9/11 attack to Islam and Muslims – whether directly or indirectly, explicitly or implicitly. In this light, the lower prominence of CONFLICT words in the 2005 sub-corpus can be seen as an indication that the link of the 7/7 bombings to Islam and/or Muslims was less pronounced than that of the 9/11 attack. A similar, but more tentative, explanation can be put forward for the drop in references to conflict in the 2002 sub-corpus: the initial strong association of the 9/11 attack with Islam/Muslims in UK newspaper reporting was followed by a more reflective and balanced discussion, which depended less on stereotyping (see, for example, *The Sun*'s post-9/11 'Islam is not an evil religion' article described in Chapter 3). The subsequent frequency rise of CONFLICT words in the 2003 sub-corpus can thus be ascribed to the invasion of (and war in) Iraq.

Diachronic keywords

The keyword analysis carried out earlier in the chapter was useful in showing which stories and concepts occurred in a single year, although this presents only a partial picture, as many topics could appear over multiple years. For this reason, it was decided to extend the keyword analysis in order to consider all keywords (rather than the 100 with the highest log-likelihood values) for each year. Additionally, rather than looking only at keywords that were unique to a particular year, we considered grouping keywords into sets that tended to have similar meanings and functions. This allowed us to plot the development of particular topics. For example, consider Table 4.2. This table shows keywords

Table 4.2 Nationality keywords over time

	98	99	00	01	02	03	04	05	06	07	08	09
Afghanis				✓								
Arab		✓	✓	✓	✓	✓						
Arabs			✓	✓	✓	✓	✓					
Arabian	✓			✓								
British						✓	✓	✓	✓	✓		✓
Briton				✓	✓	✓	✓	✓				
Britons				✓	✓	✓		✓				
Chechens		✓	✓	✓	✓		✓					
foreign				✓	✓	✓	✓	✓				
French	✓		✓		✓	✓	✓	✓				
German	✓	✓	✓	✓	✓	✓						
Saudi				✓	✓	✓	✓					
Yugoslav	✓	✓	✓	✓	✓							

Table 4.3 Terrorism keywords over time

	98	99	00	01	02	03	04	05	06	07	08	09
counterterrorism										✓		✓
Osama				✓	✓							
hijack			✓	✓	✓							
hijacked			✓	✓	✓							
hijackers			✓	✓	✓							
hijacking			✓	✓	✓							
terror				✓	✓		✓	✓	✓	✓		
terrorism				✓	✓		✓	✓	✓			
terrorist				✓	✓	✓	✓	✓				
terrorists				✓	✓	✓	✓	✓				

that relate to particular nationalities. A tick in a cell means that a particular word was key in that year.

It is notable here how the majority of these nationality keywords appear between 2001 and 2005, with only *British* continuing to be key after that point. The keywords thus suggest a gradual focus on international contexts up until around 2004/5, and then, after that point, more concern with Muslims in the United Kingdom. This is backed up by the fact that the word *foreign* is key between 2001 and 2005. Individual keywords also reveal their own stories: *Yugoslav* is key only up until 2002,[2] whereas *Arab* is not key until 2000,[3] and *Saudi* does not become key till the following year.[4]

Another set of keywords involves terrorism (Table 4.3). As we would expect, these keywords tend to be most numerous in 2001 and 2002, though terms relating to hijacking only go as far as 2002. There were other words that could potentially have been included in this table, such as *bomb*, although *bomb* tends to occur in contexts other than terrorism, so we have tried to be as specific as possible in identifying words that fit unambiguously into particular categories. The presence of *counterterrorism*, becoming key after 2007, is also of note. The lack of other terror keywords in 2008 and 2009 might suggest that stories about Muslims that involve terrorism (or vice versa) are on the decline.

[2] *Yugoslav* was key prior to 2003, on account of stories relating to the Yugoslav wars (which led to the dissolution of Yugoslavia) and Slobodan Milošević, the former Yugoslav leader who was captured and charged with corruption and abuse of power in 2001.

[3] *Arab* and *Arabs* are key from 2000 to 2004 because of stories about the conflict in Palestine and references to Arab members of the Taliban during the US-led invasion of Afghanistan in 2001.

[4] *Saudi* is key from 2001 to 2004 as a result of an increasing focus on Saudi Arabia after the 9/11 attacks; Osama Bin Laden, who planned the attacks, was a Saudi. By 2004 there are increasing references to Saudi Arabia's oil wealth in the corpus.

Table 4.4 Immigration keywords over time

	98	99	00	01	02	03	04	05	06	07	08	09
asylum			✓	✓	✓	✓		✓				
illegals										✓		
immigrant			✓					✓	✓			
immigrants			✓					✓	✓	✓	✓	
immigration			✓				✓	✓	✓	✓		
migrant									✓	✓		
migrants									✓	✓	✓	✓
migration									✓	✓	✓	
refugee		✓	✓	✓	✓							
refugees		✓	✓	✓								
seeker						✓		✓				
seekers			✓	✓	✓	✓		✓				

Table 4.4 shows keywords relating to the concept of immigration over time. Here, the keywords appear to be dispersed more broadly over the different time periods of the corpus, although 1998 is unique in that it features no immigration keywords. The first immigration topic that seems to emerge as important in the corpus is that of refugees, referring to situations in Albania, Kosovo, Macedonia, Chechnya, Bosnia, Afghanistan and Palestine. While refugees are generally represented as a 'problem' in the corpus, they are not normally seen as a direct threat to British interests, and instead there are cases such as the article below, in which Britain is seen as playing a role in helping refugees:

A BRITISH transport aircraft loaded with tents and blankets left yesterday for Albania as Western governments and international relief agencies began a massive effort to rush supplies to the thousands of destitute refugees pouring out of Kosovo (*Times*, 31 March 1999).

The above example contains a fairly representative picture of refugees in the British press, characterising them with the adjective *destitute*, which emphasises their plight, while also using a water metaphor (*pouring*), which appears to collectivise, dehumanise and problematise their existence. However, by 2002 references to refugees are no longer key.

A second immigration topic is that of asylum seeking, which is key between 2000 and 2005. This topic is one that provokes more concern, especially in the tabloids and right-leaning press:

The truth is New Labour cares more about bogus asylum seekers and militant homosexuals than it does about pensioners (Richard Littlejohn, *Sun*, 18 April 2000).

However, the left-leaning broadsheets provide a counter-discourse to that of the unwanted and frequently 'bogus' asylum seeker, by accusing the tabloids of a disproportionate reaction:

FOR THE past two months asylum seekers have been vilified by the tabloids for preying on our good nature and misusing our welfare state. In a climate of increasing hysteria, they have been denounced by a government minister for the habit of begging with children and threatened with internment by the leader of the opposition. With record numbers of would-be refugees arriving on these shores, the asylum issue becomes increasingly contentious almost by the day. Immigration staff are under intense pressure to process claims, with the backlog in cases standing at around 98,000 – despite a record 11,340 decisions being made last month (*Independent*, 2 May 2000).

In 2002 a new topic of concern, immigration itself, arises, and *immigration* emerges as a keyword. This concept is rarer in 2003 and 2004 but then becomes popular again from 2005 to 2007. In the right-leaning press, immigration tends to occur in contexts of illegal immigration (similar to Richard Littlejohn's bogus asylum seekers), and there are calls for tighter controls:

If the Government really believed in dumping multiculturalism, it would have introduced a far tighter immigration policy instead of continuing to allow at least 600,000 people from the Third World and Eastern Europe to settle here every year. The surest way to stop neighbourhoods becoming cohesive is to keep altering their structures with massive new influxes of migrants who have no language, culture or traditions in common (Leo McKinstry, *Daily Express*, 28 August 2006).

The final immigration concept to become key in the corpus is *migration*, appearing as a keyword from 2006 onwards. *Migration* tends to have a slightly more positive discourse prosody in the corpus; there are fewer calls for controls on migrants than immigrants or asylum seekers, and migrants are less likely to be called *illegal* or *bogus*. Instead, there are references to economic migration and discussion of the possible benefits of migration, although some newspapers are characteristically dismissive, as can be seen from the following example:

Economically, our public services are under intolerable strain. Contrary to what ministers claim with their prattle about the economic benefits of migration, the tidal wave of newcomers has actually been a huge burden on the taxpayer, particularly since migrants are twice as likely as the indigenous population to be unemployed or claiming benefits (Leo McKinstry, *Daily Express*, 8 September 2008).

It should be noted that, when newspapers write about immigration and Islam in the same story, they do not refer to *Muslim immigrants* (a term that never appears in the corpus). Instead, Islam and immigration are often linked together in other ways, as in the following two excerpts:

Wearing his most fearsome Glaswegian scowl, Home Secretary John Reid promises for the umpteenth time to get tough. Remember how he was going to boot out foreign ex-prisoners, crack down on lenient judges, slash illegal immigration and stand up to Muslim extremists? Well, now he is promising to kick antisocial families out of their homes, children and all (*Daily Mail*, 15 November 2006).

In an article in the New York Times Rose argues that Europe's left is deceiving itself about immigration, integration and Islamic radicalism in the same way 'young hippies' like him fooled themselves about Marxism and communism 30 years ago (*Guardian*, 30 September 2006).

The *Mail* article problematises a type of immigration (illegal) and a type of Islam (extremism), linking the two concepts together, while a similar process occurs in the *Guardian* article, which quotes the cultural editor of a Danish newspaper that published a cartoon depicting the prophet Muhammad. More explicit associations between Islam and immigration such as the one below (which combines concern about political correctness, immigration and Islam) are rarer:

Hundreds of migrants massing in Calais as they try to break into Britain were treated to a Christmas party yesterday. But folk songs replaced carols for fear of offending the mainly Muslim asylum seekers from Africa, Asia and the Middle East (*Daily Express*, 24 December 2007).

Another set of keywords involves concepts relating to hate and tolerance (see Table 4.5). Here it is interesting to note the complete lack of these keywords in the first three years of the corpus (1998 to 2000). The next three years (2001 to 2003) have only a few keywords, *xenophobia*, *racism* (and related words), *tolerance* (and related words) and *hatred(s)*, although they become more frequent after 2004 and are particularly notable in 2006. While words that refer to racism seem to be more widely dispersed in the corpus, the concept of Islamophobia is key only between 2004 and 2006, while multicul-turalism is key between 2005 and 2008 and discrimination is generally more of a focus between 2006 and 2009.

It is difficult to guess at the context of some of these keywords without conducting more detailed concordance and collocational searches of them. For example, does a term such as *intolerant* refer to Muslims being intolerant of non-Muslims or vice versa, both or something else? Even a term that has a clearer meaning, such as *Islamophobia*, may be used in order to refute the concept. Below, we explore the contexts of these terms in some detail.

There are 890 occurrences of the word *intolerant* in the corpus, being most frequent in 2006, and with sixty-nine cases of *intolerant* collocating with *Islam* overall. Of these sixty-nine cases of collocation, sixty-two of them refer to (the possibility of) Islam as intolerant while seven refer to (the possibility of) non-Muslims as being intolerant towards Islam. The sixty-two cases tend to present Islam straightforwardly as intolerant, as shown in the next example:

Table 4.5 Hate and tolerance keywords over time

	98	99	00	01	02	03	04	05	06	07	08	09
alienate							✓	✓				
alienating								✓				
alienation							✓	✓				
bigot								✓				✓
bigoted								✓	✓			
bigotry								✓	✓			
bigots								✓				
demonisation								✓				
discrimination								✓	✓	✓	✓	✓
discriminated								✓		✓		
discriminatory							✓					✓
discriminate									✓			
discriminating								✓				
diversity								✓	✓	✓	✓	✓
hate								✓	✓	✓	✓	✓
hatred				✓			✓	✓	✓			
hateful												✓
hating										✓		
hatreds				✓								
integrate							✓	✓	✓	✓		
integration								✓	✓	✓		
integrating									✓			
intolerant									✓			
Islamophobia							✓	✓	✓			
Islamophobic							✓	✓	✓			
multicultural								✓	✓			
multiculturalism								✓	✓	✓	✓	
prejudice									✓			
prejudiced										✓		
racism				✓	✓					✓		✓
racists				✓	✓		✓					
racist					✓				✓	✓		✓
tolerant					✓			✓	✓	✓		
tolerance				✓				✓	✓			
tolerated									✓			
toleration									✓			
xenophobia				✓	✓		✓					

We must not bow to the intolerant ways of Islam (*Sunday Telegraph*, 16 August 2009).

Only three cases were found in which the view of Islam as intolerant is questioned:

He spoke of his anger at the caricature in some quarters of the peaceful religion of Islam as intolerant and violent. 'We do need a better understanding in the West of the great achievement of Muslim societies and people and of Islam as a religion of peace, which rejects violence against fellow human beings' (*Times*, 21 May 2004).

However, about a half of the sixty-two cases do not refer to Islam as a whole as being intolerant but, instead, reference certain strands, brands, aspects or forms of Islam as being more intolerant than others:

Wahhabism is the most intransigent and intolerant form of Islam, and is wreaking havoc in many places urgently in need of more tolerant, mainstream styles of the religion (*Independent*, 5 October 2001).

Of the seven instances that suggest that non-Muslims are intolerant, three are dismissive of this claim. The example below shows two opposing arguments:

This small minority must learn that we will not put up with this, not because we are intolerant of Islam, but because we are intolerant of treachery. Those who take up arms against their own country's soldiers should be prosecuted on their return (*Mail on Sunday*, 4 November 2001).

I suspect that some of the public anguish that was present when Mr de Menezes was shot on the Tube last summer but seems so far to be absent over Mr Kahar is because Britain is becoming dangerously intolerant of Islam (Alice Miles, *Times*, 7 June 2006).

The general picture here, then, is not of a concern about intolerance towards Islam (and, in the rare cases when this happens, it is likely to be refuted anyway) but of Islam itself being intolerant. There are a few cases in which this view is criticised as a stereotype, and many writers limit the impact to specific types of Islam, but the pattern is more one of an association of Islam with intolerance rather than a portrayal of Islam as the object of intolerance.

What about the word *Islamophobia*, which more clearly indicates hatred toward Islam? There are 1,574 occurrences of this word in the corpus. A close analysis of 100 occurrences, taken at random, reveals that thirty-three of them use the term sarcastically or to deny that the concept exists. The use of scare quotes in the following two examples is fairly typical.

Only this month, Whitehall banned ministers from using the words 'Islamist', 'fundamentalist' and 'jihadist' in case they suggest terrorists may be Muslim! Even 'Islamophobia' – invented by hand-wringing Lefties to gag us all – is banned because it makes an 'explicit link' between Muslims and terror (Trevor Kavanagh, *Sun*, 21 December 2009).

The growth of militant Islam in Britain is one of the least discussed but most important developments of our era. A politically correct [PC] fear of committing 'Islamophobia' has prevented a much-needed debate on this subject for far too long (*Mail on Sunday*, 1 August 2004).

Thus, we should not take the increased presence of words such as *intolerance* and *Islamophobia* from 2004 onwards to suggest that the British press, as a whole, became more concerned about prejudice towards Muslims from this

Table 4.6 Sexuality and gender keywords over time

	98	99	00	01	02	03	04	05	06	07	08	09
gay			✓						✓	✓	✓	✓
gays									✓	✓		✓
gender											✓	✓
heterosexual	✓		✓							✓		
homophobia										✓	✓	✓
homophobic									✓	✓		✓
homosexual	✓		✓									
homosexuality	✓		✓						✓		✓	✓
homosexuals			✓						✓	✓	✓	✓
lesbian	✓										✓	✓
lesbians							✓					
sex	✓	✓	✓				✓				✓	
sexed							✓					
sexes		✓										
sexist										✓		✓
sexual	✓	✓	✓									✓
sexually			✓								✓	✓
sexuality	✓		✓								✓	✓

point. Clearly, some sections of the press do seem to have shown more interest in this topic, although the concern also resulted in a backlash, with parts of the press keen to argue that it is Islam (or parts of it) that is intolerant, and that Islamophobia is an irrelevant or unhelpful concept. It is perhaps of most interest, therefore, to note that, prior to 9/11, there seems to be much less discussion in the British press with regard to whether Islam is linked to intolerance. By 2005, and for the remainder of the period under examination, there is much more discussion – though little consensus.

Another set of keywords that we wish to highlight in this chapter consists of those relating to sexuality and gender (see Table 4.6). The pattern in this table is somewhat distinct from the other sets of keywords examined so far. There appears to be discussion of sexuality and gender at the beginning of the corpus (1998 to 2000), then an absence of such keywords from 2001 to 2005 (apart from *lesbians*, *sex* and *sexed* in 2004), followed by a renewed and intensified focus on these subjects during the period from 2006 to 2009. A possible explanation for this rather disjointed pattern can be found by comparing Table 4.6 with Table 4.3 (keywords relating to terrorism). The two tables are almost mirror images of each other, and we would hypothesise that, because of the fact that discourse around Islam becomes concerned with terrorism, stories linking Islam to other issues are backgrounded between 2001 and 2005, including the issues of sexuality and gender.

A number of questions arise as a result of looking at Table 4.6. Is it the case that stories linking gender and sexuality to Islam remain stable over time? Are the sorts of representations found from 1998 to 2000 also present by the period from 2006 to 2009, when the topic becomes an issue again? Alternatively, do the later set of stories differ in some way from the earlier ones? The legal and political status of gay people changed over the course of the period under question, with section 28 of the Local Government Act 1988 (which forbade the 'promotion of homosexuality' by local education authorities) being repealed in 2000, as was the ban on gay people in the armed forces. The age of consent was equalised to sixteen for gay men in 2001, and legislation allowing gay civil partnerships was enacted in 2005. It is notable that words relating to homophobia are key from 2006 onwards, suggesting one different way that homosexuality may be related to Islam in the latter part of the corpus. However, bearing in mind how references to Islamophobia are sometimes critical of the concept, equally we should not assume that homophobia is viewed as a valid concept by the British press.

Let us first consider how the word *homosexuals* is constructed during the early and later parts of the corpus. In 2000 there are 106 references to homosexuals. The concordance lines of every case were examined. Only eight cases were found to relate homosexuality and Islam together directly. Of these, three construct Islam (or branches of Islam) as homophobic, as in the two cases below:

As Dr Zaki Badawi of the Muslim College, London, points out, homosexuality's incompatibility with Islam does not mean we can deny gays the right to call themselves Muslim: 'We can say that homosexuals are not good Muslims because they are practising an unacceptable sin, but we cannot completely write them out of Islam' (*Guardian*, 17 January 2000).

The Islamic fundamentalist group that now runs 90 per cent of Afghanistan has imposed a harsh brand of Islamic, or sharia, law with savage punishments. In the four years since the Taliban took control, such grisly penalties have become a regular spectacle after Friday prayers in a country where television, films and music are banned. Homosexuals have been buried alive under walls... (*Daily Mail*, 8 August 2000).

The other five cases equate homosexuality and Islam, in terms of being similar minority groups who were often oppressed:

Signor Berlusconi, the media tycoon, has been forced to reassure minority groups that are concerned over Signor Bossi's eccentric outbursts against a variety of supposed enemies, ranging from homosexuals and Freemasons to communists and Muslims (*Times*, 28 October 2000).

The issue is, what group is going to be hounded next by the *News of the World*? Next year will it be homosexuals? The year after will it be the mentally ill? Then asylum seekers? Muslims? Jews? Critics of the tabloid press? (*Independent*, 'Letters', 9 August 2000).

Let us compare an equivalent concordance of *homosexuals* from 2009, when there are 202 occurrences. A random examination of 106 cases (the same number examined for 2000) found that thirty-five of them refer to Muslims who were homophobic, five make equivalencies between Islam and homosexuality (although in the majority of cases this is to argue that both groups are unfairly given preferential treatment) and two refer to cases in which Muslims tried to reconcile homosexuality with their religion.

Here, there seems to have been a significant change in the discourse, with many more cases in which Islam or Muslims are represented as homophobic. Cases such as the following become much more typical in 2009:

ALL HOMOSEXUALS SHOULD BE STONED TO DEATH SAYS PREACHER OF HATE (*Daily Mail*, 21 March 2009).

As argued by Baker (2005), in the past the *Daily Mail* has regularly contained negative characterisations of gay people (constructing them as militant, promiscuous, shameful or shameless). In October 2009 another *Daily Mail* article, by columnist Jan Moir about the death of gay pop star Stephen Gatley, was perceived as homophobic and resulted in the highest number of complaints to the Press Complaints Commission ever recorded (over 25,000). It is perhaps ironic therefore that articles such as the one above present the *Daily Mail* as being outraged over someone else's homophobia. At other points in the corpus, the *Daily Mail* paints gay people as militant and attacking Muslims:

DRIVEN OUT BY THE GAY MAFIA; leading Scots Muslim forced to quit charity group after objections to his support for traditional family values. Leading Muslim forced to resign by gay activists (15 June 2006).

It could be argued that the *Mail* is simply against anyone who appears militant or extreme, although another interpretation is that the newspaper is negatively biased towards both Muslims and gay people, and will strategically print stories that construct members of these two social groups as behaving unfairly towards each other.

For the sake of completeness, two final tables are included, although we do not provide a detailed analysis of them, as they are covered in later chapters. First we have keywords relating to the subject of veiling (Table 4.7). It is worth noting here that veiling is of less interest to the British press up until 2004, while the most important year appears to be 2006. This line of enquiry is pursued further in Chapter 8, when we look at a debate on veiling that was triggered by a single article by the leader of the House of Commons, Jack Straw, in 2006.

Finally, Table 4.8 shows keywords referring to extremist belief. Words relating to extremism appear to be less frequent in the early part of the corpus (1998 to 2000), although the word *hardliners* is key here. After that there appears

Table 4.7 Veiling keywords over time

	98	99	00	01	02	03	04	05	06	07	08	09
burqa				✓					✓	✓		✓
burqas				✓								✓
headscarf							✓		✓	✓		
headscarves					✓	✓						
hijab							✓	✓	✓	✓		✓
hijabs									✓			
jilbab						✓	✓	✓				
niqab									✓	✓		
veil									✓	✓		
veils									✓	✓		
veiled									✓			

Table 4.8 Extremism keywords over time

	98	99	00	01	02	03	04	05	06	07	08	09
fanatical				✓		✓	✓	✓				
fanatic				✓					✓	✓		
fanaticism				✓				✓				
fanatics				✓			✓				✓	
firebrand							✓	✓	✓			
extremism								✓	✓	✓	✓	✓
extremist								✓	✓	✓	✓	✓
extremists								✓	✓	✓	✓	✓
fundamentalism				✓			✓					
hardline												✓
hardliner								✓				
hardliners	✓		✓									✓
militancy					✓			✓	✓			
militant				✓	✓	✓	✓	✓				
radical							✓	✓	✓	✓		
radicalism								✓	✓	✓	✓	
radicals								✓	✓	✓		

to be a shifting pattern, with certain concepts appearing popular for short periods of time, which overlap each other. References to fanaticism seem to be prevalent in 2001, militants are key from 2002 to 2006, then radicals occupy the period between 2004 and 2008, and finally extremism takes up 2005 to 2009. The contexts of these words, such as whether they actually refer to Muslims, the extent to which the terms are synonymous and how they relate to other terms such as *moderate* or *pious*, are all considered in Chapter 6.

Words relating directly to Muslims and Islam

As in the previous chapter, it is worth considering whether there is any variation across the corpus in terms of the four most frequent words that directly reference Islam: *Muslim, Muslims, Islam* and *Islamic*. This information is given for each year of the corpus in Figure 4.6.

Figure 4.6 again shows the '9/11 effect', with direct references to Muslims and Islam being much more frequent since 2001 (even taking into account the fact that not all the data was available from 1998 to 2000). It is worth noting the increasing references to all words between 2002 and 2006, as well as the relatively high number of references to the word *Islamic* in 2001 and the words *Muslim(s)* and *Islam* in 2006. As with Chapter 3, it is interesting to consider whether the proportional relationship between *Muslim(s)* and *Islam(ic)* has altered over time (see Figure 4.7).

An advantage of Figure 4.7 is that it comprises proportional data, so the missing data from 1998 to 2000 is of less importance. Here, the longer bars show which periods tend to favour the use of *Muslim(s)* over *Islam(ic)*. In the early parts of the corpus, from 1998 to 2001, it mainly seems to be the case that the concept of Islam is considered more newsworthy than the people who practise the religion. Reporting during this period is thus likely to have been (slightly) more abstract, rather than personalised. However, over time, this picture gradually reverses, with greater emphasis on Muslim(s) occurring between 2003 and 2006. By 2006, for every reference to *Islam* the religion, there are almost two references to a *Muslim* or *Muslims*. There is evidence that the pattern could be changing again, as the size of the bars starts to decrease after 2006.

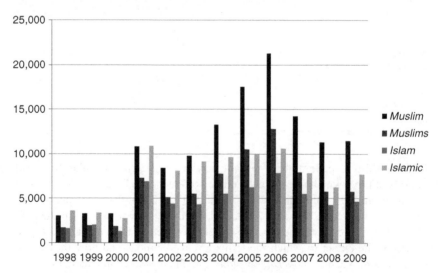

Figure 4.6 Frequencies of main terms relating to Islam over time, 1998–2009

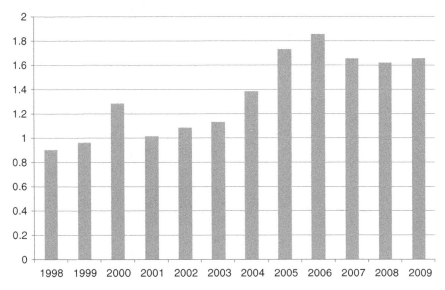

Figure 4.7 Ratio of *Muslim(s)* to *Islam(ic)* over time, 1998–2009

Changing collocates

A more detailed way of examining change over time is to consider frequent collocates surrounding important words in the corpus. We decided to examine the highly frequent word *Muslim* (occurring 126,913 times across the whole corpus) and focus purely on words that come directly after it (to use corpus linguistics terminology, we would refer to these as R1 collocates, as they occur one place to the right of *Muslim*). Table 4.9 shows the most frequent R1 collocates for each time period (each collocate scored higher than three for the T-score, MI and log-dice tests).

A number of interesting trends can be elicited from this table, some of which are examined in more detail in later chapters. The only two words that ever appear at the number one position in the table, in any column, are *community* and *world*. The prominence of these words (plus the plural term *Muslim communities*) and the fact that *Muslim world* appears in top position from 2001 to 2003 (again linking this term to 9/11) naturally suggest a direction for more detailed analysis. It is notable that *Muslim country* appears in the top ten in the years 1998 to 2003. However, it is not present in the top ten between 2004 and 2007, although *Muslim countries* is, being particularly common in 2006 (and also 2001).

Another related term, *Muslim population*, though not as popular as the other words, is also in the top ten in five years. As well as words that collectivise Muslims in terms of belonging to a group (*community*, *world*, *population* and *country*) there are words that identify political or religious

Table 4.9 Top ten R1 collocates of Muslim across all newspapers for each year (grammatical words not included)

	1998	1999	2000	2001	2002	2003	2004	2005	2006	2007	2008	2009	All years
1	community	community	community	world	world	world	community	community	community	community	community	world	community
2	world	world	rebels	community	community	community	council	council	women	council	women	community	world
3	holy	cleric	world	countries	country	cleric	cleric	leaders	council	women	men	women	council
4	schools	women	holy	leaders	countries	countries	world	world	world	world	world	extremists	women
5	women	countries	population	women	cleric	country	leaders	women	leaders	leaders	communities	woman	leaders
6	country	population	country	country	men	council	women	communities	countries	woman	council	council	countries
7	countries	country	women	council	council	leaders	countries	men	woman	extremists	countries	population	cleric
8	leaders	extremists	cleric	extremists	extremists	women	men	cleric	communities	communities	extremists	men	country
9	woman	council	men	cleric	women	population	population	brotherhood	cleric	soldier	country	countries	men
10	fundamentalists	MP	fighters	men	population	association	communities	countries	extremists	men	convert	country	communities

leadership (*leaders*, *MP*, *cleric* and *Council*). There is a sharp rise in *Muslim Council* from 2004 to 2007, while the term *Muslim leaders* is popular in 2001 and then again between 2005 and 2007. The collocates *community*, *world*, *country*, *Council* and *leaders* are examined more closely in Chapter 5.

Two terms in Table 4.9 reference extremist positions: *fundamentalists* in 1998 and *extremists* in 1999 and from 2001 to 2002 and 2006 to 2009. Such terms show both a difference over time and across newspapers, and it was thus decided to focus on these terms and others like them in more detail in Chapter 6. Similarly, the presence of gendered terms – *women*, *men* and occasionally *woman* – is also suggestive of another important focus in the press. It is notable that references to *Muslim women* are usually more frequent than *Muslim men* except in 2002 (the year after 9/11). These terms are investigated in Chapter 8.

It is also of interest to note words that occur only infrequently in the top ten lists: *holy* (1998, 2000), *rebels* (2000), *association* (2003), *brotherhood* (2005), *soldier* (2007) and *convert* (2008). These tend to be associated with particular news stories at various points in time. For example, *Muslim holy* is mainly used in the construction *the Muslim holy month of Ramadan*, and occurs in stories about Operation Desert Fox, a four-day bombing campaign on Iraqi targets by the United States and the United Kingdom that took place in December 1998. Newspapers reported on whether or not the bombing would continue into Ramadan (the final attacks apparently stopped just before the sunrise of 19 December, which signified the start of Ramadan). The term *Muslim rebels* in 2000 refers to hostage taking in the Philippines as well as attacks by Muslim rebels in Algeria. *Muslim Brotherhood* refers to the Sunni transnational movement, which was banned in Egypt at the time. In 2005 the members of the Muslim Brotherhood, standing as independents, won about 20 per cent of seats in Egypt's elections, becoming the largest opposition bloc. This story was reported mainly in the left-leaning broadsheets. *Muslim soldier* refers to an alleged plot in 2007 to kidnap and behead a British Muslim soldier. The term *Muslim convert* is frequent in 2008, because of a number of stories regarding Muslim converts who are terrorist suspects, as well as a story about Angela Gordon, a convert who was jailed for starving her seven-year-old daughter to death. Such stories tend to associate conversion to Islam with terrorism or other forms of cruelty. Concordance 4.1 also shows how conversion to Islam is linked to a range of other negative states, such as alcoholism, vagrancy, drug dealing, mental illness, sexism and being easily led.

Are the references to Muslim converts any different in the years before 9/11? There are only twenty-one mentions of *Muslim convert* before 9/11 in the corpus, of which samples are shown in Concordance 4.2.

Prior to 9/11 there are still cases of Muslim converts being involved in terrorism; for example, line 3 refers to terrorist suspect Abu Izzadeen. However, other concordance lines describe Muslim converts as victims; in line 5 a Muslim

Concordance 4.1 Muslim convert *(sample), 2008*

his estranged eldest son, Harilal, a	Muslim convert	, alcoholic and vagrant, either boycotted
Andrew Rowe, 38, a	Muslim convert	and former drug dealer, was caught in
A	Muslim convert	with a history of mental illness who was
Neighbour Ali Turner said he had seen	Muslim convert	Reilly, a vulnerable misfit with a history
Newswire service Wenn alleged the	Muslim convert	was a sexist bigot who snubbed women
EASILY LED: Nicky Reilly,	Muslim convert	, lived with his single mother Kim, below
	Muslim convert	Yeshi Girma, 32, knew of his plot to kill

Concordance 4.2 Muslim convert *(sample), prior to 9/11*

white convert to Islam married to another	Muslim convert	. My case is not unusual. The vast majority
naive, overweight, rather lost young man, a	Muslim convert	, child of a black father and a white mother
Kalashnikovs. Abu Izzadeen, a 25-year-old black	Muslim convert	, said: 'I have been with the Islamic movement
Islam and was put in touch with another	Muslim convert	in her area. Then Isabel came home one
terrorist bomb plot, while a 24-year-old	Muslim convert	from Birmingham was reportedly killed in
relationship with his present wife, Queen Noor, a	Muslim convert	who has pressed for her eldest son, Hamzah
hospital in Jolo city. Mr Schilling, a	Muslim convert	and resident of California, was taken hostage

convert is killed in a US missile attack on Osama Bin Laden's Afghanistan base, while line 6 refers to Jeffrey Schilling, a Muslim convert who was taken hostage when he visited a rebel camp in the Philippines. Schilling is negatively described in line 2 as *naive, overweight* and *rather lost*. However, despite such cases, in general the constructions of *Muslim convert*, prior to 9/11, while still referencing terrorism, do not seem to contain the full range of negative constructions about Muslim converts that are found in the later period of the corpus.

When *Muslim* occurs before a noun, it tends to function as an adjective, modifying other nouns. However, another term, *Islamic*, has a similar function. What sort of words does *Islamic* modify? Table 4.10 shows its immediate right-hand collocates, again ordered in terms of frequency.

While there are some similarities between the collocates of *Muslim* and *Islamic*, there are also notable differences, with the collocates of *Islamic* carrying a much stronger discourse prosody for extremism and militancy. The word *militants* appears as a top ten collocate in every time period, while references to *extremists* are in the top ten of every time period except 2000, and *Jihad* (referring

Table 4.10 Top ten R1 collocates of **Islamic** across all newspapers for each year (grammatical words not included)

	1998	1999	2000	2001	2002	2003	2004	2005	2006	2007	2008	2009	All years
1	militants	militants	Jihad	Jihad	Jihad	Jihad	militants	Jihad	world	extremists	law	Republic	Jihad
2	Jihad	law	law	world	militants	militants	Jihad	extremists	extremists	militants	extremists	revolution	militants
3	law	state	militants	militants	world	world	extremists	militants	Jihad	law	extremism	extremists	extremists
4	fundamentalists	extremists	state	fundamentalists	extremists	extremists	world	world	law	world	Jihad	world	world
5	world	fundamentalists	Republic	law	militant	terrorists	terrorists	state	terrorism	courts	militants	extremism	law
6	extremists	revolution	world	extremists	terrorists	state	law	Law	courts	Jihad	terrorists	law	terrorists
7	fundamentalist	fundamentalist	groups	state	groups	revolution	army	terrorists	state	state	world	state	state
8	fundamentalism	world	revolution	terrorists	group	law	fundamentalists	revolution	terrorists	terrorists	state	militants	Republic
9	Republic	Jihad	fundamentalists	fundamentalists	law	group	fundamentalism	extremism	militants	extremism	Republic	regime	fundamentalists
10	group	army	fundamentalist	groups	state	fundamentalists	terrorism	terrorism	extremism	terrorism	revolution	terrorism	fundamentalism

to the group Islamic Jihad) is in every time period except 2009. Another term, *Islamic Army*, refers to several armies around the world: the Islamic Army of Aden (based in Yemen), the Islamic Army in Iraq, and Al Qaeda, which is sometimes referred to as the Islamic Army for the Liberation of Holy Places.

References to *Islamic fundamentalism* seem to be popular until 2004, but after that *fundamentalism* is no longer a top ten collocate. However, one concept that appears to become more popular over time is terrorism, which appears in 2001 and remains in every top ten after that point. From Table 4.9, we have seen how *Muslim* also tends to attract references to extremism, although *Muslim* does not frequently collocate with *terrorism*. This may reflect an attempt by the British press to associate the more controversial topic, terrorism, with the more abstract modifying term, *Islamic*.

Like *Muslim*, there are a number of collocates that suggest collectivising processes at work in the corpus. However, while *Muslim* tends to attract *community*, this is not the case with *Islamic* (*Muslim community* occurs 8,265 times while *Islamic community* has only 735 occurrences). Both *Muslim* and *Islamic* tend to collocate with *world*, though *Muslim world* is the more frequent (5,081 times versus 3,083). However, the collectivising *Islamic group(s)* is a popular combination, whereas *Muslim group(s)* is not. Islamic groups in the corpus have a tendency to be military (*armed, militant*), politically or religiously extreme (*radical, extremist, fanatical, fundamentalist, hardline*) and often illegal (*outlawed, banned, shadowy*). The term *Muslim groups* also tends to attract the extremism collocates, but not the militancy or illegality ones, and there are also almost twice as many references in the corpus to *moderate Muslim groups* as there are to *moderate Islamic groups*.

Additionally, while there are references to *Muslim countries*, there are alternative constructions such as *Islamic state* and *Islamic regime*. Islamic regimes tend to be described as *radical, hardline, oppressive, repressive, strict* and *anti-Western*, although Islamic states do not attract such negative terms.

Clearly, the word *Islamic* carries a more negative set of discourse prosodies than *Muslim*, although, as we shall see in the following chapter, when we begin to examine phrases such as *Muslim world* and *Muslim community* in more detail, it becomes clear that these terms do not always have positive associations. The close associations of *Islamic* with militancy are not fully the responsibility of the British press, as it is simply referring to the names of organisations or groups such as Islamic Jihad or the Islamic Army, which have been coined by others. Generally, the prosodies for *Islamic* seem to be more stable over time than those for *Muslim*, and there are fewer cases of unique collocates in the top ten lists for *Islamic* (*courts* in 2006 and *regime* in 2009). The word *courts* refers to the Union of Islamic Courts (UIC), a group that wants to bring sharia law to Somalia, while, in 2009, *Islamic regime* reflects a growing media unease with the political situation in Iran (see Concordance 4.3).

Concordance 4.3 Islamic regime, *2009*

Iranians have demonstrated that the violent	Islamic regime	won't suppress their desire to live freely and fairly
Thirty years ago, as a young revolutionary, he helped to topple the Shah, putting today's	Islamic regime	in power and working as a speechwriter for its founding father, Ayatollah Ruhollah Khomeini
Montazeri's death could hardly have come at a worse time for Iran's	Islamic regime	, which has sought to isolate Mousavi and Karroubi as puppets of foreign 'enemies'.
The alleged incident follows complaints by other Iranian exiles that agents of the	Islamic regime	have tried to intimidate them into silence since they escaped
Ahmadinejad's hardline	Islamic regime	has tried to prevent images of the bloodshed getting out of Iran.
David Miliband refused to rule out military action if Tehran's hardline	Islamic regime	does not halt its nuclear weapons programme.
CRACKS appeared in the	Islamic regime	's control of Iran yesterday as security forces failed to quell protests across the country.

The term *Islamic regime* is a good example of 'convergence' (Hall *et al.* 1978: 223). Both words are loaded with negative meanings, so they will reinforce each other when paired together. Moreover, at early points in the corpus the phrase *Islamic regime* has been used to refer to the Taliban in Afghanistan (especially in 2001).

Conclusion

The analysis in this chapter reveals a number of notable findings: a gradual move towards news stories that are personalising (referring to Muslims), rather than the more abstract concept of Islam the religion. Additionally, there is a gradually increasing focus on stories about Muslims in the UK context, as opposed to Muslims in other countries. It is interesting to note how the concept of extremism appears to be fairly prevalent across the corpus, although this is referred to by changing terms: *hardliner*, *fanatic*, *militant*, *radical* and *extremist*. Other concepts are restricted to particular periods, such as veiling and references to tolerance/hatred, which tend to be more common towards the end of the corpus data, although they do not necessarily indicate that the British press has become more tolerant of Islam. Another notable case is to do with words relating to homosexuality – initially a relatively common topic, which then dies out around 2002, possibly as a result of 9/11 putting terrorism and its consequences into sharp focus, but returning around 2006. However, although the concept of homosexuality resurfaces in the corpus, the way that it is characterised has changed somewhat, with the British press more likely to be critical of Islam for homophobia in the later years rather than suggesting that Muslims and gay people share common ground because they are oppressed groups. Some newspapers indicate disapproval with Islam for not meeting 'British' standards of tolerance, although they rarely acknowledge their own role in perpetuating homophobic discourses in other articles.

Some of the analysis in this chapter reaffirms findings made in earlier chapters, such as the focus on conflict across the corpus, and the more negative discourse prosody of the word *Islamic* as opposed to *Muslim*, while other areas of interest have proved to be too complex to examine in this chapter (such as veiling and extremism), and thus have warranted a more detailed focus in later chapters.

This chapter, and the two before it, have therefore been useful in terms of the early stages of the analytical framework presented in Figure 1.3. Stage 3 of this model involved an analysis of frequencies, clusters, keywords, dispersion, etc. in order to identify potential sites of interest in the corpus, along with possible discourses/topoi/strategies. In Chapters 2 to 4 we took a 'naive' approach to the corpus, not really knowing what we would find, but using mainly frequency and keyword analyses in order to consider the corpus as a whole, as well as variation within it. From these three chapters we were able to move to develop new hypotheses and research questions, which allowed us to move on to the later stages of the model. Specifically, we identified the following topics as worthy of more detailed enquiry: collectivisation and differentiation, strength of belief, Muslims who receive government benefits, and differences between Muslim men and women. Obviously, this is not a definitive list of 'sites of interest', but we felt that focusing in more detail on these topics would help us to approach the subject of the representation of Muslims and Islam from a number of interrelated but unique perspectives. Our first 'non-naive' chapter concerns a deeper look at terms such as *Muslim world* and *Muslim community*, which were highlighted as frequent earlier in this chapter.

5 Welcome to *Muslim world*: collectivisation and differentiation

Introduction

In this chapter we focus on uses of language in the corpus that (a) collectivise Muslims into a single group and (b) differentiate them from others. Our earlier analyses (see Chapter 4) found that some of the most frequent phrases that directly referred to Muslims in the corpus were terms that were potentially collectivising and differentiating: *Muslim world, Muslim community, Muslim country*. Clearly, with so many references to these terms, it is worthwhile spending some time examining them in more detail. Are such terms mainly used in ways to imply that all Muslims are the same as each other, and, if so, in what ways are they viewed as the same? When journalists write about *Muslim countries*, which countries are they actually referring to, and how often do articles attempt to signal difference within Islam, for example by referencing terms for different branches of the faith, such as *Sunni* and *Shia*?

Other writers have pointed out the importance of considering these processes when examining the representation of social groups. John Richardson (2004: 231–2, emphasis in original) argues that

British broadsheets divide and reject Muslims via a three part process: first they identify a 'space' – which can be social or mental or physical (etc.) – and rhetorically separate it from 'Our own' space; second, they explain the workings or composition of this space in contrast to 'Our own'; and third British broadsheet newspapers place a (negative) social value on both this space and its composition. These are, in turn, processes of *separation*; *differentiation* and *negativisation*.

Another author, Said (1997: xv–xvi), argues that media uses of the term *Islam* actually define a 'relatively small proportion of what actually takes place in the Islamic world, which numbers a billion people and includes dozens of countries, societies, traditions, languages, and, of course, an infinite number of different experiences'. Said goes on to say that 'this is unacceptable generalization of the most irresponsible sort, and could never be used for any other religious, cultural, or demographic group on earth'. Said made this argument prior to 9/11, and we therefore wondered whether or not the increased focus on Islam after 9/11 would have resulted in the British media attempting to make a greater effort to be aware of the wide range of distinctions and experiences that Said refers to. On the other hand, it could be the case that, after 9/11, newspapers would be even less likely to make such distinctions, but instead refer to Islam as a more collective, homogeneous entity.

We begin by examining phrases that (on the surface) appear to represent Muslims as a single group − such as *Muslim world*. We then consider terms that refer to specific branches or movements within Islam, such as *Shia*, *Sunni* and *Wahhabi*. How frequently do newspapers use these terms, and in what contexts do they appear?

Muslim community

Let us start with the term *Muslim community*. In the previous chapter (Table 4.9) we saw how *community* is the most frequent immediate right-hand collocate of *Muslim* in the majority of years in the corpus (1998 to 2000 and 2004 to 2008). *Muslim community* occurs 6,553 times in the corpus, and in 4,656 cases (71 per cent), it is prefaced by the definite article *the*, suggesting that the British press normally references the notion of Muslim community as a single, homogeneous mass. Only a handful of articles are critical of the term, so examples such as the one below are extremely rare:

What the list also shows is that the idea of a one-size-fits-all 'Muslim community', or a commonality of experience, is a myth... Some talk about 'the Muslim community', others feel there is no such thing (*Times*, 21 March 2009).

I'm irritated, too, with the boneheadedness of some of our discussion about the Muslim community, as though it was homogeneous, as though it was somehow responsible itself for the bombings, as though, by an act of will, it could stop this madness from happening (David Aaronovitch, *Times*, 26 July 2005).

There are twenty-six uses of '*the Muslim community*' in scare quotes, most of which express similar scepticism about the term, in order to note the plurality of Muslim experience. However, the television presenter Jeremy Clarkson, writing in *The Sun*, uses the term in scare quotes in a different way. Clarkson's 1,200-word article relates to Tony Blair's resignation as prime minister; in it he attacks Blair, ID cards, bus lanes, the civil service, speed limits, speed cameras, health and safety training and police bureaucracy, as well as bans on fox hunting, hooded tops, littering, public smoking, fur farming, advertising to children and Christian religious symbols. He also claims that Blair used '*The Guardian* and others from the metropolitan elite...to change the way we speak':

In fact, we can no longer upset any 'community' which is why the 'Muslim community' was allowed to parade through London urging passers-by to blow up a skyscraper and behead the infidels (30 June 2007).

One reading of Clarkson's use of 'Muslim community' here is that people who (allegedly) urge people to blow up skyscrapers should not be referred to as a community, and that people who use the term are legitimising terrorist sentiments. The association of a monolithic term such as *Muslim community* (even in scare quotes) with incitement to terrorism is worrying, although Clarkson's position appears to be at the extreme end of what is considered printable for British journalism.

However, generally, the term *Muslim community* is not questioned, and is instead used in three ways. First, the term can refer to all the Muslims in a particular town or city. For example, there are references to the Muslim community in places such as Bradford, Bristol, Edinburgh, Glasgow, Gloucester, Liverpool, London and Luton. However, a second use of *Muslim community* refers to a single community that spans the whole of the United Kingdom, and is often used in constructions such as the *British Muslim community* (237 occurrences). A third way involves references to an *international Muslim community* (eleven instances), *global Muslim community* (twenty instances) or *world(wide) Muslim community* (nineteen). The term *Muslim community*, when used without markers such as *Bradford*, *British* or *worldwide*, must therefore be understood via context.

A detailed analysis of 100 concordance lines of the term, taken at random, found that seventy-eight cases referred to community at the national level (usually the United Kingdom), seventeen referred to local Muslim communities, and only five referred to the concept of a global Muslim community. If these figures are representative, it appears, then, that *Muslim community* is generally used in the UK press to refer to all British Muslims. Such a conceptualisation has already been problematised by others. For example, Halliday (2006: 31) writes that 'there is no such thing as a single "Muslim" community in the UK, any more than there is a single "Jewish" or "Christian" one'.

However, it was not always easy to determine exactly what the term referred to. For example, in *The Independent* (27 August 2005), the Pope is described as visiting Cologne: 'Then he meets the Muslim community and I see them on the screen, heads slightly bowed, eyes glancing furtively towards the cameras.' Here the Muslim community could possibly refer to a small number of representatives rather than the large numbers that the term *community* implies.[1] Additionally, in the *Daily Express* (16 June 2009), the celebrity heiress Paris Hilton is described as visiting Dubai and employing 'a "cultural guide" to chaperone her around the city and

---

[1] As an aside, the use of the adverb 'furtively' is notable here, implying guilt.

Concordance 5.1 Muslim communities as offended

anxious that the move could antagonise	Muslim communities	and increase feelings of resentment
They're scared of anything that might go down badly with the	Muslim community	.
might be offensive to some in the	Muslim community	and that it could 'incite acts of violence
The broadcaster also enraged sections of the	Muslim community	and the West Midlands Police over
move would cause resentment in the	Muslim community	.
in a dawn raid that caused uproar in	Muslim community	.
to avoid upsetting Muslims, the	Muslim community	will find it insulting because

ensure she didn't make any gaffes that could offend the entire Muslim community'. Here it is unclear whether 'entire Muslim community' refers to Muslims only in Dubai, in the United Arab Emirates or in the whole world. (This case was categorised by us as referring to the whole world, on account of the use of the word 'entire', though other interpretations are possible.)

A reasonably common way (eighty-seven occurrences) to refer to a Muslim community is to describe how many members it has, particularly by using a number followed by the word *strong* (e.g. 'Luton has a 30,000-strong Muslim community'; *The Independent*, 11 March 2009). Other collocates that denote the size of such communities are *large* (117 times as an L1 collocate of *community* or *communities*), *growing* (seventeen), *biggest* (thirteen), *largest* (thirty-four), *sizeable* (five), *substantial* (four), *significant* (three) and *vast* (two).

Further examination of concordance lines reveals two clear discourse prosodies surrounding the term *Muslim community*. The first occurs with collocates such as *antagonise*, *offensive*, *upset*, *uproar*, *resentment* and *anger*, and constructs the Muslim community as having the potential to be offended (as with the Paris Hilton example above). Concordance 5.1 shows a small sample of this discourse prosody.

While there are many cases that portray the Muslim community as angry or offended, a subset of these stories is interesting in that they describe other people (non-Muslims) as attempting to ban certain things in order *not* to offend Muslims:

[T]he ridiculous decision by a Government quango who rejected a story based on the *Three Little Pigs* classic in case it offended the Muslim community. The digital remake of the children's story – made by a small Newcastle publisher – was criticised by Becta, the education technology agency who refused to put it forward for an award. Muslims, however, have made it clear they weren't offended by the computer based program and a spokesman for the Muslim Council of Britain said it should be welcome in schools (*Sun*, 31 January 2008).

Such stories, which characterise officials or other PC people as misguided and oversensitive, tend to contain a quote from a representative Muslim who is described as not being offended, and normally occur in the right-leaning tabloids:[2]

PIGGYBANKS are facing the axe – because some Muslims could take offence. Britain's top High Street banks have ruled the money-boxes are politically incorrect. But last night the move sparked snoutrage. And one of Britain's four Muslim MPs, Khalid Mahmoud, said: 'A piggybank is just an ornament. Muslims would never be seriously offended' (*Daily Star*, 24 October 2005).

However, despite the fact that the article stresses that Muslims would not be offended, such stories may be interpreted by readers somewhat differently. The following day the *Daily Star*'s 'Text maniacs' column (which prints text messages from members of the public) contained several messages about the proposed banning of piggy banks:

why do we have to bend over backwards so we dont offend the muslim community? we cant even have piggy banks! we cant even have a st george flag without bein told it's offensive. what's next – ban england football shirts?

muslims r offended by our piggy banks!? Then the £56 me n ma wife n ma 4 girls have got in our piggy bank 2 help the ppl in pakistan wil b spent on a fry up.

Y shud we change r way of life just 2 stop offending muslims. they aint neva gonna change theirs. Maybe they shud try eating pork. a nice bacon sarnie cud change any1's mind.

This misinterpretation of the original story casts Muslims as easily offended and paints *them*, rather than the alleged bank bosses, as being oversensitive. The *Daily Star* also published some texts from Muslims who were not offended by piggy banks, but it could be argued that the newspaper was irresponsible in publishing the texts quoted above. First, because of their hostile tone: it is insensitive to suggest that Muslims try eating pork or to exaggerate the story to refer to banning football shirts. Second, the text messages are likely to give a false impression to readers who had not read the previous day's article (which did not cite any examples of offended Muslims). However, with such a large number of references in the press to outraged responses within 'the Muslim community', it is unsurprising that some readers misinterpret stories when it is not Muslims who actually are angry.

A second discourse prosody of the Muslim community concerns the view of the Muslim community as separate from the rest of Britain. This is referred to via phrases such as *non-assimilation*, *driving a wedge*, *too little understanding* and *simmering conflict*. There are also many references to actions that need to be taken or are being taken in order to encourage integration, assimilation,

---

[2] The stories about banning *Three Little Pigs* and piggybanks show how two right-leaning tabloid concerns (Muslims and political correctness) are combined. The *Daily Mail* and the *Daily Express* are particularly interested in stories that highlight cases of 'political correctness', and have the highest frequencies of this term in the corpus.

Concordance 5.2 Implication of a divide between the Muslim community and 'the rest of the UK'

Britain's record in integrating the	Muslim community	and in fostering a secure, strong
creating a wedge between the	Muslim community	and mainstream society."
conclusion that the non-assimilation of	Muslim communities	and the misogyny of Islamic
by the simmering conflict between the	Muslim community	and the white British.
is too little understanding between the	Muslim community	and the wider community, and vi
to help officers interact better with the	Muslim community	across Sheffield.
ould kickstart its engagement with the	Muslim community	.
44% of all British voters who say that	Muslim community	should do more to integrate

better interaction and engagement between the Muslim community and 'the wider community' (see Concordance 5.2).

Common topics associated with Muslim communities are: the notion of a backlash or attacks on them; concerns about relations between such communities and non-Muslims; and the extent to which such communities are alienated, resulting in extremism, radicalisation and terrorism:

'The war on terror has had a devastating effect,' he said. 'We have become targets of the security apparatus and are seen as an enemy within unjustifiably. This has resulted in a backlash against the Muslim community. We have become the hidden victims' (*Guardian*, 23 April 2005).

A former pub has been transformed into Britain's most prominent sharia court operating brazenly in the heart of a Muslim community beset by radical extremism (*Daily Express*, 9 February 2008).

Although the Muslim community is normally represented as homogeneous, there are times when certain members are viewed as different, and often as dangerous, as the following examples containing *within the Muslim community/communities* show:

I am also sometimes confronted by those who point out that there are elements within the Muslim community who pose a threat to our very security (*Daily Express*, 26 November 2008).

I think some of the extremists within the Muslim community essentially want to win a battle, particularly for young Muslims, and persuade them that being a Muslim is incompatible with being British (*Guardian*, 24 March 2003).

These results show there are people within the Muslim communities who are so far away from the mainstream of society, as well as the mainstream of British Muslims (*Daily Mail*, 4 July 2006).

Similar constructions are found with the phrase *sections of the Muslim community*:

It is undeniable that certain sections of the Muslim community are hotbeds of fundamentalism and misogyny, perhaps to a greater extent than any other modern religion (*Observer*, 25 June 2006).

The support among sections of the Muslim community for Bin Laden's cause was also underlined by the numbers who headed for Afghanistan 18 months ago to try to repel American-led forces (*Independent*, 1 May 2003).

Comparable patterns are found for *part(s) of the Muslim community*, *members of the Muslim community* and *elements of the Muslim community*.

The term *Muslim community* is particularly frequent in 2005 and 2006. This raises the question of the reasons behind this increased frequency, as well as the question of whether the higher frequency correlates with different discourses. In these two years frequent lexical collocates of *Muslim community* include *Britain*, *British*, *leaders*, *members* and *people*. A frequent grammatical collocate in this period is *within* (196 cases), which tends to be used in the construction *within the Muslim community* and refers to extremists, extreme factions, unrest, fear, attacks, problems, fractures, disunity, divisions, tension, ill-feeling, ructions and debate. The collocates of *Muslim community* for the other years are identical, including the high frequency of *within* being used to refer to divisions, tensions and extremism. So *Muslim community* is not referred to differently in 2005 and 2006; such concerns about the Muslim community simply appear to peak in this period. An indication for the reason is other frequent collocates of *Muslim community* during 2005 and 2006: *London, police, attacks* and *terrorism*, which mainly refer to the London transport bombings of July 2005. Examining the fifty-three occurrences of *Muslim community/communities* and *London* together in 2005–6, there are a wide range of references to the London bombs: some concordance lines containing warnings against a backlash, others claiming that the bombers came from Muslim communities:

The last reaction needed to the London attacks is reprisals against Muslim communities. The criminals responsible were inhuman and their actions have nothing to do with religion (*Daily Mirror*, 14 July 2005).

The absence also suggests that America, the nation of immigrants, is not home to the sort of disaffected, unassimilated Muslim community from which Britain's London Underground bombers sprang (*Independent*, 11 September 2006).

Thus, there is support for the hypothesis that the London bombings of 2005 caused the British press to turn more attention to the concept of a reified, single British Muslim community – a community constructed as easy to anger, disengaged from the remainder of Britain, home to a number of extremists (who had the potential to become terrorists) and also at risk from a backlash (perhaps unsurprisingly, considering that list of qualities ascribed to the community by the press).

Muslim world

If the term *Muslim community* is used as a way of referring to a mainly homogeneous group of British Muslims (containing some dangerous elements), how does *Muslim world* fare? After *community*, *world* is the second most frequent immediate right-hand collocate of *Muslim*, with *Muslim world* occurring 5,081 times. This phrase is used with less variation than *Muslim community* in the corpus; it tends simply to refer to all Muslims across the world, particularly countries that have significant Muslim populations:

'We would be doing it regardless of religion,' he said. 'But it does give the Muslim world and the rest of the world an opportunity to see American generosity, American values in action' (*Daily Telegraph*, 6 January 2005).

Iran, Iraq and Syria have been the only Muslim countries to condemn the US and British bombings, though the mood on the streets in much of the Muslim world has been hostile (*Guardian*, 11 October 2001).

Scanning the 5,000-odd concordance lines of *Muslim world*, we tried to find cases that used the term in order to imply that the Muslim world was *not* a homogeneous group. We initially looked for constructions such as *within the Muslim world* (forty-six cases), although only ten of these cases actually refer to the Muslim world as containing different perspectives or types of people. Other phrases that imply differences are *parts/part of the Muslim world* (eighty-eight cases) and *sections of the Muslim world* (five cases). These low frequencies suggest what we did find – numerous constructions that imply homogeneity: *throughout the Muslim world* (162 cases), *across the Muslim world* (323 cases), *the entire Muslim world* (sixty-five cases), *the wider Muslim world* (fifty-four cases), *whole (of the) Muslim world* (thirty-six cases), *relations/relationships with the Muslim world* (eighty-two cases), *reach* out to the Muslim world* (forty cases), *address/message/speech/dialogue to the Muslim world* (sixty-six cases) and *all over the Muslim world* (twenty-six cases). A construction that implies that the Muslim world consists of a majority is *much/most of the Muslim world* (seventy-seven cases). It is clear, then, that, for the most part, the press represents *the Muslim world* as a single entity.

One way to understand more fully how *Muslim world* is used is to see what other concepts it occurs with. Examining the phrase *Muslim world and*, it was found that it is most frequently referred to in connection with the West (sixty-three cases), and in most cases a distinction is made about differences between the Muslim world and the West (a random sample of ten of these cases is shown in Concordance 5.3).

As with the British Muslim community's relationship to the 'wider community' in Britain, the Muslim world here is characterised in terms of poor relations with the West. This is directly referenced by terms such as *bitterly*

Concordance 5.3 Muslim world and the

a distinction these days between the	Muslim world and the	western world rather than the
damage" to relations between the	Muslim world and the	west, Mr Sacranie added.
bridges between a bitterly resentful	Muslim world and the	West; between an anti-American
such heightened unease between the	Muslim world and the	West, and when many Turks are
city's bid to build bridges between the	Muslim world and the	West. He said 'A unique
help to heal the divisions between the	Muslim world and the	West. He asked 'Is it really going
increase in tension between the	Muslim world and the	West. There would also be the
deepened the alienation between the	Muslim world and the	West – with consequences not
. It will define relations between the	Muslim world and the	West." Turning to the
better understanding between the	Muslim world and the	West. In Cambridge, the HRH

resentful, *heightened unease*, *divisions* and *increase in tension*, whereas terms such as *build bridges*, *better understanding* and *help to heal* clearly imply that there are poor relationships that need to be overcome.[3] It is perhaps interesting to note a disparity in the labelling of Muslims as belonging to a 'world' and 'the West', which is simply named as a point on the compass. The term *Muslim world* seems to imply a different world from the default world of the West, which does not seem to require being labelled as a 'world'. *Muslim world* occurs 5,081 times in the corpus while a similar term, *Islamic world*, occurs 3,083 times. The term *Western world* occurs only 1,051 times, so it is rarer, though still reasonably frequent. However, there are 39,612 references to *the West* in the corpus. Even if we discount such cases as *the West Bank/Midlands/ Indies/coast/End/Country*, we are still left with over 25,000 cases of *the West* in the corpus, so *Western world* is clearly not the dominant form used to refer to the West. There is no direct equivalent of 'the West' that one can use to refer to Islam, meaning that *Muslim world* and *Islamic world* are, unlike *Western world*, the dominant phrases used to refer to Islam worldwide.

What other types of *world* are commonly found? To answer this question, it is useful to refer to a different corpus, composed of a wider range of texts. The ukWaC corpus consists of about 1.5 billion words of general English

---

[3] Less frequently, the Muslim world is also sometimes referred to along with the Arab world (thirty-two cases), although here these two 'worlds' are constructed as linked together. A typical example would be: 'There is a gulf of misunderstanding between the Arab and Muslim world and the western world' (*The Independent*, 4 November 2001).

(collected via internet sources) and is available from the online Sketch Engine interface. Common left-hand descriptors of *world* in this corpus are *Arab*, *Western*, *English-speaking*, *Islamic* and *Muslim*. Interestingly, adjectives for other religions, such as *Jewish*, *Christian* and *Catholic*, were not commonly used with reference to *world*. In addition, terms that distinguish between different branches of Islam were not common as collocates of *world*; there were only a handful of references to *Sunni world* or *Shia world*.[4] Instead, *Muslim world* seems to construct Muslims as belonging to a homogeneous group that is distinctly separate from non-Muslims. Clearly, the same thing is happening with terms such as *English-speaking world* or *Western world* – but, rather than defining people by religion, members of these 'worlds' are instead explicitly defined by the language that they speak or where they live. The terms *Western world* and *the West*, often occurring, as they do, in opposition to *Muslim world*, are potentially problematic for Muslims who actually do live in 'the West'. Does a British Muslim inhabit the Muslim world, a Western one, or both? The way that the terms are used makes them appear to be mutually exclusive categories. One way to explain the apparent discrepancy is to interpret the terms *the West* and *Muslim/Islamic world* as referring not to a geographical area and a religion, respectively, but to socio-cultural values and practices.

The term *Muslim world* has been strongly criticised by Carpenter and Cagaptay (2009), who write that it 'is not only an analytical error – it's also a critical public diplomacy mistake… Muslim world unfairly and singularly assigns adherents of Islam into a figurative ghetto. And particularly in the post-September 11 [sic], this relegation carries a real moral hazard. Extremists are the only Muslim group that strongly advocates tying all Muslims together politically, in a united global community… Every time the United States speaks to the Muslim world, then it inadvertently legitimizes the extremists' vision.'

A related point is made by Said (1997: 10), who argues that the terms *Islam* and *the West* are often used in ignorance: 'How many people who use the labels angrily or assertively have a solid grip on all aspects of Western tradition, or on Islamic jurisprudence, or on the actual languages of the Islamic world? Very few, obviously, but this does not prevent people from confidently characterising "Islam" and "the West", or from believing that they know exactly what it is they are talking about.'

John Richardson (2006: 231) also remarks on *Muslim world* as being a rhetorical process of textual exclusion, pointing to 'the referential ambiguity, fuzziness and indeterminacy of this phrase paradoxically adding to its utility, its breadth and its power'. We would agree that there is potential danger in using

---

[4] There were eleven references to 'Sunni world' in ukWAC, four to 'Shia world' and 1,837 to 'Muslim world'.

Muslim world, particularly as other religions are not normally characterised in this way, and because the term seems to background differences between branches of Islam. However, it is doubtful whether most journalists and others who use *Muslim world* are aware of this critical reading of the term.[5] Additionally, we should note that there are other potential interpretations of *Muslim world* and that the term is incorporated in the name of the Muslim World League, one of the largest Islamic non-governmental organisations, while there are journals entitled *The Muslim World* and *Muslim World Journal of Human Rights*. Perhaps, then, the term can become more problematic depending on the context of its use. For example, if it is used repeatedly to suggest that there are problems between 'the Muslim world' and 'the West', then the sense of two disparate entities will be exaggerated. As suggested by Concordance 5.3, such a construction does appear to be frequent in the corpus. Common collocates of *Muslim world* include references to the 'other' (*west, western, America, American, British, Britain*), relationships (*relations, relationship, between, against*) and words that indicate conflict (*war, protests, anger, outrage, violent, provoked, attack, inflamed, fury, hatred, conflict, resentment, damaged*), as well as words that imply attempts to resolve conflict (*friendship, peace, dialogue, bridge, bridges, unity, understand*).

One question that might be asked at this point concerns agency. If journalists write about the Muslim world and the West as experiencing problems, then who is seen as responsible for trying to resolve the problems? Is the Muslim world (or anyone who apparently belongs to it) constructed as actively trying to improve the situation? In order to investigate this question further, we examined a concordance of *Muslim world* that contained the words *bridge/bridges*. Of the twenty-seven cases that were found, nine were attributed to attempts by the United States or Americans to build bridges between the Muslim world and the west (*America* one, *Barack Obama* seven, *Colin Powell* one), four were linked to British attempts (*Tony Blair* two, *Britain* two), one to *Europe*, eight to *Turkey*, three to *British Muslims* and two to others. Although this is only a small sample, it suggests that, in general, leaders of Muslim countries tend to be represented less in terms of attempting to 'build bridges' than Western leaders, although Turkey – which is sometimes viewed in newspaper articles as occupying a kind of 'middle ground' – is associated with bridge building. An example of this is:

An Islamic democracy in Turkey would allow Europe to build bridges east to the Muslim world, just as Europe must build bridges across the Atlantic to North and South America (*Observer*, 24 November 2002).

---

[5] Indeed, we note that, in a similar way, in previous research one of the authors of this book has also used this term uncritically; see Baker (2010: 328).

The following two examples demonstrate how members of 'the Muslim world' are positioned as uncooperative or resentful:

When the US President offered a hand of peace to Iran, he was rebuffed. When he eloquently sought to build bridges with the Muslim world, Iran denounced his offer as a trick (*Times*, 13 June 2009).

For a world that is certainly more divided and dangerous than at any time since the first half of the 20th century, here was a moment of hope: an opportunity to build bridges between a bitterly resentful Muslim world and the West (*Daily Mail*, 6 November 2008).

Are the collocates any different when we consider 2001, which is when *Muslim world* overtook *Muslim community* (see Table 4.9) in terms of frequency?[6] Collocates of *Muslim world* in 2001 are *Bin, Laden, Taliban, America, American, West, US* and *war*, suggesting that the increased references to *Muslim world* in this time period are linked to the 9/11 attacks. It would be interesting to examine how the press conceived of the relationship between Bin Laden and the Muslim world during this period,. Was Bin Laden viewed as a dissident, a representative or as having the approval of the Muslim world? A concordance of *Muslim world* co-occurring with *Bin Laden* in 2001 was examined, producing twenty-four lines. Some cases represented the Muslim world as against Bin Laden:

The message came as the Muslim world closed ranks against Bin Laden in an amazing show of solidarity (*Sun*, 18 September 2001).

An international panel of top Muslims has BACKED the attacks on Afghanistan... A No10 spokesman said: 'It gives the lie to the idea that bin Laden speaks for the Muslim world' (*Sun*, 13 October 2001).

However, other examples involve representations of the Muslim world as not believing that Bin Laden was responsible for the attacks:

Some officials hope that making the tape public could counter concern in the Muslim world that bin Laden has been unjustly accused of involvement in the attacks, the *Washington Post* said (*Daily Telegraph*, 10 December 2001).

Given the sketchiness of the evidence released to the public by the US and UK governments there is widespread denial in the Arab and Muslim world that Osama bin Laden had any involvement in the attack on America on September 11 (*Guardian*, 24 October 2001).

Other examples imply that Bin Laden is able to influence the Muslim world, or parts of it:

Bin Laden electrified parts of the Muslim world within hours of the first bombs by releasing a video in which he tried to polarise the conflict between the west and Islam... (*Guardian*, 12 October 2001).

---

[6] The frequency of 'Muslim world' also peaked in 2001, compared to other years in the corpus.

Perhaps we Britons have simply decided that aerial bombardment is not an effective way to defeat al-Qaeda. Maybe some of them accept that aerial assault can only boost Osama bin Laden's standing in the Muslim world, spectacularly confirming his claim that this really is a clash of the west against Islam – pitting the richest country in the world against the poorest (*Daily Mirror*, 1 November 2001).

Thus, while the British press do not represent the 'Muslim world' as being generally supportive of Bin Laden directly after 9/11, there are other concerns: about the 'widespread denial' in the Muslim world of his involvement, or in the danger that he may succeed in polarising the conflict by influencing the Muslim world.

Muslim Council **and** *Muslim leaders*

Although the *Muslim world* is represented as being in conflict with the West, it rarely seems to be the case that the term is problematised in the press. Will this be the case with two other frequent constructions that are examined in this chapter – *Muslim Council* and *Muslim leaders*? The two terms are considered together, as they tend to have very similar representations. After *community* and *world*, *council* is the next most frequent word to occur after *Muslim* in the corpus, occurring 3,753 times. Of these, 2,936 instances (78 per cent) occur in the phrase *Muslim Council of Britain*, and the majority of the other occurrences also refer to the same council. On its website, the MCB describes itself as 'a national representative Muslim umbrella body with over 500 affiliated national, regional and local organisations, mosques, charities and schools. The MCB is pledged to work for the common good of society as a whole; encouraging individual Muslims and Muslim organisations to play a full and participatory role in public life.' In terms of dispersion across the corpus, *Muslim Council* tends to occur most often in the broadsheet newspapers (particularly *The Times* and *The Guardian*), and almost 60 per cent of its occurrences are between 2004 and 2006, with the peak year being 2005.

Muslim leaders (2,663 occurrences in total) was most popular in the years 2005 to 2007, as well as in 2001, suggesting that there was more focus on this construction as a result of 9/11 and 7/7. However, unlike *Muslim world* and *Muslim community*, there are a noticeable number of cases in which the term is questioned. In the right-leaning tabloid press, a number of columnists question the authenticity of Muslim leaders, referring to them as *so-called*, *self-styled* or *self-appointed*. Such leaders are viewed by some columnists as benefiting unjustly from their position, and their opinions are characterised negatively as *whines* and *bleats*:

Grants have been dished out like confetti to Muslim organisations, and knighthoods and peerages to self-styled Muslim leaders (Leo McKinstry, *Daily Express*, 20 February 2006).

Indeed, far from blaming those who committed these atrocities in the name of Allah, we are encouraged to treat seriously the murderous grievances of self-styled Muslim leaders as if their bleats about British foreign policy justified such carnage (Leo McKinstry, *Daily Express*, 22 May 2006).

I don't normally want to hear the whines and bleats of so-called 'Muslim leaders' or terrorist suspects' mate Shami Chakrabarti, but their silence over the sentencing of madman Parviz Khan has been deafening (Jon Gaunt, *Sun*, 22 February 2008).

Since 9/11, self-appointed Muslim leaders have seized every opportunity to advance their agenda (Richard Littlejohn, *Daily Mail*, February 21, 2006).

A strong discourse prosody surrounding Muslim leaders is that they are viewed as prone to offence (in much the same way as Muslim communities). Concordance 5.4 gives a small sample of some of the ways that this discourse prosody is realised. In this concordance, Muslim leaders are presented as being offended, angry, outraged, hostile, indignant and unsmiling, as well as making demands. The following example demonstrates the sense of hypocrisy that is felt about Muslim leaders, particularly in the right-leaning tabloids:

Given the scale of the slaughter envisaged by the airline plotters, it is grotesque of Muslim leaders now to pose as the injured party. They should be apologising for the misery that their fellow believers have inflicted on the mainstream British public (Leo McKinstry, *Daily Express*, 14 August 2006).

How strong is this discourse prosody, though? An examination of 100 random concordance lines of the term *Muslim leaders* found that in twenty-one cases they were represented as condemning something, in six cases they were shown to be angry at something, in five cases they were seen to be making demands, in four cases they were represented as raising fears or concerns about something, in four cases they were constructed as hypocritical, in three

Concordance 5.4 Muslim leaders as prone to offence

drowned out by the indignant chorus of	Muslim leaders	and Western liberals vibrating with
concern will be the hostile attitude of	Muslim leaders	. The Imam's Council said they had not
of Number 10, the unsmiling faces of	Muslim leaders	behind him, can all be scripted by his
They divided it to meet the demands of	Muslim leaders	who said that Muslims and Hindus
and based upon a fear of offending	Muslim leaders	. "Someone is not telling the truth here
TV host Kilroy-Silk had earlier outraged	Muslim leaders	by branding Arabs "Suicide bombers,
Archbishop of Canterbury has angered	Muslim leaders	by saying the faith was no longer
demand wholesale exemptions. Some	Muslim leaders	are appalled by the legislation. The
two people were later arrested.	Muslim leaders	slammed the Jewish rally. Massoud
At the time of Lord Carey's comments	Muslim leaders	responded with anger and

cases they were seen as being upset about something and in two cases they were viewed as supporting something. In the other fifty-five cases they were represented in various other ways, such as meeting people, or being called upon to do something. The random sample does suggest, then, that Muslim leaders are regularly constructed in terms of their disapproval (about a third of the concordance lines), with only a small minority of cases representing them as approving of something.

Additional evidence was found by looking at collocates. The most frequent lexical lemma collocate of *Muslim leaders* is CONDEMN, occurring 165 times within a −5 to +5 span of the term. Other collocates that hold a similar or related meaning are *angered* (nine), *complained* (eight), *criticised* (thirty-four), *demanded* (nineteen), *denounced* (seven), *dismissed* (eight), *furious* (seven), *fury* (eleven), *grievances* (six), *outrage(d)* (sixteen), *protest(ed)* (ten), *slammed* (seven) and *warned* (thirty-one). However, we should not jump to the conclusion that such collocates always position Muslim leaders as subjects who are doing the condemning. They may be recipients of someone else's condemnations. An examination of the 165 concordance lines of *Muslim leaders* co-occurring with CONDEMN was undertaken. The majority (113) cases involved Muslim leaders condemning a range of different things (mainly terrorism, including 9/11 and 7/7, but also other phenomena such as forced marriage or Israel). Twenty cases involved people saying that Muslim leaders *should* be condemning something (usually terrorist attacks), as in the following example:

The trigger for his comments was a Commons statement the previous day on the Istanbul attacks in which Jack Straw, who as Foreign Secretary is his boss, called on Muslim leaders to condemn the bombings in response to an MP's question (*Times*, 22 November 2003).

Another twenty-eight cases involved statements that Muslim leaders were *not* condemning something (again, almost always terrorist attacks), with the strong implication that they ought to be:

He was the first senior churchman to attack moderate Muslim leaders for not condemning Islamic suicide bombers 'clearly and unequivocally' (*Daily Telegraph*, 24 November 2006).

Finally, four cases involved Muslim leaders being condemned by others for something:

MUSLIM leaders were condemned by Tony Blair yesterday for appearing to sympathise with extremists who hate the West (*Daily Mail*, 6 July 2006).

The examination of CONDEMN therefore suggests an interesting pattern. Muslim leaders are regularly described as making condemnations, resulting in them being represented as disapproving or even angry. However, the press also reports an expectation that Muslim leaders *should* be engaged in condemning (terrorist attacks), and that some people have accused them of not being condemnatory enough. Despite these different 'takes' on Muslim leaders, it appears that the press has constructed the main role of Muslim leaders as to condemn things. The focus on Muslim leaders thus increased in the periods following terrorist attacks, as a debate took place around whether they were condemning the attacks sufficiently. At other times they were seen merely as engaging in a range of different types of condemnation, thus resulting in an expectation that this is what Muslim leaders do. Clearly, a Muslim leader's condemnation (or lack of it) counts as newsworthy. Other actions that Muslim leaders engage in may not be viewed as so interesting.

Similar patterns were found for *Muslim Council*, although the two most common verb collocates were opposites: *welcomed* (forty-nine cases) and *condemned* (forty-two cases). Other verb collocates included *urging, urged, criticised, branded, backed, complained, accused* and *denounced*. This indicates that the MCB tends to be represented as involved in a wider range of evaluative and persuasive processes, compared to Muslim leaders, who tend to be represented mainly as condemning.

Often the Muslim Council of Britain is represented as welcoming or backing decisions or moves that appear to benefit Muslims. This can include apologies for or investigations of Islamophobic remarks or policies that help Muslims, such as:

Mr Vine, 50, said in a statement: 'I accept that the joke was in poor taste and I apologise profusely for any offence caused.' Bashir Mann, a spokesman for the Muslim Council of Great Britain, welcomed the apology and said the joke appeared out of character (*Daily Mirror*, 17 April 2006).

Last year, HSBC was also the first UK bank to offer sharia-compliant mortgages and current accounts, both of which were welcomed as landmarks by the Muslim Council of Britain. Another welcome reform came courtesy of the Chancellor, Gordon Brown, when he announced in the budget last year that stamp duty would be reformed to make sure Muslims no longer had to pay it twice (*Guardian*, 17 April 2004).

However, the MCB is also shown to welcome other phenomena, which benefit the whole of the United Kingdom:

The Muslim Council of Britain welcomed London's Olympic victory. 'This reflects well on London's leading position as a vibrant, multicultural city,' said the organisation's recently knighted secretary-general, Sir Iqbal Sacranie (*Guardian*, 7 July 2005).

It is also shown to welcome decisions that suggest a moderate interpretation of Islamic law. For example, in 2007 a British schoolteacher in Sudan was arrested, accused of insulting Islam's prophet. She had named a class teddy bear 'Muhammad', and several parents complained. When she was released, the *Daily Mirror* reported that the MCB 'welcomed the release' (4 December 2007).

Similarly, the MCB is reported to have welcomed the departure of Omar Bakri (see Chapter 7) from the United Kingdom (*Daily Telegraph*, 9 August 2005).

In terms of condemning, again it is often the case that the MCB appears to be represented as advocating peace. For example, the MCB is described as condemning bombings, killings, hostage taking and terrorists. However, there are cases when some newspapers print disapproval of the MCB's actions. For example, a letter to *The Sun* questions why the MCB condemned a chief constable who made a joke about suicide bombers:

TAYSIDE Chief Constable John Vine was forced to apologise for a joke about suicide bombers. Why? Suicide bombers are murdering people in Iraq including coalition forces. During the war there were many jokes about Hitler and his henchmen. It was the same with the IRA when they were planting bombs in Britain. But the Muslim Council for Great Britain has condemned Vine rather than show they are British and are firmly against al-Qaeda (*Sun*, 'Letters', 19 April 2006).

Additionally, the *Daily Mail* appears to be defensive of gay rights when it runs a story about an investigation of the head of the MCB, who is described as condemning civil partnerships for gay and lesbian couples:

SCOTLAND Yard has begun an investigation into one of Britain's most senior Muslims after he described homosexuality as 'harmful'. Sir Iqbal Sacranie, head of the Muslim Council of Britain, also condemned civil partnerships for gay and lesbian couples (*Daily Mail*, 12 January 2006).

For both the Muslim Council and Muslim leaders, the two most frequent adjectives used to describe them are *moderate* and *mainstream*. At first glance, these adjectives appear to suggest a representation that is intended to be positive. However, this is not always the case. For example, there are two cases of *supposedly mainstream Muslim Council* in the corpus (both from *The Times* in 2005). Moreover, *The Guardian*, in an article that is supportive of the Muslim Council, refers to it as a *relatively mainstream organisation* (25 March 2009). Leo McKinstry, writing in the *Daily Express* (15 August 2005), reports on a televised documentary programme that 'shows that the Muslim Council is not the moderate body it is so often portrayed as'. Claudia Joseph in the *Daily Mail* (4 September 2005), referring to the same programme, uses the term *supposedly moderate Muslim Council*. Around the same time, *The Observer* (14 August 2005) carried out its own investigation, claiming that, 'far from being moderate, the Muslim Council of Britain has its origins in the extreme orthodox politics in Pakistan'. There are also three cases of journalists using ironic distancing quotes around 'moderate' Muslim Council (once in *The Daily Telegraph* and twice in the *Daily Mail*). Questions about the extent of the moderation of the Muslim Council are therefore present across the entire British press, regardless of political stance or tabloid/broadsheet distinction. Similarly, out of 104 cases of *moderate Muslim leaders*, ten of them put the word *moderate* in ironic quotes.

Generally, then, Muslim leaders have a slightly more negative discourse prosody than the Muslim Council, perhaps because the term *Muslim leaders* is a less specific term that does not require hostile newspapers actually to name anybody. However, irrespective of their presentation, the high frequency of the terms *Muslim leaders* and *Muslim Council* in the corpus further reinforces the presentation of Muslims by the British press as a coherent group.

Muslim country/countries

Another pair of collectivising terms to examine in this chapter is *Muslim country* (1,841 occurrences) and *Muslim countries* (2,106 occurrences). One set of collocates of *Muslim country/countries* consists of adverbs of scale: *predominantly, mainly, overwhelmingly, largely, mostly, particularly*. These words are used to indicate that a country has a large population of people who practise Islam, but allows for exceptions. The phrase *overwhelmingly Muslim country* (almost always occurring in the broadsheets) is worth taking note of, particularly as this adverb suggests that the writer has a somewhat negative stance. Examination of concordance lines also indicates that the phrase tends to occur in negative descriptions:

There had been fears that the match at the New Den would be a target for far-right groups following the bombings in London by Islamist terrorists, as Iran is an over-whelmingly Muslim country (*Daily Telegraph*, 27 July 2005).

And in a sign of how the affair has dangerously escalated religious tensions in the overwhelmingly Muslim country, a furious mob of several hundred militant Muslims went on the rampage in a Christian village near where the funeral ceremony was taking place, setting houses on fire and terrorising residents (*Independent*, 11 May 1998).

Another set of collocates refers to bans or strictness: *strict* (fifty-nine), *alcohol* (thirty-five), *strictly* (thirteen), *forbidden* (nine), *booze* (eight), *topless* (four). While bans on alcohol or going topless are referred to as strict, they do not usually contain any other form of evaluation (such as being (un)fair), and occasionally note exceptions to the rule:

His Dubai bar will have to be in a hotel – the only place where the strict Muslim country allows westerners to drink alcohol (*Sun*, 2 April 2005).

A third set of collocates refers to *moderate* (twenty-seven), *secular* (twenty-six), *democratic* (twelve), *liberal* (fifteen), *friendly* (nine) or *tolerant* (six) Muslim countries. Although the concept of a liberal Muslim country is approvingly evaluated in the press, the extent of liberality is frequently questioned:

Tunisia boasts that it's the most liberal Muslim country in Africa, but evidently Tunisians are not so loose-moraled that they can feel a woman's arm any day of the week (*Mail on Sunday*, 4 April 1999).

In other cases, the concept of a liberal Muslim country is described as relative:

They have similar climates, they are fairly liberal Muslim countries (compared to Saudi and Pakistan at least), and both are trying to cater to the European second home and investment market and bolster their tourist traffic (*Daily Mail*, 12 October 2007).

Overall, then, the use of positive modifiers, such as *moderate* or *liberal*, has the potential effect of implying that attitudes and practices in *Muslim countries* are not expected to be accurately described by these adjectives.

A fourth common set of collocates refers to names of countries. Those countries that are most likely to be described as a Muslim country are *Turkey* (144 times), *Saudi Arabia* (seventy-seven), *Pakistan* (sixty-six), *Indonesia* (sixty-three) and *Iran* (forty-eight). However, there are many other cases when these countries are referred to without being explicitly called a Muslim country, and therefore a question arises with regard to which Muslim countries are actually being written about in the British press. Table 5.1 shows the twenty countries with populations with the highest proportions of Muslims in them. All of them contain at least 1 per cent of the world's Muslim population, and collectively they account for 83.8 per cent of the world's Muslims. The last column of Table 5.1 shows how many times each country is referred to in the corpus.

Comparing the last two columns of figures, it is clear that there is not a particularly strong correlation between the number of Muslims in a country and the importance that country is assigned in terms of it occurring in articles about Muslims in the British press. The country that contains the most Muslims, Indonesia (where 12.9 per cent of Muslims live), is actually the twelfth most frequently named country in the corpus. On the other hand, Iraq, which has only 2 per cent of the world's Muslims, is the most commonly discussed country in the corpus. Other countries that are frequently mentioned are Iran, Afghanistan and Pakistan. In other words, the British press tends to overlook the place that contains the most Muslims, and instead focuses on countries where there are smaller concentrations of them. This finding is congruent with John Richardson's (2004: xvii) argument that the 'Muslimness' of countries such as Indonesia is often backgrounded in the British press. On the other hand, the Muslim countries that *are* foregrounded tend to be those that are involved in major conflicts or are viewed as dangerous and problematic in other ways. In terms of 'news value', this is not surprising, although an unforeseen consequence of the focus on such countries is that it will create an association between Islam and problems.

Table 5.1 Top twenty countries with the highest numbers of Muslims

Country	Total Muslim population	Percentage of world Muslim population	Frequency in the corpus
Indonesia	202,867,000	12.9	7,890
Pakistan	174,082,000	11.1	40,985
India	160,945,000	10.3	28,479
Bangladesh	145,312,000	9.3	4,651
Egypt	78,513,000	5.0	13,807
Nigeria	78,056,000	5.0	5,039
Iran	73,777,000	4.7	55,115
Turkey	73,619,000	4.7	22,812
Algeria	34,199,000	2.2	4,831
Iraq	30,428,000	2.0	145,266
Morocco	31,933,000	2.0	6,720
Saudi Arabia	24,949,000	2.0	30,915
Sudan	30,121,000	1.9	8,560
Afghanistan	28,072,000	1.9	58,171
Ethiopia	28,063,000	1.8	2,934
Uzbekistan	26,469,000	1.7	3,122
Yemen	23,363,000	1.5	5,827
China	21,667,000	1.4	14,559
Syria	20,196,000	1.3	13,538
Malaysia	16,581,000	1.1	3,978

Source: Pew Research Center (2009).

Branches of Islam

The final section of this chapter is concerned with different branches and movements within Islam, and the extent to which different newspapers make such distinctions. Just as Christianity can be divided into various large and small denominations (Catholic, Protestant, Orthodox, Pentecostal, Adventist, Anglican, Baptist, Methodist, Lutheran, etc), Islam can also be categorised as consisting of numerous groupings, the largest group being Sunni Muslims, then Shia. Other groupings or approaches include Sufis, Ahmaddiyans and the Kharijites. The two main branches can be further subdivided. For example, the Sunni branch comprises a number of schools of thought: Hanafi, Maliki, Shafi'i and Hanbali, as well as Salafi or Wahhabi Islam. It is beyond the remit of this book to provide a description of how these groupings differ from each other; instead, we are more concerned with whether such groupings are recognised by different newspapers, and whether there has been a growing awareness over time of such distinctions, particularly considering that numbers of articles about Islam have grown since 9/11. Has this sudden interest in Islam resulted in a more nuanced understanding of the different branches of Islam among the British press, or is the popularity of the term *Muslim world* a clear indication that little attempt is made to acknowledge these branches?

Figure 5.1 shows the joint frequencies of *Sunni*, *Shia*, *Sufi*, *Salafi* and *Wahhabi*[7] for each newspaper. We did not include some terms because they tended to refer mainly to names of people rather than branches of the religion (e.g. *Maliki, Hanabli*). There were 47,847 references to these terms across the corpus, of which 59 per cent consisted of the term *Shia* and 37 per cent *Sunni* (the other terms were rarer, with *Wahhabi* and *Sufi* being about 2 per cent each and *Salafi* having fewer than 1 per cent).

Such terms are most common in the two left-leaning broadsheets, then the two right-leaning broadsheets, with the 'popular' press making fewer distinctions. However, before we conclude that the broadsheets more frequently acknowledge different branches within Islam, we need to take into account the fact that the 'quality' newspapers contain more text. Therefore, Figure 5.2 shows the number of references to these branches of Islam divided by the number of times the newspaper mentions the word *Islam* itself. (Cases such as *Sunni Islam* were excluded from the count of Islam.) This figure gives a better idea of how often the branches of Islam are referred to, in relation to the hypernymic term.

In this figure, the bars indicate which newspapers refer to different branches of Islam (as opposed to Islam itself). The larger the bar, the more frequently the newspaper refers to branches of Islam. All the broadsheets, apart from *The Observer*, make more references to the branches of Islam than the word *Islam*. On the other hand, the tabloids tend to make more references to *Islam*, although the one left-leaning tabloid, the *Daily Mirror*, does have a notably higher proportion of references to branches of Islam than the right-leaning tabloids. A distinction can therefore be made between newspapers referring to Sunnis, Shias, Sufis, etc. (which tend to be broadsheets) and those that are more likely to refer merely to Islam (which tend to be tabloids). Additionally, it is notable that, in both groups, it is a left-leaning newspaper (*The Independent* and the *Daily Mirror*) that has the highest number of references to branches of Islam.

On the one hand, it is encouraging that the broadsheets do appear to make an effort to distinguish between different branches of Islam, rather than relying merely on a single term, *Islam*, which, if used heavily, is likely to have a homogenising effect, backgrounding differences between Muslims and emphasising sameness (in a similar way to the term *Muslim world*). However,

---

[7] We took into account the various spellings of 'Wahhabi' in the corpus, such as 'Wahabbi', 'Wahabi', 'Wahhabbi' and 'Whahabi'. We also counted cases such as 'Shiite' and considered all plural forms of the terms, as well as terms that ended in '-ism'.

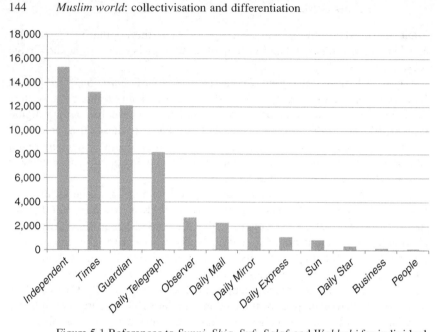

Figure 5.1 References to *Sunni*, *Shia*, *Sufi*, *Salafi* and *Wahhabi* for individual newspapers

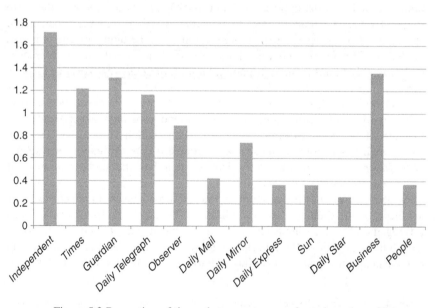

Figure 5.2 Proportion of times that newspapers refer to branches of Islam as opposed to Islam itself

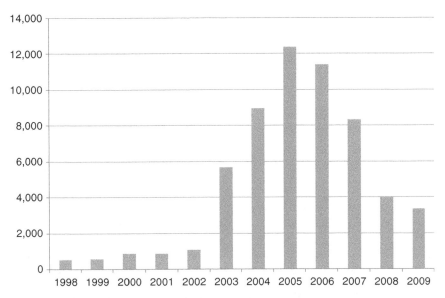

Figure 5.3 References to *Sunni*, *Shia*, *Sufi*, *Salafi* and *Wahhabi* over time, 1998–2009

it should also be noted that, collectively, these words tend to collocate with words such as *militia*, *insurgents*, *Baghdad*, *Iraq*, *Kurdish* and *radical*, so they tend to be used in contexts that refer to conflict or extremism. This pattern of representation thus echoes the earlier findings from Chapter 2: just as Islam is reported on in contexts of conflict, the same is true for the branches of Islam.

Figure 5.3 shows how references to these branches of Islam changed over time. Interestingly, it seems that the '9/11 effect' is not so strong here, with very few references to different branches until 2003, and then a sharp rise until 2005. What happened in 2003 to cause this rise? An examination of collocates of these words that year reveals that they reference terms that refer to the Iraq war, such as *Saddam*, *Baghdad* and *Iraq*. The invasion of Iraq resulted in a focus on the distinctions between Shia and Sunni Muslims, particularly those who were living in Iraq who engaged in both a long period of factional communal violence and insurgency against the Western forces in the country.

Figure 5.4 shows the relationship between references to Islam and branches of Islam. As with Figure 5.3, the longer the bar for a particular year, the more times that branches of Islam are referred to, as opposed to Islam itself. This figure does not differ much from Figure 5.3, although it is notable that the two years when different branches of Islam are referred to least, compared to Islam itself, are 2001 and 2002. There is an 'inverse 9/11 effect' here, with the discourse

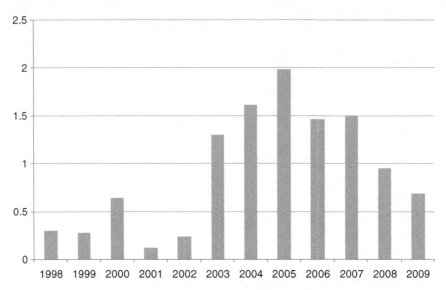

Figure 5.4 Proportion of times that newspapers refer to branches of Islam as opposed to Islam itself over time, 1998–2009

directly after 9/11 being less concerned about making distinctions between branches of Islam, but more likely simply to discuss Islam as a single concept.

Even if we consider only words relating to *Wahhabism*, the branch of Islam that is often most strongly associated with Osama Bin Laden (although scholars such as Commins, 2006, have pointed out that Bin Laden's ideology differed from Wahhabism in crucial ways), again these words are most frequent from 2003 to 2005. Thus, in the period after 9/11 the British press appears to have been especially unwilling to acknowledge different branches of Islam, instead adopting the strategy of referring to Islam as a unified whole.

Conclusion

Overall, our examination of collectivisation and differentiation processes in the corpus has confirmed John Richardson's (2004) findings. The highly frequent terms *Muslim community* and *Muslim world* tend to be used uncritic-ally, to signify a mainly homogeneous group of Muslims (in the United Kingdom and globally, respectively), although there are also references to a problematic minority within. These constructs are frequently represented as separate from, and in tension with, the rest of the United Kingdom or 'the West'. Analysis of the terms for branches of Islam provided evidence that the tabloids in particular seem more likely to conceive of Islam as homogeneous, and that during 2001 and 2002 this phenomenon is particularly pronounced. However, when newspapers begin to acknowledge concepts such as Sunni and Shia Islam, it is mainly in the context of the Iraq war. *Muslim countries* tend to be discussed in terms of how strict or liberal they are, while the countries that attract the most attention are not those with the most Muslims but those that are seen as the most dangerous, oppressive or problematic.

It is interesting to consider the findings in this chapter in connection with the results of a Gallup survey of the attitudes of 500 London Muslims and 1,200 members of the UK general public (Mogahed 2007). Of the London Muslims, 57 per cent said they identified strongly with the United Kingdom, as opposed to 48 per cent of the general public. Additionally, London Muslims were less likely to say that they wanted to live in a neighbourhood made up of people who mostly shared their religious or ethnic background (25 per cent versus 35 per cent of the general public) and were more likely to have positive views of Catholics and fundamentalist Christians than the general public did. London Muslims also had higher levels of confidence in the local police, the honesty of elections, the judicial system and the national government than the general public.

Mogahed (2007: 2) argues that the survey 'provides a new perspective on the growing debate over multiculturalism vs. assimilation in the UK. Contrary to the typical zero-sum framing of the issue, the study indicates that, particularly for London's Muslims, strong identification with one's religion and one's nationality are not mutually exclusive.' While these findings reflect the opinions only of Muslims living in London, they are an indication that, in some areas of the United Kingdom, British Muslims tend to feel a stronger relationship to Britain and are more tolerant of other religions and ethnic groups than the average. Such a picture is at odds with the reporting in the British media, which tends to stress problems between Muslim communities and the rest of the United Kingdom, and depicts Muslim leaders as being easily offended and either needlessly condemnatory or insufficiently condemnatory. If anything, considering the picture in the press, the results of the attitude survey perhaps go against expectations. It might be assumed that the Muslims surveyed would have developed more cynical and separatist attitudes as a result of the ways that they are written about in the media. The survey results are thus a testament to people who have shown remarkable tolerance in the face of misrepresentation.

6   What's a devout Muslim? Ways of believing

Introduction

This chapter focuses on how the British press makes distinctions between the strength or manifestations of belief among Muslims. We are interested in how journalists represent identities such as *extremist*, *moderate* or *devout Muslim* and in finding out which of these identities are most frequent and what they are used to mean. Are extremists always bad and moderates always good, and do terms such as 'devout' imply a kind of neutral stance? We are also interested in where these modifying terms occur in relation to the word *Muslim*; is there a difference between a *moderate Muslim* and a *Muslim moderate*? Finally, are some terms that appear synonymous, such as *fanatic*, *extremist* and *hardliner*, used interchangeably or do they indicate more subtle shades of meaning?

There are a number of reasons why we felt that this topic was worth devoting a chapter to. First, other researchers have already identified how certain belief terms play a particularly important role in shaping stereotypes. For example, Partington (1998: 74) has indicated that the words *extremists*, *fanatics*, *fundamentalists* and *militants* tend to be words that we use to refer to other people, rather than ourselves. These words are therefore good examples of an 'othering' strategy, or a means of creating a distinction between 'us' and 'them'. They help to create another group as apart from us, different from us and dangerous to us.

Akbarzadeh and Smith (2005: 4) report that the 'recurring language used to describe Islam and Muslims (such as "Islamic terrorism", "Muslim fanatics") can come to be representative of all Muslims and Islam as a religion'. Said (1997: xvi–xvii) makes a similar point with regard to the concept of fundamentalism:

The deliberately created associations between Islam and fundamentalism ensure that the average reader comes to see Islam and fundamentalism as essentially the same thing. Given the tendency to reduce Islam to a handful of rules, stereotypes, and generalizations about the faith, its founder, and all of its people, then the reinforcement of every negative fact associated with Islam – its violence, primitiveness, atavism, threatening qualities – is perpetuated. And all this without any serious effort at defining the term 'fundamentalism', or giving precise meaning either to 'radicalism' or 'extremism', or giving those phenomena some context (for example, saying that 5 percent, or 10 percent, or 50 percent of all Muslims are fundamentalists).

Our pilot study (Baker 2010), which compared tabloid and broadsheet newspapers, identified the fact that tabloids more frequently make use of the words *fanatic, fanatics, fanatical, extremist* and *extremists* in stories about Islam and Muslims, whereas the broadsheets are more likely to use words such as *radical, radicalism, hardline, fundamentalism, orthodox* and *separatist*, which, on the surface, may seem slightly less negatively biased, but reference a very similar concept. However, the broadsheets are also more likely to use the terms *moderate, progressive* and *progressives*, which suggests that these newspapers are more likely to acknowledge a wider range of religious positions – although it could also be argued that a term such as *moderate* could be used as a marker of exceptionality, implying that the default state is not moderation (a point we examine in more detail in a later section).

In this chapter, then, we have decided to return to these words, in order to look more closely at patterns associated with them. Are certain terms preferred by certain newspapers, do certain terms go in or out of vogue and how do the different contexts of usage help to furnish newspaper readers with implicit meanings of the words?

Types of belief

A word sketch of *Muslim* was used to identify the sorts of words that reference different ways of believing that commonly occur in the corpus. Three types of words that frequently occur near or next to *Muslim* were identified. First, there was a set of words indicating that someone holds a very extreme position: *fanatic, extremist, militant, fundamentalist, separatist, hardliner, firebrand* and *radical*. These words tend to occur after the word *Muslim*, and were often nouns (e.g. *Muslim fanatic*).

Second, there are words that indicate that someone has strong beliefs, but that tend *not* (at least on the surface) to suggest extremism: *orthodox, pious, committed, observant, strict, devout* and *faithful*. These words tend to occur before the word *Muslim*, as adjectives (e.g. *pious Muslim*), the exception being *faithful*, which occurs more often as a noun in the phrase *Muslim faithful*.

The distinction between these two sets of words and their grammatical relationship to the word *Muslim* is interesting. If we want to show that a Muslim holds an extreme belief (that we do not approve of), we are more likely to label the person with a noun – such as *fanatic*. However, if we want to suggest that he/she holds a strong belief we do not necessarily disapprove of, then we use an adjective such as *devout*. Why is the distinction important? Labelling people's belief with a noun such as *fanatic* is a way of implying that they have become the sum of their beliefs, that their identity is the same as the way that they believe, and there is no more to them than being a fanatic or extremist. On the other hand, referring to people's belief via an adjective such as *devout* implies that there are potentially other ways that they could be represented.[1] Their devoutness is just one potential way of referring to them.

This strategy does not necessarily occur only with Muslims. In the ukWaC reference corpus of internet texts, the noun *fanatic* can be used in a more humorous way to refer to people who love sport (e.g. *football fanatic*), whereas the noun *extremist* can refer to people who are against abortion, care about animal rights, have extreme political views or belong to a range of different religions. The strategy of 'nouning' extreme belief words seems to be a more general way of reducing people to the sum of their beliefs, as a way of emphasising and essentialising their difference from others.

A third set of 'belief' words in the Muslim news corpus were more difficult to classify with a single meaning, but they seem to indicate that belief is not strong: *moderate, progressive, liberal, secular*. As with the non-extremist strong belief words such as *devout* and *strict*, these words also tend to be used as adjectives when modifying *Muslim* (e.g. *Muslim moderate (s)* occurs forty-five times in the corpus whereas *moderate Muslim(s)* occurs 514 times).

It is difficult to quantify exactly how frequently these words are used to refer to Muslims or Islam in the corpus because the words themselves can be used in different ways and contexts. For example, *extremist* can be both an adjective and a noun (with singular and plural forms). It can occur as a premodifier, in contexts such as *extremist Islam*, or it can be premodified by *Muslim*, as in *Muslim extremists*. It can occur on its own to refer to Muslims (e.g. *extremists*), but it can also be used to refer to people who are not Muslims. As there are tens of thousands of cases in the corpus, it is not feasible to examine each one by hand. We have therefore tried to focus on examples that directly modify *Muslims*, though we acknowledge that this method gives a representative rather than an exhaustive account.

---

[1] The same process can be used with words that refer to sexuality or ethnicity. Compare the ideological effect of 'he's a gay' versus 'he is gay'.

Table 6.1 Frequencies of belief terms used to modify Muslim

Extreme belief		Strong belief		Moderate belief	
Muslim extremist	2,060	*devout Muslim*	1,144	*moderate Muslim*	514
Muslim fanatic	985	*strict Muslim*	466	*secular Muslim*	72
Muslim fundamentalist	662	*orthodox Muslim*	60	*liberal Muslim*	37
Muslim militant	459	*committed Muslim*	47	*progressive Muslim*	15
Muslim radical	259	*pious Muslim*	41		
Muslim separatist	257	*observant Muslim*	34		
Muslim hardliner	79	*faithful Muslim*	17		
Muslim firebrand	27				

Table 6.1 shows the frequencies of these terms as they are most commonly used to modify the word *Muslim* (plural instances such as *Muslim fanatics* or *moderate Muslims* are also included).

We cannot claim that we have found every single word that references a type of belief, although, from our analyses, we are confident that we have covered the majority of cases. In addition, we should not assume that all the words in each category have exactly the same meaning. For example, some people may consider a term such as *strict Muslim* to imply a stronger, perhaps more uncompromising, position than *faithful Muslim*. Even so, the frequencies of these terms give an interesting picture of the ways that Muslims tend to be described in terms of the type of belief that they possess. *Muslim extremists* are the most common type of Muslim (at least for the terms in Table 6.1). There are also relatively high frequencies of *Muslim fanatics*, *devout Muslims* and *Muslim fundamentalists*. A second set of less frequent terms involves *militants*, *separatists* and *radicals*, as well as *strict* and *moderate Muslims*. The remaining terms – *hardliner, firebrand, orthodox, pious, committed, faithful, progressive, secular, liberal* – are relatively rare, occurring fewer than 100 times each with *Muslim* in the corpus. It is worth noticing how the more frequent terms tend to reference extreme or strong belief.

A question arises regarding whether a term such as *Islam* is more likely to attract words to do with belief, especially strong belief. While *Muslim* denotes an individual who holds a religion, *Islam* references the religion itself. Therefore, if journalists do write about extreme, strong or moderate beliefs, do they tend to personalise such references to people, or do they write about them in more abstract terms? This question is tackled later in the chapter, along with a closer examination of trends across different newspapers and over time.

Table 6.2 Dictionary definitions of extreme belief terms

Word	Meaning from Merriam-Webster dictionary[2]
fanatic	Excessive enthusiasm and intense, uncritical devotion
extremist	The quality or state of being extreme
militant	Engaged in warfare and combat, aggressively active
fundamentalist	A movement or attitude stressing strict and literal adherence to a set of basic principles
separatist	An advocate of racial or cultural separation
hardliner	Advocating or involving a rigidly uncompromising course of action
firebrand	One that creates unrest or strife (as in aggressively promoting a cause)
radical	Advocating extreme measures to retain or restore a political state of affairs

Ways of representing extreme belief

As the set of words that reference extreme belief is so common, it was first decided to spend some time looking at them in more detail. These extreme words are perhaps also of most concern from a critical discourse analysis perspective, as they tend to offer a somewhat negative, uncompromising and potentially dangerous view of the people who are believed to have such characteristics. Therefore, this set of words warrants further investigation.

We chose the words *fanatic*, *extremist*, *militant*, *fundamentalist*, *separatist*, *hardliner*, *firebrand* and *radical* (and their plurals). Most of these words can be used as nouns or adjectives, except for *fanatic* and *hardliner*, which are only nouns. For this reason, we also included their adjectival counterparts: *fanatical* and *hardline*. Table 6.2 shows dictionary definition meanings of these words (although we should not assume that readers or journalists make distinctions between the terms according to such definitions).

Table 6.2 suggests that dictionary definitions make distinctions between some of the words. *Militant* appears to be the only word that directly references warfare and combat, though *firebrand* suggests aggression. *Radical* and *extremist* both seem to suggest an extreme point of view, whereas *fundamentalist* and *hardliner* both seem to reference the concept of rigidity. It is useful to bear these distinctions in mind when considering how the terms are used in examples quoted later from newspapers.

In Chapter 4 we briefly looked at how certain strong belief words gained popularity at particular points in time (Table 4.8). Words referring to hardliners were initially popular, then fanaticism gained precedence as a result of 9/11. Later, the terms *militant*, *radical* and *extremist* become more frequent. A relevant question that arises here is whether these terms actually refer to distinctly separate things or whether the words have interchangeable meanings, with a form of

---

[2] See www.merriam-webster.com/dictionary.

Concordance 6.1 Extremist *co-occurring near* militant

1	militant training, including indoctrination into	extremist	beliefs and at least some weapons training
2	The militant group led by Jordanian	extremist	Abu Musab al-Zarqawi
3	There is a growing network of militant	extremist	Islamic groups throughout the
4	fully paid up members of terrorist,	extremist	or militant groups.
5	An	extremist	Islamic group set up by militant cleric Omar Bakri
6	Notorious Islam	extremist	Hilarion del Rosario Santos III, a militant with links to Osama
7	a Muslim militant who praised the July 7 bombers. Abu Izzadeen, the	extremist	who branded John Reid, the Home Secretary, an 'enemy of Muslims
8	Osama Bin Laden, the Islamic militant	extremist	living in Afghanistan
9	Young Hamas 'activist' – for which read 'guerrilla/terrorist/	extremist	/militant', depending on your point of view
10	In which case they become 'terrorist' or	'extremist' or 'militant' or – my favourite, this – 'fiery'	

rewording taking place such that, for example, what used to be called *militant* later became an *extremist*. To explore this question, a search was carried out to find all cases of *militant* and *extremist* occurring within ten words of each other. Seventy-eight cases were found; a selection is shown in Concordance 6.1.

The concordance shows a range of different ways that *extremist* and *militant* are used. In line 1 *militant* is associated with receiving training, whereas *extremist* is used to refer to beliefs. Line 2 refers to a militant group that is led by an extremist, whereas line 3 refers to a group that is both militant and extremist. Line 4 implies that some groups are militant whereas others are extremist, whereas line 5 seems to be the opposite of line 2: here it is the group that is extremist, whereas the leader is militant. In line 6 a person is referred to first as an *extremist* and then later in the same sentence he is a *militant*. This pattern is reversed in line 7, with the person being a militant first, and then a sentence later he is called an extremist. In line 8 the two terms are used consecutively, so Osama Bin Laden is an *Islamic militant extremist*. Finally, lines 9 and 10 are interesting in that they refer to meta-linguistic uses of the terms, which are in scare quotes. In line 9 the term *activist* is also said to mean *guerrilla, terrorist, extremist* or *militant* 'depending on your point of view', whereas in line 10 the terms *terrorist, extremist, militant* and *fiery* are suggested, rather ironically, to be equivalent. Both lines 9 and 10 are from *The Independent*. Line 10, which is an article on clichés by the columnist Robert Fisk, is expanded on below:

[R]emember how Protestants in Northern Ireland were always 'staunch' and Catholics always 'devout'? Indeed, 'devout' is a definition more recently inherited by Muslims, unless they display violent tendencies, in which case they become 'terrorist' or

Concordance 6.2 Fanatic *co-occurring with* extremist, fundamentalist *and* radical

1 MUSLIM extremist Jalal Ahmed went into hiding yesterday. The	fanatic	didn't have the guts to stand up
2	Mackray branded the Islamic	fanatic	a 'murderous and perverted extremist'
3	Issued by extremist cleric Omar Bakri. The Syrian-born	fanatic	singled out the show after it emerged
4	He is not a Muslim extremist and he's not a	fanatic	. It's nonsense because he has no terror
5		Fanatic	in TA bid. A Muslim extremist who
6	El-Faisal, 'a	fanatic	and extremist', used religion to mask his
7	He was, however, an Islamist extremist, believing in an ideology that would provide the	fanatic	with a proximate cause
8	'Makhmalbaf was a religious	fanatic	, a fundamentalist,' he says
9	George Robertson warned that the fundamentalist	fanatic	is ready for attacks even more lethal
10	Muktar Ibrahim was a '	fanatic	radical' who had travelled to the Sudan

'extremist' or 'militant' or – my favourite, this – 'fiery': as in 'the firebrand cleric Muqtada al-Sadr' (*Independent*, 9 August 2008).

Concordance 6.1 suggests that the terms *militant* and *extremist* have related, overlapping meanings. A similar pattern is found for *fanatic* and *extremist*, with cases in the corpus of people being labelled as fanatics and then extremists (see Concordance 6.2). There were no cases of fanatics being referred to as militants or separatists, although there were a handful of cases of fanatics also being described as fundamentalists or radicals.

The term *radical* is also linked to the other belief words, with references in the corpus to *radical militants*, *radical fundamentalists*, *radical separatists* and *radical extremists*. In addition, we found people being referred to as *militant fundamentalists*. Such terms appear to be tautological (such as *free gift* or *added bonus*), used more for emphasis, in order to mark a person as dangerous, rather than aiming to provide an accurate description based on any pre-existing categorisation scheme:

The shoot-outs began when up to 300 armed Islamic militants stormed the city of Nalchik, near Chechnya, after the arrest of a radical extremist (*Daily Star*, 14 October 2005).

These words are not the product of a radical extremist. They come from the pen of one of the most acclaimed scholars in the Deobandi tradition (*Times*, 8 September 2007).

The security service also plays down the importance of radical extremist clerics, saying their influence in radicalising British terrorists has moved into the background in recent years (*Guardian*, 21 August 2008).

If someone is labelled as a *radical extremist* then this would appear to imply that other forms of extremists exist, such as non-radical ones. Yet the term *non-radical extremist* is an oxymoron, considering that the dictionary definition of *radical* also involves 'advocating extreme measures'.

Another way of considering how meaning is attached to these words is by considering word sketches of them. Using Sketch Engine, we derived lists of the most salient verb and adjective collocates of the words, which are presented in Table 6.3. The word sketches differentiate between verbs that show, say, fanatics as the subject (e.g. *A fanatic plotted...*) or fanatics as the object (e.g. *A fanatic was deported*). We present only the ten most statistically salient terms (using the logDice metric) for each category in the table.

The table shows some interesting differences and similarities between the words. *Islamic* is strongly associated with *fanatic, extremist, militant, fundamentalist* and *radical*. The term *fanatic* has the most strongly negative adjectives associated with it (*evil, murderous, hate-filled* and *ruthless*). The term *suspected* appears as a salient adjective of *extremist, militant, separatist* and *radical*. *Suspected* often occurs with these words in news stories about arrests being made (e.g. 'THREE suspected Islamic radicals arrested in a dawn raid may have been planning a chemical attack on Paris, security officials said yesterday' (*Daily Telegraph*, 18 December 2002)). The term thus suggests that newspapers are sometimes cautious, particularly in dealing with stories in which a person has been arrested, but misdoing has not yet been proven. *Suspect* also appears as a verb that positions separatists, fundamentalists, militants, radicals and extremists as a grammatical object. The only words not associated with *suspect* or *suspected* are *fanatic, hardliner* and *firebrand*. These words (favoured by the 'popular' press) appear to be more straightforward labels that do not require hedging. Either fanatics make no attempt to disguise their fanaticism, or the press does not feel obliged to protect itself from accusations of libel from people whom they claim to be fanatics. Not all the adjectives are intrinsically negative in meaning: militants and hardliners are sometimes described as *loyal*, while radicals may be *non-violent*.

In terms of actions that these types of people are described to be doing, a distinction appears to be made between physical violence (*behead, hijack, bomb, ambush, kidnap*) and 'ideological' violence (*brainwash, preach, hate, threaten, exploit, recruit, influence*). Militants tend to be described as engaging mainly in physical violence, whereas fundamentalists, hardliners and firebrands appear to carry out ideological violence. Radicals, extremists and fanatics appear to use a mixture of the two, while the verbs attributed to separatists do not appear to be as violent as for the other groups.

Another shared verb is *appease*, which is used to refer to fanatics, extremists, fundamentalists and hardliners. This verb often occurs in political commentary that is critical of the British government:

Table 6.3 Word sketch of extreme belief words

Extreme belief word	Adjectives	Verbs (subject)	Verbs (object)
fanatic	*murderous, Islamic, Muslim, religious, home-grown, evil, suicidal, fundamentalist, ruthless, hate-filled*	*brainwash, plot, behead, plan, abuse, hate, preach, target, hijack, rant*	*brainwash, deport, appease, defeat, fear, curb, isolate, link, brand, prepare*
extremist	*Islamic, Muslim, violent, suspected, right-wing, religious, home-grown, far-right, Algerian, animal*	*target, brainwash, infiltrate, plot, hijack, preach, exploit, murder, plan, pose*	*isolate, deport, tackle, link, suspect, determine, prosecute, appease, defeat, confront*
militant	*Islamic, suspected, Palestinian, Hamas, Kashmiri, wanted, loyal, armed, alleged, Pakistani*	*fire, kidnap, storm, attack, threaten, seize, behead, target, bomb, ambush*	*suspect, link, hole, arrest, arm, assassinate, blame, mask, kill, disarm*
fundamentalist	*Islamic, Christian, Muslim, religious, reluctant, Protestant, crazed, fanatical, extreme, Algerian*	*infiltrate, object, wish, favour, preach, hate, target, threaten, wage, exploit*	*poise, appease, anger, offend, upset, fuel, oppose, link, criticise, suspect*
separatist	*Basque, Kashmiri, Kurdish, Tamil, Flemish, Croat, Sikh, Albanian, suspected, Muslim*	*operate, seize, try, fight, threaten, seek, want, begin, claim, call*	*blame, crush, defeat, suspect, encourage, support, fight, accuse, join, include*
radical	*Islamic, British-based, left-wing, non-violent, suspected, homegrown, Islamist, Muslim, anti-Western, so-called*	*brainwash, plot, preach, exploit, influence, recruit, hijack, kidnap, pose, want*	*deport, inflame, counter, determine, suspect, tackle, jail, confront, investigate, invite*
hardliner	*embattled, unelected, incumbent, clerical, Iranian, Croat, Hamas, loyal, furious, outspoken*	*wield, control, oppose, exploit, dominate, ally, block, attempt, fear, replace*	*appease, embolden, anger, galvanise, infuriate, strengthen, isolate, alienate, enable, oppose*
firebrand	*left-wing, one-eyed, Unionist, populist, one-time, bearded, socialist, far-right, clerical, Protestant*	*endanger, head, launch, support, lead, run, tell*	–

Hasn't Britain indeed become, in the words of Nile Gardiner of the Heritage Foundation, 'a hornets' nest of Islamic extremists'? How have we let this come about? Much
of the answer lies in our authorities' spineless refusal to confront Islamic extremism
for fear of being thought anti-Muslim. Americans gape in disbelief when our senior
policemen's first reaction to every terrorist atrocity is to try to appease religious
extremists. Or when Ministers employ apologists for terrorism as special advisers at
the Foreign Office (*Daily Mail*, 30 August 2006).

Related to *appease* are the verbs *offend*, *anger* and *upset*, which are
particularly salient to fundamentalists and hardliners who are regularly
described as prone to anger (like the patterns found with *Muslim leaders* in
Chapter 5). The verb *deport* co-occurs with *fanatic*, *radical* and *extremist* and
tends to refer to the government's promises of legislation to 'deport fanatics'
(e.g. 'Mr Blair vowed to deport foreign fanatics and promised new laws to
cage extremists who whip up hatred' (*Sun*, 14 July 2005)). Such stories were
most frequent in the right-leaning press in 2005 after the 7/7 attacks. There
are many other verbs across the entire table that refer to defeat: *defeat*, *isolate*,
tackle, *prosecute*, *confront*, *arrest*, *kill*, *disarm*, *oppose*, *crush*, *counter*,
tackle. A final interesting observation is that, for *fanatics*, *brainwash* is the
most salient verb regardless of whether *fanatics* is in subject or object
position. In the following two examples, fanatics (who caused 9/11 and 7/7)
have been brainwashed (although it is not clear who or what has caused the
brainwashing):

They were brainwashed fanatics, utterly bereft of anything recognisable as human
feeling (*Daily Telegraph*, 28 September 2001).

We have seen elsewhere that such fanatics are brainwashed into a state of fervour and
the belief that they will be martyrs if they kill others and themselves (*Daily Express*, 13
July 2005).

However, in the next two examples, it is fanatics who are carrying out the
brainwashing on other people:

He travelled to Pakistan in 2004 where he was brainwashed by fanatics (*Sun*, 6 January
2005).

INNOCENT school pupils in their early teens are being groomed to become suicide
bombers, The People can reveal. They are being brainwashed by hardened Muslim
fanatics to turn them into teeny terrorists even before they sit their GCSEs (*People*,
10 September 2006).

Although newspapers do not explicitly acknowledge the fact that *fanatics* are
both represented as brainwashed and brainwashers, this interesting use of
grammatical agency makes fanaticism and brainwashing appear to be rather
like a disease that can be spread from one person to the other, and it is difficult
to know where or how fanaticism actually originated.

Extreme belief and proportional usage

The word sketch in Table 6.3 can tell us only how words such as *fanatic* are grammatically positioned in articles that are about Muslims and/or Islam. As mentioned at the beginning of the chapter, it might be the case that the words do not actually refer to Muslims but to other people. For example, there are thirty-four references to *radical feminists* in the corpus, none of which actually refer to Muslims, and some of the collocates in Table 6.3 clearly do not refer to Islam (*Protestant, Unionist, Socialist*).

Therefore, Figure 6.1 shows the overall frequencies of times that a newspaper uses an 'extreme belief' word either directly before or after the word *Muslim, Muslims, Islam* or *Islamic*. The frequencies for *Muslim* and *Muslims* have been aggregated. Again, we selected *fanatic(al), militant, extremist, fundamentalist, radical, separatist, hardline(r)* and *firebrand* as 'extremist belief' words, along with the plurals of these terms. Thus we considered terms such as *fanatical Muslims* and *Muslim extremist*. It should be noted that *Muslim* can be used in the corpus as a noun or an adjective, so a term such as *fanatical Muslim* may actually be part of a longer noun phrase such as *fanatical Muslim group*. We have included such cases because they still make an association between strong belief and Muslims. We have considered only cases that directly modify the words *Muslim(s), Islam* or *Islamic* – so a word such as *firebrand* must occur either immediately beforehand or afterwards. There are, of course, cases when *firebrand* may be used as a modifier, but not actually occur next to the word but two or more places away from it. Therefore, the actual numbers of extreme belief words being used to modify *Muslim(s), Islam* and *Islamic* is likely to be higher, although, by considering collocates at L1 and R1, the resultant data is certainly sufficient to allow us to make synchronic and diachronic comparisons between the newspapers in the corpus.

From Figure 6.1 it can be seen that the extreme belief words tend to be used more frequently to modify the word *Islamic*, especially in *The Times, The Daily Telegraph* and *The Independent*. There are somewhat fewer cases of extreme belief words being used to modify *Muslim(s)*, while cases for *Islam* are quite rare. There are lower frequencies in the Sunday newspapers and the weekly magazine *The Business*, obviously because these newspapers have fewer editions. Additionally, the 'quality' newspapers tend to contain more text, so it is perhaps not surprising that *The Times, The Independent* and *The Daily Telegraph* have high frequencies. It is perhaps notable that another broadsheet newspaper that contains a lot of text, *The Guardian*, actually appears to connect the extreme belief words with Muslims and Islam fairly infrequently, having quite a similar profile to the *Daily Mirror* – a newspaper that contains much less text.

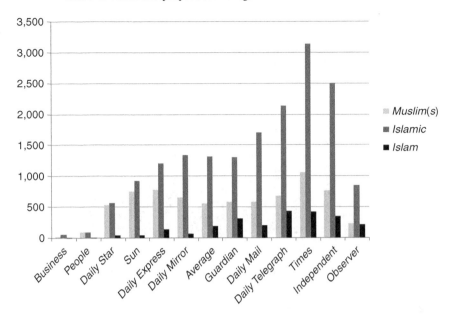

Figure 6.1 Overall frequencies of extreme belief words occurring before or after *Muslim(s)*, *Islamic* and *Islam* for each newspaper

We can continue this line of analysis by taking into account the number of times that each newspaper uses the word *Muslim(s)* and then considering what proportion or percentage of those occurrences actually occur with the extreme belief words. For example, *The Guardian* mentions the word *Muslim(s)* 20,388 times in total. It refers to Muslims who have extreme beliefs in 572 of these cases, or 2.81 per cent of all cases. Compare this to the *Daily Star*, which mentions the word *Muslim(s)* only 5,141 times. Of these, 515 refer to Muslims with extreme beliefs (fewer cases than *The Guardian*), but, proportionally, this gives a much higher total: 10.02 per cent of cases. Figure 6.2 thus shows the *proportion* of times that each newspaper refers to Muslims as having extreme beliefs.[3]

---

[3] Proportions were calculated by counting the number of times that an extreme belief word occurred either at the R1 or L1 position for *Muslim(s)* for each newspaper (and time period), and then dividing this by the total number of occurrences of *Muslim(s)* for that newspaper, then multiplying by 100. However, this method did not take into account the possibility that a strong belief word may occur at both L1 and R1 in the same case (e.g. *radical Muslim separatist*). Such cases would get counted twice and artificially raise the overall proportion. Therefore, all such cases (only thirty-six in total) were found and subtracted from the count before dividing by the overall number of occurrences of *Muslim(s)*. Interestingly, a third of these 'double' cases occurred in 2002, the year after 9/11, with the *Daily Star* and the *Daily Mirror* accounting for 55 per cent of all cases between them.

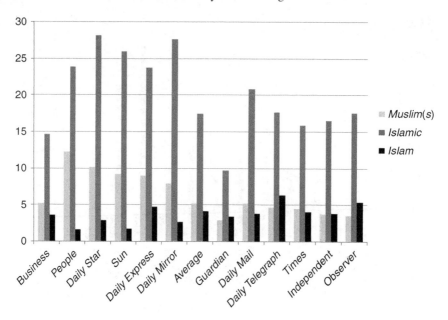

Figure 6.2 Proportion of times that extreme belief words occur before or after *Muslim(s)*, *Islamic* and *Islam* for each newspaper

Here a somewhat different picture emerges. It is the 'popular' or tabloid newspapers that have the highest proportions, with the Sunday-only news-paper *The People* using a modifying word such as *fanatic* 12.34 per cent of the time when it uses the word *Muslim(s)*. In other words, for every eight times that *The People* writes *Muslim(s)*, one of those cases will be next to an extreme belief word such as *fanatic* or *extremist*. *The Guardian*, which is close to the average frequencies in Figure 6.1, actually tends to be one of the newspapers that directly associates this concept with Muslims the least, proportionately.

Figures 6.1 and 6.2, when considered together, tell an interesting story. The broadsheets refer to Muslims having extreme beliefs a lot, simply because there is so much text in them. So, even though they also refer to Muslims in lots of other ways, the sheer amount of text in broadsheets means that their readers will regularly encounter depictions of Muslims as fanatical or extreme. On the other hand, the tabloids, while containing less text, and thus referring to Muslims less often, tend to be much more likely to associate Muslims with extremism when they do write about them. Therefore, both sets of newspapers could be viewed as perpetuating a 'Muslims are extreme' discourse, but for different reasons.

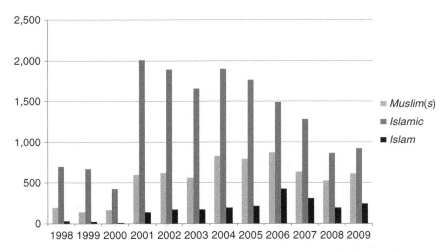

Figure 6.3 Overall frequencies of extreme belief words occurring before or after *Muslim(s)*, *Islamic* and *Islam* over time, 1998–2009

Again, it is *Islamic* that seems to be the strongest attractor of extreme belief words. Three newspapers, the *Daily Star*, *The Sun* and the *Daily Mirror*, all refer to *Islamic* in terms of extreme belief over a quarter of the time they mention this word. However, the proportions in all newspapers are high. Even *The Guardian*, which has the fewest proportional references, still connects *Islamic* to extreme beliefs almost 10 per cent of the time. While all three terms hold a discourse prosody for extreme belief, it is definitely with *Islamic* that this is strongest.

What about change over time? Figure 6.3 shows the raw frequencies of *Muslim(s)* modified by an extreme belief word over time. It can be seen that such total references peaked around 2004 to 2006. However, we need to be careful about reading too much into the early years shown in this table (1998 to 2000), as for a few newspapers we were not able to obtain data prior to 2000. Even though there is a '9/11 effect', whereby Muslims were written about more after 9/11, this is probably slightly exaggerated in Figure 6.3.

Again, there are more cases of *Islamic* being connected to extreme belief words, particularly between 2001 and 2005. The period from 2004 to 2006 is when we are most likely to see *Muslims* represented as having extreme beliefs, whereas for *Islam* it is 2006 to 2007.

Figure 6.4 shows the proportions of references to Muslims as having extreme beliefs for each year. This figure appears to show rather less variation over time, particularly for *Islamic*. Prior to 9/11, even though *Muslim(s)* and *Islam(ic)* tended to be discussed less often, when they were mentioned they still tended to be referred to as having extreme beliefs, with a similar if not

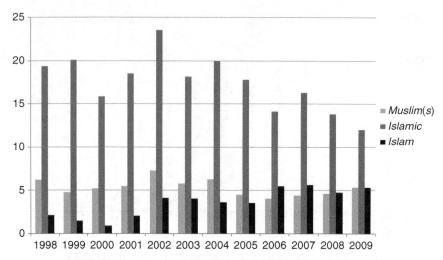

Figure 6.4 Proportion of times that extreme belief words occur before or after *Muslim(s)*, *Islamic* and *Islam* over time, 1998–2009

greater proportional frequency compared to the post-9/11 period. The 9/11 effect may have dramatically increased the number of times that newspapers wrote about Muslims, but, perhaps surprisingly, 9/11 didn't seem to have as much effect on the proportion of writing about Muslims who were directly described as extremist. The period that has the smallest amount of references to *Muslims* with extreme beliefs is the period from 2005 to 2008. There are also relatively low proportional frequencies for connecting *Islamic* with extreme beliefs in 2006 and 2008. This is also a somewhat unexpected finding, as we may hypothesise that the 7/7 attacks would have resulted in rather more cases of Muslims or the word *Islamic* being referred to as holding extreme beliefs.

There are a number of possible reasons for this strange finding. First, it could be the case that journalists decided to act 'responsibly' after 7/7, and so they attempted to curb the number of times that they referred to Muslims as holding extreme beliefs. However, the sharp fall is true only for the word *Islamic* from 2002 onwards. In fact, proportions of references to the words *Muslim(s)* and *Islam* with extreme beliefs seem to be growing again from 2006 onwards.

Moreover, in Figure 6.3 it is clear that 2006 had the most references to *Muslims* as having extreme beliefs. A second possible reason, therefore, is that, in the years immediately following 7/7, there were both more stories about Muslims and a greater *variety* of stories about Muslims. Referring to a Muslim as a *fanatic* is one way of presenting Muslims in a negative light, but there are many others, such as writing about Muslims claiming benefits (which reached a peak in 2005 – see Chapter 7), or debating the issue of the veil (which peaked in 2006 – see Chapter 8). We would therefore suggest that the proportional decrease in 'fanatical Muslims' after 7/7 was perhaps a consequence of other constructions of Muslims appearing during this time.

In this section we have considered variation, looking at change over time, between newspapers, and tracing diachronic changes in the semantic prosodies of the words *Muslim(s)* and *Islam(ic)* separately. What about the big picture, though? When all the data on extreme belief is conflated together, we find that, across the whole corpus, 8.26 per cent (about one in twelve) of all references to *Islam(ic)/Muslim(s)* occur in close connection to a word for extreme belief. It is useful to bear this figure in mind as we move on to consider the oppositional representation: moderation.

Moderation

What about words that suggest that Muslims hold moderate beliefs? Figure 6.5 shows the relative frequencies of the words *moderate(s)*, *progressive(s)*, *secular* and *liberal(s)* occurring either directly before or after *Muslim(s)*, *Islam* and *Islamic* as a proportion of all cases of those identity words, for each newspaper.

It should be noted that there are fewer terms here than in the equivalent figure that looks at extreme belief, Figure 6.2, and also the proportional frequencies for moderation are generally much lower than some of the strong belief words (particularly *fanatic*, *extremist*, *fundamentalist*, *militant* and *radical*). It is notable that some newspapers never use phrases such as *moderate Islam* (such as *The People* and the *Daily Mirror*), and that *The Business* has many more references to moderate Muslims and Islam than the other newspapers. The bars for *Muslim(s)* are higher than those for *Islamic* and *Islam*, with *Islamic* tending to attract moderation words the least. This is a different picture from that for the extreme belief words, which tend to be more likely to occur with *Islamic*.

Figure 6.6, which depicts proportional change over time for mentions of these moderation terms collectively, shows a general increase between 2000 and 2001, with the peak around 2005, suggesting again the effect of 9/11 and 7/7 on the presentation of Muslims and Islam. Perhaps ironically, these two terrorist attacks resulted in more discussion of moderation in articles about Islam, although the two attacks also coincided with frequency increases in terms such as *extremist* and *fanatic* as well.

The general pattern of these moderation words is one of rarity. First, most of the moderate words tend not to be used to modify *Muslim(s)* or *Islam(ic)*, apart from the word *moderate* itself, which accounts for around 80 per cent of

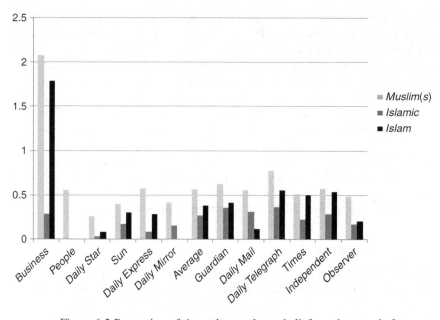

Figure 6.5 Proportion of times that moderate belief words occur before or after *Muslim(s)*, *Islamic* and *Islam* for each newspaper

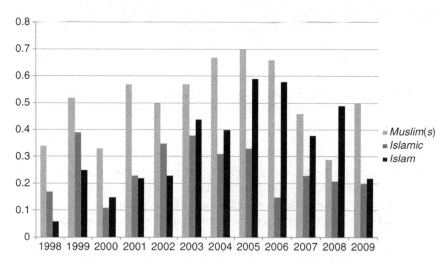

Figure 6.6 Proportion of times that moderate belief words occur before or after *Muslim(s)*, *Islamic* and *Islam* over time, 1998–2009

all cases of moderate words modifying *Muslim*(s) or *Islam*(*ic*). Across the whole corpus, there are 704 instances of these 'moderate belief' words occurring either side of *Muslim*(*s*), making up just 0.56 per cent of all cases of *Muslim*(*s*). For *Islamic* and *Islam* there was a similar picture, with moderate words (235 and 208, respectively) accounting for only 0.26 per cent and 0.38 per cent of all cases of these words.

Taken collectively across the entire corpus (all newspapers, all time periods together), the concept of moderation occurs with *Muslim*(*s*)/*Islam*(*ic*) 0.42 per cent of the time, or roughly one in every 237 cases. Compare this to the equivalent proportion of extreme beliefs (one in every eleven cases), and we can see that the extreme cases outnumber the moderate cases by twenty-one to one. In other words, for every reference to moderation with respect to Muslims and Islam in the British press, there will be twenty-one mentions of extremism.

Does the British press think that moderate Muslims are good Muslims? Moderate Muslims are generally viewed more positively than extremist ones in the corpus, often constructed as working towards integration, engaging in dialogue, condemning violence, being tolerant, or being victimised by extremists. However, terms such as *moderate* are sometimes problematised in the press, particularly in terms of where they appear in relationship to *Muslim*. In *The Independent*, an article is critical of the term *moderate Muslim*, arguing that it implies that other Muslims are *not* moderate, and that there is something fundamentally extreme about Islam. Instead, the author, Guy Keleny, suggests that *Muslim moderate* is a better term:

We called Yusuf Islam 'the most moderate of Muslims'. Only moderately Muslim, then. I do not believe this talk of 'moderate Muslims' is bigoted in intention; it could be argued that 'a moderate Muslim' unpacks as 'a Muslim who is a political moderate'. But I do believe it is likely to foster bigotry; for it looks like 'a person who is moderate in his Islam'. The implication seems to be that Mr Islam, who is a good guy, is moderately Muslim, unlike the bad guys, who are extremely Muslim. If that is the picture we are painting, then we had better be clear what we are doing. We are suggesting the anti-Islamic notion that a real, full-blooded Muslim is likely to be an extremist and a terrorist. I imagine that if I were what is being called a 'moderate' Muslim – that is to say a staunch, God-fearing, extremely enthusiastic Muslim who happens not to approve of hostage-taking or suicide bombing – I should resent that a good deal. After all, no decent person would dream of writing about 'the most moderate of Catholics' or 'the most moderate of Jews'. Mr Islam is not a moderate Muslim but a Muslim moderate (*Independent*, 2 October 2004).

As noted above, *Muslim moderate*(*s*) occurs forty-five times in the corpus whereas *moderate Muslim*(*s*) occurs 514 times. Tellingly, the opposite pattern is noted for the strong belief word *extremist*, with 2,060 cases of *Muslim extremist* and only 388 instances of *extremist Muslim*.

A letter, also in *The Independent* (29 December 2008), makes a similar point:

> The term 'moderate Muslim' in UK media and politics is a sad reflection of how Islamophobia is subtly working its way into our national mentality. The term suggests that Muslims who practise their faith in some limited capacity can be upstanding members of society, whereas those who practise more fully are a danger to us all.

This critical reading of *moderate Muslim* raises a question. If *moderate Muslim* somehow implies that the default term *Muslim* means non-moderate, then perhaps the same could be argued about *extremist Muslim* (i.e. if someone uses *extremist Muslim*, they are implying that most Muslims are *not* extremist). However, this argument holds only if a term such as *extremist Muslim* is relatively rare. As shown in Figure 6.2, on average, references to such terms occur about one in twenty times that the word *Muslim* is used (with this figure rising to one in six for *Islamic*). Therefore, the argument that extremist Muslims are the 'marked', unusual case falls down, because of the high number of references to such Muslims in the corpus. On the other hand, with references to Muslims who are moderate being so infrequent (one in 178 cases on average across the whole corpus), it definitely appears that moderate Muslims are the marked exception to the norm.

A more qualitative demonstration of this idea of the 'moderate Muslim' being the marked, exceptional case is given by columnist Madeleine Bunting in *The Guardian*, who writes about attending a meeting of a Muslim group in London:

> Pondering on the evening, it seemed to me that the most troubling aspect of this debate was how much responsibility to contain the anger among this country's Muslims is being heaped on the shoulders of a small group. Being a moderate Muslim has now become a viable career option – there are government taskforces to serve on, journalists to talk to, advice to give to charitable foundations and thinktanks, innumerable conferences to attend – although, be warned, it's not well paid and the hours are awful (27 February 2006).

Bunting implies that moderate Muslims are seen as being in the minority, and can perhaps make a career out of filling a niche. In *The Guardian*, attempts to unpack or criticise the meaning and usage of *moderate Muslim* tend to come from Muslim writers. For example, a spokesperson for the Muslim Association of Britain argues that his understanding of *moderate* is different from that of *The Sun*, in an article that comments on a visit to the United Kingdom by Yusuf al-Qaradawi, the head of the European Council for Fatwa and Research:

> When most Muslims look to Mr Qaradawi, they see a shining example of moderation: in its Islamic meaning. To us, being a moderate Muslim means to practise the religion faithfully, according to its letter and its spirit. So when he arrived in Britain on Monday in advance of his long-awaited conferences in London, the barrage of attacks against him in the media was distressing for the British Muslim community. All of a sudden, the words 'extremist', 'radical' and 'hardline' were being used liberally, and the Sun surpassed itself by calling him a 'devil', complete with a menacing-looking photograph under the headline: 'The Evil Has Landed'. Now there are demands that he be expelled from the country. This was bound to cause distress among Muslims, but not because of the personal attacks on Mr Qaradawi. This was also a sharp tug at the rug under the feet of moderate Muslims: because if he is an extremist, who is there left to be moderate? (*Guardian*, 9 July 2004).

During his 2004 visit, Mr Qaradawi gave a BBC interview in which he defended suicide attacks on Israelis as 'martyrdom in the name of God', and he was banned from entering the United Kingdom in 2008. *The Sun*'s 'The Evil Has Landed' article (7 July 2004) describes Mr Qaradawi as a 'terror fan cleric...who backs child suicide bombings', yet in *The Guardian* he is described as 'a shining example of moderation'. This discrepancy is worth investigating further, as it helps to explain how the press understands extremism and moderation. Whatever we think about Mr Qaradawi, it is notable that *The Guardian* affords a voice for Muslims to question categorisations of other Muslims as extreme or moderate; this is quite rare in the press overall. The debate over Mr Qaradawi suggests that, even if we can reach a consensus on what counts as a moderate (or non-moderate) position, which in itself is unlikely, a potential problem in defining someone as moderate or extremist means that we characterise *all* their beliefs and actions under a single label. Unless we explicitly qualify our use of the word (e.g. 'He has moderate views on X and Y, but is more extreme on Z'), we risk oversimplifying someone's position.

This observation may help to explain the differences between reports of Mr Qaradawi's stance. He has articulated views on a wide range of topics, some of which position him as (relatively) moderate, such as the danger of blindly following religion and extremism and the importance of dialogue with non-Muslims. He also has been quoted as supporting the protection of non-Muslim minorities in countries that have Muslim majorities, as well as advocating democracy in such countries and political reform in the Middle East. However, he also seems to have articulated views that people would label as 'extreme': as well as condoning suicide attacks, he apparently views wife beating as 'a method of last resort', believes that gay people should be punished, supports female circumcision and claims that Hitler was a punishment on the Jews through Allah. It is therefore possible to quote selectively from Mr Qaradawi in different ways in order to characterise him either as moderate or extremist. Mr Qaradawi shows that the moderate/extremist distinction can be an oversimplification, and that, rather than thinking about such terms as exclusive binary labels, it would be in the interests of accurate journalism to consider a person's full range of positions.

Another example of *The Guardian* publishing debate on definitions of such words is in an article by Manzoor ul Haq, who is critical of the moderate/ extremist distinction, arguing that it is politicians who decide on the boundaries:

The insistence on labelling Muslims as moderate and extremist will create dangerous divisions within the Muslim community. Tony Blair has clearly spelled out who he considers extremist – whoever criticises the Israeli occupation of Palestine, wants to live by the rules of Allah and calls for the Khilafah as a way to rid the Muslim world of its problems. A moderate Muslim is, therefore, one who surrenders to the policies of Bush and Blair, i.e. one who accepts the western invasion and occupation of our lands (5 August 2005).

One 'reading' of these articles in *The Guardian* is that the newspaper 'gives a voice' to an under-represented minority group so that it can offer an alternative position. However, it could also be argued that if the point is made only by Muslims, and non-Muslims are not shown to have such views, then it becomes easier to view the point as coming from a marginalised position.

While *The Guardian*'s publication of the above articles could be characterised as a case of the newspaper being 'well-meaning', such examples of the use of *moderate Muslim* are different from that of the *Daily Mail*, which instead has an article by another Muslim, Saira Khan, who is critical of the treatment of a British schoolteacher in Sudan, who was imprisoned for calling a teddy bear 'Muhammad':

[T]here is a real danger that, within the British Muslim community, the extremists are winning the ideological battle – making it difficult, dangerous or downright impossible for moderate Muslims to stand up and be counted. As a moderate Muslim who is outraged at the creeping tentacles of extremism, I will not be silenced (29 November 2007).

In the above article, *moderate Muslim* is used uncritically as a 'claimed' identity by the author of the article. Although *The Guardian* and the *Daily Mail* both therefore give Muslims the opportunity to put forward their own views on the concept of moderation, these two articles reflect different ideological strategies and political positions. *The Guardian* gives voice to

Muslims who are critical of the concept of *moderate Muslim* and the way that powerful opinion makers (*The Sun* and Tony Blair) apparently define who is and is not moderate, whereas the *Daily Mail* quotes a Muslim who echoes its own position about the need to fight against extremism. A similar article in the *Daily Mail* (4 August 2005) quotes a 'moderate Muslim' who is against women wearing the veil: 'A MODERATE Muslim leader has advised Islamic women to stop wearing traditional veils amid fears of a backlash.'

As Downing (1980) notes, people from minority groups who are quoted tend to be chosen either because their opinions coincide with the views of the majority or because they are extremists who are quoted in order to facilitate attack.

Strong but not extreme?

Having considered constructions of Muslims as having either extreme or moderate beliefs, it is now worth turning to a third category – a set of words that, on the surface, appear to place strength of belief somewhere between extremism and moderation. These words are *orthodox*, *pious*, *committed* (as an adjective), *devout* and *faithful*. Figure 6.7 shows the proportion of

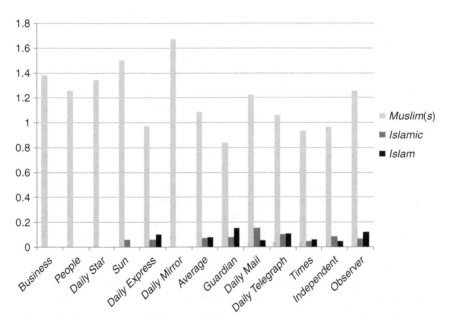

Figure 6.7 Proportion of times that strong belief words occur before or after *Muslim(s)*, *Islamic* and *Islam* for each newspaper

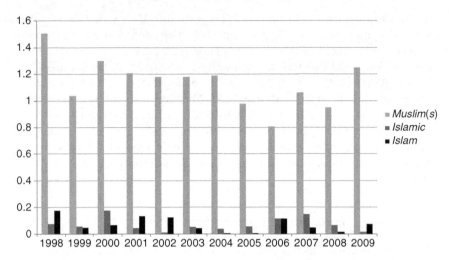

Figure 6.8 Proportion of times that strong belief words occur before or after *Muslim(s)*, *Islamic* and *Islam* over time, 1998–2009

times that these words occur either side of *Muslim(s)*, *Islamic* and *Islam* for each newspaper.

These 'strong belief' words hardly ever occur with *Islamic* and *Islam*, although they are used somewhat more often with *Muslim(s)*. Again, though, compared to the extreme belief words, they are much less frequent. Across all the newspapers, in total, 1,382 strong belief words directly modify *Muslim(s)* (either one place to the left or right), accounting for 1.08 per cent of all references to Muslims. This is higher than the moderate belief words (the equivalent figure being 0.56 per cent), but somewhat lower than the extreme belief words (which occur in 5.16 per cent of the references to Muslims). There are only a very few cases of strong belief words being used to modify *Islam* (forty-one, accounting for 0.075 per cent of all uses of *Islam*), with a similar outcome for *Islamic* (sixty-four cases, accounting for 0.071 per cent).

In terms of change over time, Figure 6.8 suggests that there is not a great deal of change, although it is worth noting the relatively low proportion of references to Muslims with strong beliefs in 2006, the year after 7/7 and a period when the British press was most concerned with a debate on Muslim women who veil.

For ease of comparison, Figure 6.9 shows the proportional frequencies (across all the newspapers) of words denoting extreme, strong and moderate belief when they directly modify *Muslim(s)*, *Islamic* and *Islam*. The figure shows that, in all cases, the extreme belief set of words is more frequent than those for strong and moderate beliefs. This is particularly marked for the word *Islamic*, which shows the highest preference for extremist belief words. The figure also shows that, relatively speaking, *Muslims* and *Islam* do not tend to

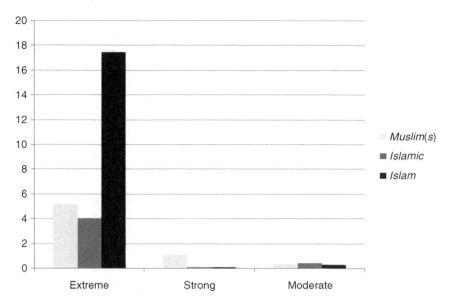

Figure 6.9 Proportion of times that *Muslim(s)*, *Islamic* and *Islam* are directly modified by different types of belief words

be represented as possessing strong (yet not extreme) or moderate beliefs, although, when these terms are referred to, they are more likely to be attributed to people rather than the abstract concept of the religion.

However, returning to the focus on the strong belief words, one question that arises is how these words are actually used. We have seen that, for Muslims and Islam, extremism tends to be viewed negatively by the British press, whereas, in general, moderation is seen as good. How is a category such as *devout Muslim* evaluated, then? Is it regarded as being somewhere between bad and good, or does a more complex and nuanced picture emerge? One pattern that did emerge as occurring with *devout Muslim* is *described/cast/projected/ regarded/portrayed/ [him/her] as a devout Muslim,* which occurs twenty-nine times in the corpus. A sample of these cases is shown in Concordance 6.3.

In Concordance 6.3, people who have been described as devout Muslims tend to be linked to criminality or terrorism. In line 3, the story concerns a judge who was involved in a sex and blackmail scandal with an illegal immigrant whom he had employed as a cleaner, while line 5 refers to one of the British residents held in Guantanamo Bay and line 7 is about a woman who carried out benefit fraud. It is interesting that the people who do the 'describing' are backgrounded. Either they are not named at all (as in lines 1, 6, 7 and 8), or the phrase is attributed to an unnamed 'close friend' or work colleague (only line 5 attributes the description to family members mentioned earlier in the article). The effect of the construction *describe(d)/regarded as a*

Concordance 6.3 Described as a devout Muslim

#			
1	David Heaton, 24, is described as a	devout Muslim	and was detained more than a week ago with an American colleague, Abdullatif Ibrahim Bilal, after allegedly being caught scuba-diving during the month of Ramadan.
2	Ragab el-Swerkie, 56, who owns a chain of clothes stores and is described by his employees as a	devout Muslim	, preyed mainly on beautiful young females, say prosecutors.
3	Colleagues had regarded him as a	devout Muslim	who had risen steadily up the legal ladder since arriving from his native Kenya.
4	…accused of attempting to detonate a bomb on the Victoria Line at Warren Street, was described by a close friend as a	devout Muslim	who performed spontaneous acts of charity.
5	They describe him as a	devout Muslim	, who occasionally preached at a Brighton mosque, but say he was no extremist and travelled
6	Palestinian mother to carry out a suicide bombing. Described as a	devout Muslim	who gave lessons on the Koran, she came from a prominent merchant family
7	mother-of-two Patel, who wears a burka and is described as a	devout Muslim	, made £70,000 from the sale of a house in nearby Wanstead in September 1996.
8	Abdulmutallab, described as a	devout Muslim	, tried to ignite an explosive device on a plane from Amsterdam to Detroit on Christmas Day

devout Muslim in these articles appears to be to highlight the contrast between someone who is perceived to have been 'devout' and his/her 'true' nature (terrorism, extremism or crime). In other words, readers are primed to suspect that (some) devout Muslims are actually not devout at all, or, worse, that *devout* is merely a euphemism for *extremist* (or other 'extreme belief' words). There are many similar cases in the corpus of other devout Muslims being described as committing crimes or acting in 'non-devout' ways, including holding extreme beliefs:

A devout Muslim has been found guilty of cruelty after he encouraged his ten-year-old son to beat himself at a mosque in Birmingham as part of a religious ceremony (*Times*, 9 January 2009).

He is described as having an ordinary upbringing in the Holbeck area of Leeds, but is reported to have changed after his parents sent him to Pakistan. He returned a devout Muslim, later praising the 9/11 terrorists as 'martyrs' (*Daily Star*, 12 May 2006).

In the meantime, although he was a devout Muslim, Major Hasan was a regular visitor to a Texas strip club, where he would sip beer while enjoying $50 (£30) lap dances (*Times*, 21 November 2009).

Being devout is sometimes implied to be not normal. For example, in the *Daily Mail*, an opposition is set up between the phrases *normal girl* and *devout Muslim*:

FORMER classmates of Miss Begum said she had gone from being a 'normal' girl to a devout Muslim almost overnight. When she turned up at school in full Islamic dress – aged 13 – she was studying the Koran daily (*Daily Mail*, 11 February 2006).

In the following article, it is interesting how the quote refers to someone as 'a devout Muslim, but...a normal kid', the use of *but* acting as a case of exception negating, resulting in the implicature that devout Muslims are usually anything but normal:

He was a devout Muslim, but he was a normal kid who loved Manchester United and played football and cricket. He was brilliant and could have played for England, but he started to lose interest when he got involved with these extremists (*Daily Mirror*, 1 April 2004).

The phrase *devout Muslim but* occurs twenty-eight times in the corpus, also being used to refer to exceptional cases in which a devout Muslim is not 'strict' or has not been involved in military activity or terrorism. Another case of exception negating in the *Daily Mirror* refers to the boxer Naseem Hamed, with the article implying that people from Yorkshire cannot be expected to be (devout) Muslims:

The former world featherweight title holder is a devout Muslim, although he was born in Yorkshire (18 September 2001).

Another noteworthy case of how a 'strong belief' word can actually reference extremism is the word *committed*. The phrase *committed Islamic* occurs only seventeen times across the corpus, but in sixteen of these cases it comes before an extremist word such as *extremist, terrorist, fundamentalist* or *jihadist*:

The 23-year-old Muslim wrote of her desire to become a martyr and listed her favourite videos as the 'beheading ones'. Described as a 'committed Islamic extremist', Malik, a WH Smith shop assistant at Heathrow, hoarded an extensive collection of terrorism manuals, the Old Bailey heard (*Daily Mail*, 9 November 2009).

This pattern does not occur with *committed Islam* and *committed Muslim*, but it appears that, when journalists talk about being committed in reference to the word *Islamic*, it is almost always used to mean that someone is committed to extremism rather than Islam per se.

Further analysis of *devout Muslim* reveals a more complex picture. In many cases, *devout Muslim* appears to be used as a more neutral descriptor, or the phrase occurs in order to explain a person's reasons for his/her actions.

In the following example, it is explained that the boxer Muhammad Ali refused the call-up to fight in the Vietnam War:

The year before the snap, devout Muslim Ali had had his heavyweight crown taken from him by boxing chiefs for refusing to fight in Vietnam (*Daily Mirror*, 6 October 2009).

Finally, in some cases *devout Muslim* can be used in stories that evoke sympathy:

A DEVOUT Muslim was killed when he was hit by a motorcycle after crossing one of Scotland's busiest roads to say a kerbside prayer (*Daily Express*, 17 November 2009).

The reporting of this story in the *Daily Express* and other newspapers is very positive about the victim of the accident, quoting friends as saying that he was charitable, kind, a good man, a friend to everyone and a dedicated member of Aberdeen's Muslim community.[4] At the same time, the above excerpt invites the question of why the attribute *devout Muslim* was treated as salient (and therefore reported).

It appears, then, that *devout Muslim* has a potentially wider range of meanings than terms such as *moderate Muslim* and *Muslim extremist*, for which it was easier to uncover more straightforward positive and negative discourse prosodies. The phrase *devout Muslim* can be used to elicit sympathy; it can be used as a shorthand explanation for unusual behaviour (or what is constructed as unusual); but it can also be used to imply abnormality, extremism or a hypocritical nature. In short, the term is good at demonstrating the sense of ambivalence that runs through the press's reporting on Muslims and Islam.

Conclusion

This chapter has demonstrated an association of Muslims and Islam with extremism in a number of ways: the higher frequency of different types of terms that reference the concept of extreme beliefs, and the higher frequency of these types of terms, in relationship to terms that reference strong or moderate beliefs. The fact that extremist terms are sometimes combined (such as *radical extremist*) is another indicator of this fascination with extreme Islam. Across the corpus, about one instance in twenty of the word *Muslim* or its plural occurs directly next to a word that refers to extremist belief. This figure rises to one in six for *Islamic*.

---

[4] Despite the sympathetic construction of the man who died in this news story, a possible 'reading' of it is that it constructs Islam as a religion that places its adherents in dangerous situations.

While 9/11 appears to have resulted in many more references to 'extremist' Muslims in the British press, this reveals only one-half of the story. In fact, the proportions of Muslims who are referred to as extreme changed little after 9/11. The overall numbers went up, but the press had a tendency to label one in twenty mentions of *Muslim(s)* with 'extreme belief' words, even before 9/11. After 7/7 the relative proportions of 'extremist Muslims' and 'extremist Islam' decreased slightly, but that may have been a reflection of a focus on other sorts of stories, such as veiling or the recipients of benefits.

Perhaps this focus on extremism is not surprising, or can be justified. People who hold 'extremist' ideas or beliefs tend to be viewed as problematic (and thus newsworthy) because they often want to change society, and sometimes the means to advocate such changes are threatening, involving violence and oppression. However, it is worth comparing frequencies and relative frequencies between newspapers. *The Guardian* has relatively few proportional references to 'extremist Muslims', compared to the tabloid newspapers. Moreover, while it is generally true that extremists tend to make newsworthy subjects, if 'extreme belief' words are used to represent an entire group, then the result is a distorted picture of that group. The repeated association of a word such as *fanatic* or *extremist* with the word for a major religion begins to look rather suspicious, and framed by ideology.

Qualitatively, we found that references to moderation, although appearing to offer a wider picture of Islam as containing a spectrum of strength of belief, could potentially confound the problem of an excessive focus on extremism, by implying that the moderate Muslim is in a minority or is an exceptional case. This is particularly illustrated by the preference for *moderate Muslim* over *Muslim moderate*. While the left-leaning broadsheets do attempt to give some voice to people (especially Muslims) who are critical of such terms, other newspapers quote from people who claim to be moderate Muslims in order to voice criticism of extremists. Again, on the surface, this strategy may appear to be inclusive, showing readers that 'not all Muslims are bad ones'. However, such voices are relatively rare; references to extreme forms of Islam or Muslims are twenty-one times more common than references to moderate Islam or Muslims. In addition, references to 'moderate' or 'non-threatening' Muslims, even if well-meaning, can result in a strengthening of the presentation of Muslims and Islam as fundamentally problematic, if not dangerous.

Finally, the term *devout Muslim* had a particularly complex and wide-ranging set of meanings attributed to it – sometimes being used in stories to imply that a devout Muslim was criminally hypocritical, engaged in strange behaviour (which needed explaining to readers), was not normal or was exceptional when viewed as normal. However, in other cases, a devout Muslim was viewed as a 'good' Muslim, and the term helped to evoke sympathy for Muslims who had suffered.

Overall, then, the picture that emerges from this chapter is one of Islam as dangerous, frightening, uncompromising and extreme. This image is borne in mind as we turn to the next chapter, which focuses on another stereotyping and negative image: that of the 'scrounger'.

7   From hate preachers to scroungers: who benefits?

Introduction

This chapter focuses on a specific aspect of the construction of Muslims in the British press, namely the issue of Muslims claiming benefits from the British government. The subject of Muslims who claim benefits potentially combines two sets of concerns that arose in the United Kingdom during the period under examination: one about (unwanted) Muslims in the country, the other about people who were perceived as work-shy or 'scroungers', who received large amounts of government benefits that they were seen as not deserving. In this chapter we trace how this combination of concerns appeared; which newspapers helped to nurture it, and to what extent did those newspapers influence the reporting of others? We also investigate which sorts of Muslims were viewed as 'fair game' for this sort of reporting and how this changed over time.

There were a number of reasons why it was decided to focus on this particular topic. First, stories about two particular Muslims who received benefits, Abu Hamza and Omar Bakri, had been identified as significantly frequent in the tabloid part of the corpus (*Hamza* and *Bakri* were keywords – see Chapter 3). A pilot project (Baker 2010), which used a smaller dataset, had also found these two words to be key. The pilot study did not examine articles containing these names in detail, but this discrepancy in their frequency was felt to represent an interesting difference between broadsheet and tabloid news reporting. Additionally, reference to financial concerns has been identified by critical discourse analysts as tending to be a feature of racist discourse. Van Dijk (1987: 58) describes four topic classes for racist discourses: they are different, they do not adapt, they are involved in negative acts and they threaten our socio-economic interests. Additionally, Karim (2006: 119–20, emphasis in original) notes four primary stereotypes of Muslims: '[H]aving fabulous but undeserved wealth (they have not *earned* it), being barbaric and regressive, indulging in sexual excess, and the most persistent image of the "violent Muslim".' Golding (1994) has also identified news articles about benefit recipients as typical of 'scroungerphobia', a phenomenon whereby the media make emotive reports on the distinction between the deserving poor (helpless and worthy) and the undeserving poor (immoral and seedy), who are seen as having benefits lavished on them.

Far from being fabulously wealthy, Muslims are more likely than non-Muslims to live in poverty in the United Kingdom. Robin Richardson (2004: 30) reports that more than a third of children born to Muslim parents live in households in which there is no work (as compared to the national average of 17.6 per cent). Muslim children are also more likely to live in overcrowded homes (41.7 per cent, compared to the national average of 12.3 per cent) with no central heating (one in eight, versus one in sixteen for non-Muslim children). In terms of health, 30.9 per cent of men aged fifty to sixty-four of Bangladeshi origin report that their health is not good, while the equivalent figures are 26.3 per cent for Pakistani men and 13.7 per cent for the national average. In addition, high unemployment rates are found in Pakistani and Bangladeshi communities (which tend to have high numbers of Muslim residents), while those who are employed tend to earn 68 per cent of what non-Muslims earn, on average. Women from these communities are also three to four times more likely to be 'housewives' than the national average.

In the current corpus, the initial quantitative analysis drew our attention again to these 'scrounger' articles. The words *fanatics*, *extremists* and *militants* were notably frequent modifiers of the word *Muslim* in the tabloid data (although not in the broadsheet data). At least one of these three words (and usually two or three) was a top ten immediate right-hand collocate of *Muslim* in each of the twelve years examined for tabloids. When concordances of these three words were examined, it was again noticed that stories about fanatics claiming benefits appeared to be particularly salient. However, it was difficult to ascertain by simply examining concordance lines of the above three words whether articles commenting on Muslims claiming benefits were generally frequent. It was thus decided to examine the entire corpus in detail in order to determine the extent to which different newspapers or time periods referred to 'Muslims on benefits', and in what ways this aspect of the presentation of Muslims was constructed.

Method

The corpus was split into 144 subsections, each containing news articles from a single paper in a particular year. As noted at the start of Chapter 4, we were not able to obtain articles for some newspapers between 1998 and 2000. While this may impact on overall frequencies for the different newspapers, and it should make us wary about reading too much into frequencies for the 1998–2000 period, it should be noted that, of the data that was available during this period, there were very few articles about Muslims receiving benefits, so it is unlikely that this pre-9/11 period would have provided large numbers of stories even if all the data had been available to us.

A search term was created in order to identify news articles that referenced people who were receiving benefits. This term was initially developed through introspection. Then a number of sample articles were read in order to identify further terms that may have been missed. The final search term was *scroung*/dole/handouts/benefits/welfare*, with the * symbol standing for any sequence of characters. It should be noted that the search term contains words that tend to characterise benefit claimants in negative ways – particularly *scroung** (which elicits *scrounger*, *scroungers*, etc) and *handouts*. On the other hand, the terms *benefits* and *welfare* did not implicitly hold such negative connotations, although it was later found that they were sometimes used in negative contexts. Additionally, in some articles these terms appeared to be used interchangeably:

HOOK-handed cleric Abu Hamza is to sue welfare bosses for thousands of pounds in extra state hand-outs, The Sun can reveal. Hamza, due in court next month on incitement to murder charges, reckons he has been fiddled out of benefits worth £200 a week for nearly three years (*Sun*, 21 December 2004).

Concordances of this search term were carried out across the sub-corpora separately. Each concordance line was then examined in order to ascertain whether it referred to Muslims who were receiving benefits. Some cases needed to be discounted, either because the word *dole* referred to a person's surname (e.g. Bob Dole) or because they referred to non-Muslims on benefits. There were also articles that referred to asylum seekers receiving benefits. These articles, too, were discarded – unless it was clear that the asylum seeker in question was also a Muslim. Articles that referred to a person by name were included if the person in question was known to be a Muslim, or was referred to as a Muslim, or it was strongly implied that he/she was a Muslim elsewhere in the article (when expanded concordance lines were examined). Articles that referred to an unnamed Muslim or Muslims in general receiving benefits (either in hypothetical or actual cases) were included. After all the irrelevant articles had been set aside, the frequency of references to Muslims receiving benefits was calculated.

As the concordance lines from each newspaper and time period were examined, it was possible to notice trends over time, as well as identifying particular Muslims who were frequently described as being on benefits. We were particularly interested in how newspapers used evaluation in such stories, and we tried to identify evaluation strategies from the concordance lines, as well as focusing on patterns of referencing – such as when newspapers quoted from other newspapers.

Results

Table 7.1 shows the frequencies of the words in the search term for each newspaper, tabulated by time period.

A couple of points need to be made about this table. First, it does not tell us how many *articles* were written about Muslims on benefits. Instead, it tells us about *overall references* to Muslims on benefits. The data is presented in this way because a single article may contain multiple references to Muslims on benefits, thus strengthening a cognitive model or representation of Muslims in a certain way. Additionally, the table does not take into account the relative frequencies of these occurrences in relation to the overall number of words that each newspaper printed in each year. As noted elsewhere, the tabloids contain less text overall than the broadsheets. As a result, it could be argued that the higher frequencies found in some of the tabloids are particularly salient. However, for the purposes of this chapter, we are more concerned with overall frequencies. We want to consider the following: if a person reads every issue of *The Sun* (or another newspaper) for a given year, how many times will he/she read about a Muslim (or Muslims) receiving benefits? How many times does the newspaper link the two concepts (Muslims and benefits) together in the course of one year?

In total, there were almost 2,000 references to Muslims receiving benefits during the period examined. Clearly, this is a topic that the British press (or at least some parts of it) found to be newsworthy during the first

Table 7.1 Frequency of references to Muslims on benefits per newspaper per year, 1998–2009

	98	99	00	01	02	03	04	05	06	07	08	09	Total
Express	n/a	0	0	9	5	71	54	194	60	52	127	62	634
Sun	n/a	n/a	7	31	4	56	61	85	78	41	80	60	503
Mail	4	10	6	30	7	59	8	104	47	29	57	47	408
Star	n/a	n/a	n/a	12	0	18	20	22	15	15	24	23	149
Mirror	3	0	0	14	4	6	3	30	14	2	8	1	85
People	0	0	1	6	0	17	4	4	11	14	0	0	57
Telegraph	n/a	n/a	0	8	1	4	1	4	3	1	19	4	45
Times	0	0	0	11	2	9	0	14	0	6	0	0	42
Business	n/a	0	0	0	0	0	0	9	0	0	0	0	9
Guardian	0	0	0	0	0	0	0	1	1	0	1	0	3
Observer	0	0	0	0	0	1	0	0	0	0	0	0	1
Independent	0	0	0	0	0	0	0	0	0	0	0	0	0
Total	7	10	14	121	23	241	151	467	229	160	316	197	1,936

Note: 'n/a' = not available.

decade of the twenty-first century. However, this figure does not take into account the fact that these references were not evenly distributed across newspapers or over time. The newspapers that referenced Muslims receiving benefits the most were all right-leaning tabloids: the *Daily Express*, *The Sun* and the *Daily Mail*. These newspapers all referenced Muslims on benefits at least 400 times in the period under examination − together accounting for 79.8 per cent of all such references in the corpus as a whole. Another set of newspapers also had moderately frequent references: three tabloids, *The People*, the *Daily Star* and the *Daily Mirror*, and two right-leaning broadsheets, *The Daily Telegraph* and *The Times*. During the period under examination these newspapers each referred to Muslims on benefits between forty-two and 149 times. A third set of newspapers had hardly any references to Muslims on benefits. These were all broadsheets: *The Business*, and three left-leaning newspapers, namely *The Guardian*, *The Independent* and *The Observer*. None of these newspapers made more than nine references to Muslims receiving benefits within the twelve-year period covered in the corpus. *The Independent* was particularly notable, as no such articles were found. Such a topic can therefore be considered to have no or little 'news value' to the writers (and readers) of left-leaning broadsheets, although it would appear to be of much more interest to the right-leaning tabloids.

In terms of the distribution of such references over time, another pattern can be observed. The first three years considered (1998 to 2000) show very few references to Muslims on benefits, even in the right-wing tabloids (although, to an extent, this could be attributed to the fact that we could not obtain a full set of data for these years). There are then three surges of interest in the subject, in 2001, 2003 and 2005. After each peak, the following year shows a reduction, although each peak is stronger than the one preceding it. There is a further, smaller, peak in 2008. However, the bulk of the references occur in 2003 or afterwards. Table 7.1 shows that the peak point for articles about Muslims on benefits comes in 2005, the most prolific year for this topic for six newspapers, when almost a quarter (24.1 per cent) of all corpus articles on Muslims on benefits occur. Even *The Guardian* and *The Business* have the most references to Muslims on benefits during 2005.

It is likely that the first peak in 2001 is attributable to the response to the 9/11 terrorist attacks, whereas the peak in 2005 is attributable to reaction to the 7/7 bombings of London transport, as at these points there is a general rise in stories about Muslims. It is notable that articles published during these periods make an explicit link between victims of the terrorist attacks and a small set of Muslims receiving benefits, particularly those believed or found to be involved in the attacks:

Qatada had been claiming £400 a week in state benefits but his social security payments were stopped and his bank account frozen after his name appeared on a US list of terrorist suspects. Treasury investigators seized £180,000 in cash – believed to help fund the terrorist network – from his home last month (*Sunday Express*, 16 December 2001).

[I]f these fanatics hate the West so much, why are they still here and claiming benefits? (*Daily Mirror*, 23 September 2001).

PLANS to slash benefits for London bomb victims, while the families of extremists continue to receive state handouts, were attacked last night (*Daily Express*, 12 September 2005).

The following sections examine how Muslims on benefits are constructed, looking in more detail at change over time and between newspapers.

Early tabloid fears

Prior to the 9/11 attacks, Muslims on benefits were of only tangential interest to British newspapers, even those that would later become very focused on the subject. Although the full picture is incomplete, due to the fact that we could not obtain earlier articles from the *Daily Star* and *The Sun*, of the early data that we do have it is the *Daily Mail* that has by far the most mentions of Muslims receiving benefits from 1998 to 2000 – accounting for almost two-thirds (64.5 per cent) of the references during this period. The *Daily Mail* therefore appears to have played an important role in developing this discourse at its early stage, before it became a more mainstream tabloid staple in the following years. One of the earliest articles in the corpus data is a letter in the *Daily Mail* in 1999, in which the writer gives an 'eyewitness account' that all Bosnian Moslems (sic) are set on moving to parts of the European Union and receiving 'big handouts':

DROVE through much of Bosnia this year and most Bosnian Croats and Bosnian Serbs I met seem resigned to working hard to rebuild their devastated country. But I never met one Bosnian Moslem who did. To a man, they intended to leave to start new lives in Germany, America or the UK. These people genuinely believe that they have an overriding right given to them by the EU or similar to settle wherever they choose, be given nice homes and big handouts, and bring over vast extended families (1 December 1999).

However, during this period, when such Muslims are referred to, their religion almost appears to be secondary to the fact that the people in question are asylum seekers above all, as indicated by the following *Daily Mail* article:

An asylum seeker with two wives and 15 children has received more than £32,000 in benefits while his case is being considered. The Algerian family, headed by Moham-med Kinewa, who is in his 60s, arrived 15 months ago. They have also been given the use of two fully-furnished four-bedroom houses with satellite TV, one for each wife and her children. They receive £617.72 a week in benefits alone. The yearly estimated cost rises to more than £50,000 when council tax relief, educating the school-age children, translators, solicitors, and English classes for the family are taken into account (30 March 2000).

In a 1998 article entitled 'London ban on four Egypt terror suspects', the *Daily Mail* refers to a terrorist group that claimed responsibility for a massacre in Luxor in 1997. In the seventh paragraph, the article links an asylum seeker called Yasser al-Serri to the group:

Three of the other four are seeking asylum, including Yasser al-Serri, 35, unemployed and receiving benefits (31 March 1998).

Again, here the focus does not seem to be on the fact that al-Serri is receiving benefits, but the article instead appears to foreground the fact that the terrorists were Muslims, which is referred to in the first sentence of the article. The fact that al-Serri is receiving benefits is therefore secondary to the fact that he is an asylum seeker who is suspected to be linked to terrorism, although after 9/11 Yasser al-Serri assumes more prominence in stories about benefit recipients.

However, it is before 9/11 that we first find references to one of the most well-known 'scroungers', Omar Bakri Mohammed. An article by *The People*, in 2000, reports: 'A British charity run by Islamic Fundamentalists which trains young men to get involved in "Holy Wars" has had its special privileges revoked.' The article then quotes Bakri's response:

Omar Bakri Mohammed said: 'It gives the impression that the British Government is an enemy. That sort of attitude could lead some people to carry out violent acts.' By rights he should be chucked out of the country for uttering threats like that. But of course he won't be and will probably get benefits instead (16 January 2000).

Although Bakri *was* receiving benefits, the article only tangentially refers to this. This was not the case with a letter to the *Daily Mirror* on 27 August 1998, in which Bakri is described as 'nothing but a rich scrounger'. Clearly, some readers and reporters were aware of Bakri, although at this point he had not yet gained national notoriety in the press. This was set to change after 9/11.

Hate clerics and bombers: the tabloids find their villains

In the years following 9/11 the number of articles about specific Muslims who were described as receiving benefits increased notably, particularly after 2003. It might perhaps be expected that the surge in such articles would have been instantaneous, occurring from September 2001 onwards. However, the actual development was quite different: there were 121 articles in 2001 (the majority occurring in the final quarter of the year), then only twenty-three in 2002, while the first big peak came in 2003 (241 articles). A possible reason for this 'delayed' response could be that the newspapers had bigger fish to fry. In the immediate aftermath of 9/11, and the year following it, there was a huge media focus on the founder of al-Qaeda, the group that carried out the 9/11 attacks: Osama Bin Laden. He received 19,470 mentions in our corpus in 2001 and a further 5,525 in 2002. References to him decreased even more in 2003, to 3,489, and by 2009 they had slid to 1,092. In the immediate weeks after 9/11 some articles appeared optimistic that Bin Laden would soon be caught: 'We can find bin Laden in days, say guerillas' (*Daily Telegraph*, 3 October 2001). However, as the weeks and months passed, the discourse on finding Bin Laden became increasingly incredulous:

You may remember Tone's confident answer to the question: 'Will you catch Bin Laden?' – 'Yes...of that I have no doubt.' It then turned out – funny how information about this operation trickles out in dribs and drabs – that we could be facing an army of 10,000 Al Qaeda fanatics, maybe even double that number, prepared for a bitter guerilla war (*Daily Mail*, 21 March 2002).

Bin Laden evaded American forces until 2 May 2011, and therefore, during the years after 9/11, we would argue that some British newspapers began to turn their attention towards people who were more accessible and could be seen as having similar ideologies. Focusing on such people who were living in the United Kingdom therefore gave the British press a more tangible set of villains to focus on. At the beginning of this 'campaign', such villains tended to be either terrorists, terrorist plotters, Muslims linked to terrorist groups or Muslims who held politically extreme views. They were also often asylum seekers. 'Hate preachers' Abu Hamza and Omar Bakri were given prominent attention. Robin Richardson (2004: 66–7) reports how Hamza in particular represented a 'top attraction' for the British media: 'Here, just waiting for an unquestioning press, was a villain straight out of central casting. He has an eye patch, a hook replacing an amputated hand, a claimed association with Taliban training camps and a knack for issuing blood-curdling threats.'

EVIL hook-handed Muslim cleric Abu Hamza is using a legal trick to delay getting the boot from Britain for THREE years and rake in thousands more in hand-outs (*People*, 21 March 2004).

RANTING Muslim cleric Omar Bakri Mohammed pulled off another handouts coup by claiming disability benefit to get a £28,000 car, complete with satellite navigation system. Yet he walked into the showroom with barely a limp. Readers – some of them disabled but refused lesser benefits – are appalled (*Sun*, 16 May 2005).

Such articles quickly begin to make use of a formulaic discourse structure, which is demonstrated in the following three extracts:

THE mastermind behind the July 7 bombings raked in nearly £5,000 in sick leave pay while plotting the massacre which killed 52 innocent people. Mohammad Sidique Khan, 31, was signed off from his primary school teaching job as he planned Britain's worst terror atrocity. The benefits cheat even travelled to Pakistan while claiming up to £250-a-week in sick pay – effectively funding his double life as an Islamic extremist with council taxpayers' money (*Daily Express*, 1 February 2006).

A MUSLIM extremist who advocates indiscriminate terror bombing has just been given a £400,000 council home from which to launch atrocities on the British people. The three-storey London town house provides superbly comfortable living for Abtul Lakhouane, who draws £300 a week benefits for himself and his family of six. And the icing on the cake for the dangerous Moroccan fanatic is that, under the right-to-buy scheme, he is entitled to purchase it – as he fully intends to do – for the knockdown price of £89,000, giving him a potential £311,000 profit (*Daily Express*, 29 September 2002).

Hate on handouts... A FANATICAL preacher of hate has been recorded urging impressionable young British Muslims to go to WAR against our troops. Yet, sickeningly, crazed cleric Anjem Choudary and his wife rake in more than £25,000 a year in welfare BENEFITS – while he plots to destroy British society (*Sun*, 23 March 2008).

In these articles, first the subject is identified by referring to his extremist views or terrorist activities (*mastermind behind...bombings; Muslim extremist who advocates...terror bombing; fanatical preacher of hate*). Then the subject is described as having received specific amounts of money or other benefits as a result of British policies (*raked in nearly £5,000 in sick leave pay; has just been given a £400,000 council home; rake in more than £25,000 a year in welfare BENEFITS*). Some articles go into great detail, listing all the benefits and luxurious items that the subject has been entitled to, as in the following *Sun* article about Omar Bakri:

Bakri – who sponged £300,000 in benefits – has also spent more than £100,000 kitting out the four-bedroom apartment. It is in the exclusive Doha area of the Lebanese capital and overlooks the Mediterranean and a paradise beach fringed with palm trees. His neighbours include local sports and TV stars as well as the Egyptian Ambassador. The flat – which has two bathrooms and FOUR loos – is furnished with antiques from the Far East and has THREE widescreen TVs (*Sun*, 29 March 2006).

The use of verbs describing the process of receiving money is notable. As well as *raking in* money, there are a range of other metaphorical verb processes connected to receiving money. Such metaphors both emphasise the amount of money being received (*showered with benefits, cream in benefits, let them roll in*) and are suggestive that the recipients constitute a drain on society (*leech off, sponge*), are greedy (*pocket, milk the system*) or are illegal (*pull off a handouts coup*). While some verb processes appear to cast the recipients of benefits as having agency (e.g. when they *rake in* money or *milk* the system), other processes construct them more as passive beneficiaries of a 'soft' government (*showered* with benefits, *let* [benefits] *roll in*). Another aspect of many of these articles is in the description of the number of dependants who are attached to the main recipient (e.g. *dad of 7*, *father of 5*, *wife and 7 kids*). Such claimants are therefore also implied to be irresponsible, by having many children that the government or taxpayer must then care for.

Such recipients of benefits are also described in a variety of negative ways. For example, a list of adjectives ascribed to Abu Hamza includes *hook-handed*, *radical*, *evil*, *notorious*, *one-eyed*, *hate-filled* and *claw-handed*. He is also referred to with nominals, including *scum*, *hatemonger*, *extremist*, *militant*, *terrorist mastermind*, *prophet of poison*, *hate preacher* and *renegade*. In terms of actions, he is ascribed the following: *connived*, *conned*, *incited*, *infuriated*, *masterminded*, *taunted* and *trumpeted*. During his court case he 'gloated over the killing of 17 sailors in a suicide bomb attack' (*Sun*, 14 January 2006). After he has been imprisoned for seven years in a high-security prison he is described in the *Daily Mail* (12 October 2006) as 'laughing at us from Belmarsh' and 'laughing himself to sleep' due to his continuing prosperity.

However, as the years progress, and particularly after the 7/7 bombings, it appears that the criteria for being a newsworthy Muslim 'scrounger' begin to shift. Later examples focus on Muslims who are merely asylum seekers, or who have been involved in political protests that are potentially more 'peaceful'. For example, Mohammad Salim, an ex-teacher who runs a political party called Islam Zinda Badd (Long Live Islam), stood as an anti-war candidate in Rochdale and went on hunger strike as a protest at the publication of *The Satanic Verses*:

Unemployed scrounger Mohammad Salim is getting the state to pay for him, his wife and their ELEVEN kids – because he can't be bothered to go to work… And he has much more time to devote to his Islamic political party – which ATTACKS the British government, even though this country gives his family their food, clothes and house for free (*News of the World*, 10 February 2008).

Another article exposes a benefit fraudster:

LURKING behind this burkhah is Muslim grandmother Hansa Patel who swindled £30,000 in benefits – then dodged prison by pleading illness (*Daily Star*, 6 April 2005).

An article by the *Daily Express* in 2009 uses the example of Afghan single mother Toorakai Saiedi as a way of criticising the government's policy on Afghanistan:

THIS enfeebled language makes a mockery of Miliband's claim that we are fighting Islamic extremism. Indeed, the whole Afghan policy is riddled with contradictions and hypocrisies. So the courageous young men who are battling in Helmand Province are on basic pay of just £16,500 a year, yet Afghan single mother Toorakai Saiedi is given £170,000 a year in state benefits to live in a mansion in west London (29 July 2009).

Then, in 2006, the *Daily Mail* wrote an article on Shahbaz Chauhdry, a contestant on the reality television programme *Big Brother*:

After all, in real life, the misfit from Glasgow has never had a proper job, preferring to make a career out of indolence funded by dole handouts of £57.45 a week. At the ripe old age of 37, he can already look back on 21 glorious years of continuous unemployment (27 May 2006).

Clearly, by the latter half of the decade the 'scrounger' discourse has been expanded to refer not only to those deemed terrorists and hate preachers but, potentially, any Muslim who receives benefits.

The other villain

It is easy to identify Muslims as the targets of a 'scrounger' moral panic conducted by the tabloids during the 2000s. However, a closer look at some of the articles (particularly those written by right-leaning columnists) reveals that a further target can be identified: Britain's Labour government. While the 'scroungers' are sometimes constructed as actively claiming benefits, at other times, as noted above, they are represented as more passive recipients of benefits via verb processes such as *showered with benefits*.

[I]f Bin Laden was discovered living above a kebab shop in Finsbury Park, he'd be given indefinite leave to stay, showered with benefits and given access to the best 'yuman rites' lawyers taxpayers' money could buy (Richard Littlejohn, *Daily Mail*, 20 February).

The tabloids (particularly the *Daily Mail*, *The Sun* and the *Daily Express*) refer to Britain's welfare state in terms of it being too big (*belching, swollen, bloated, vast, enormous, expensive, over-stretched, sprawling, monster*), too kind (*cushy, generous, compliant, cosseting, lax*) and inefficient (*creaking, wasteful, uncontrolled, hopeless, abused*):

The people whose uncontrolled, bloated welfare state gives handouts to hate-merchants and leaves widows pleading for means-tested dole, claim to be the guardians of justice (Peter Hitchens, *Mail on Sunday*, 7 August 2005).

Thus, it is the government that is viewed as being responsible for creating an unfair system that can be exploited by certain Muslims who want to destroy Britain's way of life:

Hamza did so well from the social security system that he could afford private school fees for some of his children, as well as the purchase of a £220,000 house in north London, which he rented out to Poles. This kind of lunacy has come about directly as a result of Government policy for more than a decade (Leo McKinstry, *Daily Express*, 20 February 2008).

At other times, the government is represented as trying to 'do the right thing' but hampered by rules (such as the Court of Appeal or Human Rights legislation):

ONE of the world's most dangerous terror suspects could be back on our streets and claiming handouts after the Government yesterday lost a battle to kick him out. Evil cleric Abu Qatada, dubbed Al Qaeda's ambassador in Europe, won his human rights appeal against deportation back to Jordan (*Daily Express*, 10 April 2008).

In this article, about terror suspect Yasser al-Serri, the British government seem to be represented as being unduly obstructionist:

He is also thought to have helped in the recent murder of the Taliban's main opponent in Afghanistan. He draws thousands of pounds in British welfare benefits while the Government says there is not enough evidence against him (*Mail on Sunday*, 30 September 2001).

In other articles, it is not the government but local councils that are jointly targeted along with the 'scroungers'. For example, in the following article, a 'scrounger' who was found guilty of conspiracy to murder is linked to another story about councils that are responsible for placing children in danger. In 2009 the British media focused on the social services of Haringey Council, which was seen as indirectly responsible for the death of 'Baby P' – a seventeen-month-old boy who died after suffering more than fifty injuries from his mother's boyfriend, despite the fact that the child had been repeatedly seen by Haringey's children's services and health professionals:

BUNGLING Baby P social services bosses sent a foster child to live with the terrorist leader behind the airline liquid bomb plot. Muslim fanatic Abdulla Ahmed Ali, 28, was amazingly approved as a carer by Haringey Council, North London, despite being under police surveillance. Dole-scrounging Ali was approved as a foster carer despite a poor employment record and being a known Taliban supporter (*Daily Star*, 12 September 2009).

Articles about 'Muslim scroungers' therefore also have a secondary function, allowing newspapers that do not support the Labour government to portray it as at best impotent at resolving the problem, at worst enabling it. This helps to explain why the majority of references to Muslims on benefits occur in right-leaning newspapers.

Fanatics versus maniacs

In Chapter 1 we described how the use of columnists enables newspapers to print opinions that are perhaps more extreme or controversial than those in articles or editorials. Petley (2006) and Robin Richardson (2004) have described how the Press Complaints Commission generally does not uphold reader complaints that are made about columnists, as they are described as simply giving their personal views or 'robust opinions'. Thus it could be argued that the deployment of columnists could be one way in which more negative constructions of Muslims are legitimated by certain newspapers.

However, using named columnists is not the only legitimation strategy that newspapers use in order to publish more controversial representations of Muslims. Another way is to print letters written by members of the public, which often appear the day after the original article. On 18 January 2005 the *Daily Express* published several articles about Omar Bakri, including an editorial entitled 'THIS EVIL SCROUNGER MUST BE DEPORTED – RIGHT NOW'. The following day a letter in the same newspaper said: 'After a lifetime working and paying taxes, my wife and I have a joint income less than half the amount this scrounging parasite receives each week.' In this case, the letter simply repeats the sentiment in the original article (with an additional label – *parasite*). However, in other cases, letters can represent a more simplified version of a story. For example, a few months later the *Daily Express* published the following:

DAVID Blunkett has ordered a benefits blitz on Islamic hate clerics who sponge off the state (17 August 2005).

The following day, a member of the public referred to this story in a letter:

SO, David Blunkett is to have a blitz on Muslim clerics who sponge off the state ('Benefits blitz on the hate preachers', August 17) (18 August 2005).

It is interesting here how the original article referred to 'Islamic hate clerics', while the letter writer (or the person who edited the letter) reworded this as 'Muslim clerics'. This may seem like a small or unimportant alteration, but it could be argued that it has several effects. First, the replacement of *Islamic* (a word that connotes the religion) to *Muslim* (a word that connotes the person who practises the religion) serves to personalise the story and potentially contributes to a negative prosody of the word *Muslim*. Additionally, the change from 'hate clerics' to 'clerics' is a generalising strategy. No longer is a specific set of 'hate clerics' the problem; we are now prompted to think in terms of just 'clerics'. To be fair, the term 'hate preachers' occurs in the following line, but here the implication is that terms such as 'hate preachers', 'Islamic hate clerics' and 'Muslim clerics' are all somehow interchangeable and equivalent. A similar letter in the same newspaper the following month asks: 'Now have the clerics scrounging benefits in the UK been thrown out?' (8 September 2005).

The *Daily Star* also uses opinions from members of the public, which are elicited through encouraging readers to send text messages. A selection of these are then published in a regular column called Text maniacs (a pun on the term 'sex maniacs'). As with the *Daily Express*, there is some evidence that opinions in this column are extending the ideas of a small number of people, who voice very abhorrent views, to a wider set of people. For example, on 6 August 6 2005 the *Star* ran the headline 'BLAIR: I'LL THROW OUT THE MUSLIMS WHO PREACH HATE; PM WARNS FANATICS OF NEW LAWS ON WAY'. Two days later a text maniac wrote: 'WELL DONE TONY BLAIR NOW DELIVER THE GOODS CLERICS PANICKING ALREADY COS NO MORE HANDOUTS' (8 August 2005). Again, the generalising term *clerics* is used. On 18 September 2008 another text maniac wrote: 'The credit crunch could be a blessing in disguise. All the poles and muslim scroungers will go home if theres no money left to give out!' Here, the scroungers are not represented as a small number of clerics who preach hatred, or even clerics as a class, but as 'muslim'. It could be argued that letters, and, in particular, text messages, are effective vehicles for the spread of generalising negative discourses, because the need for brevity means that they do not encourage nuanced description or discussion.

Widening the focus

Stories about such 'scroungers' peaked in 2005, although in the following years they remained more popular than they had been before this point. From 2006 there was a new focus, which was concerned with male Muslims having multiple wives and claiming benefits for all of them, particularly having brought such wives from overseas. This was of particular concern to the *Daily Mail*, which had the most stories about Muslim polygamists:

Now husbands can get benefits for every wife... THE right of men to claim welfare benefits for each of their multiple wives has been endorsed by the Government. The decision by the Department for Work and Pensions (DWP) means that each of the estimated 1,000 polygamous partnerships in Britain, mainly Muslims, is now recognised formally by the state but only if the weddings took place in countries where the arrangement is legal (3 February 2008).

Estimates about the numbers of polygamous marriages tend to differ. In the above article the estimate is 1,000 such marriages, although *The Sun* quotes a source who says that it may be more: '[A]ccording to the leader of the Muslim Parliament of Great Britain, thousands of men are taking two, three, even five wives' (30 May 2007).

In March 2006 the *Daily Star* ran a series of articles about 'four Muslim immigrants' who had attempted to claim money to have their deceased spouses buried in their 'countries of origin'. Their claims had been rejected by the DWP and they had lost their appeal. In an editorial entitled 'Taking us for a ride', the *Daily Star* made extensive use of inclusive (*us*, *we*) and exclusive (*they*, *you*) pronouns to create a division between every Briton and the 'four Muslim immigrants':

[W]e showered houses and benefits on those who made it to our shores, legally or otherwise. But while we may be a soft touch, we are not so soft in the head as to allow the claim by four Muslim immigrants that we pay for them to transport their spouses' bodies back to their home countries for burial. An appeal court judge had to tell them in legal language what every Briton would have told them in far more basic words: You must be joking (24 March 2006).

The *Star* also ran a telephone poll about the story, asking readers to vote about whether the outcome had been fair. The following day, they reported: 'A WHOPPING 98% of Daily Star readers say Muslims should not get handouts to bury their dead overseas' (25 March 2006). These two stories, on polygamists and burying the dead, suggest that the 'scrounger' discourse was robust, not simply connected to terrorists or 'hate preachers' but part of an ongoing campaign to represent Muslims negatively.

So far, the majority of quoted articles have been from tabloid newspapers. This is because it is these papers that published most of the stories and helped to propagate the idea of Muslims claiming benefits as newsworthy. Although there is a smaller amount of data to examine in the broadsheets, it is also worth looking at how they tackle the same subject.

The broadsheets: reporting the reporters

The average broadsheet reader would have been very unlikely to have encountered articles about Muslims on benefits. There are only 100 non-ironic or uncritical mentions of the search term in the broadsheets, of which most appear in the more right-leaning *Telegraph* and *Times*, compared to over 1,800 such mentions in the tabloids.

On the rare occasions when the left-leaning broadsheets refer to Muslims on benefits, it often involves intertextuality: references to reports from other newspapers. For example, *The Observer*'s football column sometimes reports on racist chanting at matches. As part of such articles, it occasionally reprints messages from the *Daily Star*'s 'Text maniacs' columns. On 2 November 2008, in a column entitled 'RACISM LATEST: BAK IN STONEAGE', *The Observer* printed several *Star* reader texts about Muslims, with no other commentary. This included the text: 'All the poles and muslim scroungers will go home if theres recession.' Then, on 7 December 2008, in another football column entitled 'DO U FEEL PROUD?', *The Observer* published another *Star* text message: 'where in Quran does it say jihadists should scrounge 25k a year of benefits?'

The Guardian also comments on tabloid discourses of Muslims on benefits, perhaps less directly than *The Observer*'s explicit labelling of this discourse as racist. In the following article a columnist discusses Abu Qatada in a humorous tone (painting an image of him being made to use cheap toilet paper). However, the money given to Qatada is downplayed, then contrasted with an expensive anti-missile defence system called 'Son of Star Wars':

Of course it's a nuisance that Qatada is on benefits, and I'd have preferred to see him limit himself to off-brand loo paper. But if you want to talk about depressingly misdirected public funds, you'll find rather more has been lavished on things like son of star wars than on keeping this troublemaker in a rented semi (Marina Hyde, 12 July 2008).

The left-leaning broadsheets, therefore, when they do write of the most notorious Muslims on benefits, tend to engage in meta-reporting. Of Abu Hamza, *The Guardian* writes:

That he claimed more than £1,000 a week in benefits for himself and his family at his modest home in Ealing, west London, further angered his opponents in the media (8 February 2006).

Then, in 2000, *The Guardian* is explicit in naming the *Daily Mail* as combining discourses of terrorism, scrounging and Islamic fundamentalism:

Hijacking this aircraft was a desperate act by desperate men who would appear to have had good reason to fear for the safety of themselves and their families. This does not excuse the hijacking – but it does put the media hysteria into context, where the hijackers are simultaneously portrayed as Islamic fundamentalists, international terrorists and dole scroungers – a *Daily Mail* leader writer's dream (Nick Hardwick, 11 February 2000).

In contrast to the tabloid reporting of Abu Hamza as a gloating villain and laughing himself to sleep thinking of his money, *The Observer* paints a more nuanced picture of an unhappy yet ungrateful Hamza:

Hamza certainly isn't happy here. The prevalence of sex and nudity in Soho and elsewhere has convinced him that the British 'live in obscenity'. The state benefits he has received for years have failed to ignite a spark of gratitude (30 March 2003).

There is no love lost between the left-leaning broadsheets and the right-leaning tabloids. In the following article, written just after 9/11, Richard Littlejohn in *The Sun* accuses *Guardian* readers (mockingly referred to as *Guardianistas*) of turning London into one of the 'terrorist capitals of the world', as well as suggesting that such people would give benefits to Bin Laden:

The Guardian is the bible of the people who run the country, day in, day out... They are often described as 'dogooders'. They are not. They are bad bastards. This country has been hijacked as ruthlessly and comprehensively as any airliner. It is the Guardianistas who have turned London into one of the terrorist capitals of the world, who have perverted the notion of 'human rights' while lining their pockets out of the legal aid budget... [I]f bin Laden pitched up in Haringey tomorrow there'd be plenty of apologists and left-wing lawyers queuing up to support his right to live here on benefits (22 September 2001).

The right-leaning broadsheets use more restrained language than the tabloids, and at times paint a complex picture, which simultaneously appears to be sympathetic towards Muslims in poverty, characterising them as being vulnerable to being recruited into terrorism, yet at the same time criticising the Labour government's welfare policy as actually damaging Muslims rather than helping them:

The New Labour slums of welfare dependency are more likely to trap British Muslims (overwhelmingly of Pakistani and Bangladeshi origin) than any other strata of British society, including that of British Indians, who are mainly Sikh and Hindu. Only 10% of Anglo-Indian households are workless, a far healthier figure than the 15% for indigenous whites. But more than 30% of British Muslims of Pakistani origins are workless; over 30% of working-age Muslims have no qualifications, twice the national average; and Muslims are least likely to own their own homes of any British ethnic group. To be workless is an option in Britain, in a way it is not in America; and the problem of welfare-dependency – a problem made very much worse by the Labour government – is particularly acute amongst Muslims. Still not sure what this has to do with the terrorist attacks? Then consider the case, among others, of Yasin Hassan Omar, the 24-year-old would be suicide bomber (*The Business*, 1 August 2005).

In 2001 *The Daily Telegraph* reported in passing on Abu Qatada as receiving benefits:

INVESTIGATORS discovered £180,000 in a London bank account held by a radical Muslim cleric accused of fomenting and financing terrorism. Sheikh Abu Qatada, who lives on benefits in Acton, west London, had his assets frozen at the weekend after appearing on a Treasury list of people suspected of 'committing or providing material support for acts of terrorism' (18 October 2001).

However, as the decade progressed, *The Daily Telegraph*'s reporting style became more similar to the tabloids, referencing 'the taxpayer', and giving a more detailed description of how much money Qatada receives in benefits, suggesting that it has been 'led' by the tabloid discourse:

The taxpayer will also fund at least £12,000 per year in benefits for Qatada, his wife and five children, even though Qatada was once found to be carrying £170,000 in cash when he was stopped by police (18 June 2008).

The Telegraph is also opposed to people in polygamous marriages receiving benefits, as with other newspapers, using this as an example to be critical of the government. However, an argument about women's rights is used, rather than focusing on other aspects of the story, such as the cost of the benefits, which tends to be more of a tabloid concern:

[The Government has just taken the dismally retrograde step of recognising polygamy: men with more than one wife will be able to claim benefits for each additional spouse. How this can be squared with the Government's rhetoric of commitment to women's rights is beyond us: it is a quite clear incitement to the humiliating and blatantly unjust practice of allowing men, but only men, to take more than one spouse (*Sunday Telegraph*, 3 February 2008).

Similarly, just as left-leaning broadsheet writers are critical of the right-leaning tabloids, *The Daily Telegraph* is disparaging of 'liberal columnists' in this article:

According to the Office of National Statistics, 35 per cent of Muslim households have no adult in employment, more than twice the national average, though no liberal columnist would dream of ever writing about 'Muslim scroungers' (15 November 2006).

This is one of only two direct references to *Muslim scroungers* in the entire corpus (the other being the 'Text maniacs' described above). It is perhaps odd, then, to single out liberal columnists (as no columnists use the term, even those in right-leaning tabloids). *The Daily Telegraph* has used scare quotes around the term, although one reading of this article is that the hypothetical situation that is set up and the scare quotes are a way of justifying the inclusion of a term that otherwise would be unacceptable.

Conclusion

In the process of carrying out the analysis, a number of issues were raised. One is to do with news values. Clearly, the tabloids and broadsheets have a very different perspective on whether stories about Muslims who claim benefits count as 'news'. This perspective is also subject to each newspaper's own political perspective. So, at one extreme is a right-leaning tabloid such as the *Daily Express* (634 references), and at the other is a left-leaning broadsheet such as *The Independent* (no references). Depending on one's own perspective, it could be argued that the *Daily Express* over-focuses on such stories, or that *The Independent* is ignoring a newsworthy issue completely. Political perspectives apart, another reason for the varying focus across different newspapers in the corpus could be linked to the correlation between the socio-economic profile of broadsheet and tabloid readers (see Figure 3.2) and the frequency of reporting of Muslims on benefits. Poorer readers may be a more receptive audience regarding stories about who should or should not receive government support.

Another issue concerns the way that such stories are reported. Articles that report that a particular Muslim is receiving benefits can either do so 'in passing', as a way of providing some descriptive information about the person who is the subject of a story, or they can choose to make the benefits the focus of the story – which is regularly the case in the right-leaning tabloids. It could be argued that both types of references play a role in furthering negative representation. The detailed stories clearly spell out the negative representation, while the 'in passing' references implicitly present 'scrounging Muslims' as a form of common knowledge that needs no elaboration.

Additionally, the way that the benefits are represented is of importance. A term such as 'receiving welfare' is perhaps more objective than 'scrounging benefits'. There is a quantitative and qualitative correlation here: the more a newspaper tends to refer to the topic, the more likely it would be to report it in more negative ways and do so in a manner that foregrounds the benefits as the key part of the story (*The Sun* and the *Daily Star* use the term *scrounger(s)* the most). A noun such as *scrounger* is purposefully disrespectful and implies that some people are undeserving of benefits (and that *scrounger* is the whole sum of their identity). Regardless of whether they are deserving, it is potentially dangerous to allow such decisions to be made by newspapers and their readers. The use of the word legitimates decisions about who is 'deserving' or not to be made by anybody about anybody. Reports on 'scroungers' are certainly not restricted to Muslims in the right-leaning newspapers, and such stories appear to be explicitly attacking Britain's welfare system, which is seen as too soft – so the 'scrounger' stories are not just about Muslims. It is interesting how some newspapers regularly combine the two topics, resulting in a cumulative effect that helps to create an association between one stigmatised group and another.

Leading on from this is a further concern about the extent to which such stories can become generalised to refer to a wider class of people. It could be argued that stories about a single Muslim such as Abu Hamza cannot be extended beyond him. However, if readers regularly encounter such stories and do not meet, read or hear about Muslims in other contexts, then it is not unlikely that the qualities that Hamza is characterised as possessing will promote stereotyping, as he may come to typify Muslims for such readers. A question that thus arises is this: to what extent do the main proponents of these stories – the *Daily Express*, the *Daily Mail* and *The Sun* – report about Muslims in other capacities? Do these newspapers attempt to achieve a more balanced representation by including other stories that portray Muslims as hard-working, or giving rather than taking? For example, one of the 'five pillars' of Sunni Islam (duties that are incumbent on all Muslims) is to give alms to the poor. The word *alms* occurs 111 times in the corpus, of which eighteen instances appear in the three newspapers above. However, none of these cases actually refer to Muslims giving alms to the poor. Instead, they refer to other religions such as Catholicism, or to Muslims *begging* for alms, or using alms in order to support terrorism. As shown in Chapter 2, the most frequent context in which Muslims are written about in the British press is to do with conflict. British newspapers, in particular the right-leaning tabloids, have many more stories about Muslims on benefits than they do about Muslims who are characterised as hard-working or charitable.

There are attempts made by some newspapers to distance the 'scroungers' from the majority of Muslims. This is sometimes achieved by quoting from other Muslims:

Yesterday Muslim leaders described Bakri as an 'utterly repellent' fringe extremist who represented 'an Islamic version of the British National Party'. Inayat Bunglawala, a spokesman for the Muslim Council of Britain, said: 'Omar Bakri and his outbursts are pure poison and are despised by the vast majority of British Muslims' (*Daily Express*, 18 January 2005).

The following day a letter on the same subject opines: 'This man is not a religious person and is in no way typical of the Muslim faith' (19 January 2005). Such cases perhaps help to restrict the danger of generalising, although in other cases there seems to be evidence that readers of the newspapers are already making generalisations from the evidence in their letters and texts to the newspapers (e.g. by replacing a term such as *Islamic hate clerics* with *Muslim clerics* or *clerics*, or using a term such as *Muslim scroungers*).

We should perhaps end by repeating the purposefully ambiguous question that was included in the title of this chapter: who benefits? While the newspapers have answered this question by arguing that it is Muslims who are benefiting (often unfairly), we would suggest that the true beneficiaries of these stories are newspaper editors and their readers, who are presented with an opportunity to voice hatred in a way that appears to be 'legitimate' while potentially being harmful to all Muslims.

8 Burqas and brainwashing: Muslims and gender

Introduction

This chapter examines how the British press writes about gender in relation to Islam. In particular, we focus on two very common constructions of Muslims that are gender-specific: the veil-wearing Muslim woman and the Muslim man at risk of radicalisation. First we explore an ongoing debate about whether British Muslim women should wear veils, which reached a peak in 2006, shortly after the then leader of the House of Commons, Jack Straw, published an article on the topic in a local UK newspaper. We examine linguistic patterns around Muslim women who veil. Is veiling presented more often as a demand, an imposition, a right or a choice? Are certain types of veils viewed as more acceptable than others, and, indeed, do newspapers always make such distinctions? Additionally, what sort of arguments do newspapers utilise in this debate, and how are Muslim women (de)personalised via a range of negative metaphors? Second, we examine the term *radicalisation*, which was found to refer mainly to Muslim men. We ask: which sort of men are seen to be at risk and what sort of places are viewed as dangerous? Finally, we look at the range of reasons that different newspapers posit for radicalisation, and how such reasons help to further the political stances of individual newspapers.

Why is it worth spending a chapter to focus on separate constructions of men and women? As shown in Chapter 4, two very frequent modifiers of *Muslim* are *women* and *men* (see Table 4.9). *Women* is a consistent right-hand collocate of *Muslim*, always appearing as a top ten collocate for every year of the corpus (3,325 occurrences in total), while *men* is in the top ten for eight out of twelve years (1,835 occurrences). Gender is one of the foremost ways in which people conceive identity, and many societies tend to place a great deal of emphasis on gender-appropriate ways of behaving, working, thinking, speaking and dressing. Clearly, gender distinctions appear to be important in our Islam corpus, although it is interesting that Muslim women are referred to almost twice as often as Muslim men. We have noted elsewhere that a study of newspaper visuals by Moore, Mason and Lewis (2008) found that Muslim men were actually far more visible than Muslim women. It is interesting, then, that there are more *pictures* of Muslim men but more *references* to Muslim women in the British press. This could possibly be due to an assumption that the default Muslim (or person) is male, so is not normally gender-marked in writing.

Alternatively, it could be due to a particular type of focus on female Muslims in the British press. Certainly, other researchers have noticed and analysed the media's preoccupation with Muslim women. For example, Kabbani (1994: ix) discusses how she was interviewed by the magazine *Vanity Fair* for an article about Islam, and was disappointed that the article 'ignored any of the important debate within Islam about the rights of women. It distorted every sentence I had uttered.' Kabbani concludes that 'the whole Western debate about Muslim women is a dishonest one'. Al-Hejin (2009) carried out a corpus analysis of articles from the BBC News website between 1997 and 2007 that focused on Muslim women, concluding that the articles tended to focus on dress (different types of covering) or restrictions of women's rights. Byng (2010) examined seventy-two stories about veiling in France, the United Kingdom and the United States in *The New York Times* and *Washington Post* between 2004 and 2006. She found that the two US newspapers positioned the three countries as ideologically alike in spite of their different framings of religious freedom. The reporting tended to support Western values and constructed a common-sense view that Muslim women would not veil in public.

Therefore, due to the high frequency of *Muslim women* and *Muslim men* in the corpus, as well as indications from other studies that Muslim women in particular tend to be written about in restricted ways, we decided to carry out more detailed examinations of these two terms, in order to identify the most common contexts in which gender and Islam were written about, and the accompanying discourses that were articulated.

We first decided to examine the frequencies with which the two terms occurred over time (see Figure 8.1). A number of points can be made about this figure. First, a very large peak for *Muslim women* is noticeable in 2006. Additionally, it should be noted that, for most years, there are more references to *Muslim women* than *Muslim men*, although this pattern is reversed in 2002.

Why was 2006 such a marked year for articles about Muslim women? The most frequent lexical collocates of *Muslim women* in 2006 articles are *veil*, *veils*, *wear*, *wearing*, *remove*, *Straw*, *Jack*, *right* and *faces*. Further examination of these collocates in context reveals that they were concerned with a single, politically salient story. On 5 October 2006 the leader of the House of Commons, Jack Straw, wrote in his local newspaper, the *Lancashire Evening Telegraph*, that Muslim women should abandon wearing the veil,

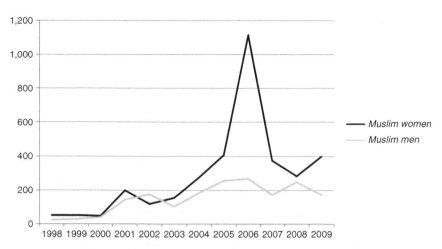

Figure 8.1 Frequencies of *Muslim women* and *Muslim men* over time, 1998–2009

as a way of breaking down barriers between communities. He argued that the full veil was a 'visible statement of separation and difference'. This article resulted in a media debate about Muslim women and the veil in the latter months of 2006, with quotes from Straw's article being repeated dozens of times.

We may also ask why the term *Muslim men* constitutes a more popular subject than *Muslim women* in 2002. It was hypothesised that this could be a result of the '9/11 effect', which had been demonstrated in other analyses of the corpus; for example, 9/11 resulted in increased numbers of stories about Muslims in its immediate aftermath. Perhaps because the people involved in planning and executing the 9/11 terror attacks were men, we would see articles referring to the terrorists as Muslim men, or there would be articles warning that Muslim men were in danger of being radicalised. There are a small number of articles along these lines:

A GANG of terrorists with links to al-Qaeda plotted to launch a devastating cyanide gas attack on the London Underground which could have have[1] killed thousands of people. Anti-Terrorist Branch officers from Scotland Yard arrested the six Muslim men after a six-month operation by MI5 (*Daily Mirror*, 17 November 2002).

However, it soon became clear to me that issues such as institutional Islamophobia directly leading to the social exclusion of the Muslim community and the criminalisation of young Muslim men were not issues that we were going into (*Guardian*, 'Letters', 5 July 2002).

---

[1] The repetition of 'have' is in the original document obtained from Nexis UK.

However, the most frequent lexical collocates of *Muslim men* in 2002 are *boys*, *7,000*, *Bosnian*, *young*, *women*, *massacre*, *8,000*, *Srebrenica*, *massacred* and *1995*. These collocates are used in stories that referred to the mass murder of several thousand[2] Bosnian Muslim men and boys in Srebrenica in July 1995 by Serb forces. A report, published in April 2002, blamed the Netherlands government, its army and the United Nations for the massacre, which helps to explain why references to Muslim men overtake references to Muslim women in that year.

Nevertheless, the highest number of references to *Muslim men* occurs in 2006. Can this perhaps be attributed to concerns about the potential criminality of Muslim men after the 7/7 attacks on London transport in 2005? At a first glance, some of the most frequent collocates are similar to 2002: *young*, *boys*, *women*, *8,000*, *Srebrenica*, *British*, *massacre*, *Bosnian*. However, a closer look at the 2005 collocates tells a different story from 2002. The most frequent collocate *young* (ninety occurrences) mainly refers to fears about radicalisation, which was not the case when this collocate was examined in 2002. Some articles argue that the police should use 'profiling' to examine young Muslim men more carefully in airports or other situations:

There isn't much point in pulling out middle-aged dads with their kids going to watch a match abroad. Common sense will tell you that traditionally it is olive-skinned young Muslim men who have been involved in terrorist activities (*Sun*, 16 August 2006).

In an article on 4 July 2006, called '20 unanswered questions', the *Daily Mirror* asks, 'How many young Muslim men are flirting with extremist ideology, and what is it that is radicalising them?', and in August the same newspaper notes, '[W]hile there can never be excuses offered for mass murder, those angry young Muslim men who feel strangers in their own land have a point. This country has been shamed by a Prime Minister who has sucked up to America to a degree where we no longer have an independent foreign policy.'

The word *British*, which collocates seventeen times with *Muslim men* in 2006, is also suggestive of concerns about 'radicalisation' and terrorism, referring directly to the 7/7 attacks:

Ahmed was also linked to Lashkar-i-Taiba and had been in contact with three British Muslim men arrested in London on terrorism charges in November 2005 (*Observer*, 13 August 2006).

The war in Iraq has become a 'convenient excuse' for a generation of young British Muslim men to take part in a violent jihad, the Government's independent reviewer of terrorism laws has warned (*Independent*, 13 November 2006).

---

[2] Reports in the newspapers range from 6,500 to 8,000.

Comparatively, the references to the Bosnian massacre are less frequent. Therefore, it seems that the British press became interested in the radicalisation of Muslim men (particularly those who were young and British) after the London transport bombings in 2005, but not after 9/11.

Notably, 2006 is when stories about Muslim women also peak, although they do not tend to be written about as potential terrorists. As noted, the key story here is about Muslim women veiling in public, and was triggered by Jack Straw's article. Straw's article does not refer to the 7/7 attacks of 2005, but it could be argued that the attacks, or the national mood towards Islam in the following months, could have contributed towards Straw's mindset, as well as towards the way that the media heavily debated his article. Veiling in itself could therefore be viewed as a more 'passive' form of radicalisation for Muslim women, whereas Muslim men are viewed as more 'active' threats – that is, as potential terrorists.

Comparing collocates

Having briefly examined change in frequency over time, we move on to consider differences between the ways that Muslim men and Muslim women are represented. To do this, we first obtained lexical collocates of both terms using a span of five words either side of the search term. To limit the number of collocates examined, we considered only those that occur ten times or more. Collocates were then grouped together, on the basis of terms that seemed to reference the same semantic category (see Tables 8.1 and 8.2).

The two tables are suggestive of some of the main differences surrounding the representation of Muslim men and women. Both terms also have some similar categories: identity words, reporting and feeling, and locations. This would probably be expected; on account of the fact that the genre we are examining is newspaper discourse, it would be unusual not to find words such as *said, saying, told* and *feel*. Additionally, some of the location words overlap, and also reference the country of origin of the newspapers (*London, British, Britain, Western, Europe, English*). Other location words reference the Srebrenica massacre (*Srebrenica, Bosnia, Bosnian, Serb*), which as we have already seen was a frequently mentioned story, particularly in 2002. However, there are also some differences in the sets of collocates of *Muslim men* and *Muslim women*. Three related categories for *Muslim men* are law and order, radicalisation and terrorism, and killing. While some of the collocates in these categories refer again to the Bosnian massacre, many of them relate to concerns about the radicalisation of young British Muslim men. On the other hand, three closely related categories of collocates for *Muslim women* are: the veil, freedom and oppression. These two sets of topics for men and women were the same ones identified when looking at the context of *Muslim*

Table 8.1 Frequent (ten or higher) collocates of Muslim men

Category	Collocates
Identity words (age, gender and relationships)	*young, boys, women, children, wives, whore, dating*
Locations	*Srebrenica, Bosnian, British, Britain, Serb, Serbs, Iraq, London, Asian, town*
Killing	*massacre, killed, massacred, slaughter, murder, murdered, slaughtered, died, war, killing, suicide, bombers*
Reporting and feeling	*said, say, believed, feel, says, told*
Law and order	*arrested, accused, executed, innocent, alleged, trial, law*
Radicalisation/terrorism	*impressionable, disaffected, radicalised, radicalisation, training, terror, radical, Abu*
Other	*white, allowed, disgraceful, angry, born, beards, forces, gathered, way, dignity, see, get*

Table 8.2 Frequent (ten or higher) collocates of Muslim women

Category	Collocates
The veil	*wear, veils, veil, wearing, remove, worn, hijab, full, Straw, cover, Jack, niqab, faces, face, headscarves, veiled, Straw's, dress, covering, head, headscarf, traditional, burkas, burka, wore, dressed, covered, veiling, burqa, burkha*
Identity words (age, gender and relationships)	*young, men, children, women, people, girls, old, generation, husbands, marry*
Reporting and feeling	*said, saying, feel, asked, call, told, asking, comments, say, ask, talk, revealed, believe, suggested, called, calling, urged, prefer, hope, know, wants, claimed, speak, question, warned, understand*
Locations	*British, Britain, country, world, London, English, Western, Bosnian, constituency, society, Blackburn, France, Europe, street, Serb, town, French, Arab, community*
Freedom	*rights, allowed, forced, ban, issue, choose, debate, power, support, help, free, allow, row, required, banned, encourage, campaign, choice, freedom*
Oppression	*rape, abuse, attacks, oppressed, oppression, raping, raped, fear, honour, fearful, attacked, bodies, abused, killed, spat, torture*
Law and order	*law, police, courts, laws, accused*
Religion	*Islamic, religious, sharia, devout, Mosques, extremists*
Other	*get, go, stop, way, role, work, educated, given, lives, living, growing, release, separation, give, good, fact, consequences, make, held, life, working, film, live*

men and *Muslim women* in the most frequent years that these two terms appear in. Is it the case, then, that the collocates examined here have been skewed by two stories (veiling and fears of the radicalisation of Muslim men) that seem to have been covered in a relatively brief time period? In order to investigate this, we carried out searches on two relatively frequent 'gendered' terms: *veil* and *radicalisation*.

There are 9,681 references to the word *veil* in the corpus in total. Of these, 4,488 (46 per cent) occur in 2006. For the other years in the corpus there are between 153 and 1,212 references to the veil, so, while 2006 is clearly the key year that veiling was mentioned (due to Jack Straw's involvement in the issue), it is also a relatively popular story in other years. *Radicalisation* is less frequent in total (occurring 1,038 times). However, 956 of these occurrences (92 per cent) occur in 2005 or later. Linking this to the earlier examination of *Muslim men* in 2006, the high frequency after 2005 seems to be further evidence of the 7/7 bombings resulting in a concern about the radicalisation of Muslim men. In the following sections, we focus more closely on examining how the British press represented these two gendered issues: the veil and the radicalisation of Muslim men.

The veil

The veil is the most frequent topic that is directly associated with Muslim women. The top ten lexical collocates of the term *Muslim women* are *wear* (284 occurrences), *veils* (243), *veil* (234), *wearing* (216), *young* (118), *remove* (108), *worn* (seventy-three), *hijab* (seventy-two), *full* (seventy) and *cover* (sixty). In this section we approach an analysis of the veil from a number of perspectives. These include looking at whether veiling is represented as a choice or as something that is forced upon Muslim women, differences between the ways that various garments are described, the arguments given as to why Muslim women should not veil and the range of dysphemistic (intentionally harsh) references that are used to denigrate the veil and other garments associated with Muslim women.

It should be noted that the term *veil* was used in the newspaper corpus in a range of different ways. There are references in the corpus to *the full veil*, *the full-body veil* and *the face-covering veil*, or to the veil covering the *face, head, everything* or *all but the eyes*. Additionally, there are cases that describe people as wearing a *veil over the head* (but possibly not over the face). This suggests that veiling can be an ambiguous concept, which may be interpreted differently, particularly if a reference to veiling is not explicit about what is actually being covered.

Moreover, sometimes there is confusion over the relationship between the veil and other garments such as the *hijab* (head/hair covering), *niqab* (face covering), *jilbab* (body covering apart from hands, face and head) and *burqa* (whole body covering, usually comprising jilbab and hijab). This is the case when these terms are used in the same sentence. For example, *The Guardian* (22 March 2007) writes that 'headteachers are to be given the right to ban Muslim girls from wearing the niqab or veil in school'. It is unclear from the wording here whether *niqab* and *veil* are viewed as equivalent, or whether they are seen as different from each other. An article in *The Times* (28 May 1998) translates the full-body burqa as a veil: 'A film called *Bombay* drew fire for not using the city's local name, Mumbai, and for showing a Hindu boy flirting with a girl in a burqa (veil).' Meanwhile, in the *Daily Mirror* (7 February 2005), the hijab (which covers only the hair) is similarly described as a veil in an article that translates a speech by Abu Hamza: 'And women sin when they wear make-up outside the house and "tight trousers with a hijab (veil)".' Clearly, in the British press, *veil* can refer to different types of clothing worn by Muslim women.

As a result of the indeterminate meaning of the word *veil*, it can have the effect of conflating different types of clothing together, making them appear potentially equivalent to each other. For example, when columnist Jon Gaunt (*Sun*, 12 December 2006) asks of Tony Blair 'When is he actually going to discover a backbone and openly ban the veil in public life?', some readers may take this to mean that Gaunt disapproves of the burqa while others may think he disapproves of the niqab or the hijab, or all three.

A choice or an imposition?

Examining concordance lines containing the terms *Muslim women* and *veil*, it was noticed that one way that newspapers represent the veil has to do with the extent to which it is characterised as a choice. Some concordance lines contain phrases such as 'Muslim women who choose to wear the veil', whereas others use verbs such as *forced*, *compelled*, *obliged* or *required*, or modal verbs that imply that the veil is imposed on them, such as 'must wear the veil'. Another set of verbs interprets the position of Muslim women differently again, constructing them as *insisting* or *demanding* to wear the veil. With such women, the concept of choice is indexed, although here the women are constructed more negatively, and as politically militant. A fourth category of representation involves the veil being described as a *right*, as in 'the right of Muslim women to wear the veil'.

In order to examine the extent to which these four strategies occur across the whole corpus, as well as to see whether certain newspapers use certain representations more than others, a concordance of *Muslim women* was examined. This resulted in 3,325 concordance lines. Each line was examined in order to determine whether the Muslim women are characterised as (a) choosing to wear the veil, (b) being forced to wear the veil, (c) demanding to wear the veil or (d) having the 'right' to wear the veil. Not only did we consider the word *veil*, we also included all terms that involve any sort of religious covering worn by Muslim women. This includes *hijab, niqab, jilbab, headscarf* and *scarf*, as well as related words such as *garment* or dysphemisms such as 'swathes of black cloth' (differences between these terms are considered in more detail in the following section). Sometimes writers use phrases such as 'Muslim women who choose to wear the veil' in order to argue that such women do not really exist. Such cases were noted, but they were not counted as examples of a newspaper using 'choose to wear the veil'.

However, a potential limitation of analysing these concordance lines was that it revealed only cases that refer to *Muslim women*. There are potentially many more cases in which the veil can be represented as a choice, a right, a demand or an imposition, which may involve other terms such as *a woman*, *girls* or the names of individual people. It was thus decided to supplement the analysis by taking a different approach. This approach involved carrying out concordance analyses of the following phrases:

CHOOSE to WEAR the
FORCE to WEAR the
OBLIGE to WEAR the
COMPEL to WEAR the
REQUIRE to WEAR the
RIGHT to WEAR the
INSIST on WEAR the
DEMAND to WEAR the

Here the words in small capitals denote all noun and verb forms of the words; so DEMAND may refer to *demand* and *demands* (as both nouns and verbs), as well as *demanding* and *demanded*, while WEAR refers to *wear, wearing, wears* and *wore*.

These searches found a different set of concordance lines from the ones for *Muslim women*. However, some lines were found not to refer to people wearing the veil or related concepts, and these were removed. Additionally, some of these new concordance searches duplicated the concordance lines for *Muslim women*, and these were removed also. Finally, as before, cases in which a term is used as part of a refutation (e.g. 'there is no such thing as women who choose to wear the veil') were also deleted. The frequencies from these concordance searches were then combined with those gathered for the analysis of *Muslim women*. These are given for each newspaper in Table 8.3. It should be noted that the searches for *insist* and *demand* were combined. The figures for *The Guardian* and *The Observer* were also combined, as *The Observer* is often viewed as the Sunday edition of *The Guardian*.

Table 8.3 Representation of the veil as an imposition, right, choice or demand

	Forced to wear it	Right to wear it	Choosing to wear it	Demanding to wear it
Times	21	16	12	7
Telegraph	21	3	10	1
Sun	1	4	10	1
Mail	11	13	5	7
Express	3	17	9	6
Star	0	16	2	4
Mirror	3	2	3	0
Guardian/Observer	30	25	16	1
Independent	16	9	10	6
Business	0	0	0	0
Total	103	105	77	33
Total (percentage of cases)	32.4	33.1	24.1	10.4

From the 'Total' row in Table 8.3, it can be seen that the veil appears to be described most frequently as either a right or an imposition. The representation of the veil as a demand is relatively infrequent, though not non-existent. *The Guardian* and its Sunday equivalent, *The Observer*, seem to write the most about Muslim women being forced into wearing the veil. However, these same newspapers also write more about the right of Muslim women to wear it, or present their wearing of the veil as a choice. The only representation that is not frequent in *The Guardian/Observer* is the view that Muslim women are insisting upon wearing or demanding to wear the veil. While this more militant representation is somewhat less frequent than the other representations examined, it is notable in *The Times*, the *Daily Mail*, the *Daily Express* and *The Independent*. The *Daily Mail*, *The Independent* and *The Times* have similar dispersion patterns to *The Guardian/Observer*, except that they sometimes write about Muslim women demanding to wear the veil.

Rather surprisingly, the *Daily Star* and *The Sun* tend to frame the veil more in terms of rights or choice than Muslim women being forced or demanding to wear it. These patterns are perhaps confusing and unexpected, as at first glance they do not appear to fit with expectations about tabloid/broadsheet or left/right distinctions. One reason for this could have to do with multiple interpretations and understandings of what the veil actually signifies. For example, some left-leaning newspapers and columnists write about the veil from a feminist perspective, either explicitly arguing that it is 'a symbol of subjugation' (such as *The Independent* article below) or giving examples, either of particular political systems (such as *The Guardian* article below) or specific cases (*The Observer* article below) in which an individual woman is viewed as being controlled by an individual man:

Wearing a headscarf is a symbol of women's subjugation and those apologists, be they Muslims or so-called liberals, who want us to believe that Muslim women are given a choice of wearing the headscarf forget about the very strong sense of tradition coupled with intense intimidation by male relatives (*Independent*, 'Letters', 30 December 2003).

Muslim women are being forced to cover up in a number of countries as part of a political backlash against growing freedoms (*Guardian*, 13 October 2006).

Right after that, the misery began. Khalid tried to control her and force her to wear the hijab, the headscarf worn by devout Muslim women (*Observer*, 23 April 2006).

In the following *Guardian* article, the writer views the niqab as an emblem of sexism within British Islam:

While middle-aged male Muslims queue up to defend the right of women to wear the niqab, most Muslim women in Britain today are far from being in a position to make free, informed choices about their lives, least of all about what to wear (*Guardian*, 7 October 2006).

The columnist, Yasmin Alibhai-Brown, is one of the strongest opponents of the niqab. Writing in *The Independent* (9 October 2006), she argues that it is used to hide and thus perpetuate the physical abuse of women: 'I have seen appallingly beaten Muslim women forced into the niqab to keep their wounds hidden.'

Some articles in the left-leaning broadsheets, then, express concern about the niqab or hijab as being incompatible with sexual equality, and view such garments as imposed upon women by men. When the right-leaning news-papers (particularly the *Daily Mail*, *The Times* and *The Daily Telegraph*) write about the imposition of the veil (or related garments), they are also negative, but tend not to make an explicit argument about sexual equality. Instead, they are more likely to write of the veil as being one component in a list of criticisms of particular Muslim-based societies, which are constructed as generally being extremist and controlling. Such articles are often focused on the Taliban in Afghanistan:

After international aid agencies helped restore Kabul's stadium, the Taliban promptly used it to stage public executions. Men were obliged to wear beards and attend prayers, televisions were banned and women forced to wear the burqa, an all-enveloping robe with only a mesh window allowing a glimpse of the world. Education for girls over eight was banned and women were barred from work (*Sunday Times*, 4 March 2001).

Many of the representations of women who insist on or demand to wear a veil or related form of dress occur within the context of news stories about court cases in the United Kingdom in which women have lost their jobs for refusing not to wear the veil. These particularly involve teachers, and in the majority of cases the newspapers are not sympathetic towards the women involved. This article, by *The Independent*, presents a woman whose 'demands' to wear the veil have caused her to be marginalised within her own community by Muslims and non-Muslims alike:

Her fight for the right to wear the veil in class may have divided politicians but there was little support for the teaching assistant Aishah Azmi yesterday among parents at her school in Dewsbury, West Yorkshire. Muslims and non-Muslims alike challenged Ms Azmi's demands to wear the veil in class (*Independent*, 17 October 2006).

While *The Independent*'s disapproval of Azmi is quite subtle, and must be inferred through the use of the term *demands*, as well as the focus on her as marginalised within her own community and having 'divided politicians', other newspapers are more forthcoming. For example, Fraser Nelson in the *News of the World* (22 October 2006) refers to Azmi as a 'stroppy, confrontational battleaxe'. Similarly, Ruth Dudley Edwards in the *Daily Mail* (3 August 2005) quotes the case of a fourteen-year-old girl who was excluded from school for 'insisting on wearing the jilbab'. The girl appealed against the decision with the help of the then prime minister's wife, Cherie Blair (who is a barrister). The *Daily Mail* argues that '[t]he elite cared nothing about the threat posed by Muslim extremism', and writes that Cherie Blair was 'a clever woman with as little common sense as she has an understanding of what she and her kind have done to make Britain a haven for murdering bigots'. Thus, although Muslims who want to wear the veil are represented as a problematic out-group, they are also linked to another out-group: non-Muslim members of 'the elite' who are viewed as conspiring with Muslims for their own reasons. Ms Blair is characterised by the *Daily Mail* as ignorant, although another reason is cited to explain her actions when the *Daily Express* covers the Azmi case on 20 October 2006: 'Specialist employment lawyers warned last night that the classroom rebel's vow to go to Brussels would mean a taxpayer-funded bonanza for lawyers while the case took years to rumble through the legal system.' Here, lawyers are implied to be greedy and amoral, willing to take on a case so they can profit from it, while benefiting from the 'taxpayer'.

Returning to the idea that some women insist upon wearing or demand to wear the veil, in a *Mail on Sunday* article (5 December 2004) the columnist Peter Hitchens takes this argument a stage further, writing: 'By the way, I was told by a leading Arab militant that Muslim women often wear the Hijab headscarf as a gesture of defiance, to wind up the rest of us. As I have long suspected.' It is worth considering how Hitchens refers to Muslim women, himself and his readers in this article. First, he constructs his readers as non-Muslim by using the personal pronoun *us* to create an in-group that includes himself. It is interesting that he privileges the opinion of an unnamed source in the article column, making the claim difficult to refute, while his statement that this is something he has 'long suspected' helps to legitimate his overall stance; he can say he was right about Muslim women all along. Meanwhile, the out-group is constructed as women using the veil as a way of showing defiance, rather than for, say, religious reasons, or even because they are forced to wear it by their male relatives. This is a view of Muslim women not as victims but as agitators. Moreover, the claim is not specific; it is generalised to 'Muslim women', and the frequency with which they are supposed to wear the veil to cause others to be upset is described as 'often'. Hitchens thus paints a picture of a nation of defiant Muslim women, taking pleasure in upsetting non-Muslims.

Adjectival collocates of *veil*

Moving away from the issue of whether the veil is viewed as a choice, right, imposition or demand, it is useful to consider what other ways it is referred to. In order to do this, it is helpful to consider adjectival collocates. As pointed out earlier, the word *veil* is often used to refer to a range of different items of clothing, so it is useful to consider the more commonly used terms separately. Table 8.4 therefore shows adjectival collocates of *veil* and other related words, derived from Sketch Engine. Perhaps what is most striking about this table is that the different words have very similar collocates, which can be grouped into a number of semantic preferences or discourse prosodies. Terms that describe these garments in terms of full cover (*all-enveloping, all-covering, all-encompassing, full, full-length, full-body* and *all-embracing*) are very common. Additionally, there are terms that describe the garments in terms of their colour or pattern (*white, black, red, blue, pale, green, floral*). Another group of words describe them as forced (*obligatory, compulsory, essential*) or wrong (*not welcome, not desirable, wrong, unnecessary, bad*), or at least controversial (*contrary, controversial, divisive*). Another set of collocates indexes the religious nature of these garments (*Muslim, religious, Islamic, Islamic-style*), while a final small set describes them in more positive terms (*special, important*). Tellingly, the collocates for the English word *headscarf* tend to be less negative overall than the other terms. A headscarf does not involve covering the face, and it seems as if, the more of the woman the garment covers, the more negative the collocates of that term will be, with the more disapproving collocates tending to be reserved for the Arabic words *burqa, niqab* and *hijab*.

The overall picture in the newspapers therefore seems to be one of viewing these garments as problematic. Before looking in more detail at some of the arguments that are used to explain why they are problematic, it is useful to examine the more positive-sounding collocates. We therefore looked at *important, essential* and *special* in more detail. An examination of these cases

Table 8.4 Adjectival collocates of veil *and related words*

Term (frequency)	Adjectival collocates
veil (9,681)	*full, full-length, all-enveloping, all-encompassing, full-body, obligatory, discreet, facial, Muslim, compulsory, divisive, black, thin, Islamic, traditional, blue, white, heavy, different, long, religious*
burqa (3,411)	*all-enveloping, all-covering, tent-like, all-encompassing, full-length, obligatory, (not) welcome, full, compulsory, unnecessary, wrong, traditional, pale, black, white, blue, Afghan, Muslim*
headscarf (2,466)	*Islamic-style, floral, traditional, obligatory, coloured, pink, black, Islamic, Muslim, white, green, essential, red, blue, simple, Arab, important, small, religious, own*
hijab (2,247)	*full-length, obligatory, contrary, compulsory, full, grey, traditional, correct, blue, black, bad, green, special, Muslim, white*
niqab (1,060)	*(not) desirable, full, controversial, black, Muslim*
jilbab (620)	*full-length, all-embracing, flowing, loose, full, traditional, black, Islamic, Muslim*

revealed that they were not straightforwardly positive representations. For example, the *Daily Star* (9 November 2007) writes about Bushra Noah, who sued a hair salon after it refused to hire her because she wore a headscarf. The article begins with the headline 'Crimper sued for refusing job to Muslim in headscarf'. It then gives a summary of the case and has an eighty-eight-word quote from the owner of the hair salon, who justified her position as not racist, but more to do with how the job involved displaying hair, and how, if she lost the case, she would also lose her business. The article ends with a single sentence about Bushra, which also contains a fourteen-word quote from her: 'Bushra, who has been rejected for 25 hairdressing jobs, insisted: "Wearing a headscarf is very important in my religion. I could have fitted in."' In terms of perspectivisation, the article de-emphasises Bushra, by writing about her last and affording her less space. In addition, Bushra's quote is prefaced with the word *insisted*, which implies that she is militant in her views. The fact that the headscarf is described as *important* is thus diminished by the overall discursive thrust of the article. The headscarf's importance is ascribed only to Bushra, rather than to the editorial voice of the newspaper. Bushra is also attributed a similar quote in an article by the *Daily Mail* (18 June 2008), in which she says: 'Wearing a headscarf is essential to my beliefs.' However, again, this article marks its disapproval of Bushra's position by beginning the article like this: 'It seems too lunatic to be true. But here a hair salon boss reveals how she was driven to the brink of ruin and forced to pay £4000 for "hurt feelings".'

What about the collocate *special*? The term *special hijab* occurs in a humorous article by the columnist Dominik Diamond in the *Daily Star*

(16 January 2008). In the article, Diamond comments on the fact that Princess Diana's mother did not approve of her dating a Muslim man. Diamond then jokes that, when *he* dates a Muslim man, his mother 'puts on her special tartan hijab'. This article thus uses the hijab as a prop in a joke, rather than suggesting that there is anything intrinsically special about it to its wearers. The trend for positive collocates, then, is that they are not really used to view such items of clothing as positive, but either to construct their proponents as militant or to make jokes.

Arguments against the veil

What arguments, therefore, are given by the newspapers to justify the overall hostile position towards the veil and related garments? As described above, the left-leaning broadsheets sometimes employ the argument that the veil contradicts women's rights or equal rights. However, numerous reasons are cited in other newspapers. In a letter to *The Times* (30 August 2005), the writer takes a different stance from the gender equality argument, by claiming that the full veil is an insult to men, as it implies that men cannot control themselves: 'It seems to me that the real offence conveyed by the wearing of the full veil by Muslim women lies in the implication that no man can look on any woman without being consumed by unholy lust.'

Another approach is taken by the *Daily Express* (6 October 2006), which uses a health argument: 'A growing number of Muslim women who wear the head-to-toe veil are being treated for rickets.' In *The Independent* (9 October 2006), Yasmin Alibhai-Brown argues that veiled women are denied the ordinary pleasures derived from nature: 'Veiled women cannot swim in the sea, smile at their babies in parks, feel the sun on their skin.' A related argument is that the veil prevents Muslim women from performing their jobs properly. For example, *The Sun* (2 April 2009) features a text message by a reader: 'How will a Muslim firefighter climb a ladder in a full-length skirt? And surely a hijab would interfere with breathing apparatus?'

A different argument is that the veil threatens *the British way of life* (a phrase that occurs 308 times in the corpus and is most frequent in the right-leaning *Express, Mail* and *Telegraph*). The *Daily Express* (19 July 2007) writes: 'Anyone sincerely wishing to integrate into the British way of life would never wear such an alien and threatening outfit.' Related to this are arguments that the sight of a veiled woman provokes fear or unease. The *Daily Express* (24 June 2009), in an article entitled 'Why Britain should ban the burqa', describes a German woman living in Leeds who finds them 'frightening and intimidating'. The same attribution first occurs in an article written by Phil Woolas, then Britain's race minister, in the *Sunday Mirror* (8 October 2006). The *Daily Express* (19 July 2007) also refers to burqas as unsettling: 'The sight of Muslim women dressed head to toe in burkas is unsettling enough at the best of times.'

Linked to the idea of the 'frightening' veil are arguments that people could use the coverings in order to commit crimes, particularly terrorist crimes. This is quite typical of tabloid arguments. For example:

I can't think of anything more maddening than wasting hours in a freezing terminal, being groped and interrogated at the security gate while veiled Muslim women (or police killers in disguise) are waved through with a smile (*Sun*, 22 December 2006).

This was the moment two armed robbers disguised as Muslim women in burkas were about to pounce (*Daily Mirror*, 3 June 2002).

In the following article in *The Daily Telegraph*, it is interesting that the burqas are foregrounded. We are told what the extremists are wearing, as well as given a translation of the term, before we are told what they did and who they did it to:

Two extremists wearing burqas, the veil worn by some Muslim women, threw a grenade into the middle of 50 worshippers at a Christmas service in Chianwala, about 40 miles north of Lahore (27 December 2002).

Taking a different stance, the *News of the World* (22 October 2006) argues that veil wearing is a minority position of Muslim women in the United Kingdom: '95% of Britain's Muslim women don't wear the veil. They are normal people who want to integrate.' Wearing the veil thus becomes something that is viewed as 'not normal' and not integrationist. The same article warns of the dangers of eschewing integrationism, by claiming that the British National Party and Islamo-fascists want to 'whip up a clash of civilisations in the UK. Their evil agenda has failed so far in Britain because the country is famously tolerant and Muslims mostly moderate.' *The Times* (20 June 2007) also presents statistics, but is more subtle in hinting that there is something problematic about the veil: 'Muslims make up nearly 14 per cent of India's 1.1 billion people and many Indian Muslim women still wear headscarves and veils.' Here, the temporal adverb *still* implies that the information that follows is somehow surprising or unpleasant, and that the expectation would be that Muslim women would not wear the veil any more. Wearing the veil is thus implied to show a lack of social progress.

Another argument is that the veil is not required by Islam. A letter writer in the *News of the World* (29 October 2006) categorically argues that 'Muslim women should be stopped from wearing veils because they have no religious significance'. The columnist Janet Street-Porter, in *The Independent* on 7 December 2006, writes that 'the wearing of the veil is demeaning to women, not required by the Islamic faith and has no place in an integrated Britain', while Jon Gaunt (20 June 2008), in *The Sun*, writes, 'Nowhere in the Quran does it say a woman should be fully covered, and as a result there is no place for the full veil in 21st Century, tolerant, liberal Britain.' Some readers may view Gaunt's argument about tolerant, liberal Britain to be somewhat paradoxical, as he advocates that people should be intolerant of an item of clothing, to the point of banning it. Yasmin Alibhai-Brown, writing in *The Independent* (9 October 2006), gives a detailed account of the origin of the veil, arguing: 'The sacred texts have no specific injunctions about covering the hair or face. The veil predates Islam and was common among the Assyrian royalty, Byzantine upper-class Christians, and Bedouins – men and women – when sandstorms blasted their faces.'

However, in other articles, writers or people being interviewed give the opposite view, that Islam requires women to cover their bodies. For example, in an article on 30 September 2001, the *Sunday Express* conducts interviews with two 'Moslem' women. The article's title, 'Two Moslem women who love Britain explain why their faith is far removed from the creed of hatred preached by Afghanistan's fanatics', suggests that this is an example of the tabloid sensitivity that occurred directly after 9/11. In the article, one woman is quoted as saying: 'When I first started reading about Islam, I was learning my rights. I could say, "Islam requires me to cover my body except my hands and face but whether I wear a sari or skirt and shirt is my choice."'

Arguments are not always made against the veil, but, at times, veiling can be used as an argument against something else. For example, *The Guardian* (27 July 2005), in an article that is disapproving of a Labour-led plan to make members of the public use identity cards, claims: 'Facial recognition technology raises problems for veiled Muslim women; it reads odd-shaped faces badly.' The article is notable (and atypical) because it problematises ID cards rather than the veil itself or the women who wear them.

Table 8.5 shows the results of an analysis of 100 concordance lines of *veil* and related words that give arguments against veiling, selected randomly across all newspapers and time periods in the corpus. Although the table reflects only a small sample of the corpus, it suggests that the two most frequently cited arguments against the veil are that it oppresses women and it makes community relations difficult. The former argument is perhaps so popular because of its representation in the left-leaning broadsheets, which tend to contain longer articles. However, this argument is also cited in other types of newspapers (tabloids and right-leaning broadsheets), although not as often. The argument that the veil makes community relations difficult became popular due to the frequent references in 2006 to Jack Straw's article in the *Lancashire Evening Telegraph*. Taken together, these two arguments represent almost two-thirds of all reasons given for a dislike of veiling. Additionally, the argument that the veil is a form of religious or political extremism (often articulated in right-leaning newspapers) is strongly linked to the view of the veil as oppressing women.

Table 8.5 Arguments against veiling

Argument	Number
Oppression of women	38
Makes community relations difficult	26
It's a form of religious or political extremism	10
Religious reasons are invalid	7
Veiled women can't do their jobs properly	7
Veiling is against national values	2
Threat to security	2
No one should be disguised in public	1
Most parents don't want their daughters to veil	1
It's frightening and intimidating	1
It's unhealthy (causing rickets)	1
It's insulting to men	1
It puts pressure on other women to wear it	1
In the current climate, veiling women could face attack	1

The final two arguments in Table 8.5 are interesting to consider, as they both seem to acknowledge the dominant discourse of the veil as problematic, which is then used, almost as a form of circular reasoning, to justify not wearing it. First is the view that wearing the veil should be banned because doing so puts pressure on other women and girls to wear it. This argument contains two potential implicatures: that putting pressure on others is bad, but also that the veil in itself is bad. (However, it could, equally, be argued that banning the veil would put pressure on Muslim women *not* to wear it.) Second is the view that women should not veil because the current climate of prejudice could subject them to attacks by members of the public:

A leading British Islamic scholar has advised Muslim women not to wear the traditional hijab head scarf to protect themselves from attack after the July 7 bombings. Professor Zaki Badawi, head of the Muslim College in London and chairman of the Council of Mosques and Imams, made his call amid fears that wearing the hijab would make women more vulnerable to attack or abuse (*Guardian*, 4 August 2005).

This argument is noteworthy, because Badawi says nothing negative about the veil itself, but recommends that, because people are likely to be hostile to Muslims, they should refrain from acting in a particular way associated with being a Muslim. Thus, existing hostility about veil wearing is used to discourage further veil wearing. However, the problem is framed as being about veil wearing rather than the hostility towards veiling.

Shroud-swishing zombies: dysphemistic representations

While most newspapers tend to use terms such as *veil* and *headscarf*, with terms such as *niqab* and *hijab* being less frequent (see Table 8.4), it is also notable that some journalists reconceptualise these items of clothing by using their own ad hoc constructions, which generally have negative connotations. One set of words that references veil wearers consists of verbs that describe certain types of movement.

For example, the *Daily Mail* (10 November 2005) writes about a veiled woman (in this case the author Tanya Gold, who has decided to wear the veil for a week as a social experiment) as 'waddling around a 21st-century supermarket'. Here, Gold constructs her own movement as akin to that of a duck. Ducks are not normally viewed as particularly graceful when walking, but other metaphors also characterise veil wearers as objects that take to water. In another *Daily Mail* article (9 August 2008) there is reference to 'elaborately-veiled Muslim women gliding along New Bond Street in London', while in *The Guardian* (22 January 2004) veiled Muslim women are described by Catherine Bennett as 'sailing along'. Such verbs help to dehumanise veil wearers, functioning as othering strategies and making the veil wearer appear more different and unusual to others.

The gliding metaphor is also implicitly referenced by Jon Gaunt in *The Sun* (20 June 2008) when he writes that 'we wasted thousands in legal aid on silly little misguided Muslim girls to take schools to court for the right to dress like a Dalek in a full veil'. Gaunt refers to Muslim women who veil as 'Daleks' several times in the corpus, using the same construction the following year (7 August 2009), when he writes that 'women are being forced to dress like daleks'. Daleks are machine-like monsters in the popular British science fiction television programme *Dr Who*. They have a gliding movement, as if on wheels or hovering slightly above the ground. They are also obsessed with 'exterminating' creatures that are not like them. The suggestion that burqa-wearing women are Daleks is interesting, because it also references this form of clothing as frightening, contributing to the discourse of the veil as being frightening, mentioned earlier. These two articles are also notable because of the fact that, in the first, Gaunt constructs Moslem girls as insisting on wearing the veil (and prepared to go to court to argue that it is a right) while, in the second, he uses the contradictory 'forced to wear the veil' discourse. However, whichever way Gaunt chooses to represent Muslim women, it is negative: they are either victims of their own religion or agitators.

Other than referring to Muslim women as Daleks, what other noun phrases do journalists use to describe the veil? *The Guardian* article described above also refers to 'eyes peeping from yards of leg-tangling, windblown drapery', and then later suggests: 'Maybe, inside all that dark material, they are brimming with self-esteem.' The term 'dark material' warrants comment, as it could be an intertextual reference to a popular fantasy novel by Philip Pullman called *His Dark Materials*, first published in 1995. The novel involves fantasy elements including witches, and one possible reading of this article is that it implies a subtle connotation about veil wearers. The *Daily Mail* writer who wears the veil as a social experiment begins her article with a joke: '"I love soft furnishings," I tell my laughing flatmates. "But that doesn't mean I want to be one."' Later on her criticism becomes more serious, and she refers to the full-body veils as 'medieval costume' and 'fabric prisons', whereas in the *Daily Express* (24 June 2009) veils are alliteratively labelled as 'restrictive robes'. Another columnist, Julie Burchill, in *The Times* (6 August 2005) describes veiling as 'rigging yourself up like a parrot's cage with the covering on', while in *The Guardian* (22 December 2001) burqas are described as 'flowing blue tents'. Clearly, such dysphemistic labels are not the preserve of right-leaning tabloids but are dispersed across the entire corpus.

Other verbs refer to the act of veiling itself in negative ways. For example, the *Daily Mirror* (17 October 2006) refers to 'Muslim women who hide themselves away from the world', while *The Times* (2 November 2006) says Muslim women 'swathe themselves in shapeless black cloth'. As other aspects of the analysis have found, the columnists tend to articulate the more extremely negative views. Peter Hitchens, in the *Mail on Sunday* (16 July 2006), asks: 'How long before non-Muslim women are compelled to dress like bats to enter certain parts of certain British cities?' Julie Burchill, this time writing in *The Sun* (24 June 2009), emphasises the 'us'/'them' construction by using block capitals when she writes: 'We let shroud-swishing zombies flout OUR standards of freedom and tolerance every day.'

Readers may have noticed that, collectively, a number of these constructions of veil-wearing women reference the concept of the supernatural. These references are either explicit, as in Burchill's zombies, or more implicit – such as Hitchens referring to bats (which have associations with vampires and horror fiction in general); alternatively, they are made through intertextual references, such as 'dark materials', or through verbs such as *glide* and *sail*, which imply that Muslim women's movement somehow happens unnaturally, as well as the use of adjectives such as *frightening* and *intimidating*. Any one of these examples, viewed in isolation, does not necessarily amount to a stable construction, but we would argue that the wide range of ways in which veil wearing is associated with the supernatural suggests that writers are, unconsciously or not, articulating the same discourse. The label *zombie* to refer to women who veil fulfils a number of purposes. First, it implies that the person veiling is completely without agency. She is, to all intents and purposes, the living dead. The zombie construction is forceful, because it renders the issue of whether women choose or are forced to wear the veil somewhat moot.

If they have no real desires of their own then they can neither choose something freely nor be forced to do something against their will. Additionally, a zombie conjures up a frightening mental image, with associations of rotting flesh, violent attack, infection (in popular culture, a person bitten by a zombie normally becomes a zombie him-/herself) and unnaturalness (dead people do not walk around).

The term *shroud*, used by Burchill, also characterises this discourse of the veil as being associated with death or the supernatural 'undead'. *Shroud* with reference to full-body veiling occurs in other right-leaning newspapers, sometimes as a verb (e.g. 'Crowds of faceless women, shrouded in their burqas' (*Daily Telegraph*, 8 May 2004), '[D]ozens more, shrouded in traditional black burqas, chant their hatred of Pakistan and the US' (*Daily Mail*, 25 September 2001)), with a good number of these cases being from letter writers. One letter writer in the *Daily Mail* (1 March 2007) refers to young Muslim women who 'shroud themselves in black cloth', whereas in the *Daily Express* (8 September 2006) another letter writer uses a number of dysphemisms, including 'swathes of material', 'this sheet' and 'the living shroud'. The letter ends by drawing further on the (un)dead discourse: 'I'm sick of divisive foreign cultures being accepted in Britain as the norm and the NHS burka is the last straw. Who wants to wake from an operation to see a swaddled figure in the next bed?' One interpretation of this is that people who have undergone an operation under general anaesthetic will wake up, see a Muslim woman wearing a burqa and draw the conclusion that they are in a room with a dead person, or perhaps that they have died themselves. The NHS burqa seems to have struck a chord with *Express* readers: another letter writer says, 'We are appalled at the idea of "shadowy figures" walking around hospital wards, particularly at night, in NHS-supplied burkas' (7 September 2006).

Balance or ambivalence?

Although the general picture across the British press is disapproval of veiling, at times some newspapers do attempt to present a more balanced picture or show concern about media representations. This can make it difficult to attribute a single 'position' to some newspapers. Catherine Bennett, writing in *The Guardian* (22 January 2004), for example, asks: 'Even if hijab-wearing is a genuine choice, does that make it obligatory for us to respect it? Any more than hijab-wearers respect women who wear shamefully little? What we would not ban, we do not have to condone.' Such a position, while not wanting to ban the veil, is still negative, in that veiling is explicitly not afforded concepts such as *respect* or *condone*. This position is similar to the one found by Byng (2010), that American newspapers created the notion that, even though the restrictions on veiling were questionable, they were understandable, and it was 'common sense' for Muslim women not to veil in public.

However, during the peak of the Jack Straw controversy in 2006, *The Guardian* expressed concern about the way that other newspapers have represented the veil:

Last week *The Times* splashed on 'Suspect in terror hunt used veil to evade arrest'. That sat alongside yesterday's lead in the *Daily Express*: 'Veil should be banned say 98%'. Nearly all those who rang the *Express* agreed that 'a restriction would help to safeguard racial harmony and improve communication'. At the weekend the *Sunday Telegraph* led on 'Tories accuse Muslims of "creating apartheid by shutting themselves off"'. That's how it's been almost every day since Jack Straw raised the matter of the veil nearly two weeks ago... The result is turning ugly and has, predictably, spilled on to the streets. Muslim organisations report a surge in physical and verbal attacks on Muslims; women have had their head coverings removed by force (*Guardian*, 18 October 2006).

Similarly, *The Observer* (8 October 2006) takes the position that women have the right to wear the veil, although it also notes that people have the right to voice concerns: 'If Muslim women in Lancashire want to use the niqab to veil their faces, that is their right. But their MP is entitled to voice his concern that wearing it restricts his constituents' full participation in British society.' Perhaps more surprisingly, the *Daily Mail* occasionally attempts to give both sides of the debate a voice, for example by printing two letters of about equal length, one pro-veil and one anti-veil, alongside each other (27 October 2006). *The Times* (10 October 2006) has a 392-word article written by Rajnaara Akhtar – chair of the society Protect-Hijab. Akhtar writes that Jack Straw's comments have 'built up the walls of ignorance and division ever higher', that wearing the veil is a basic right in a democracy and that the real issue is the 'ghettoisation of minorities, exacerbated by poor housing, second-rate education and inadequate job opportunities'. Another columnist in *The Times* (26 June 2009), the sometime comedian Frank Skinner, writes: 'I'm not sure that the burqa is objectively wrong. Some Muslim women clearly feel oppressed by it, but then some clearly don't. To ban it is to remove women's choice, using oppression to combat oppression.'

One contradiction involves how writers construct the Labour government's position in relation to the veil. Not all newspapers are critical of Labour. In the *News of the World* (8 October 2006), Jack Straw's anti-veiling position is described thus: 'While the Tories mince about, Labour could be on the winning side of a cultural war', although the article later insinuates that Straw is looking for a seat in the House of Lords and his anti-veil stance is thus strategic. However, in other newspapers, a more negative interpretation of Labour is given, no matter what Labour's opinion appears to be. One position, perhaps to be expected by the right-leaning press, is that Labour is in favour of the veil (e.g. 'It is Labour that allows misguided Muslim women to think it is OK for them to wear a veil at school or, even more ludicrously, in court' (*Sun*, 3 July 2007)). However, at other times, Labour is represented in the opposite light: 'As we sleepwalk into a New Labour police state, fashion fascist Jack Straw's denunciation of the right of Muslim women to wear the veil is racist and must be challenged' (*Daily Express*, 'Letters', 11 October 2007). The *Daily Mail* (21 October 2006) criticises Labour for being inconsistent in its stance, referring to Straw's position as 'a breathtaking U-turn on multiculturalism by a Government that once promoted it to the point of obsession'. The reason for this 'U-turn' is that Labour politicians 'hope to advance their careers by appearing "tough" (though any Tory who tried the same tactic would of course be denounced as "racist")'.

While it is not surprising in itself that right-leaning newspapers will paint Labour in a negative light, no matter what it does, these attacks also demonstrate a deep sense of ambivalence among the British public and journalists about the veil. This is perhaps summed up well by the *Daily Mail* article (10 November 2005) in which the journalist decides to wear the burqa for a week. After making jokes about the veil, the article becomes more serious in tone, as the author describes how she encountered curiosity, pity and contempt from members of the public. She ends by writing: 'My week is over. I am confused. I saw my burqa as a prison imposed by the frailties of men. But I also hated the judgmental stares and the hostility. The week was a strange window into a different culture, but I have no answers.' The journalist's final two words, 'no answers', amply encapsulate the ambivalent stance on the veil in the British media, while her use of the adjectives *strange* and *different* are further examples of the media's 'othering' of Islam.

In conclusion, the general position of the British press towards veiling is ambivalent and conflicted; this ranges from the belief that Muslim women have the right to wear the veil (although they should expect 'concern' rather than 'respect') to expressions of mocking hatred and rage. The controversy around veiling, peaking after Jack Straw's article,[3] presents almost all newspapers with various dilemmas. The left-leaning press deplores veiling from a feminist perspective, although it would find condoning a ban to be problematic, and is concerned at the way that the right-leaning newspapers seem to be using the issue to stir up hatred. On the other hand, the right-leaning press finds itself in the unusual position of having to agree with a Labour minister,

---

[3] In 2010 Straw gave a public speech about his article in 2006, in which he said: 'To be blunt, if I had realised the scale of publicity that [my comments] received in October 2006, I wouldn't have made them, and I am sorry that it has caused problems and I offer that apology.' Some commentators criticised him for trying to win votes before an election.

Jack Straw. After hundreds of thousands of words of reporting and opinion in the press, Muslim women who cover themselves are still described as controversial, and the 'issue' does not appear to have been happily resolved for anybody.

Radicalisation

Let us turn now to *Muslim men* and one of its frequent collocates, *radicalisation*. A concordance search of *radicalisation* was conducted across the whole corpus, resulting in 1,038 hits. The word *radicalisation* is a nominalisation, created from the verb *radicalise* (itself derived from the adjective *radical*). Nominalisations are potentially useful constructions, because they do not necessarily need to reveal specific subjects or objects but, instead, allow the process itself to be expressed as an abstract or generalised concept – as in this example from *The Times* (4 April 2009): '[T]he Home Office's Prevent strategy, which intends to counter radicalisation in Britain.' When required, though, the author has the option of labelling who is being radicalised, as in 'the radicalisation of young British Muslims' (*Times*, 9 July 2009), or who is doing the radicalisation, as with 'these Muslims proved easy prey for radicalisation by exiled clerics from hardline groups' (*Guardian*, 29 October 2008). This makes the word *radicalisation* interesting to examine, as, unlike a word such as *brainwashing*, it does not necessarily imply a particular cause.

An initial question we decided to examine was: to what extent is radicalisation seen as occurring within the United Kingdom? The overwhelming majority of concordance lines of *radicalisation* present it as in existence and as a growing problem. A number of metaphors that are used in conjunction with radicalisation help to demonstrate this. First, a 'water' metaphor is used, to refer to radicalisation as a *wave*, a *tide* or an *upsurge*. There is also talk of needing to *stem* radicalisation. A second metaphor thus links radicalisation to plants: radicalisation is described as having taken *root*, or the *roots* of radicalisation need to be explained. Additionally, some authors refer to the *seeds* or *fruits* or radicalisation. A third metaphorical construction conceptualises radicalisation as something that is moving. Accordingly, we are referred to its *acceleration* and its *speed*, we are told that it is *snowballing*, *rapid* or *runaway*, and that action is needed in order to *slow* it down or *curb*, *halt* or *forestall* it. A related metaphor conceptualises radicalisation as a place, implying that there are *paths* to it or that certain actions can *lead* to it. Less frequent metaphors involve reference to heat – for example by describing universities or prisons as *hotbeds* of radicalisation, or writing about factors that *fuel* radicalisation.

While these metaphors are different, their utilisation is almost always used in ways to refer to a *growing* problem. A minority position is that radicalisation is rare or non-existent, although even this position is articulated by needing to address the received wisdom, as in the following article in *The Guardian* (7 October 2007), which quotes a Muslim television producer: 'We did not find any evidence of this radicalisation that's supposed to be everywhere.' At the other extreme is columnist Jan Moir, who writes of the trial of Omar Khyam, who was found guilty of plotting terror attacks in the United Kingdom, which the media refer to as the 'fertiliser bomb plot'. Moir argues:

It has become horribly clear over recent years that a number of British-born Muslims, many of them from comfortable middle-class backgrounds, have somehow evolved into terrorists determined to perpetrate mass murder on their fellow citizens... Perhaps the most unsettling thing to emerge from the terror trial that ended this week is that Khyam was once just another bloke from the burbs, and that there are plenty more like him out there, full of hate and rage (*Daily Telegraph*, 2 May 2007).

The use of the vague quantifications 'a number of', 'many of them' and 'plenty more like him out there' help to evoke an impression of a widespread danger. While the metaphors described above tend to refer to radicalisation as being on the increase, most writers are not so explicit as Moir about the extent to which they perceive radicalisation to be occurring but, instead, tend to present the concept as undoubtedly already in existence within UK Muslim communities, with phrases such as 'the fight against radicalisation' (*Times*, 18 July 2009), 'the Home Office invited him to discuss radicalisation in Britain's Muslim communities' (*Daily Mail*, 11 May 2008) and '[b]ringing an end to the radicalisation of young Muslims in Britain could take 30 years' (*Independent*, 22 October 2008).

After excluding a small number of lines that do not refer to the radicalisation of Muslims, each concordance line was then carefully examined in order to identify whether a reason for the radicalisation is given. A categorisation scheme was then created, in order to group similar reasons together. It should be noted that, in the majority of cases, reasons tend to be reported as part of quotes from a government source, report or other stakeholder (such as the leader of a Muslim community). Such cases may not then be viewed as the actual stance of the newspaper. However, newspapers have a wide range of opinions and reports to draw on, and therefore a newspaper's decisions as to which positions to present can be seen as revealing something about its stance. In tallying the types of explanations that different newspapers give, we ignored those that were duplicated in the same article, and we also discounted cases when an explanation was clearly given simply in order for it to be refuted in the course of the article. The results are given in Table 8.6 (the *Daily Star*, *The People* and *The Business* are excluded as no relevant cases were found).

Table 8.6 Reasons attributed for radicalisation of Muslims

	Extremist Islam	Government policy	Alienation	Arab-Israeli conflict	Multiculturalism	Economic factors	Grievance culture	Others	Total
Guardian/ Observer	9	20	6	4	2	2	0	0	43
Telegraph	11	7	5	0	0	1	1	1	26
Times	8	4	5	1	2	1	2	0	23
Mail	6	8	1	0	0	1	0	1	17
Independent	10	3	1	0	0	0	1	0	15
Express	1	5	1	0	1	1	0	0	9
Sun	1	0	1	0	0	0	0	0	2
Mirror	2	4	0	1	0	0	0	0	7
Total	48	51	20	6	5	6	4	2	142

Table 8.6 does not show every case in the corpus of attributions made in connection with radicalisation. The concordance search examined only one word, *radicalisation*, and there may be other ways of expressing the same concept – such as 'become radicalised'. Additionally, phrases such as 'turn to extremism', 'brainwashed' or 'become a suicide bomber' may be used as synonyms for *radicalisation*. The term is clearly less popular with tabloid newspapers such as the *Daily Star* and *The Sun*, which use the term *brainwashed* far more often. We have retained our focus upon the term *radicalisation* for this part of the analysis because it is one of the strongest collocates of *Muslim men* across the whole corpus, and even this analysis of a single word allows patterns to be identified, although it should be acknowledged that our analysis is limited to this (particularly frequent) way of expressing the concept of becoming radical.[4] Moreover, as noted above, *radicalisation*, being a nominalisation, does not automatically imply agency or blame to anyone. Thus, writers who use this term have a wide range of ways of conceptualising it, which serves to highlight when particular choices are being made.

First, it is *The Guardian* that clearly seems to be the most likely to be explicit in attempting to assign reasons for the radicalisation of Muslims, although, if *The Times* and *The Daily Telegraph* are added, these three newspapers account for almost two-thirds of the attribution in the corpus. Two major 'discourses' of attribution are given, being referenced almost equally frequently. The first is a discourse (which tends to come from government sources and reports) that blames different forms of extreme Islam for radicalisation. Although this discourse appears to be only one of two majority discourses (the other being to cite UK foreign policy for radicalisation), it should be noted that many newspapers refer to this discourse via a wide range of other terms. This is done, for example, through the use of terms such as *brainwash* and related forms (occurring 1,381 times in the corpus, and almost always referring to proponents of radical Islam), or *become a suicide bomber*, which also is normally used to refer to someone who has become involved with an existing radical group.

The 'radicalisation through extreme Islam' discourse is roughly equally spread between the broadsheets, and, on further analysis, can take a variety of forms. The most common form is to assign blame to *extremist, militant, hardline* or *firebrand* preachers in the United Kingdom:

[4] The phrase 'BECOME radical' occurs 195 occurrences in the corpus while 'BECOME a suicide bomber' occurs 222 times. When we examined 'BECOME a suicide bomber', we found that it is almost always used to refer to cases in which Muslims have been 'brainwashed' by radical Muslims or political/religious groups. However, the word *radicalisation* was potentially more interesting to examine, because a wide number of reasons are attributed to it, suggesting that the term does not in itself hold a particular connotation as to its causes.

Extremists are engaged in fundraising, radicalisation and training and in providing support to fellow extremists overseas (*Sunday Telegraph*, 1 April 2007).

As for the process of radicalisation, the report says 'attendance at a mosque linked to extremists may be a factor' (*Guardian*, 12 May 2006).

Khan's rapid radicalisation came in adulthood, when he became friendly with a group of radicals from Leeds and Huddersfield, West Yorkshire, the associates suggest (*Independent*, 18 November 2005).

An interesting aspect of such an argument is that it tends not to address how such radicalisation arose initially. The discourse makes a very clear distinction between people who are already radical (their radical status requires no explanation; they just appear to have materialised that way) and people who are not radical but are at risk of becoming radical if they come into contact with members of the first group. Additionally, this distinction between existent radicals and non-radicals at risk seems to imply that the status of being radical is an either/or one, rather than allowing for more complex understandings, such as people being radical in some ways and not others, or as some people being more radical than others. Radicalisation, therefore, is presented as a binary change of state – from being completely non-radical to being fully radical.

Four sites that are seen as particularly dangerous are mosques, prisons, universities and the internet:

[G]reater efforts must be made to prevent the radicalisation of young Muslims by extremist Imams within British jails (*Times*, 1 May 2007).

Although mosques, where firebrand imams sometimes preach, can contribute to the radicalisation of young Muslims, the main sources of fundamentalist propaganda are Islamist websites (*Daily Telegraph*, 8 November 2006).

'Radicalisation is extremely serious and something we have to blame ourselves for,' says Ahmed. 'The leadership has not been effective in dealing with young people. We have left them to the mercy of extremist groups, who have preyed on them at colleges and universities' (*Observer*, 7 December 2003).

Occasionally there are warnings in the press that almost no place is safe from radicalisation:

Their radicalisation seems to have taken place in local gyms, not mosques (*Independent*, 25 April 2005).

They [extremists] look for ungoverned spaces where they can approach the vulnerable: places like cafes, bookshops and gyms... (*Daily Mirror*, 1 November 2007).

Moreover, a headline in *The Times* (11 December 2009) reads 'Terror police monitor nurseries; four-year-olds vulnerable to Islamic radicalisation, officers say', although the article foregrounds criticisms of this claim from Liberal and Conservative politicians, who call it 'absurd'. The article could therefore be read as drawing both on a discourse of 'no one is safe from radicalisation' and on a discourse of 'exaggerated fears over radicalisation'.

A second explanation for radicalisation is most common in *The Guardian*, although it is also found in other newspapers. This explanation blames British foreign policy for the radicalisation of British Muslims, particularly citing the invasions of Iraq and Afghanistan:

It does for the first time officially acknowledge what the rest of the world has known for most of the past decade: that Muslim 'perception' of the West's support for Israel, the Iraq and Afghan wars and the wider war on terror plays a 'key role' in fuelling 'radicalisation' *(Guardian,* 26 March 2009).

They accused Mr Blair who again ruled out a public inquiry into the London bomb attacks of being responsible for the 'radicalisation' of young Muslims by waging wars in Iraq and Afghanistan *(Daily Mail,* 5 July 2006).

Not only has the prime minister continually refused to accept a public inquiry, he has vociferously denied a link between Western foreign policy and radicalisation *(Guardian,* 'Letters', 7 July 2006).

This explanation is reported as being against the Labour government's (and particularly Tony Blair's) understanding of radicalisation for the majority of the period under which the data was collected. Blair's stance is constructed as being in opposition to reports and the beliefs of high-ranking security and military officials:

The war in Iraq contributed to the radicalisation of the July 7 London bombers and is likely to continue to provoke extremism among British Muslims, according to reports based on secret assessments by security and intelligence chiefs *(Guardian,* 3 April 2006).

[Stella Rimington, former director general of MI5] challenges claims, notably made by Tony Blair, that the war in Iraq was not related to the radicalisation of Muslim youth in Britain *(Guardian,* 18 October 2008).

The former head of the Royal Navy told a conference in London: 'Tony Blair would never accept that our foreign policy actually had any impact on radicalisation... Well that is clearly b*******' *(Daily Mail,* 28 January 2009).

Muslim sources are often cited as putting forward the British foreign policy explanation for radicalisation:

Abdullah, 46, said some young people were pushed towards radicalisation because of Afghanistan and Iraq *(Guardian,* 9 September 2009).

Inayat Bunglawala, of the Muslim Council of Britain, said: 'The fact is that many Muslims believe the UK's participation in the wars against Afghanistan and Iraq have been a key contributory factor in the radicalisation of some young Muslims' *(Daily Mirror,* 5 July 2006).

The Muslim leaders voiced their concerns that British foreign policy over Iraq and Lebanon was leading to a radicalisation of young Muslims *(Daily Telegraph,* 15 August 2006).

However, one of the Muslim leaders blamed the Iraq war for increasing the reach of extremists (*Daily Mail*, 20 July 2005).

A related argument is that the Arab-Israeli conflict contributes towards radicalisation, again with *The Guardian* drawing on this view more often:

Government efforts to prevent the radicalisation of British Muslims have been set back by Israel's assault on Gaza, the security and counter-terrorism minister, Lord West of Spithead, said yesterday (*Guardian*, 28 January 2009).

Beckett also admitted 'great concern' that the conflict could increase the radicalisation of young Muslims in Britain angered by the scenes of Arab suffering (*Observer*, 6 August 2006).

THE bloodshed in Gaza could lead to more home-grown suicide bombers, Home Secretary Jacqui Smith fears... An aide added: 'Awful images are beamed back on TV every night and we know that could well lead to radicalisation' (*Daily Mirror*, 16 January 2009).

The examples above do not explicitly condone Muslims who are believed to have become radicalised on account of the invasions of Iraq and Afghanistan, but, on the other hand, they do not criticise them either; instead, the bulk of the criticism is laid directly on Tony Blair. Conversely, there are a smaller number of cases in the corpus in which the invasions are referenced as contributory factors in radicalisation. However, unlike the above cases, these writers refer to a 'grievance culture', and imply that people have simply used the invasions as a 'convenient excuse'. Newspapers that publish this view tend to use distancing strategies, either by printing it in letters, or attributing it to a specific interviewee:

Lord Carlile of Berriew QC said: [...] It is now clearly the case that although the Iraq war did not create violent jihad it has become a convenient excuse for violent jihad (*Independent*, 13 November 2006).

[W]orrying, perhaps, is the depth of a grievance culture which even moderate Muslim leaders feed with their talk of a war on Muslims (what about the war against Orthodox Christians on behalf of Muslims in Bosnia and Kosovo?) and their emphasis on socioeconomic failure in Britain (much of it the result of origins in poor and traditionalist cultures in Pakistan and Bangladesh – and, in any case, half of all British Muslim youth now goes to college) (*Times*, 'Letters', 7 July 2006).

I have heard two proclaimed British Muslim leaders attempting to explain radicalisation. On offer as an explanation was extreme hostility towards British foreign policy. Neither was challenged by any statement that it is unacceptable for an elected Government's policy to be met with violence if that policy does not accord with a minority view (*Daily Telegraph*, 'Letters', 12 August 2006).

A fourth explanation also cites grievances by Muslims, although this one does not refer directly to the invasions and also reports on such grievances in terms of Islamophobia, or Muslims being disenfranchised, disadvantaged, disengaged and alienated, as well as a lack of integration and cohesion. For example, policies such as 'stop and search' are said to lead directly to radicalisation:

[S]top and search may prove to be the tipping point to radicalisation for some British Muslims who already feel alienated from British society (*Independent*, 'Letters', 3 August 2005).

[O]n returning to Britain last week, I felt a stranger in my own country for the first time. It will be a long time before I can take a rucksack or bag on the Tube without being looked at suspiciously by my fellow passengers and police. I do not blame them. The blame firmly lies with those who brought about this situation (*Daily Telegraph*, 'Letters', 6 August 2005).

Additionally, negative representations are held to be a contributing factor:

Journalism has a duty to reflect and not condemn the views of people such as Abu Muhammed. In denying them a voice, it is contributing to the radicalisation of British Muslims (*Guardian*, 6 August 2007).

If all the Muslim organisations are squeezed into being extremists and hardliners – there is nowhere left for youngsters to go and it adds to the radicalisation of youths (*Observer*, 21 August 2005).

Related to the view that radicalisation is caused by Muslims' suffering is a minority view that economic factors contribute towards radicalisation:

In some of the northern towns, Oldham and Burnley, there is a lot of deprivation and unemployment – is that the breeding ground for radicalisation? (*Daily Telegraph*, 19 July 2004).

The relationship to radicalisation is complex…but there is a possibility that [a downturn] will increase the pool of those susceptible to radicalisation (*Guardian*, 1 September 2008).

But we're also being told that one of the reasons for the radicalisation of Muslim youth is the high levels of unemployment among minority Britons (*Times*, 6 April 2004).

However, a different perspective blames the government's strategy of 'multiculturalism' for radicalisation:

[M]ulticultural policies have encouraged ethnic-minority groups to believe they are in need of special recognition… Islamic radicalisation is, in part, an acute expression of broader trends that affect us all (*Guardian*, 2 February 2007).

The Tories' security spokesman, Lilian Pauline Neville-Jones, said the government should have acted sooner to tackle the roots of radicalisation and claimed the government's 'failed strategy of multiculturalism' was partly to blame (*Guardian*, 18 January 2008).

They turn multiculturalism into the central dogma of the state then wail about lack of integration and the radicalisation of Muslims. But the demented nature of New Labour goes even deeper (*Daily Express*, 5 February 2007).

This argument blames both the government, for its failed strategy, and Muslims, who have 'encouraged ethnic-minority groups to believe they are in need of special recognition' (*Guardian*, 2 February 2007). This perspective therefore links to the idea of Muslims having unreasonable 'grievances', outlined above with reference to the invasions of Iraq and Afghanistan. Melanie Phillips, writing in *The Times*, merges both perspectives together in this article:

The doctrines of multiculturalism and minority rights, themselves the outcome of a systematic onslaught by the British elite against the country's own identity and values, have paralysed the establishment, which accordingly shies away from criticising any minority for fear of being labelled as bigoted... Minority rights doctrine has produced a moral inversion, in which those doing wrong are excused if they belong to a 'victim' group, while those at the receiving end of their behaviour are blamed simply because they belong to the 'oppressive' majority (*Times*, 6 June 2006).

A final, and perhaps even more extreme, explanation for radicalisation is given in *The Daily Telegraph* by Sam Leith. He writes that suicide bombers (whom he refers to as 'teenage numpties who blow themselves up') are adolescent:

It occurs to me that you might view the radicalisation of young Muslim men in the chip-shops of Britain not as a response to American foreign policy, or a backlash against the decadence of the West, but in terms of something outside politics: a playground craze – something that spreads like pogs, or happy-slapping, or Pokmon [sic] (*Daily Telegraph*, 13 August 2005).

This explanation views radicalisation in terms of a 'craze', like the skateboard craze in the 1970s, and is perhaps an extension of the 'grievance culture' perspective, in that it does not attribute a valid justification.

Some aspects surrounding the issue of the radicalisation of young, mainly male, British Muslims are characterised by agreement in the British press; for example, most journalists who refer to the issue seem to view it as a problem that exists and/or one that is growing. Additionally, the term often appears to imply binary states – between radicalised and not radicalised. However, journalists tend to disagree on the causes of this perceived radicalisation. Existing radical imams and preachers are widely believed to be responsible (although it is unclear how they became radical in the first place). However, other perspectives hold Tony Blair's foreign policy to account. This is particularly so in the left-leaning *Guardian*, although, in citing this argument, right-leaning newspapers such as like the *Daily Mail* are able to cast Blair in a negative light. As with the view that the veil oppresses women, this therefore becomes one of the issues in British journalism whereby left-leaning and right-leaning newspapers appear to agree (although, again, perhaps for differ-ent reasons). As with Chapter 7, which examined the case of Muslims on benefits, it seems to be the case that this 'issue' is a convenient one with which to attack government policy – and it is the domestic policy of 'multiculturalism' that also fares badly (though less so than Labour's foreign policy). While some newspapers cite economic deprivation, social alienation or other feelings of injustice, there are smaller numbers of writers who are critical of such positions, believing that they are simply excuses or that they do not justify radicalisation. However, any possible role that newspapers themselves have to play, such as considering whether their representation of Muslims and Islam could contribute towards such radicalisation, tends to go unremarked.

Conclusion

Whatever the stance of the corpus newspapers towards Islamic modes of dress for women, or the reasons they may cite regarding the radicalisation of (male) British Muslims, what the discourses discussed in this chapter collectively achieve is to describe Islam as, at the same time, oppressive and radical – and to paint a picture of growing radicalisation among British Muslims.

A final difference we noted after reading hundreds of concordance lines relating to Muslim men and women was that the corpus data occasionally displays a dislike or disapproval of Muslim women, which did not seem to be as salient for Muslim men. Constructions such as *silly little misguided Muslim girls* or *stroppy, confrontational battleaxe* keyed into negative stereotypes that, we felt, betrayed a dislike of females as much as Muslims; we did not find equivalent stereotypes for males. Muslim women therefore appeared to be doubly problematised in the corpus, because of their religion and their gender, in a way that Muslim men were not.

Over the course of the last seven chapters we have examined the discursive construction of Muslims in our corpus of mainly twenty-first-century news data. The following chapter considers constructions within a much older corpus of newspaper articles, in order to examine whether the representations of Islam occurring around 9/11 are actually 'old news'.

9 Does history rhyme? Earlier news representations of Muslims

Introduction

This book so far has focused exclusively on the representation of Islam in the UK press from 1998 to 2009. However, Islam has been a subject of discussion in British newspapers for a much longer period of time than this. While the study has drawn conclusions about the early twenty-first-century representation of Islam in the UK press, it is more difficult to infer whether this representation is new, or simply a modern version of a representation that has deep historical roots. For example, have Muslims always been associated with extremism and conflict in British journalism? Have Muslim women traditionally been viewed as oppressed, and is *Muslim world* an historic othering concept dating back over many centuries? As noted in Chapter 1, a quote attributed to Mark Twain is 'History does not repeat itself, but it does rhyme'.

Therefore, this chapter explores the extent to which the picture emerging from the analysis presented in the previous chapters is only the latest manifestation of a representation that has been current in British newspapers for a very long time. Fortunately, it is now possible to look, on a large scale, at such a representation over an extended period of time, because of the wealth of data that is now becoming available in machine-readable form that permits the study of English in an historic context. Old books, papers and pamphlets are being scanned to provide online facsimiles of them by organisations such as the British Library and Google. For the moment, we are assuming that the sources are accurate enough to be of use (though we return shortly to the issue of their accuracy). The potential of such resources is enormous: if the World Wide Web has revolutionised the access that linguists have to language data from the late twentieth century onwards, initiatives such as the British Library Online Newspaper collections, Early English Books Online (EEBO) and Google Books are slowly expanding this revolution to earlier centuries. This makes it feasible to address the representation of Islam on a much longer time scale using the methods presented in this book. To demonstrate this, and to explore the representation of Islam in historic depth, we look at two time periods in this chapter: 1475 to 1720 and the nineteenth century. This diachronic examination will also enable us to draw parallels with, and note differences from, early twenty-first-century representations of Islam in the UK press. Although the main discussion falls on the nineteenth century, as will be seen, it is important to be able to push the study of this representation back further.

Choosing a century

We begin by looking briefly at the representation of Muslims in English books in the period from 1475 to 1720. It is possible to do this due to the existence of Early English Books Online, a collection of material that includes some 125,000 texts covering the period in question. Most of this material is composed simply of images of the original texts, and is not ideal for our purpose. However, a subset of 12,284 texts, totalling 624,277,146 words, is available to us as so-called 'full texts' – fully machine-readable text files analogous to the files used to study modern newspaper material in the earlier chapters of this book. Nonetheless, using this material to look at the representation of Muslims is not straightforward, for a relatively trivial reason: the word *Muslim* was rarely used in this time period, as other words were used to refer to Muslims instead. In the whole of the corpus there is only one occurrence of the word *Muslim*. It appears in a dictionary of sorts from 1610,[1] in which it is cross-referenced to the word *Mussulman* – which occurs fifty-eight times in the EEBO. More frequent still is *Mahometan*, with 1,427 examples in the EEBO corpus. This leads to an obvious point: when searching in an historical context, one needs to be mindful that lexis is prone to change over time. The meanings of words shift, and words themselves fall out of and come into use. Table 9.1 shows, for the nineteenth and twentieth centuries, the changing pattern of words used to refer to Muslims in one British newspaper, *The Times*. Assuming that *The Times* is a fair proxy for general newspaper English, it is clear that a preference to use the word *Muslim* to refer to adherents of Islam is a relatively recent phenomenon, with the word becoming preferred over *Moslem* and *Mussulman* only from the 1940s onwards. *Mussulman* was the preferred form for the nineteenth century, and *Moslem* was the preferred form from 1900 to 1940.

Returning to the EEBO material, we decided to explore the word *Mahometan* to see whether it had any similarities in terms of collocates with the word *Muslim*. Figure 9.1 shows, in rank order from strongest to weakest

---

[1] EEBO text reference A07603.

Table 9.1 The number of newspaper articles using the words Muslim, Moslem *and* Mussulman *in ten-year periods from the 1790s to the 1970s*[2]

Decade	Muslim	Moslem	Mussulman
1790s	0	0	0
1800s	0	0	3
1810s	0	0	5
1820s	0	23	42
1830s	0	20	50
1840s	1	45	164
1850s	0	79	398
1860s	4	89	242
1870s	19	321	774
1880s	9	242	703
1890s	3	250	320
1900s	22	467	249
1910s	18	918	7
1920s	65	2,000	16
1930s	84	2,179	10
1940s	1,269	808	7
1950s	2,195	53	19
1960s	1,854	92	2
1970s	1,937	102	2

religion, superstition, princes, a, the, pagan, heathen, law, Christian, turn, or, Jew, infidel, kings, constitute, Jewish, mosque, professors, doctors, paradise, women, countries, sect, Morocco, poor, Turkish, temples, instructed, empire, Asia

Figure 9.1 Top thirty collocates of *Mahometan* in the EEBO corpus

certainty that a word is a collocate, the top thirty collocates of *Mahometan* in the EEBO corpus.[3]

There are themes apparent in these collocates that have been touched upon earlier in this book. Consider Table 3.1; the categorisation of keywords presented there provides categories that some of these collocates could fit into, though the words themselves may not be present in that table. For

---

[2] Ideally, one would normalise these frequencies. However, it is not possible to extract the number of words printed in each decade by *The Times*, and so normalisation is not possible.

[3] For the purposes of this analysis we have discarded punctuation that collocated with the words. We have also standardised collocates appearing with multiple spellings to one standardised form. Collocates were searched for in a $+5/-5$ window, with the log-likelihood statistic being used to determine the collocates of the word. A minimum frequency of five occurrences was required for any word to be considered a candidate collocate.

example, the 'Places/nationalities' (*Morocco*, *Turkish*, *Asia*) and 'Religion' (*pagan*, *heathen*, *Christian*, *Jew*, *infidel*, *Jewish*, *sect*) categories are evident in the list of collocates. The representation is clearly negative at times; consider, for example, the collocate *poor*. This always occurs one or two words to the left of *Mahometan*, modifying the word itself, and has the sense of pitiful rather than impoverished:

Can a poor deluded Mahometan rejoyce in expectation of a feigned sensual Paradise? (EEBO file A27017).

[C]ould meet with no body to Instruct that poor Mahometan, for want of Understanding his Language (EEBO file A26262).

Similarly, *heathen* is negative. This co-occurs with *Mahometan* thirty-six times. The dominant pattern of collocation for *heathen* is for it to occur either two words to the left (twenty-one times) or two words to the right (ten times) of *Mahometan*. However, in both cases one pattern dominates: *Mahometan* and *heathen* are being equated with one another by a coordinating conjunction (twelve examples) – as can be seen in the following examples:

I consider'd what I should first advise an Heathen or Mahometan to do, who had been bred up to Idolatry and Fables (EEBO file A42822).

[T]he Infidel, Mahometan and Heathen World, are kept from Faith in Jesus Christ, and many millions of Souls destroyed by them (EEBO file A26917).

As is apparent from the last example above, the coordination of *Mahometan* and *heathen* may also include other disapproved-of groups, in this case so-called infidels. This can include Christian groups or sects that are being criticised, as is evident in the following example:

Pretend no more, poor man, to great knowledge, as the sight of a Grave and a rotten Carcass may humble the Fool that is proud of Beauty, so the thought of the Popish, Mahometan and Heathen World, may humble him that is proud of his understanding (EEBO file A27051).

This in turn leads to some of the words coordinating in this way also collocating with *Mahometan*, notably *popish* and *papist*, both of which are strongly tied to *Mahometan* by conjunctions, as can be seen in the following examples:

[T]here never was a consciencious Pagan, Papist, or Mahometan (EEBO file A59850).

The Popish, Mahometan, Sun, Moon, and Devil Worshipping Religions (EEBO file A43026).

While similarities to the twenty-first century have been noted, there are also superficial differences in the list of collocates. Among countries in which Islam is the predominant religion, Iraq was considered notable in the early twenty-first century, whereas Morocco and Turkey appear to have been most worthy of note in the fifteenth, sixteenth and seventeenth centuries. More interesting differences also exist: an association between Islam and medicine would seem to be present in the data, as evidenced by the collocate *doctor*. However, a closer examination of the data shows once again how the meaning of a word can change over time. In each case in which *doctor* collocates with *Mahometan*, the reference is in fact to an Islamic jurist (a *faqih*), as the following example shows:

About this time (by the suggestion of Cara Rustemes a Doctor of the Mahometan Law) Zinderlu Chelil, then Cadelesher or chief Justice among the Turks... (EEBO file A47555).

This is a very rare usage in present-day English; there are only 527 examples of the phrase 'doctor of Muslim law' on the World Wide Web. By contrast, the term *faqih* is much more common, with 2,890,000 examples on the World Wide Web in English-language documents, contrasting with no mentions of the term in the EEBO corpus.[4]

The investigation so far, while of interest, is also somewhat flawed. The EEBO corpus is not directly comparable to the newspaper data used in the rest of this book, as it contains very little press material. While there were early newspapers – so called newsbooks – during the reign of Henry VIII, newsbooks became a popular and relatively stable genre only in the seventeenth century (see Cranfield 1978 for an excellent history of the early English newsbooks). Yet, even if we focused upon newsbooks and limited our study to the seventeenth century, problems would persist. The genre of newsbooks is very different from the genre of newspapers; they were mainly composed of reports reproduced from letters from correspondents abroad, for example, rather than by journalists working for a specific newspaper. Moreover, the newsbooks in this period vary somewhat; titles opened and closed quite rapidly at times, and wildly varying regimes of censorship mean that the number of papers and what they were allowed to report are not consistent.

However, if we did wish to conduct such a study, it would be possible to use another corpus: the English Newsbooks corpus (Hardie and McEnery 2010). This is a corpus composed of all the surviving newsbooks published from the second half of December 1653 to the end of May 1654, consisting of 999,248 words of data. However, a corpus analysis conducted on these newsbooks found that they were not particularly concerned with reporting distant events in general, or with reporting on Islam in particular. The word *Mahometan* does not occur in the corpus at all, although there are indirect mentions of Muslims. For instance, the word *Turk* is mentioned, albeit only seventeen times. Interestingly, these few examples include some patterns that

---

[4] Frequencies on the web as at 8 July 2011, searched using Google.

are present in the brief study of the EEBO material discussed already, notably the use of coordinating conjunctions to form equivalence between groups disapproved of by the newsbooks, in a process similar to that described by McEnery (2006: 146–8), as in the sentence 'Beware the Turk and Pope!'.[5] There are several reports referring to a supposed disaster at Mecca, where the tomb of Muhammad is claimed to have fallen into a fiery chasm that opened before it.[6]

However, other than these rather indirect and quite negative references to Islam, the newsbooks of the seventeenth century, at least as represented by this selection of newsbooks, are a poor source of data to use to explore the representation of Islam. The focus of the newsbooks is rather domestic, or focused upon northern Europe, as shown by Gregory and Hardie (2011). Given the very small Muslim population in England at the time (see Ansari 2004: 27), the near-invisibility of Islam in the newsbooks of this period is understandable.

Additionally, regulatory practices around the press altered between the seventeenth and twenty-first centuries, making direct comparisons difficult. For example, in the seventeenth century the state (whether based on the authority of the monarch or, in the Commonwealth, the Lord Protector) decided who could own and operate a printing press, and it was thus used to support the ruler or other powerful institutions, such as the church. The only exception to this was shortly before, during and after the English Civil War, when press regulation broke down. For most of the period the press was not supposed to question authority, and licensing and censorship systems were set up to control the increasing number of new books, broadsides and pamphlets that had emerged since the 1500s. The situation changed in the eighteenth century with the emergence of an unlicensed press. Reporting on Parliament was allowed in 1771, although the government was more repressive of radical publications in the late 1700s, being afraid of revolution. However, a modern free press did not really emerge until the nineteenth century.

Hence, while it is of interest to see how Muslims are represented in early modern English writing in general, it seems that the sixteenth and seventeenth centuries are not ideal periods for an attempt to compare the representation of Muslims in the twenty-first-century press with that in the press of an earlier period. To do this, considering the issues raised so far, it seems best to select the earliest time period in which:

---

[5] Newsbooks Corpus, file ModIntell174.xml.
[6] This mention of Mecca by many of the newsbooks is an error; the grave in question is in Medina. Some newsbooks also mistakenly identify Mecca as a 'Church or Temple' (see PerfAcc158.xml in the Newsbooks corpus, for example). The story is entirely apocryphal.

- newspapers have taken a form similar to that seen today;
- newspapers have a less parochial focus and/or a significant Muslim community has developed in the United Kingdom;
- journalistic and editorial practices are similar to those seen today; and
- the regulatory environment in which the press was operating was stable and broadly analogous to that experienced now.

Fortunately, the British Library has made available online its collection of nineteenth-century newspapers. This is a time in which newspapers have a form similar to those of today: the British press is writing about Britain in the world, notably through the British Empire; journalistic and editorial practices are at least somewhat comparable to those of today; and the regulatory environment is broadly analogous to that in the twenty-first century. It is for these reasons that we focus in the rest of this chapter on the representation of Islam in the British press of the nineteenth century.

However, before doing so, we should consider briefly what words we should examine, because, as is apparent from Table 9.1, the word *Muslim* entered general usage only in the middle of the nineteenth century – with *Moslem* and *Mussulman* also being in general use at the same time. Was there a notable difference in the meaning of the three words? Their use in the corpus indicates that this is not the case. Consider the following extracts from an article in *The Standard*, 23 December 1898, in which the terms MOSLEM, MUSSULMAN and MAHOMMEDAN are essentially used as synonyms (emphasis added):

THE REJOICINGS AT CANEA. ATTITUDE OF THE **MOSLEMS**. The popular rejoicings over the arrival and investiture of Prince George are continuing with unabatable vigour. Last night the town was brilliantly illuminated, even the **Moslem** Beys contributing to the display… This morning the Prince paid a visit to the principal mosque. He was received by the **Moslem** priests and notables, and engaged them in conversation, taking a kindly interest in the repairs of the building, and speaking in most encouraging tones to those who, up to yesterday, had looked upon him as their enemy. Nothing could have been better calculated to reconcile the **Mahommedans** to the changed conditions. The Prince also had a private interview with the Mayor, who is a **Mussulman**, in which he assured that official that the minority might have implicit confidence in him, as he had resolved to show no preference to either creed.

Our study established that a range of lexis, including *Muslim*, *Mussulman*, *Moslem* and *Mahommedan*, was used interchangeably to refer to Muslims in the nineteenth century.[7] Given that there is no discernible difference in the meanings of these terms in the nineteenth century, and there is no evidence

---

[7] We have established this by reading the texts and undertaking concordancing of all the stories about Muslims in the nineteenth century as represented in the Muslim Excerpts corpus, which is introduced shortly.

that the different spellings caused notable offence, as they have in the twenty-first century (see Chapter 3), in the analysis that follows we have counted the words together as equivalent. This is denoted in the discussion that follows by the notation {MUSLIM}, which signifies the set of words equivalent in meaning to *Muslim* and its plural form. For the purposes of this study, this set is: *Mahommedan, Mahommedans, Moslem, Moslems, Muslim, Muslims, Mussulman, Mussulmans* and *Mussulmen*.

Focusing on the nineteenth century

To explain how the nineteenth-century newspaper collection (henceforth NCNC) was exploited, it is necessary to return to a point that was passed by earlier in this chapter: the issue of the accuracy of the searches one may undertake with historic materials. It is entirely possible to carry out highly accurate searches with some such materials; for example, the English Newsbooks corpus used in the previous section was hand-typed in from original documents, with the typing itself being checked meticulously. However, such hand-typing of material is very time-consuming. Hence, the approach taken by the creators of the NCNC was to use optical character recognition (OCR), so that a rough machine-readable corpus is made from the original texts. This is then linked to scanned images of the original page. Therefore, although searches are carried out on the rough (digitised) corpus, the user is presented with the original (scanned) pages. The 'rough' corpus is rough in the sense that the resulting machine-readable text contains errors; it is not hand-corrected to the extent that it provides a near-perfect machine-readable version of the text — as the Newsbooks corpus does.

Nonetheless, this rough corpus allows users to search for a specific word or phrase, and to be fairly sure of getting the right answers most of the time. The user may note from time to time that the OCR was in error and some of the examples returned are not of the word requested (a class of error we call false positives). It may also be the case that some OCR errors lead to relevant pages not being shown at all; such errors, which we call false negatives, are very hard for the user to find. However, the system also returns true positives; that is, the OCR successfully reads the text, and this can be seen as the pages retrieved and displayed do indeed contain the desired word or phrase. It was through such an interface that the data for this study was collected. A search was undertaken for all the words that may be used to refer to Muslims in the NCNC newspaper stories. The pages thus returned were then checked, with pages being identified either as false positives or true positives. False positives were often caused by words that are similar in form to the word searched for. For example, the word *muslin* led to a number of false positives. This manual check enabled the study to focus upon the true positives.

These true positives were then subject to transcription. Given that (a) the goal of the study was to look at collocates and keywords and (b) limited time and money were available to undertake the transcription, short excerpts of the relevant news stories were transcribed. More precisely, what was transcribed was the sentence containing the one or more words from the set {MUSLIM}, as well as the previous and following sentences. The resultant dataset, which we call the Muslim Excerpt corpus (MEC), contains 55,360 words in 572 excerpts. This gave a sound basis on which to calculate collocates of {MUSLIM} within the usual span of five words to the left and right of the node. However, without a reference corpus it is not possible to generate a set of keywords for the MEC. Fortunately, the corpus of nineteenth-century newspaper English (the CNNE) was being developed at the time of writing by Erik Smitterberg at the University of Uppsala. This corpus, covering both editorial and reportage, contains 190 newspaper articles, amounting to some 300,000 words, sampled from a range of British newspapers in the nineteenth century. Erik kindly agreed to give us access to his data, so that we were able to: (a) contrast the MEC with a general corpus of nineteenth-century news-paper material in order to generate a keyword list; (b) explore the keywords and collocates of the MEC in the CNNE; and (c) carry out concordances of keywords and collocates found in the MEC in the CNNE.[8]

In the analysis that follows we first present the results of the keyword analysis of the MEC. Following from that, we consider how the keywords compare to those found in twenty-first-century reporting. An analysis of the collocates of {MUSLIM} in the MEC then allows us both to explore what we may term *key collocates* – those keywords that are also collocates of {MUSLIM} – and to look at the general representation of Muslims arising from the data. The analysis concludes with a broad comparison of twenty-first-century and nineteenth-century representations of Muslims in the UK press.

Keywords

What words occur in the context of {MUSLIM} more frequently than we would expect by chance? Table 9.2 gives the keywords in the MEC derived by a comparison to the CNNE. Similar keywords have been grouped together into semantic fields.

One keyword – *Mahdi* – is present in two fields, as the word represents an intersection between the two fields in question (i.e. the Mahdi was a religious leader). Within the fields, further subdivisions are clearly possible. For

---

[8] The authors would like to express their thanks to Erik, both for allowing us access to the CNNE and for carrying out the searches of the corpus on our behalf.

Table 9.2 Keywords in the MEC, grouped into semantic fields

Semantic field	Keywords in this field
Armed fighters	*insurgents, troops*
Conflict	*insurrection, war*
Fanatic	*fanaticism*
Leader	*consul, governor, Mahdi, sultan*
Government	*authorities, Porte*
Places	*Asia, Bulgaria, Candia, Canea, Constantinople, Crete, Europe, India, Philippopolis, Russia, Salonica, Syria, Turkey, village, villages, world*
Nationality	*Armenian, Armenians, British, Bulgarian, Bulgarians, Cretans, European, Greek, Indian, Ottoman, Russian, Turkish, Turks*
Outrage	*atrocities, killed, massacre*
Population	*population, subjects*
Religion	*faith, Islam, Mahdi, mosque, prophet, religion, religious*
Religious identity	*Christian, Christians*
Victims of conflict	*refugees*

example, under 'Nationality', it would be possible to distinguish the nationality itself (e.g. *Turkish*) from the plural noun form referring to a group of people with that nationality (i.e. *Turks*). However, in this study we are seeking to examine the broadest fields possible – although some of the fields are subdivided when it aids the analysis.

Some of these keywords are linked to each other in a complex way. For example, fanatics are seen to promote violence, violence leads to outrages, and outrages have victims. We are setting aside a discussion of the links between the categories for the moment as it is important first to see how these words relate to {MUSLIM} and, consequently, how the connections between the categories play upon {MUSLIM}. It is also important to note that, while we have developed a categorisation system that arises from the examination of the particular dataset, the resultant categories do bear more than a passing resemblance to those emerging from the twentieth-/twenty-first-century data in Chapter 3, even though the words categorised in Chapter 3 were derived by a different technique. This is an early indication that perhaps a similar representation is present in the data. Notably, both analyses include a conflict category. We have also chosen here to subdivide some of the categories, with the 'Places/ nationalities' category from Chapter 3 becoming two categories in this chapter: 'Nationality' and 'Places'. The reason for this is that in the nineteenth century, as will become apparent, there was a much less easy mapping between locations and nationalities than is currently the case. So, for example, the Ottoman Empire, while one geographical entity, contained many nationalities. Hence,

riot, rising, fanatical, Liverpool, world, Reuter, Crete, agitation, fanaticism, population, feeling, refugees, Cretan, Bulgaria

Figure 9.2 Collocates of {MUSLIM} in the MEC in descending order of association with the word

we have found it useful here in this instance, and some others, to subdivide what is a unitary category in Chapter 3 as context dictates.

Nevertheless, before discussing these keywords, it is useful to distinguish between those keywords that are also collocates of {MUSLIM} and those that do not collocate with {MUSLIM}. Figure 9.2 shows the words in the MEC that collocate with {MUSLIM}. For the purposes of this study, collocates were looked for five words either side of {MUSLIM}. Words with a frequency of below ten were discarded, and a minimum mutual information score threshold of six was used to identify collocates.[9]

It is of interest to note that the semantic fields that categorise the keywords can also be used to categorise most of the collocates of {MUSLIM}. This indicates that these categories/topics are not only represented by words frequently in the close vicinity of {MUSLIM}, but also comprise words that are significantly more frequent in the corpus (which comprises articles pertaining to Muslims) when compared to an appropriate general corpus. This is important to note, as the same observation regarding collocates and frequent topics was made in the analysis of the contemporary corpus (Chapter 2).

In Table 9.3 the semantic fields of the keywords of the MEC are shown once more. Words that collocate with {MUSLIM} are also shown, as well as words that are both keywords and collocates. Collocates that do not fit into the semantic fields are shown in a new field, 'Unclassified'.

To explore these keywords and collocates, we begin with the 'Places' category, for, as will become apparent, this category is important in revealing the underlying issues and representations, as they refer to elements of the physical/geographic context in which the events reported in the articles take place. Towards the end of the section a clear link will be made back to the studies already presented earlier in this book.

'Places'

The most dominant set of keywords relating to the MEC consists of the keywords focused upon places. Geopolitics obviously influences this set of keywords, and one political entity in particular, the Ottoman Empire, is the

---

[9] This threshold was used because it was identified by Durrant and Doherty (2010) as the minimum threshold at which collocations seem to reflect a mind-internal process.

Table 9.3 Collocates and keywords of {'MUSLIM'}

Semantic field	Keywords in this field	Collocates of {MUSLIM}	Both key and collocate
Armed fighters	insurgents, troops		
Conflict	insurrection, war	agitation, feeling,[10] riot, rising	
Fanatic		fanatical	fanaticism
Leader	consul, governor, Mahdi, sultan		
Government	authorities, Porte		
Places	Asia, Candia, Canea, Constantinople, Europe, India, Philippopolis, Russia, Salonica, Syria, Turkey, village, villages	Liverpool	Bulgaria, Crete, world
Nationality	Armenian, Armenians, British, Bulgarian, Bulgarians, Cretans, European, Greek, Indian, Ottoman, Russian, Turkish, Turks	Cretan	
Outrage[11]	atrocities, killed, massacre		
Population	subjects		population
Religion	faith, Islam, Mahdi, mosque, prophet, religion, religious		
Religious identity	Christian, Christians		
Unclassified		Reuter[12]	
Victims of conflict			refugees

obvious source of many of the 'Places' keywords. The modern countries of Bulgaria, Syria and Turkey were all parts of the Ottoman Empire. Similarly, Crete and the cities of Candia (modern-day Heraklion in Crete), Canea (modern-day Chania in Crete), Constantinople (modern-day Istanbul in Turkey), Salonica (modern-day Thessalonica in Greece) and Philippopolis (modern-day Plovdiv in Bulgaria) were part of the Ottoman Empire in the nineteenth century.

Turkey is present in the corpus as the leading geopolitical entity of the Ottoman Empire. Its only collocate is *sultan*, which further reinforces this

---

[10] In the MEC the word *feeling* is linked to feelings of ill-will bordering upon violence. When co-occurring with Muslims, these feelings are *fanatical* (twice), *unpleasant*, *deep* and *sore* (from a total of six). The *feelings* also *exasperate* and manifest in an *outburst*.

[11] This category can be viewed as a subcategory of conflict. It is identified as a subset here as it highlights the consequences of violence, often in a context in which clear disapproval of the outcomes is shown.

[12] This collocate is a clear reference to the source of the news (i.e. the Reuters news agency).

point. Similarly, Constantinople, as capital of the empire, is also frequently mentioned. Of more interest are the apparently non-specific mentions of places, *village* and *villages*; some indeed are non-specific, but in other cases, when a specific village is named, there is rarely ever more than one example of the name of that village in the corpus, which is why, although *village* is a keyword, the names of individual villages are not. The over-whelming majority of the villages in the MEC are villages in the Ottoman Empire, with thirty-two out of thirty-seven examples of *village* and all thirty-six examples of *villages* referring to villages in the Ottoman Empire. Therefore, *village* and *villages* are also references to locations within the empire. Given some of the notable massacres of Christians that occurred in the Ottoman Empire, especially those in Bulgaria (see Rodogno 2012), it would be tempting to conclude that the locations mentioned are those where the massacres of Christians by Ottoman troops and irregulars being reported in the British press took place. However, a look at *village* and *villages* shows that this would be an unwise assumption to make: if we look at collocates of VILLAGE, and restrict the window in which we look for collocates to two words either side of VILLAGE in order to explore what type of village is mentioned, e.g. *Muslim village*, *villages of Candia*, the top two content words to collocate with VILLAGE are {MUSLIM} and *population*.

The reason for this becomes apparent when the stories are examined in some detail. A frequent theme of the press reports relates to attacks by the Muslim population of an area, rather than Ottoman troops, on neighbouring Christians. Overall, in the MCE, forty-one examples of the use of the term VILLAGE appear in a context in which Muslims are attacking Christians. The attackers are almost invariably civilians, though one report specifies that the civilians are aided by what one may presume are Ottoman troops, and another claims that the Muslims were armed by the government. In only twelve cases are the attacks being carried out by local Christians on their Muslim neighbours. Two examples follow demonstrating how Muslim villagers are shown to engage in violence against Christian neighbours:

The Bashi-Bazouks of the Moslem village of Justina – that is to say, all the lowest roughs of the place – armed by Government with full permission to kill, violate, and rob, determined to destroy Pernshtitza unless its inhabitants would consent to surrender all the arms and ten of their leading families as hostages (*Northern Echo*, 24 June 1876).

The Armenian village of Topaje, in the provinces of Sivas, was the scene of an attack by the Mahommedan population on the 13th of February last (*Daily News*, 21 May 1895).

In a further eight cases, attacks are being carried out on Muslim villagers by Russian or Bulgarian soldiers. Muslims are never reported in a positive light in these stories, yet on at least five occasions helpful acts by Christians, sometimes directed at Muslims, are reported. It is difficult to tell whether the proportion of reported Muslim attacks to Christian attacks is a fair reflection of what happened over the century. However, there is some clear evidence of partiality in the reporting, which would suggest that the stance of the newspaper with regard to Muslims and Christians is not even-handed. Strategies are used either to reduce the sympathy that we may have for Muslim victims or to excuse the actions of violent Christians. The following examples show each:

[T]he Mussulmans having killed two Christians, were attacked by the Christian inhabitants (*Morning Post*, 29 August 1896).

CRETE. OBSTINATE MUSSULMANS. Three French officers of high rank arrived here to-day to consult the British authorities regarding the means to be adopted to facilitate the return of the Mussulman refugees of the Province of Sitia, who decline to return to their villages without material assistance. Their return is stated to be impossible, and the Mussulmans declare that they would rather emigrate to Turkey than return to live with the Christians. They also recall with much bitterness the massacre of Mussulmans by Christians at Sitia, which has remained unpunished. Moreover, unless they receive assistance they have little inducement to return to their homes, as their houses are completely destroyed, their fields ravaged, and their cattle carried off (*Dundee Courier and Argus*, 17 December 1898).

In the first example, the violent actions of Christians towards Muslims are explained, and mitigated in part, by the mention of the murder of two Christians by Muslims. In the second example, a tale that should evoke pity (one of homeless Muslims forced to become refugees by Christian attacks upon their villages) is headed by the headline 'OBSTINATE MUSSUL-MANS' − a far from sympathetic, or even neutral, introduction to the story.

The examples involving the Russian army in the Balkans show similar strategies to those normally employed against Muslims. In the face of the Russian attacks on Turkey in the context of the 1877–1878 Russo-Turkish war, the newspapers report Russian army attacks on Muslim villages, and also continue to report the aftermath of the conflict in a way that is not favourable to Russia:

THE MUSSULMAN REFUGEES. The Russian Government has contributed six thousand francs towards the fund for the repatriation of the Mussulman refugees of East Roumelia. Unfortunately, the Russian officers almost exclusively commanding the Bulgarian and East Roumelian forces in the Mahometan villages, recently burnt by them have been destroying property to a much larger amount (*The Standard*, 4 May 1880).

Here, the generosity of Russia is set against what appear to be covert acts of barbarism by the Russian army. The overall picture in the MEC, therefore, is more subtle than one may think at first glance. Muslims are both the perpetrators of crimes and the victims of crimes; however, when they are the victims of crimes, their suffering may be downplayed. Christians are also reported as the perpetrators of crimes and the victims of crimes, yet sometimes their crimes are excused, and, on occasion, they are shown to be helpful to Muslims. Only the Russians and Bulgarians are, in some cases, subject to the same strategies of presentation, when in the role of aggressor, that the Muslims are.

The cities and countries mentioned are largely related to violent disorder and insurrection; *Candia, Canea* and *Crete* are key because of the reporting of a series of uprisings that occurred in Crete against Ottoman rule (in the 1820s, 1851, 1858 and 1878), but mainly in the context of the final uprising against Ottoman authority from 1895 to 1897, which led to independence from the Ottoman Empire and eventual union with Greece in 1913. *Bulgaria, Philippopolis* and *Russia* occur in the context of the massacre of Christian insurgents by Ottoman troops and the subsequent intervention by Russia that triggered the Russo-Turkish war of 1877–1878. Such is the intensity of reporting around the two areas that both *Crete* and *Bulgaria* are collocates of {MUSLIM} as well as keywords. Their collocation with {MUSLIM}, considered alongside the analysis of VILLAGE already presented, shows the clear religious nature of the dispute in these countries. *Salonica* attests to the unstable situation in the Balkans, with a number of collocates of *Salonica* relating to murder either directly or indirectly, such as (in descending order of strength of collocation) *unpremeditated, assassinations, murders, assassinated, murder* and *murdered*. Reporting on *Syria* also includes mentions of religion-related conflict in the 1860s and 1890s: seven of the twenty-one examples of *Syria* in the MEC focus upon religious violence. Although, in four cases, all from the early 1860s, Muslims are presented as the aggressors, there are no cases in which Christians are presented as the aggressors until the late 1890s, when, on three occasions, both sides are presented as being culpable.

Given that the Ottoman Empire was a large empire of over 35,000,000 people, governed and largely populated by Muslims[13] with European and Asian territories, its prevalence in the news of the period is understandable, as are the keywords *Europe* and *Asia*. The mention of larger geographical regions relates mainly to geopolitical entities. For example, *Asia* has two collocates in the MEC (in descending order): *Minor* and *central*. *Asia Minor*

---

[13] The estimated Muslim population of the Ottoman Empire was 20,550,000 (Michelsen 1854: 140).

is used as a synonym of Turkey, tying it clearly into discussions of Ottoman affairs. The collocate *central* relates to reporting in 1897 of Muslim unrest in the Caucasus and on the border of British India occasioned by Turkish victories over the Greeks in the Turco-Greek war of that year:

For some time past a general movement of unrest has manifested itself among the Moslem population throughout Asia, possessing both a religious and a political character. The movement first made its appearance immediately after the Turco-Greek war, the results of which in an amplified and exaggerated form were brought to the knowledge of the whole Mahommedan world... The Mullahs and other Mussulman emissaries bore the tale far and wide to the followers of the Prophet, who not only believed it, but spread the great tidings, which swelled with each repetition, in every direction, and while the prestige of Turkey and the Sultan thus grew more and more in the Orient, that of Russia and of Great Britain gradually waned. Hence the insurrectionary outbreak on the Indian frontier, and hence, too, the danger which Russia begins to perceive and to fear of a revolt in the Caucasus, where an extreme ferment is going on (*Glasgow Herald*, 10 December 1897).

Once again, therefore, the central role of the Ottoman state and Muslim insurgents is evident in the data. A surprise is that the role of Muslims in the British Empire is not as central to the reporting of stories relating to Muslims as one might expect. India is mentioned in relation to Muslims, and tales of religious violence from India are also present in the press, yet they are apparently few in number, with only one story falling inside the same general frame as could be applied to villages in the Ottoman Empire:

A MUSSULMAN REBEL AND IMPOSTOR. The Sealkote Fuqeer, Hubeeb Shah, was hanged at the Lahore district on Saturday last (*Morning Chronicle*, 24 October 1859).

Yet *India* is a keyword in the corpus; the MEC mentions Muslims more often in relation to India than the general British press of the nineteenth century. The answer to why this is the case rests in part on lexis: in reporting British India, the papers do not necessarily talk of Muslims, using instead labels that make it clear that individuals are Muslims without expressly identifying them as such, for example through words such as *Fuqeer*, *mullah* and *sultan*. Consider the word *Fuqeer*, as used in the newspaper headline quoted above. It clearly refers to a Muslim, usually an initiate of Sufism, but not every newspaper article mentioning *Fuqeer* need say that the person in question is a Muslim or a Sufi. This is assumed knowledge on the reader's part.

The examples in the MEC in which *India* is discussed in the context of Islam show a very different picture from the more numerous examples relating to the Ottoman Empire. Muslims in India are represented negatively – as aggressively expanding their religion through conversion (twice), as being in thrall to the Ottoman sultan (three times), as being intolerant of other religions (once), being violent in the context of Muslim 'Islamism' (once), engaging in an uprising (twice), engaging in communal violence (once), rioting (once) and supporting or having sympathy for the Mahdi (twice). The mention of the Mahdi in this list – the Muslim leader Muhammad Ahmad, who led Sudanese armies against Egyptian armies and whose successors entered into direct conflict with the British – gives a clue as to the broader attitude of the British newspapers to Muslims in India. Muslims are framed negatively when they are reported as (a) reacting against British rule, (b) being in thrall to a power outside British control (specifically the Ottoman sultan) or (c) sympathising with a power in direct confrontation with the British. However, unlike in the Ottoman Empire, these 'bad' Indian Muslims are counterbalanced by 'good' Indian Muslims who are framed positively. These are Muslims who exert independence from the Ottoman sultan (twice), are loyal to the British Empire (four times) and tolerant of other religions (once).

This positive portrayal of Muslims continues in the final city keyword, *Liverpool*. The mention of Liverpool relates to the establishment of the Muslim Institute in the city. Press coverage is positive, as is apparent in the following quote:

A MOSLEM WEDDING AT LIVERPOOL. The first Mahomedan marriage ever celebrated in England took place last Saturday at the Moslem Institute, Liverpool, where the followers of the Prophet in that city regularly assemble. The bride was Miss Charlotte Fitch, eldest daughter of Charles Fitch, J.P. of London; and the bridegroom a Mahomedan barrister in London, whose father is revenue secretary to the Nizam of Hyderabad (*Leicester Chronicle and Leicestershire Mercury*, 25 April 1891).

This piece of reporting is of interest for two reasons. First, it is positive. Second, it is not from a Liverpool newspaper. In Liverpool, the Muslim Institute was a significant cause of disturbance, with the local population being so against its establishment that a threat was made on the life of its founder, William Quilliam, a convert to Islam (Ansari 2004: 83), who opened the institute as Britain's first mosque in 1889. So, while newspaper reporting of this event outside Liverpool may have been positive, the institute itself was a focus of significant unrest and violence from an intolerant local population in the city. This goes unreported in the national press. Consequently, while the piece is positive, one should not assume that the events themselves were viewed positively by all in the United Kingdom, particularly in Liverpool.

We conclude this section by considering the last keyword, which is also a collocate of {MUSLIM}: *world*. If the 'Places' collocates in general show that the association of Muslims with violence is not new, this word shows that another finding presented earlier in this book, relating to the phrase {MUSLIM} *world*, has deep historical roots. Of the thirty-eight cases of the word *world* collocating with {MUSLIM} in the MEC, thirty appear as {MUSLIM} *world*. The collectivisation and othering of Muslims by this device, as discussed in Chapter 5, is as readily apparent in the nineteenth century as it was in the study of the late twentieth and early twenty-first century, as shown in the following example, in which Muslims are not simply othered, they are beyond the pale:

> The tendency of the Ottoman Christians in the present century to throw off their old Eastern habits, and adopt the manners and opinions of Europe must, in a great measure, be attributed to the Frankish ideas which have always accompanied the teaching of the Catholics. Yet these active and well-organised missionaries have never been able to make any impression on the Mussulman world. Their influence has been confined to those who were already within the pale of Christiandom (*Glasgow Herald*, 6 August 1864).

Those roots go deeper than the nineteenth century. Using the EEBO corpus, we have explored earlier manifestations of this phrase; *Mahometan world* occurs four times in EEBO. While these constitute admittedly very few examples, they all come from the latter part of the seventeenth century. They also all link the *Mahometan world* with the *Heathen* or *Infidel* world, in phrases such as 'Especially the sottish Opinions which the Heathen and Mahometan World do generally entertain, do tell us how dark a Creature man is' (EEBO file A27051).

There are two further examples in which *Mahometan* and *heathen* change places (*Heathen and Mahometan world*), again in the latter half of the seventeenth century. The coupling of *Mahometan* with *heathen* or *infidel* is expressly an othering strategy: Islam is being equated with heathenism, with both being placed in contrast with Christianity. Although only six examples exist in the corpus, they suggest that the phrase *Muslim world* has its roots in the late seventeenth century, and was an othering device from its first usage. The growth of this othering strategy stands in contrast to the more dominant use of *world* in relation to religion in EEBO – *Christian world* is much more common in this period. There are 4,083 instances of *Christian world* in the EEBO corpus.[14] Table 9.4 shows how the phrase is distributed across two centuries in the EEBO corpus.

It would be tempting to conclude that *Christian world* stands in contrast to {MUSLIM} *world* as a marker of an in-group in the corpus, identifying the reader with a transnational religious community of which he or she is a part. Given the rarity of this expression now, but the prevalence of *Muslim world*, one must ask how the in-group marking construct *Christian world* fell out of use, but an out-group marking phrase *Muslim world* came into use.

---

[14] Note that two of these examples come from the 1460s and are not shown in Table 9.4.

Table 9.4 Occurrences of Christian world *by decade in the sixteenth, seventeenth and early eighteenth century in the EEBO corpus*

Decade	Frequency of occurrences	Frequency per million words	Amount of data for this decade
1500s	0	0	803,172
1510s	0	0	403,813
1520s	0	0	2,509,535
1530s	1	0.17	5,792,267
1540s	0	0	7,143,879
1550s	1	0.18	5,465,739
1560s	1	0.08	12,908,535
1570s	3	0.18	16,975,981
1580s	24	0.93	25,916,909
1590s	24	1.14	21,007,880
1600s	184	4.95	37,192,294
1610s	148	3.86	38,355,454
1620s	280	7.9	35,435,497
1630s	185	4.79	38,636,699
1640s	269	7.94	33,864,127
1650s	614	8.66	70,921,278
1660s	481	8.99	53,506,260
1670s	659	10.04	65,638,094
1680s	744	9.86	75,442,055
1690s	438	6.77	64,681,105
1700s	17	2.69	6,319,035

The answer lies in the collocates of *Christian world*. Figure 9.3 shows the top thirty collocates of *Christian world* in the EEBO corpus, in descending order of significance.

---

the, whole, throughout, all, in, parts, over, of, part, ages, through, almost, churches, divisions, hath, rest, ever, bishops, renowned, been, consent, divider, moiety, peace, divided, most, controversies, innovators, map, combustion

---

Figure 9.3 Top thirty collocates of *Christian world* in the EEBO corpus

While the top three collocates suggest a united Christian world (*whole, throughout, all*), other collocates show one of *parts* or *divisions*, in which some people are acting as a *divider* of Christian unity, *controversies* reign and sectarian violence is setting the Christian world alight, as the following text from the 1670s shows:

For they have no regard of any, they spare not to root up the very Catholicks themselves, so that they may pleasure the Popes Holiness therein, though it were with the betraying of their Countreys, and setting the whole Christian world in a combustion. And therefore because they are in daily fear to be massacred by those among whom they live, they make this provident and timely prevention by Warlike preparation (EEBO file A65789).

Europe was riven by sectarian violence in the seventeenth century as wars of religion, such as the Thirty Years War, raged across the continent. The discussion of the *Christian world* occurs in this context – not quite the in-group one might expect. In this context, the following is a speculative explanation for the rise of the phrase *Mahometan world* in the late seventeenth century, based upon one of the examples of *Mahometan world* in the data in EEBO file A26917. In this text, the writer complains about the effects of disunity in Christianity:

For these miscarriages of many well-meaning zealous persons, the Land mourneth, the Churches groan; Kingdoms are disturbed by them; Families are disquieted by them; Godliness is hindered, and much dishonoured by them; the Wicked are hardened by them, and encouraged to hate and blaspheme and oppose Religion; the glory of the Christian Faith is obscured by them; and the Infidel, Mahometan and Heathen World, are kept from Faith in Jesus Christ, and many millions of Souls destroyed by them.

It may be that the fracturing of the Christian world in the sixteenth and seventeenth centuries and the threat from a powerful Islamic state in the East, the Ottoman Empire, which reached its apogee with the second siege of Vienna in 1683, led to a focus away from the fractured and conflict-ridden 'us' of the *Christian world* to the 'them' of the *Muslim world*. Much work needs to be undertaken before any such hypothesis can be 'proved', but as a starting hypothesis this strikes us both as historically plausible and in concord with the examples we have found in EEBO. In any case, we would argue that the noun *world* can be employed as an effective othering device when modified by an adjective denoting a characteristic of a population that the author wants to present as (negatively) different – belonging to a domain that the author and intended readers do not (and, presumably, would not want to).

Returning to the 'Places' category, one last, somewhat obvious, point needs to be made. As a further token of the othering of Muslims, the locations they are linked to, with the notable exception of *Liverpool*, are beyond the United Kingdom. Muslims are abroad, not in the United Kingdom – or, rather, they are identified abroad as Muslims and in the United Kingdom by nationality or other ethnic traits. In the nineteenth century the United Kingdom had notable Muslim populations living in Cardiff, Liverpool, London, Manchester and South Shields (Ansari 2004). Yet these populations 'did not publicly act under the label "Muslim" and were not perceived as such by wider society' (Ansari 2004: 24). The Liverpool example is one of the very earliest instances of a public media debate about Muslims in the United Kingdom. However, in the nineteenth century it is a rarity, with Islam being a matter of foreign, not domestic, policy.

Conflict categories

The following categories link clearly into the conflicts revealed by the analysis of the 'Places' keywords in the previous section: 'Armed fighters', 'Conflict', 'Fanatic', 'Leader', 'Government', 'Nationality', 'Outrage' and 'Population'. This focus on conflict mirrors much of what was shown in Chapter 2. Notably, the 'Fanatic' category is a clear echo of the discussion of extremism in the representation of Islam discussed in Chapter 6: *radicals* and *extremists* in the twenty-first century, *fanatical* and *fanaticism* in the nineteenth century. These categories work together in the MEC, much as they do in the contemporary corpus, with the discussion of conflicts in specific locations linking Muslims not merely to a range of conflicts but to a number of semantic preferences, as the following example shows:

All the native Christians of the place either slept in the houses of the European residents (under the impression that they would be safer there than in their own places of residence), or else on board boats and vessels in the harbour. The local government was powerless, and although it had more than 2500 regular troops at its command, and could at any moment have had 1300 Europeans landed from the ships of war, it allowed itself to be dictated to the whole of Saturday by a fanatic Moslem mob of not more than 400 persons. On Sunday, as of the preceding day, whenever a native Christian appeared armed, his gun, sword, and every weapon he had were taken from him by the Turkish police; but not only were the Moslems permitted to go about in armed bands, but did so shouting out that the time had now come to murder every dog of a Christian. On both Sunday and Monday, large bands of armed Druses, fresh from the massacre of whole Christian villages in Lebanon, came into town and were everywhere feted by the Moslems. Any Druse who could show a gun that had killed a Christian had the weapon ornamented with flowers by the Moslems of Beyrout. All this while the Turkish authorities looked on and did nothing (*Glasgow Herald*, 17 July 1860).

Here the semantic preferences of {MUSLIM} are accessed as a complex, generating a negative representation of Muslims; within the article they are othered by being linked to a place outside the United Kingdom (*Beirut*). Muslims are acting as irregular armed fighters (*armed bands, large bands*), are involved in outrages (*murder, massacre*) and are represented as fanatics (*fanatic*). Other nationalities are linked to their violent acts (*European, Europeans, Turkish*), as are government agents (*police, Turkish authorities*). Additionally, religious identities are important (*Christian, Christians, Muslim, Muslims*). A complex of semantic preferences is coming into play when an event at a specific location is mentioned: this event is violent; the violence is religious. As noted, Muslims are represented more often than not as the sinners, not those sinned against. Their actions are seen as outrageous and are sometimes directed by a leader with religious authority, such as the sultan or Mahdi. They act violently and collectively. Importantly – and this example shows this well – the Muslim authorities are described as slow to act, or, as the example in question shows, maybe even complicit in the actions undertaken. The overall impression given is that Christians are not safe under Muslim rule. This general representation is not far removed from that explored in the twentieth and twenty-first centuries earlier in this book. Figures such as the Mahdi in particular can be seen as equivalents of the 'tabloid villains' discussed in Chapter 3.[15] Muslims are seen as prone to be influenced and led by such figures (though some may not be), in a process echoing the discussion of radicalisation in Chapter 8 – as the example below shows:

Next morning the Mahdi went through the bazaars urging the Mahometans to attack the Armenians. Two young men who thought it safest to arm themselves, were set upon the same day, their arms taken from them, and were beaten and badly wounded (*Daily News*, 21 May 1895).

There is an intimate link between the representation of Muslims and a capacity for religious violence realised through collective action, resulting in outrages. Again, this process is not dissimilar to that outlined in Chapters 3 and 4, and even moves towards what might be viewed as terrorism at times, especially when Muslims are linked to assassinations, as in the following example:

MUSSULMAN RIOT IN SALONICA. ASSASSINATIONS OF THE FRENCH AND GERMAN CONSULS. The consul of France and the consul of Germany in this town have been assassinated by Mussulmans. The riot which led to these murders arose in the following manner: – a young Christian girl wishing to embrace the Mahometan religion was prevented from carrying out her intention by a body of Greeks, who carried her away from the Mussulmans. Further disturbances are apprehended (*The Star*, 9 May 1876).

Conclusion: similarities, but differences

The discussion so far has noted a series of similarities between the representation of Muslims in the twenty-first-century British press and the nineteenth-century British press. However, these similarities, striking as they are, distract

---

[15] While the Mahdi of Sudan is the most frequently referred to Mahdi in the nineteenth-century press, reports of other Mahdis, such as the one here, also appear in the years after the death of the Sudanese Mahdi.

one from some very real differences. Some are based upon the change in historical context. There is no possibility of Muslims being represented as 'scroungers' (see Chapter 7) in the nineteenth century, for example, as the United Kingdom did not have a welfare state at that time. Such differences are hardly surprising. What is more surprising, perhaps, is the absence of collocates such as *men* and *women* (see Chapter 8) for {MUSLIM}. In the MEC there are only four examples of {MUSLIM} *women*. In one case their lamentations are noted, in two cases the Muslim women of Syria are discussed and in the fourth example it is noted – ironically – that no Muslim women have been violated in an outbreak of religious violence, by contrast with Christian women, who have been. There is only one mention of a *Muslim woman*, and the woman in question is mentioned because she is injured by a stray bullet.

There is no mention of the veil in the context of {MUSLIM} *woman* or {MUSLIM} *women*. In total, *veil* is mentioned only three times, and is not discussed in either positive or negative terms. The absence of a discussion of the veil and Muslim women as a topic is, again, linked to cultural change, but more subtly so. An acceptance of veiling as a common practice in the West at the time is clearly not an explanation; it was not common practice – certainly not in the United Kingdom. However, the salience of women and the struggle for equal rights for women had yet to be realised in the West. As a result, perhaps, the explanation for the lack of salience of issues relating to women, including veiling, in the MEC relates to a similarity in the position of females in both Muslim countries and the West at the time. Although the specifics of their treatment in each culture may differ, with one using the veil and the other the whalebone corset, the status of women in both societies was equivalent, hence the lack of comparability between the two groups, which was to develop in the next century, simply did not exist, and was not a cause for comment. Nor was it a source of contention.

One last difference between the nineteenth and twenty-first centuries needs to be noted. While an obvious point to make, it must be stressed that the frequency of reporting of Muslims in the nineteenth century was very low. The whole century of British national newspapers yielded only 322 newspaper articles in which Muslims are mentioned. While there is the possibility that false negatives mean that there are some articles that use one of the words in the {MUSLIM} set, these are likely to be far fewer than the number of true positives recovered. Yet this lower frequency does not impact markedly upon representation; the representation of Muslims in the nineteenth-century press and the twenty-first century press is, we believe, broadly comparable. This leads to the question of why the frequency of reporting on Muslims in the nineteenth century is so much lower. One answer has been explored already: the lack of a domestic focus upon Muslims, at least until the establishment of the Liverpool Muslim Institute, when some domestic reporting of Muslims in the United Kingdom begins. The other answer relates to newsworthiness and representation. Only when Muslims are engaged in notable acts of violence are they newsworthy. It beggars belief to think that nothing of newsworthiness that was not tinged with tragedy happened in the Ottoman Empire, for example, in the nineteenth century. The link between newsworthiness, Muslims and conflict, noted in Chapter 2, is as marked in the nineteenth century as it is in the twenty-first.

10   Conclusion

In this chapter we collectively revisit the main findings from each of the analysis chapters, asking what we can conclude about the overall picture of representation of Muslims and Islam in the British press between 1998 and 2009, and how that might be understood in a broader historical context. We address the issues of explicit and implicit bias, arguing that, while the picture emerging from the corpus analysis is negative overall, it would be wrong to consider the British press as monolithic, and it would also be an oversimplification always to attribute Islamophobic motives to journalists. We then discuss some of the more problematic words and phrases that were found in different parts of the analysis. Although we consider the value of 'banning' certain terms, we argue that the words themselves are not necessarily the problem; quite often the issue is the contexts and combinations that they are used in. Finally, after reviewing our methodological approach and comparing some of our findings to other studies, we address some of the impacts that the constructions in the British press may have had on the lives of Muslims. In light of our findings, we ask: 'Who really benefits?'

Explicit versus implicit bias

Having surveyed the findings of the previous chapters, we now present a number of tentative conclusions regarding the ways that the British press represents Muslims and Islam. First, while we found explicitly Islamophobic representations, particularly in the right-leaning tabloids, these representations were more of a salient than a majority pattern in the data – standing out because they were so clearly intended to be antagonistic and generalising. Some newspapers put statements in their headlines, designed to create an 'us'–'them' distinction: examples include 'MUSLIMS TELL BRITISH: GO TO HELL!' (*Daily Express*, 4 November 2010), 'BBC PUT MUSLIMS BEFORE YOU!' (*Daily Star*, 18 October 2006) and 'MUSLIM SCHOOLS BAN OUR CULTURE' (*Daily Express*, 20 February 2009). However, consider the response of one of the most conservative tabloids, *The Sun*, to 9/11: 'Islam is not an evil religion.' While one critical response would be 'Why do we need to be told this?', the newspaper at least made a very explicit statement aimed at dissuading bigotry directed at Muslims during this period.

We did find a small number of cases of individual journalists making statements about Muslims (such as Jeremy Clarkson, in Chapter 5, and Julie Burchill, in Chapter 8) that we viewed as clearly negative and offensive. The journalists who wrote such articles tended to be columnists, often writing for conservative newspapers, especially the tabloids. Additionally, the same newspapers printed letters or text messages from readers that were also questionable, and sometimes carried inaccurate interpretations of news stories. Based on the earlier decisions of the Press Complaints Commission not to uphold complaints about columnists such as Robert Kilroy-Silk and Carol Sarler (see Chapter 1, Petley 2006: 56 and Robin Richardson 2004: 68), we feel that the regulatory structures of the British media regarding 'opinions' and 'offence' would benefit from an overhaul, and we welcome reports at the time of writing that the PCC will be replaced. We would also approve of a more careful scrutiny of readers' contributions. Advising Muslims to eat a bacon sandwich (as in the *Daily Star*'s 'Text maniacs' column; see Chapter 5), particularly on the basis of an incorrect interpretation of a previous story, is clearly intended to offend, while a text message that claims that 'all our money goes on asylum & mosques' (Chapter 3) is patently untrue. Ultimately, editors must bear responsibility for the whole content of their papers.

Yet, on the whole, we did not find a great deal of explicit evidence of extremely negative and generalising stereotypes about Islam along the lines of 'Muslims hate the West' or 'Islam is a violent religion' (the Runnymede Trust's 1997 'closed views'; see Chapter 1). Most newspapers were careful to avoid making such claims, at least openly. What emerged instead is a more subtle and ambivalent picture, which indirectly contributes to negative stereotypes. For example, in Chapter 2 we saw how the British press used the word *terrorism* (and related forms, such as *terrorist*) more often in stories about Muslims and Islam than words that actually referenced the concept of *Islam*. Additionally, a wider set of words that referred to conflict occurred five times as much as the query terms relating to Islam that we used to build our corpus. Thus, a significant amount of reporting across the whole of the British press involved placing Muslims in the context of conflict. Chapter 4 showed how concepts such as terrorism, extremism and militancy tended to be more strongly associated with the abstract *Islamic* rather than the identity of the person who practises the religion: *Muslim*. This could indicate a general trend across the British press to 'depersonalise' the more unpleasant connotations (e.g. it is the religion that is bad, not its practitioners), although some people might argue that this is a legitimation strategy, which allows journalists to brand Islam as dangerous without being seen to attack anybody personally. However, Chapter 4 also showed that, between 1998 and 2009, UK news discourse shifted notably in two major ways: from Islam the religion to Muslims the people, and from international stories to an increasing focus on the United Kingdom. Overall, then, the discourse became more personalised, and concerned about British Muslims in particular.

In Chapter 5 we saw how Muslims were frequently referred to via collective nouns such as *community* and *world*, and that such nouns tended to present a picture of a monolithic Islam, indistinguishable from within and different from those outside it. The Muslim community and those who were deemed to represent this collective, Muslim leaders, were both viewed as hostile, easily angered and undeserving of the title of leader, especially by the right-leaning tabloids. Additionally, terms such as *Muslim world* and *Muslim community* tended to occur in contexts that suggested that there were tense and difficult relations between Muslims and 'the West'. Such findings echo the conclusion by John Richardson (2004: 232) that newspapers were engaging in separation, differentiation and negativisation. Chapter 9 showed that the term *Muslim world* was over 300 years old, and grew out of exactly the type of historical circumstances predicted by Richardson – a context in which the West and Muslims were in conflict. However, less predictably, we also saw that the notion of the Christian world, invisible in the modern press, declined prior to the rise of the use of the term *Muslim world* as the Christian world shattered and fragmented in sectarian conflict in the sixteenth and seventeenth centuries, adding to the false impression that the Muslim world represents a monolithic block in contrast to Christendom. This monolithic *Muslim world*, as shown in Chapter 6, is closely linked to extremism. Chapter 6 showed how one in twenty references to the word *Muslim* or its plural was directly next to a word that referred to extremist belief, while this figure was one in six for *Islamic*. References to *moderate* or *devout* Muslims were much less frequent in comparison (and qualitative analysis of these terms suggested that they were sometimes used problematically in any case). Chapters 5 and 6 suggested a tension in journalism between the 'collectivising' terms such as *Muslim world* and the segmenting ones such as *Muslim extremists* that are associated with the degree of belief or alleged extremism, although it could be argued that both types of term can be used with pejorative intent.

While newspapers usually avoided making overgeneralising claims about Muslims, it is worth noting that some newspapers (mainly right-leaning tabloids) placed great focus on a very small number of Muslims who were either extremist 'preachers of hate' or terrorists – with some in receipt of government benefits. This particular practice of the press was shown in Chapter 9 to reach back, in part at least, to the nineteenth century, with words such as *fanaticism* and *Mahdi* being key in nineteenth-century reporting of Islam, showing again a focus on extremists and religious leaders associated with violence. Chapter 7 also suggested that the original tabloid focus on high-profile 'hate preachers' who were 'scrounging' benefits gradually became extended, eventually encompassing any Muslim who received benefits, as well as appearing to influence the discourse of some of the right-leaning broadsheets.

Chapter 8 highlighted a key gender distinction, with Muslim women tending to be represented as victims, and Muslim men viewed as potential aggressors, with young Muslim men consistently written about in the context of radicalisation. Another way in which women in the representation of Islam were presented as an issue or problem is in relation to the veil. Approximately 42 per cent of the time, wearing the veil was represented as either a form of oppression or a (fairly unreasonable) demand, as opposed to a right or a choice. The conservative newspapers referenced a 'horror' discourse around veiling, by using terms such as *zombies*, *Daleks* and *shroud*, while the liberal broadsheets often appeared conflicted: concerned about oppression of women and averse to condoning veil wearing, while reluctant to support a ban explicitly. In some articles it was argued that Muslim women had the right to wear the veil, but they also had to accept criticism, while at other points the broadsheets expressed concern that the veil debate in 2006 was turning ugly. The veil, and a general focus on the role and treatment of women in Islam, is a relatively modern topic in the British press, reflecting the changing role of women in the late twentieth century in the West as much as women in Islamic societies per se, as discussed in Chapter 9. Given the relatively recent development of this aspect of the representation of Islam, it is perhaps unsurprising to discover that the British press is neither fully positive nor fully negative about the veil. Here we found criticism, both of the 'open' and 'closed' varieties, and the general impression we took from analysing this debate was one of inconsistency and ambivalence.

Collectively, such phenomena can result in a distorted picture of Islam. Even if the reporting is accurate regarding the particular people, attitudes, practices or situations in focus, it is only a partial picture of the whole. However, if these people, attitudes, practices or situations are presented (explicitly or implicitly) *as* representative of the whole, then the reporting is rendered inaccurate and misleading. The vast majority of Muslims do not spend their lives involved in conflict, are not 'scroungers' and do not condone the sorts of violent actions carried out by terrorists or advocated by 'hate preachers'. Yet the voices and experiences of these Muslims are often not considered to be newsworthy, and so they become sidelined. It is not far-fetched to assume that, if someone reads about Abu Hamza on a daily basis, and this is the main way that he/she encounters Islam, then his/her views will become deeply skewed. Even when newspapers are careful to hedge their articles with statements such as 'Most Muslims are not fanatics/terrorists...', this can sometimes feel like a legitimation strategy, similar to 'I'm not racist but…'. Indeed, in Chapter 2, over a quarter of the cases that characterised 'the majority of Muslims' as peaceful went on to focus on the dangerous minority, or questioned the original claim. In addition, such vague quantifications can invite the inference that a good proportion of Muslims are indeed dangerous. Advocates of the 'open view' of Islam might say that positioning Islam as diverse (and then claiming that the problem is with the minority) is acceptable. We would agree, although we would still point out that an excessive focus on the minority can, eventually, seem ideologically motivated.

In 2010 focus groups on religion and the media carried out by Taira, Poole and Knott (forthcoming) indicated that viewers and readers were aware of Islamophobic representations and the fact that Islamic extremists were written about a great deal, but people found it difficult not to be influenced by such stories because there were so few positive ones that offered a different perspective. However, they also recognised that bad news stories tended to be viewed as having a higher news value than good news stories. This is one argument that editors could make: that it is not that newspapers are Islamophobic, just that the media's role is to report on bad news. However, to counter this, we would point out that, when we compared our corpus of stories about Islam with other corpora of more general news in Chapter 2, we found that there were more references to conflict in the Islam corpus – a difference that was statistically significant. Even taking into account the general press tendency to focus on bad news, the amount of conflict stories regarding Islam and Muslims looked suspiciously high.

It might be asked whether newspapers ought to report on people such as Abu Hamza at all. It could be argued that the archetypical working-class tabloid reader, who works long hours for little pay, deserves to know that the government seems to be 'rewarding' individuals who appear to hate many values and traditions considered to be 'British'. On the other hand, there are likely to be many other people living in the United Kingdom who are in receipt of benefits, and will have been convicted of crimes or will hold views that are racist, sexist, homophobic or otherwise abhorrent. Such people may be Christian, Jewish or atheist, yet they do not seem to be seen as newsworthy. More to the point, even when they *are* deemed newsworthy, their religion is rarely the focus of the reporting. Perhaps Hamza is of more relevance because he is in a position of influence and preaches a hateful message. However, it could be argued that, in focusing so much on people such as him, certain parts of the press actually give such people a platform, while contributing towards negative stereotyping. In terms of social cohesion, more harm than good may be achieved by having so many of these sorts of stories in the press. We would be less critical of the negative stories about extremists if they were part of a more balanced reporting of Islam, which gave space to more positive representations. Sadly, *Muslim heroes* were harder to find in the press, as were modifying adjectives such as *brave*, *kind* and *honest*.[1]

However, not all newspapers considered such stories to be relevant. *The Guardian*, *The Observer* and *The Independent* had only four direct mentions of Muslims receiving benefits (compared to the *Daily Express*, *Daily Mail* and *Sun*, which managed 1,545 between them). Similarly, *The Guardian* directly described Muslims as extreme only about once in thirty-five times, while this figure was one in eight for *The People*. Another liberal broadsheet, *The Independent*, made the most effort to acknowledge that Islam was not a single religion but composed of different branches. We would characterise the left-leaning broadsheets as containing the most balanced reporting of Muslims, although this does not necessarily mean that a well-meaning stance is always interpreted positively, or that the broadsheets are always unequivocally positive. For example, *The Independent* had a very high number of mentions of terms such as *extremist Islam*, which is partially a function of the newspaper having so much text in it. The focus on international news means that broadsheets tend to write more about Muslims engaged in wars across the world, as well as extremely oppressive governments based in countries with majority Muslim populations. Again, news tends to follow controversy, resulting in us being more likely to read about the situation for Muslims in countries such as Afghanistan (containing 1.9 per cent of the world's Muslims) and Iran (4.7 per cent) than in Indonesia (12.9 per cent) and Bangladesh (9.3 per cent) (see Chapter 5).

Additionally, some writers in left-leaning broadsheets were critical of the practice of veiling, arguing that it oppresses women. While some people may not equate an argument against veiling with an attack on Islam, others may simply see it as yet another form of negative reporting. Generally, though, we found that the left-leaning broadsheets were critical of the more obviously Islamophobic stories in other newspapers and were more likely to give voices to Muslims and reflect on issues to do with terminology or representation. In cases when the more hostile sections of the British press gave voice to Muslims, it was to show them either as dangerous and unreasonable, or as having views that matched the ideology of the newspaper.

Interestingly, views of Muslims as holding extreme beliefs and being involved in violence and conflict were found to be prevalent in nineteenth-century articles about the behaviour of Muslims in distant countries, suggesting that some modern-day representations have been drawing on much older discourses. Such discourses are likely to have been accepted uncritically and strengthened at that time because the majority of British people had no

---

[1] *Brave Muslim(s)* had twenty occurrences, *kind Muslim(s)* zero occurrences, *honest Muslim(s)* six occurrences and *Muslim hero(es)* thirty-nine occurrences.

contact with Muslims. It is noteworthy to see that such views have been sustained into the early twenty-first century, although they have been joined by newer ones, reflecting Britain's changed society and the fact that Muslims now comprise a sizeable minority population in the United Kingdom. Stories about veiling and its relationship to gender equality, and concerns about Muslims receiving government benefits, may be new topics, but they have only continued the long-standing trend of seeing Muslims as a problem.

At times it is difficult to assign motives for the more indirect forms of negative stereotyping in the British press. Some of it may be accidental or unconscious. Clearly, there is a dilemma, in that the news media will always focus on stories that involve fear, danger, crime and conflict. Cases in which Muslims have been involved in terrorism or wars are therefore high in terms of 'news value'. We do not believe that the reporting of such stories neces-sarily aimed to represent Muslims in negative ways, although this has been an unfortunate by-product of the sheer amount of stories in the British press that involve Muslims in conflict. We would not recommend that the British press stops reporting such stories, or even that it should aim to disguise the fact that Muslims are involved. However, it is worth raising a number of points of concern. First, care should be taken to ensure that, within such stories, there are no generalising statements that imply that Muslims are 'naturally' warlike or that the relationship between 'the West' and 'the Muslim world' is one that is based on conflict. This requires writers to work against the historic roots of the term *Muslim world*, as shown in Chapter 9. We would also warn of the dangers of reifying these two concepts, especially when they are set up in opposition against one another. Finally, we need to reiterate that, although we would expect newspapers to write about conflict, when we compared the Islam corpus against two other corpora of general newspaper articles we found more references to conflict in the Islam corpus (Chapter 2) – a differ-ence that was statistically significant. There appears to be a general view across the British media that Muslims are most newsworthy when they are involved in conflict, and we would encourage newspapers to consider a more 'balanced' reporting of Muslims, which considers a wider range of contexts beyond war, terrorism and community relations (culture, education, business, leisure, human interest stories, travel, etc.).

In other cases, we suspect that some editors do hold a negative agenda, and have been using subtle (or obvious) techniques in order to get their message across. However, we wondered about the extent to which some negative stories about Islam fully have Muslims as their target. At times Muslims appeared to act as convenient scapegoats in order to attack something else. During the period that we examined (1998 to 2009) the country was run by the ('New') Labour government, which encountered increasing hostility from the right-leaning press. Thus we found numerous stories in which Labour's policy on Islam was attacked as 'too soft', politically correct or detrimental to taxpayers. Such stories sometimes emphasised that even Muslims did not want the 'special treatment' that they were receiving. In such cases, we felt that the motivation was not necessarily to attack Islam per se, but that newspapers simply had a negative bias towards the government, and so criticism of its policy towards any minority group (asylum seekers, gay people, etc.) would suffice. Of course, a consequence of such attacks is that Muslims become stereotyped as demanding, quick to take offence and generally difficult to deal with. An alternative reading of such stories is that they consist of 'spirals of signification'. Seen this way, a negative story about, say, the Red Cross banning Christmas trees in its charity shops so as not to offend Muslims (*Sun*, 21 December 2000) is essentially killing two birds with one stone, with the effect that two disliked groups, Muslims and politically correct people, are spuriously linked and therefore decline together in the estimation of *Sun* readers.

Situations in which the reverse was the case (journalists arguing for or against something because it coincides with the concerns of Muslims) were rarer. *The Guardian* argued against identity cards because facial recognition technology was not good at identifying veiled women, whereas the *Daily Mail* was critical of gay 'activists' who, it claimed, forced a Muslim to resign membership of a charity group. However, such cases are small indications that, at times, the British press has been able to align with the perceived interests of Muslims, particularly if such interests helped to further another agenda of the newspaper.

In terms of 'good practices', we point to a number of representations or strategies that we felt helped to give a more balanced picture of Islam. First is the acknowledgement that Islam is not monolithic. This can be achieved in numerous ways, as, for example, by referring to different branches of Islam such as Sunni and Shia, and not just in the context of conflict. References to Islam in countries that are not involved in wars would also be welcome. Additionally, coverage of Islamic culture (poetry, film, music, art, architecture, fiction, etc.) would help to offset the stories of war, extremism and terrorism. Newspapers that gave 'ordinary' Muslims the opportunity (and space) to present their views, such as when the *Sunday Express* interviewed two women who explained why they wanted to wear the veil (30 September 2001), also offered examples of good practice. Moreover, as a counterbalance to the large number of stories about victimised Muslim women and 'brainwashed' young Muslim men, we would like to see stories about empowered Muslim women (and not because they refuse to wear the veil), and young Muslim men who actively make a positive contribution towards British society. Finally, we would invite better reflection as to whether the religious orientation of people in stories is actually salient to the reporting.

Problematic terms?

We would shy away from asking newspapers to 'ban' the use of certain words, as words themselves are not necessarily the problem. It is the meanings that get attached to them and the contexts in which they are regularly used that are more damaging. Banning words can also have unintended consequences, as censorship can trigger a backlash, resulting in the word being used more than it was beforehand. Understandably, people instinctively tend to rebel when told by so-called 'expert' linguists that they shouldn't use a particular word. In any case, words may go out of fashion, but the concepts they refer to can be more difficult to suppress. Consider how the British press first favoured *hardliner*, then *fanatic*, then *militant*, then *radical*, then *extremist* over the course of the twelve-year period covered by the corpus data. The words may have changed but the meaning and the frequency with which the meaning was used hardly altered. Similarly, we have argued in this book that the term *Islamic* carries an extremely negative discourse prosody, heavily associated with religious and political extremism, militancy and terror. However, *Islamic* is difficult to avoid, particularly if newspapers wish to continue reporting on groups such as Islamic Jihad and the Islamic Army of Aden. Considering how the word feels 'doomed' to be used in contexts that link it to militancy, as it is embedded in the names of these groups, some newspapers may want to consider whether it is helpful to use the word in other contexts in which it may be generalised to Islam as a whole. Terms such as *Islamic community* (735 occurrences), *Islamic world* (3,083 occurrences) and *Islamic country* (1,444 occurrences) are therefore likely to garner somewhat negative associations, and we would suggest that journalists should consider carefully whether *Islamic* is always needed in such contexts, particularly when there are other forms of phrasing available.

One case in which a word was dropped from the lexicon of the British press is *Moslem*. This was at the instigation of the Muslim Council of Britain, which pointed out that its pronunciation is similar to the Arabic word for 'oppressor'. We suspect that the majority of people who read the *Daily Express* and the *Daily Mail* (the two newspapers that used 97 per cent of cases of this word) would have no idea of this particular association, thinking of it merely as an alternative spelling of the word *Muslim*, which it had been historically (as shown in Chapter 9). However, once the Muslim Council asked these two newspapers to stop using this term, we found it particularly telling that the *Daily Mail* continued to use it for up to a year afterwards, this policy suggesting a hostile stance.

We would advocate the avoidance of certain discourses or general representations. One unhelpful representation is the 'horror' discourse around veiling women. Referring to such women as zombies, bats, Daleks, etc.

is dehumanising and overshadows any relevant points that journalists might make with regard to veiling. Referring to women who fought for the right to wear the veil as stroppy or demanding is also unhelpful. Veiling is one 'issue' over which there is a difference in opinion between (and within) the general British public and Muslims, with 55 per cent of the general public believing that British Muslims should remove face veils in order to integrate into the United Kingdom, with this figure dropping to 13 per cent for London Muslims (Mogahed 2007: 6). While the British press in general is opposed to veiling, the survey suggests that the British public are more conflicted.

In some cases we have critically examined the use of frequent word combinations. For example, in Chapter 5 we examined the term *Muslim world* and noted how John Richardson (2006: 231) and Carpenter and Cagaptay (2009) view it to be problematic, as it tends to collectivise and homogenise all Muslims into one group. However, we also found cases of Muslims using the term (e.g. the Muslim World League), and it was one that we had previously used ourselves. We would argue that the context within which the term is used is of greater importance. It is possible to use the term to emphasise differences within Islam. Examples include '[T]he Muslim world is not a job lot. In each country, the nature of the debate, activism and its outcomes are determined by the particular and different circumstances of history and national experience' (*Guardian*, 1 September 2005) and 'The Muslim world is not monolithic' (*Times*, 'Letters', 2 April 2003). Additionally, the term can be used to show similarity or equivalence with 'the West', as in 'While she points to the Persian nature of her tales, she also underlines their similarities to traditions from the Muslim world and the West' (*Independent*, 1 June 2005). Nevertheless, these examples are exceptional in the corpus, and there are many more cases that refer to tension or rifts between *the Muslim world* and *the West*.

The term *moderate Muslim* was popular with *The Guardian*, and quite rare in the tabloids. Additionally, moderate Muslims were generally described in positive terms. However, in Chapter 6 we saw how a critical analysis of the term suggests that it carries certain implications with it: that Muslims can be straightforwardly labelled as 'extreme' or 'moderate', which may be an oversimplification of their beliefs. Moreover, the relatively infrequent references to moderate Muslims compared to the ubiquitous Muslim extremists suggests that moderate Muslims are the exceptional case. One writer in *The Independent* suggested that *Muslim moderate* should be used instead (which would bring the term into line with *Muslim extremist*, a term five times more common than *extremist Muslim*). The reversed ordering of the words places a different emphasis: *moderate Muslim* suggests a Muslim who is good because he/she is moderate only in his/her adherence to Islam (implying that full adherence to Islam is bad), whereas *Muslim moderate* is more likely simply to suggest a Muslim who holds politically moderate views. Considering that references to strength of belief are very common in articles about Islam, we would be inclined to suggest that journalists consider the cumulative impact of all such labels.

Methodological reflections

To our knowledge, this study takes into account the largest amount of news writing (143 million words) about Muslims and Islam that has ever been undertaken. Our method has been somewhat different from other research on the same topic, in that we used corpus-driven techniques, initially identifying frequent patterns in the data, which then provided the basis for closer examination. We did not carry out a content analysis, whereby an article was read and then placed into a category concerning whether, say, it was about terrorism or gender inequality (or both). With over 200,000 articles, this would not have been feasible. Nor did we want to simply run a larger-scale repeat of other studies that had carried out content analyses. Additionally, we did not begin our analysis with a set of clear hypotheses that we aimed to explore. Instead, hypotheses were developed as a result of early corpus-driven analyses, providing us with a smaller number of topics or constructions around Islam, which we then explored in greater detail in some of the later chapters in the book. We did not aim to prove that the British press was biased for or against Islam; rather, we approached the corpus in a 'naive' way.

While some of our findings were congruent with those of John Richardson (2004) and Moore, Mason and Lewis (2008), at times we felt that our analysis gave us a somewhat different perspective. For example, Moore, Mason and Lewis (2008: 17) report that the most common nouns used in conjunction with British Muslims in their corpus were *terrorist*, *extremist* and *cleric*. Our Table 4.9 (which considers right-hand noun collocates of *Muslim*) found nouns such as *community*, *world*, *council*, *women* and *leaders* to be the most common. Even if we considered the collocates of the four terms combined (*Muslim*, *Muslims*, *Islam* and *Islamic*), and set the span at five words either side, the most frequent noun collocates were *world* (12,085), *community* (8,235), *group* (6,173), *country* (5,618) and *women* (5,565). Our analysis thus seems to have identified processes of collectivisation as being more frequent than those to do with extremism. When we looked specifically at the term *British Muslims*, the most frequent noun collocates were *community*, *world*, *soldier*, *leaders*, *women*, *communities* and *men*. Although the techniques are different (we relied on collocation, whereas Moore, Mason and Lewis may have identified 'British Muslims' much more widely, incorporating names of individual people and pronouns such as *he*), our analysis seems to suggest a set of more frequent nouns that are less negative in nature. Similarly, while Moore, Mason and Lewis (2008: 18) report that the most frequent adjectives used with British Muslims were *radical, fanatic* and *fundamentalist*, we found that the top adjective that collocated with *Muslim(s)/Islam(ic)* was *young*.

We do not dispute that references to extremist or radical Muslims are frequent in the corpus, just that the form that our analysis took indicated that readers are more likely to see the concept of Islam paired with nouns that collectivise Muslims into large groups, rather than as extremists. Another difference concerning extremist Muslims that we found in comparison to Moore, Mason and Lewis is to do with the proportional relationships between radical and moderate Muslims in the British press. While Moore, Mason and Lewis (2008: 18) conclude that 'references to radical Muslims outnumber references to moderate Muslims by 17 to one', our analysis found that the extremist Muslims outnumbered the moderates by a lower figure, nine to one – though when we considered the words *Muslim, Muslims, Islam* and *Islamic* together, this figure rose to twenty-one to one. Again, methods of calculation will have differed between the two studies, and both give a general impression that extremism is more frequent than moderation – but the scale differs.

One issue that is raised when quantitative methods are applied to answer questions about human societies is to do with what counts as 'acceptable' or 'unacceptable' bias. For example, consider Table 8.3, which shows the extent to which wearing the veil is clearly described as an imposition, demand, choice or right. While the table gives us the frequencies of these representations in the corpus, it is difficult to reach a consensus on what a 'fair' representation would be. Can we claim that the British press is negatively biased because 32 per cent of cases describe the veil as being forced on women and 10 per cent describe veiling women as demanding? In the majority of cases (58 per cent) the veil seems to be described more positively as a choice or a right. Can we therefore conclude that, as the British press seems to represent the veil positively most of the time, we should say that the other 42 per cent of cases are acceptable? Or would we say that even 1 per cent of the imposition/demand constructions are unacceptable and unnecessary in the British press? However, could a corpus that contained no imposition/demand constructions be viewed as *too* positive, erasing the possibility that some women might demand to wear the veil or might have it imposed on them? Similarly, what proportion of Muslims is allowed to be described as extreme before the corpus starts to look negatively biased? Making comparisons between corpora is easier, so we might argue that, on this issue, *The Guardian* (one in thirty-six such constructions) seems less biased than *The People* (one in eight). However, it is difficult to find a common consensus on what an 'acceptable' range is. When it comes to any social group, is there a tipping point when the proportion of negative constructions of that group becomes unacceptably high? Even if we could decide on a number, is that number the same for every social group, or should it differ depending on the group? Should we be more accepting of journalists negatively representing a reasonably powerful identity group, such as men or white people or rich bankers, proportionally more often than they do the same to a less powerful group, such as gay people or Muslims? These are questions that require further discussion, even if the idea of finding a 'magic number' is seen as unnecessary or unreasonable.

Our approach to the corpus data began as quantitative and large-scale, and became more qualitative as it progressed. While the initial focus on frequency lists and keywords helped to pinpoint areas for further analysis, the examination of collocates and keywords in (expanded) concordance lines allowed us to investigate the contexts that words or phrases normally occurred in. It was useful to consider issues of intertextuality, such as how different papers referred to the same story, or how newspapers were critical of each other. It was also interesting to compare particular news stories with readers' letters responding to them, as well as expanding concordance lines to read whole articles in order to consider the extent to which different types of people were afforded space to put their position across.

We did not use meta-data to 'tag' and then systematically compare different types of articles (e.g. letters versus leaders versus opinion columns), although we regularly noted that the more explicitly negative constructions tended to be found in letters and opinion columns, as evidenced via concordancing. This would suggest a direction for future research, involving a wider-scale comparative study of different article types across the corpus. Additionally, with many people now accessing their news online, the comments sections of web pages would also provide a rich source of data, allowing us to gauge whether the small selection of printed letters in the press is actually representative of the wider majority, and whether the ease and anonymity afforded by online posting actually results in even more extreme positions being articulated. Another approach would be to examine news that is written by and for Muslims living in the United Kingdom. It would be particularly interesting to see the extent to which such articles represent alternative discourses, and identify what these discourses are. Do words such as *Muslim* and *Islamic* appear in similar contexts to do with conflict, or are a wider range of stories given? In addition, how do such articles construct topics such as veiling or 'hate preachers'?

Another direction any future analysis could take would be to carry out a contrastive analysis by examining accounts of Muslims in other media (radio or television) or other countries (e.g. the United States, China, Saudi Arabia, etc.) or by investigating representations of other religions (e.g. Christianity, Buddhism, etc.). Such analysis would help to provide further evidence that certain linguistic or discursive constructions are unusually frequent in particular texts, and thus worthy of comment.

Who benefits?

In Chapter 1 we noted that one of the most salient questions of critical discourse analysis is 'Who benefits?'. We incorporated this question into the title of Chapter 7, when we looked at Muslims in receipt of government benefits. Having conducted our analysis, we would now like to turn to this question again. Clearly, it is perhaps easy to answer an alternative question: 'Who doesn't benefit?' The obvious answer would be 'British Muslims', who, we would argue, would feel justified in claiming that sections of the British press were prejudiced against them.

A report produced by the group Engage in 2010 makes a number of observations relating to increased amounts of violence towards British Muslims. A report produced by the Crown Prosecution Service (CPS) in 2008 says that there was a 10 per cent increase in crimes involving racial or religious aggravation from the previous year, up by 1,300 to 13,008. Similarly, a study in 2009 that takes into account the European Union (European Union Agency for Fundamental Rights 2009) finds that 11 per cent of Muslims had experienced racially motivated 'in-person crime' (covering assault, threat or serious harassment) at least once in the previous year. About a third of respondents said they had experienced discrimination over the same period, with an average of eight incidents in that year. Additionally, many Muslims did not report such attacks or cases of discrimination to the police. The United Kingdom's 2007/8 Citizenship Survey (Department of Communities and Local Government 2009) finds that the proportion of people who believed there was more religious prejudice in the United Kingdom than five years previously had increased from 52 per cent in 2005 to 62 per cent in 2007/8. Of those people who felt there was more religious prejudice, 89 per cent of them believed that Muslims experienced more prejudice compared to other religious groups. These figures are unacceptably high, and collectively suggest that Britain (and Europe) have become less accepting of Islam in recent years. This is a pattern that matches the broad picture of representation of Islam in the British press: an increased focus on Islam, often placed within the context of conflict, providing implicit negative associations, with a smaller, yet vociferous, minority of journalists who seem to take pleasure in explicitly stirring up hatred (ironically, perhaps, considering their distaste for 'hate preachers').

Does the non-Muslim British population benefit from such representations? Uncritical readers may feel aggrieved and angry that Muslims have, apparently, unfairly benefited from 'soft' Labour policy and 'political correctness'.

If you are unhappy with your economic or social status, then it might be a consolation to feel that there is a group that you can feel superior to, that you 'belong' more than they do. Two organisations, the British National Party (BNP) and the more recently formed English Defence League (EDL), have engaged in rhetoric that echoes that of the more Islamophobic sections of the British press. For example, the BNP's 2010 election manifesto states: 'The BNP believes that the historical record shows that Islam is by its very nature incompatible with modern secular western democracy... [T]here should be absolutely no further immigration from any Muslim countries, as it presents one of the most deadly threats yet to the survival of our nation.' The EDL claims in its mission statement that it wants to 'protect the inalienable rights of all people to protest against radical Islam's encroachment into the lives of non-Muslims', arguing that it is against radical Islam, rather than British Muslims.[2] However, its members have carried placards saying 'No more mosques' on demonstrations, and on its website it argues: 'The first problem is that radical Islam *isn't* so different. Radical Islam is deeply embedded within Islam, and is not just contained within the heads of a handful of extremists.'[3] It is hardly surprising, therefore, if British Muslims feel anxious about these two groups, and we wonder if they would be as popular had certain sections of the media not reported so many stories about scrounging 'hate preachers', terrorists and oppressed or militant women in veils.

However, we would argue that, while the creation of a divisive atmosphere may dissuade the general populace from being accepting and tolerant of other forms of diversity, ultimately it benefits very few people. As the report of the independent review team that was set up in the wake of the Oldham riots of 2001 (Cantle 2001: 20) argues, 'It is unfashionable to speak of loving one's neighbour, but unless our society can move at least to a position where we can respect our neighbours as fellow human beings, we shall fail in our attempts to create a harmonious society in which conditions have changed so radically in the last 40 years.'

It is clear that, on some issues, the majority of Muslims do not hold 'extremist' views. For example, in Chapter 5 we reported on a Gallup survey (Mogahed 2007) that found that London Muslims, in comparison to the general public, tended to identify more strongly with the United Kingdom, were more tolerant of other religions and were less likely to want to live among people from the same religious or ethnic background. However, the same study also reported that London Muslims tended to be more disapproving of homosexuality (96 per cent versus 34 per cent), sex outside marriage (89 per cent versus 18 per cent) and abortion (90 per cent versus 42 per cent)

[2] See http://englishdefenceleague.org/about-us.
[3] See http://englishdefenceleague.org/edl-news-2/117-shopping-with-radical-islam-in-east-london.

than the general public. Although we find such attitudes to be problematic, in the spirit of 'open views' (Runnymede Trust 1997), we would note that even these figures do not demonstrate 100 per cent disapproval among Muslims nor 100 per cent approval among the general populace, and that social conservatism is often found in other religions too. We view homophobia and Islamophobia as equally abhorrent, and also point out that acceptance of homosexuality in the United Kingdom is relatively recent, occurring only in the last few decades. Tolerance is therefore not a 'Western' trait, but one that emerges whenever the conditions form for people to respect each other's differences and show concern for each other. We believe that people have the capacity to change their views, and that the key to change is engaging with others rather than attacking them.

So, who benefits? We would perhaps point to two potential beneficiaries. First, newspaper editors may find that they are able to cement their readership by providing it with a shared identity and focus. Stories about Islam clearly became more popular after 9/11, and, although average newspaper sales are declining, it could be that Muslims proved to be a useful focus of disapproval (rather than open hatred) as a way of stemming this decline. Two right-leaning publications, *The Sun* and the *Daily Mail*, are still by far the two best-selling newspapers in the United Kingdom. It would seem that there is an audience for stories about hook-handed clerics or politically correct organisations that want to ban Christmas, and so long as large numbers of people continue to buy these newspapers they will continue to hold immense political influence, helping to shape the direction that the United Kingdom takes in future years.

A second beneficiary relates to the subjects of so many articles in the right-leaning tabloids: the extremists. Just as Charles Manson hoped that the murders of the actress Sharon Tate and others would instigate a 'race war', which he called 'helter skelter', Osama Bin Laden wanted the 9/11 attacks to signal a call to holy war, uniting all Muslims across the world against non-Muslims. It could be argued that George W. Bush's response to the 9/11 attacks – 'You are either with us or you are with the terrorists' – also carved the world into two categories. Almost ten years after 9/11 Osama Bin Laden was located and killed, without trial, by American forces. We wonder what he might have thought of the reporting of Islam in the years following 9/11 in the British press. The way that some factions of the press focused on those Muslims who were extreme, fanatical, dangerous, repressive, easily angered and involved in conflict appears to have played directly into his hands. The more narrow such representations were, the more they were likely to make Muslims feel under attack. The result is firmly in keeping with Bin Laden's goal: to exaggerate differences between two groups and then instigate a war between them.

We therefore do not want to lay the blame for negative representations of Muslims and Islam solely at the feet of the British press. Without 9/11 and 7/7, it is unlikely that there would have been as much negative reporting about Muslims (both in terms of quality and quantity). People such as Bin Laden, who wish to achieve their goals through violence and intolerance of those who do not follow their example, are heavily implicated in the picture of negative representation in British newspapers. All the same, it is sadly ironic that some members of the British press have played an obliging role, reacting to extremists in exactly the ways that contribute towards Bin Laden's goals. It is hoped that future generations can learn to respond to intolerance by creating a more tolerant and accepting society, based upon recognising and respecting that, while everyone is essentially different, in a number of basic ways our similarities will always outweigh our differences.

References

Akbarzadeh, S., and Smith, B. 2005. *The Representation of Islam and Muslims in the Media (The Age and* Herald Sun *Newspapers)*. Melbourne: Monash University.

Al-Hejin, B. 2009. 'What matters about Muslim women? A comparison of BBC News and Arab News 1997–2008'. Paper presented at the 30th conference of the International Computer Archive for Modern and Medieval English, Lancaster, 29 May.

Anderson, B. 1983. *Imagined Communities: Reflections on the Origin and Spread of Nationalism*. London: Verso.

Ansari, H. 2004. *'The Infidel Within': Muslims in Britain since 1800*. London: C. Hurst.

Awass, O. 1996. 'The representation of Islam in the American media'. *Hamdard Islamicus* **19**: 87–102.

Baker, P. 2005. *Public Discourses of Gay Men*. London: Routledge.

2006. *Using Corpora in Discourse Analysis*. London: Continuum.

2009. 'The BE06 Corpus of British English and recent language change'. *International Journal of Corpus Linguistics* **14**: 312–37.

2010. 'Representations of Islam in British broadsheet and tabloid newspapers 1999–2005'. *Language and Politics* **9**: 310–38.

Baker, P., Gabrielatos, C., Khosravinik, M., Krzyzanowski, M., McEnery, T., and Wodak, R. 2008. 'A useful methodological synergy? Combining critical discourse analysis and corpus linguistics to examine discourses of refugees and asylum seekers in the UK press'. *Discourse and Society* **19**: 273–306.

Baker, P., Hardie, A., and McEnery, T. 2006. *A Glossary of Corpus Linguistics*. Edinburgh University Press.

Baker, P., and McEnery, T. 2005. 'A corpus-based approach to discourses of refugees and asylum seekers in UN and newspaper texts'. *Language and Politics* **4**: 197–226.

Ballaster, R., Beetham, E., Fraser, E., and Hebron, S. 1991. *Women's Worlds: Ideology, Femininity and the Women's Magazine*. London: Macmillan.

Baumeister, R. F., Bratslavsky, E., Finkenauer, C., and Vohs, K. 2001. 'Bad is stronger than good'. *Review of General Psychology* **5**: 323–70.

Biber, D., Conrad, S., and Reppen, R. 1998. *Corpus Linguistics: Investigating Language Structure and Use*. Cambridge University Press.

271

272   References

Billig, M., Deacon, D., Downey, J., Richardson, J. E., and Golding, P. 2006. *'British-ness' in the Last Three General Elections: From Ethnic Nationalism to Civil Nationalism*. London: Commission for Racial Equality.
Brescoll, V., and LaFrance, M. 2004. 'The correlates and consequences of newspaper reports of research on sex differences'. *Psychological Science* **15**: 515–20.
Burr, V. 1995. *An Introduction to Social Constructionism*. London: Routledge.
Byng, M. D. 2010. 'Symbolically Muslim: media, hijab, and the West'. *Critical Sociology*, **36**: 109–29.
Caldas-Coulthard, C. R. 1995. 'Man in the news: the misrepresentation of women speaking in news-as-narrative-discourse', in S. Mills (ed.) *Language and Gender: Interdisciplinary Perspectives*. Harlow: Longman, 226–39.
Cantle, T. 2001. *Community Cohesion: A Report of the Independent Review Team*. London: Home Office; available at http://image.guardian.co.uk/sys-files/Guardian/documents/2001/12/11/communitycohesionreport.pdf.
Carpenter, S., and Cagaptay, S. 2009. 'What Muslim world?'. *Foreign Policy*, 2 June; available at www.foreignpolicy.com/articles/2009/06/01/what_muslim_world.
Cole, P. 2006. 'Mixed communities: mixed newsrooms', in E. Poole and J. E. Richardson (eds.) *Muslims and the News Media*. London: I. B. Tauris, 63–73.
Commins, D. 2006. *The Wahhabi Mission and Saudi Arabia*. London: I. B. Tauris.
Conboy, M. 2010. *The Language of Newspapers: Socio-Historical Perspectives*. London: Continuum.
Cranfield, G. A. 1978. *The Press and Society: From Caxton to Northcliffe*. Harlow: Longman.
Crown Prosecution Service 2008. *Hate Crime Report 2007–2008*. London: CPS.
Department for Communities and Local Government 2009. *2007–08 Citizenship Survey: Race, Religion and Equalities Topic Report*. London: Department for Communities and Local Government.
Dietrich, S., Heider, D., Matschinger, H., and Angermeyer, M. C. 2006. 'Influence of newspaper reporting on adolescents' attitudes towards people with mental illness'. *Social Psychiatry and Psychiatric Epidemiology* **41**: 318–22.
Downing, J. 1980. *The Media Machine*. London: Pluto Press.
Dunn, K. 2001. 'Representations of Islam in the politics of mosque development in Sydney'. *Tijdschrift voor Economische en Sociale Geografie*, **92**: 291–308.
Durrant, P., and Doherty, A. 2010. 'Are high-frequency collocations psychologically real? Investigating the thesis of collocational priming'. *Corpus Linguistics and Linguistic Theory* **6**: 125–56.
Eatwell, R., and Goodwin, M. J. (eds.) 2010. *The New Extremism in 21st Century Britain*. London: Routledge.
Engage 2010. 'Engage briefing note for MPs'. Ilford: Engage.
Epstein, S. 1998. 'Gay politics, ethnic identity: the limits of social constructionism', in P. M. Nardi and B. E. Schneider (eds.) *Social Perspectives in Lesbian and Gay Studies*. London: Routledge, 134–59 [reprinted from *Socialist Review* 93/94 (1987): 9–54].
European Union Agency for Fundamental Rights 2009. 'Muslims', Data in Focus Report no. 2. Vienna: European Union Agency for Fundamental Rights.
Fairclough, N. 1989. *Language and Power*. London: Longman.

1995. *Critical Discourse Analysis: The Critical Study of Language*. London: Longman.

Fischhoff, B. 1975. 'Hindsight ≠ foresight: the effect of outcome knowledge on judgment under uncertainty'. *Journal of Experimental Psychology: Human Perception and Performance* **1**: 288–99.

Ford, R. 2008. 'Is racial prejudice declining in Britain?'. *British Journal of Sociology* **59**: 609–36.

Foucault, M. 1972. *The Archaeology of Knowledge* (trans. A. M. Sheridan Smith). London: Tavistock.

Fowler, R., Hodge, G., Kress, G., and Trew, T. (eds.) 1979. *Language and Control*. London: Routledge & Kegan Paul.

Gabrielatos, C. 2007. 'Selecting query terms to build a specialised corpus from a restricted-access database'. *ICAME Journal* **31**: 5–43.

Gabrielatos, C., and Baker, P. 2008. 'Fleeing, sneaking, flooding: a corpus analysis of discursive constructions of refugees and asylum seekers in the UK press 1996–2005'. *Journal of English Linguistics* **36**: 5–38.

Gavin, N., and Sanders, D. 2002. 'The press and its influence on British political attitudes under New Labour'. Paper presented at the Political Studies Association annual conference, Aberdeen, 5 April; available at www.psa.ac.uk/journals/pdf/5/2002/gavin.pdf.

Gerbner, G., Gross, L., Morgan, M., and Signorielli, N. 1986. 'Living with television: the dynamics of the cultivation process', in J. Bryant and D. Zillman (eds.) *Perspectives on Media Effects*. Hillsdale, NJ: Lawrence Erlbaum Associates, 17–40.

Gibson, O. 2003. 'Sales dip may push *Mirror* under 2m: Morgan accepts war stance could reduce circulation to 70-year low'. *Guardian*, 2 April.

Goffman, E. 1963. *Stigma: Notes on the Management of Spoiled Identity*. Englewood Cliffs, NJ: Prentice-Hall.

Golding P. 1994. 'Telling stories: sociology, journalism and the informed citizen'. *European Journal of Communication* **9**: 461–84.

Gregory, I., and Hardie, A. 2011. 'Visual GISting: bringing together corpus linguistics and geographical information systems'. *Literary and Linguistic Computing* **26**: 297–314.

Hall, S., Critcher, C., Jefferson, T., Clarke, J., and Roberts, B. 1978. *Policing the Crisis: Mugging, the State and Law and Order*. London: Macmillan.

Halliday, F. 2006. 'Anti-Arab prejudice in the UK: the Kilroy-Silk affair and the BBC response', in E. Poole and J. E. Richardson (eds.) *Muslims and the News Media*. London: I. B. Tauris, 24–34.

Hardie, A., and McEnery, T. 2010. 'Corpus linguistics and historical contexts: text reuse and the expression of bias in early modern English journalism', in R. Bowen, M. Mobärg and S. Ohlander (eds.) *Corpora and Discourse – and Stuff: Papers in Honour of Karin Aijmer*. Gothenburg: Acta Universitatis Gothoburgensis, 59–92.

Hardt-Mautner, G. 1995. 'Only connect: critical discourse analysis and corpus linguistics', UCREL Technical Paper no. 6. Lancaster University; available at www.comp.lancs.ac.uk/computing/research/ucrel/papers/techpaper/vol6.pdf.

Harré, R., Brockmeier, J., and Mühlhäusler, P. 1999. *Greenspeak: A Study of Environmental Discourse*. London: Sage.

Kabbani, R. 1994. *Imperial Fictions: Europe's Myths of the Orient.* London: Pandora.

Karim, K. H. 2006. 'American media's coverage of Muslims: the historical roots of contemporary portrayals', in E. Poole and J. E. Richardson (eds.) *Muslims and the News Media.* London: I. B. Tauris, 116–27.

Kilgarriff, A., Rychly, P., Smrz, P., and Tugwell, D. 2004. 'The Sketch Engine', in G. Williams and S. Vessier (eds.) *Proceedings of the Eleventh EURALEX International Congress: EURALEX 2004.* Lorient: Université de Bretagne-Sud, 105–16.

Krishnamurthy, R. 1996. 'Ethnic, racial and tribal: the language of racism?', in C. R. Caldas-Coulthard and M. Coulthard (eds.) *Texts and Practices: Readings in Critical Discourse Analysis.* London: Routledge, 129–49.

Leech, G., Rayson, P., and Wilson, A. 2001. *Word Frequencies in Written and Spoken English: Based on the British National Corpus.* London: Longman.

Lido, C. 2006. *Effects of the Media Priming Asylum-Seeker Stereotypes on Thoughts and Behaviour.* London: Economic and Social Research Council; available at www.esrcsocietytoday.ac.uk/ESRCInfoCentre/ViewAwardPage.aspx? AwardId=3560.

Linton, M. 1995. 'Was it *The Sun* wot won it?'. Seventh *Guardian* lecture, Nuffield College, Oxford, 30 October.

Martin, J. 2004. 'Positive discourse analysis: power, solidarity and change'. *Revista* **49**: 179–200.

Martin, J., and Rose, D. 2003. *Working with Discourse: Meaning beyond the Clause.* London: Continuum.

McEnery, T. 2006. *Swearing in English: Bad Language, Purity and Power from 1586 to the Present.* London: Routledge.

McEnery, T., and Wilson, A. 1996. *Corpus Linguistics: An Introduction.* Edinburgh University Press.

McIlvenny P. 1996. 'Heckling in Hyde Park: verbal audience participation in popular public discourse'. *Language in Society* **25**: 27–60.

McKee, D. 1995. 'Fact is free but comment is sacred; or was it *The Sun* wot won it?', in I. Crewe and B. Gosschalk (eds.) *Political Communications: The General Election Campaign of 1992.* Cambridge University Press, 121–36.

McLaren, L., and Johnson, M. 2007. 'Resources, group conflict and symbols: explaining anti-immigration hostility in Britain'. *Political Studies* **55**: 709–32.

Michelsen, E. H. 1854. *The Ottoman Empire and Its Resources with Statistical Tables of the Army, Navy, Trade, Navigation, Institutions, etc., etc.* London: Spooner.

Mogahed, D. 2007. *Beyond Multiculturalism versus Assimilation: Gallup World Poll.* Princeton, NJ: Gallup Organization.

Moore, K., Mason, P., and Lewis, J. 2008. *Images of Islam in the UK: The Representation of British Muslims in the National Print News Media 2000–2008.* Cardiff School of Journalism, Media and Cultural Studies.

Norris, P., Curtice, J., Sanders, D., Scammell, M., and Semetko, H. 1999. *On Message: Communicating the Campaign.* London: Sage.

Partington, A. 1998. *Patterns and Meanings: Using Corpora for English Language Research and Teaching.* Amsterdam: John Benjamins.

    2004. 'Corpora and discourse: a most congruous beast', in A. Partington, J. Morley and L. Haarman (eds.) *Corpora and Discourse.* Bern: Peter Lang, 11–20.

Petley, J. 2006. 'Still no redress from the PCC', in E. Poole and J. E. Richardson (eds.) *Muslims and the News Media*. London: I. B. Tauris, 53–62.

Pew Research Center (2009) *Mapping the Global Muslim Population*. Washington, DC: Pew Research Center.

Plous, S. 1993. *The Psychology of Judgment and Decision Making*. New York: McGraw-Hill.

Poole, E. 2002. *Reporting Islam: Media Presentations of British Muslims*. London. I. B. Tauris.

Poole, E., and Richardson, J. E. (eds.) 2006. *Muslims and the News Media*. London: I. B. Tauris.

Reisigl, M., and Wodak, R. 2001. *Discourse and Discrimination: Rhetorics of Racism and Antisemitism*. London: Routledge.

Richardson, J. E. 2004. *(Mis)Representing Islam: The Racism and Rhetoric of British Broadsheet Newspapers*. Amsterdam: John Benjamins.

  2006. 'Who gets to speak? A study of sources in the broadsheet press', in E. Poole and J. E. Richardson (eds.) *Muslims and the News Media*. London: I. B. Tauris, 103–15.

Richardson, R. (ed.) 2004. *Islamophobia: Issues, Challenges and Action. A Report by the Commission on British Muslims and Islamophobia*. Stoke-on-Trent: Trentham Books.

Rodogno, D. 2012. *Against Massacre: Humanitarian Interventions in the Ottoman Empire 1815–1914*. Princeton University Press.

Runnymede Trust 1997. *Islamophobia: A Challenge for Us All. A Report by the Commission on British Muslims and Islamophobia*. London: Runnymede Trust.

Said, E. W. 1997. *Covering Islam: How the Media and the Experts Determine How We Should See the Rest of the World*, rev. edn. London: Vintage.

Sanders, D., Marsh, D., and Ward, H. 1993. 'The electoral impact of press coverage of the British economy, 1979–87'. *British Journal of Political Science* **23**: 175–210.

Sebba, M. 2007. *Spelling and Society: The Culture and Politics of Orthography around the World*. Cambridge University Press.

Sparks, C. 1999. 'The press', in J. Stokes and A. Reading (eds.) *The Media in Britain: Current Debates and Developments*. Basingstoke: Macmillan, 41–60.

Stibbe, A. 2006. 'Deep ecology and language: the curtailed journey of the Atlantic salmon'. *Society and Animals* **14**: 61–77.

Stubbs, M. 1996. *Texts and Corpus Analysis*. Oxford: Blackwell.

  2001. *Words and Phrases: Corpus Studies of Lexical Semantics*. Oxford: Blackwell.

Taira, T., Poole, E., and Knott, K. (forthcoming). 'Religion in the British media today', in J. Mitchell and O. Gower (eds.) *Religion and the News*. Aldershot: Ashgate.

Tajfel, H. 1970. 'Experiments in intergroup discrimination'. *Scientific American* **223**: 96–102.

  1982. *Social Identity and Intergroup Relations*. Cambridge University Press.

Thomas, J. 2005. *Popular Newspapers, the Labour Party and British Politics*. London: Routledge.

Tognini-Bonelli, E. 2001. *Corpus Linguistics at Work*. Amsterdam: John Benjamins.

van Dijk, T. 1987. *Communicating Racism: Ethnic Prejudice in Thought and Talk*. London: Sage.

  1991. *Racism and the Press*. London: Routledge.

Van Leeuwen, T. 2007. 'Legitimation in discourse and communications'. *Discourse and Communication* **1**: 91–112.

von Restorff, H. 1933. 'Über die Wirkung von Bereichsbildungen im Spurenfeld [The effects of field formation in the trace field]'. *Psychologie Forschung* **18**: 299–342.

Widdowson, H. G. 2004. *Text, Context, Pretext: Critical Issues in Critical Discourse Analysis*. Oxford: Blackwell.

Wilmshurst, J., and MacKay, A. 1999. *The Fundamentals of Advertising*, 2nd edn. Oxford: Butterworth-Heinemann.

Wodak, R., and Meyer, M. 2009. 'Critical discourse analysis: history, agenda, theory and methodology', in R. Wodak and M. Meyer (eds.) *Methods of Critical Discourse Analysis*, 2nd edn. London: Sage, 1–33.

Zajonc, R. B. 1968. 'Attitudinal effects of mere exposure'. *Journal of Personality and Social Psychology* **9**: 1–27.

Index